CASE HISTORIES OF PSYCHOPATHOLOGY

Fourth Edition

Gloria Rakita Leon
University of Minnesota

Allyn and Bacon
Boston   London   Sydney   Toronto

Series Editor: John-Paul Lenney
Series Editorial Assistant: Susan S. Brody
Production Coordinator: Susan Freese
Editorial-Production Service: Kailyard Associates
Cover Administrator: Linda K. Dickinson
Manufacturing Buyer: Tamara McCracken

Leon, Gloria Rakita.
    Case histories of psychopathology / Gloria Rakita Leon.—
    4th ed. p. cm.
    Rev. ed. of: Case histories of deviant behavior, 3rd ed.
    © 1984.
    Includes bibliographies and index.
    ISBN 0-205-12085-7
    1. Psychiatry—Case studies. I. Leon, Gloria Rakita. Case
histories of deviant behavior. II. Title.
    [DNLM: 1. Mental Disorders—case studies. 2. Social
Behavior Disorders—case studies. WM 40 L579c]
RC465.L44 1989
616.89′09—dc20
DNLM/DLC   89-15175
for Library of Congress   CIP

Printed in the United States of America

10 9 8 7 6 5 4   94 93

For
Noah and Courtney

CONTENTS

PREFACE

The fourth edition of this book includes an update of the research literature and comprehensive information about the DSM-III-R (1987) diagnostic criteria for the psychopathological disorders covered in this text. Each of the twenty chapters presents a case history of a specific disorder, followed by a discussion that surveys and critically evaluates current findings regarding the etiology and treatment of that disorder. The "Discussion" section also presents a detailed analysis of the social learning and other environmental and biological influences that seem important in the development of the particular disorder.

This edition draws on the substantial amount of research that has been published in the last five years assessing the role of biological factors in the etiology of psychopathological disorders. This text provides the student with a unique perspective for understanding psychopathology through its coverage of recent developments in the field of behavior genetics and a discussion of the interaction of biological and social factors in the etiology of particular disorders.

The change in the title of this edition from *Case Histories of Deviant Behavior* to *Case Histories of Psychopathology* reflects the current evolution in theory and research in the field of abnormal psychology. The study of disordered behavior by behaviorally oriented researchers and clinicians has moved from an environmental, social learning conception to an interactional approach that recognizes that not all abnormal behavior can be explained by the principles of learning theory. The notion that some disorders are indeed illnesses seems to be gaining greater acceptability.

The student of abnormal psychology is able to gain a comprehensive picture of the family and peer context of each of the disorders covered in this text, as well as an understanding of the development of symptoms over time and the meaning of psychological test findings. The treatment methods used are covered in detail; behavior therapy or cognitive behavioral treatment approaches were employed in the majority of cases, and pharmacological treatments were used in some. The treatment outcome literature related to these procedures is surveyed and their efficacy examined. There are two new case histories in this edition, one of an individual suffering from catatonic schizophrenia and the other, a person with primary degenerative dementia of the Alzheimer's type. The choice of these cases strengthens the coverage in the text of more severe forms of psychopathology.

Although the DSM-III-R diagnostic criteria are specified in each case history, it is possible that another diagnostician might have chosen a somewhat different diagnosis for a particular case. In this text, the student is provided with information about the general category in which the disorder falls and the symptoms germane to the category. The fine points of differential diagnosis are not argued, as these criteria could well change over time, as they have in previous revisions of the *Diagnostic and Statistical Manual of Mental Disorders.*

The primary purpose of this text is to present a *descriptive psychopathology,* that is, a careful and detailed description of the symptoms that are exhibited by a person suffering from a particular type of abnormal behavior. Comprehensive information about the individual and family history of each patient or client and the current reactions of persons in the social milieu highlight the development of the psychopathological disorder described and its impact on current functioning.

Evolution of Theory

The changing content of the four editions of this book reflects a fifteen-year evolution of theoretical and treatment perspectives on psychopathological disorders. The first edition provided an alternative to traditional psychodynamic explanations of deviant functioning. The case history material in each chapter was analyzed from a social learning perspective, and the development of a particular pattern of behavior was assessed in relation to the individual's social learning history. In the second edition the case analyses were presented from an interactional perspective. The interactive influence of cognitions, constitutional and genetic factors, and social processes in the evolution of behavior disturbances was highlighted. The implementation of cognitive-behavioral procedures was described as appropriate to a case. The third edition presented a further update regarding developments in the treatment of psychopathological disturbances. The treatment strategies that were described demonstrated an increased emphasis on procedures that will modify maladaptive cognitions and develop effective self-control. Self-efficacy, attributions, expectancies, and self-statements were included within the domain of procedures used by therapists who identified themselves as following a general, learning theory orientation (Bandura, 1977). In this fourth edition, the stronger conception of problems in terms of psychopathology rather than deviant behavior reflects the changes in the field over the fifteen years since the first edition was published.

The social learning approach presented in the first edition suggested that one could understand an individual's behavior by studying the reinforcement and modeling influences in that person's past and present social environment. While earlier learning theories stressed the environment's impact upon an individual's behavior, the social learning focus evident in the 1960s assessed the *interaction* between the individual and the environment. Social learning theories were seen as providing a reasonable alternative to psychodynamic formulations of behavior disorders, such as Wolpe and Rachman's reinterpretation (1960) from a social learning point of view of Freud's analysis of the development of a phobia in the classic case of Little Hans.

Theories and techniques of behavior therapy also emerged during the 1960s as viable alternatives to psychodynamic or psychoanalytically oriented methods of treatment. An assessment of the client's current interaction patterns was identified as an important step in the process of selecting a particular technique of behavior modification, in evaluating the targets for behavior change, and in assessing the effectiveness of the treatment strategies used.

Rotter, presenting a cognitively based social learning theory in 1954, postulated that generalized expectancies for reinforcement were the key to understanding, predicting, and changing human behavior. Rotter, Chance, and Phares (1972) applied this particular social learning conception of personality to the analysis of abnormal behavior and the understanding of the process of psychotherapy. But, the specific assessment and modification in treatment of cognitive factors, such as expectancies for reward or punishment, was a more recent development.

Bandura and Walters (1963) emphasized the crucial role of observational learning in the development of new response patterns. They felt that Rotter's form of social learning theory was inadequate to explain the occurrence of a response that had not as yet been learned, and therefore had a zero probability value of occurrence. Bandura later expanded on modeling theory, and his explanation of the process of observational learning (Bandura, 1972) included cognitive factors such as attention, the symbolic coding and rehearsal operations governing retention, motor reproduction processes, and motivation. Bandura (1977) moved still further in a cognitive direction by proposing that self-efficacy expectations are a major predictor of therapeutic success.

A related development indicating the increasing interest of social learning theorists in cognitive variables was the behavioral formulation of the process of self-control. Thoresen and Mahoney (1974) discussed self-control as a process whereby the individual engages in overt and covert behaviors to alter the environment. These alterations, in turn, systematically modify other behaviors related to the problem situation. The basic feature of this concept of self-control is that the individual is his or her own agent of behavior change.

The growing interest in the role of constitutional factors in behavioral expression (Wing, 1974) also had an influence on social learning theory. The diathesis-stress formulation of abnormal behavior (Slater, 1971) postulated that biological predisposition or biological vulnerability interacts with environmental and interpersonal factors in the development of psychopathology. For those with a strong biological vulnerability, a relatively lesser degree of stress will precipitate a particular disorder. Those with a lesser biological vulnerability will require a greater amount of stress for the disorder to be manifested. If the biological predisposition is not present, an individual may never develop that particular disorder.

A logical outgrowth of the diathesis-stress model is the study of children at high risk for the development of disturbed functioning because of the presence of a parent with a specific disorder such as schizophrenia (e.g., research by Nuechterlein, 1983; Rutschmann, Cornblatt, & Erlenmeyer-Kimling, 1986, and others). In interpreting these findings, one should note that both genetic and social learning influences have an impact on a child growing up in a family with a psychologically disturbed member. A schizophrenic mother could not only transmit some type of biological vulnerability to her child, but her disorder could further affect the child if she manifests an indifferent and withdrawn parenting style, a social interactional influence (Rodnick & Goldstein, 1974).

It now seems clear that some forms of mental illness, particularly schizophrenia and bipolar mood disorders, are not simply mythical, as Szasz (1961) postulated. There is increasing evidence that these and other disorders have significant biological predispositional components. Individual differences in anxiety readiness, stress reactivity, and neuropsychological function may exert an important influence on the probability that an individual will develop some type of psychopathology. The behavioral genetic findings covered in this text demonstrate an increased prevalence of particular disorders in identical twins and in persons adopted at birth whose biological relatives have a history of the disorder. These findings, if replicated in methodologically stronger studies, argue persuasively for a genetic contribution to some forms of psychopathology. Further, the onset of an autistic disorder in the absence of any obvious environmental precipitants is highly suggestive of a biological although not necessarily a genetic component to autism.

On the other hand, it is extremely important that one does not overlook the fact that irrespective of biological predisposition, individuals live in a social environment. The timing and expression of a disorder, as well as treatment outcome, can be influenced by stressful interactions with family members, peers, and persons in the general social milieu. The modeling of psychopathology by others also may be important. The identification of biological etiological factors does not necessarily mean that psychological approaches cannot be effective in treating some disturbances. The promising findings using cognitive-behavioral intervention programs in the treatment of anxiety disorders and some forms of depression are but one example.

One does not simply inherit schizophrenia, depression, Alzheimer's disease, or any of the other disorders that show a higher than expected family history. An important task for future researchers is to identify the biochemical or neurological mechanisms that *are* genetically transmitted or occur in utero that place an individual at risk for the later development of a particular disorder. With the specification of these mechanisms and an understanding of their functioning, it may be possible to develop more effective biomedical as well as psychoeducational interventions for preventing or treating these disorders.

The classification system used in this edition follows the criteria established in DSM-III-R, the 1987 revision of the third edition of the *Diagnostic and Statistical Manual of Mental Disorders*. The research findings discussed in the case history chapters cover many of the findings on family history, biological, and behavioral factors that were incorporated into the DSM-III-R criteria. The advantage of the DSM-III-R system is that the various psychopathological disorders are described according to objective symptom patterns rather than presumed underlying psychodynamics.

Basing diagnostic criteria on research findings and behavioral descriptions of symptoms is a highly positive advance. However, the formulation of cases in this text according to the DSM-III-R classification system does not imply a wholehearted endorsement of that scheme. DSM-III-R provides more stringent criteria for the diagnosis of mental disorders than was evident in the DSM-III (1980) version. However, a number of the categories continue to be overinclusive or vague in their specification of nonpsychiatric problems like nicotine withdrawal or caffeine intoxication as mental disorders.

The DSM-III-R categories for child and adolescent disorders continue to be the most problematic. A normal developmental phenomenon like an identity crisis is still classified as a mental disorder. The inclusion of psychoeducational problems such as arithmetic skills, reading, and language and speech problems as mental disorders on the Axis II developmental disorders category is inappropriate.

Why, then, is diagnosis necessary in studying abnormal behavior? Accurate classification has become more important with the publication of research suggesting that biological factors influence psychopathology. An important step in specifying the biological and psychological contributions to a disorder is accurate identification. Stringent classification also may be helpful in clarifying which types of abnormal behavior are indeed mental illnesses, which other disorders seem to be specific entities that are not biologically based, and which areas of disturbed functioning are simply normal reactions to life stresses. If the process of classification reaches this stage of precision, then it will become important in the sense in which Kraeplin (1883) intended, that is, with implications for etiology, course, and outcome.

There currently is a great need to develop more effective methods of treating psychopathological disorders. Advances over the past decade in the treatment of these problems have been relatively modest. It is hoped there will be more progress in this area in the next few years concomitant with better identification of etiological mechanisms.

The cases in this book are based on information gained by permission from a number of clinics, institutions, and therapists. The chapters dealing with childhood disorders present data about mother-child interactions that were observed in a clinic setting, according to a standardized technique developed by the author (Leon, 1971; Leon and Morrow, 1972). In all of the cases, the names used are fictional names, and identifying details have been changed for teaching purposes and to protect the anonymity of the persons involved.

Acknowledgments

I would like to thank Michael Fuhrman, Marilyn Hartman, Ronald Hansod, Arthur Leon, James Mitchell, and Mary-Jo Nissen for their helpful comments on or aid with various aspects of this text. The expert typing and organizational help of Liz Anderson is most gratefully acknowledged. I also would like to thank John-Paul Lenney, my editor at Allyn and Bacon, for his encouragement and advice.

Grateful acknowledgment is due to the following individuals for their thoughtful reviews of the entire manuscript: David N. Bolocofsky, University of Northern Colorado; William Iacono, University of Minnesota, Minneapolis-St. Paul; James E. Mitchell, University of Minnesota Hospital and Clinic; and Richard Wenzlaff, The University of Texas at San Antonio.

References

American Psychiatric Association (1987). *Diagnostic and statistical manual of mental disorders* (3rd edition, revised) (DSM-III-R). Washington, DC: American Psychiatric Association.

American Psychiatric Association (1980). *Diagnostic and statistical manual of mental disorders* (3rd ed.) (DSM-III). Washington, DC: American Psychiatric Association.

American Psychiatric Association (1980). *Diagnostic and statistical manual of mental disorders* (3rd ed.) (DSM-III). Washington, DC: American Psychiatric Association.

Bandura, A. (1977). Self-efficacy: Toward a unifying theory of behavioral change. *Psychological Review, 64,* 191–213.

Bandura, A. (1972). Modeling theory: Some traditions, trends, and disputes. In R. D. Parke (Ed.), *Recent trends in social learning theory* (pp. 35–61). New York: Academic Press.

Bandura, A., & Walters, R. H. (1963). *Social learning and personality development.* New York: Holt, Rinehart, & Winston.

Kraeplin, E. (1883). *Compendium der psychiatrie.* Leipzig: Abel.

Leon, G. R. (1971). Case report. The use of a structured mother-child interaction and projective material in studying parent influence on child behavior problems. *Journal of Clinical Psychology, 27,* 413–416.

Leon, G. R., & Morrow, V. (1972). Differing patterns of maternal behavior control and their association with child behavior problems of an active or passive interpersonal nature. *Journal   Supplement Abstract Service, 2,* 136–137.

Nuechterlein, K. H. (1983). Signal detection in vigilance tasks and behavioral attributes among offspring of schizophrenic mothers and among hyperactive children. *Journal of Abnormal Psychology, 92,* 4–28.

Rodnick, E. H., & Goldstein, M. J. (1974). Premorbid adjustment and the recovery of mothering function in acute schizophrenic women. *Journal of Abnormal Psychology, 83,* 623–628.

Rotter, J. B. (1954). *Social learning and clinical psychology.* Englewood Cliffs, NJ: Prentice-Hall.

Rotter, J. B., Chance, J. E., & Phares, E. J. (1972). *Applications of social learning theory of personality.* New York: Holt, Rinehart, & Winston.

Rutschmann, J., Cornblatt, B., & Erlenmeyer-Kimling, L. (1986). Sustained attention in children at risk for schizophrenia: Findings with two visual continuous performance tests in a new sample. *Journal of Abnormal Child Psychology, 14,* 365–385.

Slater, E. A. (1971). A heuristic theory of neurosis. In J. Shields & I. I. Gottesman (Eds.), *Man, mind, and heredity. Selected papers of Eliot Slater on psychiatry and genetics* (pp. 216–227) Baltimore: Johns Hopkins Press.

Szasz, T. S. (1961). *The myth of mental illness.* New York: Harper & Row.

Thoresen, C. E., & Mahoney, M. J. (1974). *Behavioral self-control.* New York: Holt, Rinehart, & Winston.

Wing, J. (1974). *Early childhood autism* (2nd ed.). London: Pergamon Press.

Wolpe, J., & Rachman, S. (1960). Psychoanalytic "evidence": A critique based on Freud's case of Little Hans. *Journal of Nervous and Mental Disease, 131,* 135–148.

I

Childhood Disorders

1

Autistic Disorder— The Case of Jimmy Peterson

Five-year-old Jimmy Peterson was brought by his parents to an inpatient child psychiatry diagnostic unit at a large city hospital. The family's local physician referred the youngster to the hospital for intensive evaluation of his hyperactivity and failure to develop communicative speech. The parents readily agreed to a three-week hospital admission so that a coordinated team of specialists could evaluate the boy. Mr. and Mrs. Peterson indicated that Jimmy was impossible to manage, was not toilet trained, said only a few words, and generally screamed or gestured to indicate what he wanted. They had been concerned about his lack of speech for some time and welcomed the inpatient evaluation when it seemed clear that the youngster was not going to "outgrow" his various speech and behavior problems. They shared with the staff their feelings of frustration, sadness, and disappointment in Jimmy's poor and puzzling development.

Jimmy was an attractive, well-built youngster of normal height and weight. The Peterson family was white and lived on a farm in the Midwest.

Mr. and Mrs. Peterson were in their middle 30s. Jimmy had one older sister, Michelle, who was ten years old at the time of the evaluation. Her parents and the referring physican described her as "perfectly normal" and doing well in school. There was no one with a history of mental illness on either side of the parents' families.

Developmental Background

Mrs. Peterson reported that she had had a normal pregnancy with each of her children and could not recall any birth complications or postnatal problems. Jimmy had had the usual childhood diseases and the parents reported no particular medical problems or high fevers during or subsequent to these illnesses. Jimmy had never had a serious head or body injury.

The Petersons could recall nothing unusual in Jimmy's early physical development, except that he showed no clear hand preference and still used his right or left hand indiscriminately. They felt that in general his motor development compared normally to the progress of his older sister. However, he was extremely active and had a very short attention span. The parents attributed Jimmy's not being toilet trained, despite a great deal of effort on Mrs. Peterson's part, to the fact that he would not sit still long enough to be trained. They also counted Jimmy's lack of interest in pleasing his parents a factor. Mrs. Peterson stated that Michelle had been toilet trained by the time she was two-and-a-half years old. Mrs. Peterson had tried the same methods of frequent placement on the potty and praise for elimination with Jimmy, but with no success. She indicated that she still tried to place Jimmy on the potty from time to time, but essentially had given up hope of training him for the present.

The Petersons agreed that Jimmy's behavior had always seemed different. Mrs. Peterson related that Jimmy had never let her hold him close and, even as an infant, he would arch his back, cry, and struggle to get out of her arms. He never stretched out his arms to be held, nor had he ever smiled in recognition when family members walked into a room where he was. He also had never engaged in the typical infant babbling and cooing. Mrs. Peterson indicated that she had become quite concerned when Jimmy passed his second birthday and still had not developed any speech other than shrill cries. The family physician had suggested that Jimmy simply might be slower than average in developing language, and that the parents should make an extra effort to try and talk to him. He also referred them to a speech therapist who found it impossible to test Jimmy because of his high activity level.

At age three, Jimmy occasionally said a few words, but these words appeared unrelated to ongoing activities in his immediate vicinity. Efforts by family members to get him to repeat the word he had just uttered, or to imitate new words were unsuccessful. Jimmy began to smile occasionally, but the smiles were unpredictable and did not appear to be in response to behaviors by other persons in the family. Further, it was not possible to get Jimmy to smile with regular frequency. He did not follow directions and appeared to pay little attention to other persons. Mrs. Peterson said that Jimmy seemed to relate only to "things" or objects, not to people. At present, he spent a great deal of time at home spinning a toy, rhythmically banging an object, or rocking back and forth in a chair. He often masturbated while rocking, and sometimes sucked on his fingers at the same time.

Jimmy had progressed somewhat in language skills from the ages of three to five. He could say approximately 20 words, but he still tended to gain attention principally through gestures, pulling on someone's arm, or emitting a shrill cry. He showed a greater tendency to smile to appropriate social stimuli than he had previously, and his attention span seemed to have increased somewhat. However, he continued to spend a great deal of time apparently aimlessly walking about the house. He actively ran, hit, clawed, or cried if someone tried to hold him or dress him. He also strongly resisted sitting at the table throughout an entire meal.

The Observed Interaction

Jimmy was observed in a structural interaction situation with his mother. The author developed this standard interaction as a means of observing, in a clinical setting, the kinds of home behaviors parents complain about when they bring their child to a guidance clinic (Leon, 1971; Leon & Morrow, 1972). The Observed Interaction begins with a ten-minute free play period, followed by the parent and child working cooperatively on a series of tasks and puzzles devised in a manner so that both parent and child must work together to complete the requirements of the situation. The mother was told that she and her child would be observed from behind a one-way mirror.

In the free play situation, Jimmy wandered about the playroom, much as he had during the parents' just completed conference with a hospital social worker, psychologist, and psychiatrist. Mrs. Peterson sat in a chair in a corner of the playroom, smiled occasionally at Jimmy when his glance crossed hers, and watched him move around the room. After several minutes, she got up and attempted to involve her son in some cooperative play with wooden blocks. She spoke to Jimmy in an apparently cheerful tone of voice, but he did not answer her and moved to another part of the room. Mrs. Peterson made several other comments to him during the free play period but he appeared oblivious to his mother's conversation.

When it was time to begin putting a jigsaw puzzle together, Mrs. Peterson led Jimmy to a chair beside her. However, almost as soon as he sat down, Jimmy got up again and continued wandering around the room. Mrs. Peterson then got up and firmly, although not harshly, took Jimmy by the arm and brought him back to the chair. Jimmy began to whine and emit shrill cries, flap his hands, and eventually wiggled out of his mother's grasp. Several minutes later, Mrs. Peterson again called Jimmy over to the table. He came over, stood by the table, and watched as his mother explained and demonstrated how to fit together two pieces of the puzzle. Jimmy watched his mother's demonstration for a moment and then began to handle the puzzle pieces and spin them on the table. However, he subsequently put the two pieces of the puzzle together, and smiled fleetingly when his mother praised him.

Mrs. Peterson later attempted to get Jimmy to hold the basket puzzle (the next task in the standardized Observed Interaction procedure) so that she could string some rods through the basket spaces. She walked over to Jimmy, verbally instructed him to hold the basket, and then placed the basket back in his hands. However, Jimmy's response was to push the basket back at her. Mrs. Peterson then completed the task by herself and, when finished, sat quietly in her chair and observed Jimmy's wanderings around the room until the session was over. Jimmy made no apparent attempt to communicate verbally with his mother during the session.

During the interaction procedure, Mrs. Peterson engaged in numerous attempts, both verbal and nonverbal, to involve Jimmy in games or in the required task procedures. She appeared comfortable with Jimmy and did not exhibit signs of anger when he refused to interact with her. She usually was unsuccessful in gaining Jimmy's cooperation during the session. Generally, he wandered around the room, giving one the impression that he was alone. Attempts to interact with him seemed almost an intrusion on this aloneness. However, several positive signs were noted: occasionally Jimmy did respond to his mother's praise with a smile, and he had successfully imitated his mother's demonstration of how to fit two pieces of the puzzle together.

Hospital Evaluation

Jimmy separated readily from his parents and did not cry or struggle when he was brought to the children's unit of the hospital for the three-week evaluation period. The staff attendant attempted to lead Jimmy to a play area, but he pushed her away and remained standing in the middle of the room. He soon began walking about the large day room, but his movements seemed restless and aimless rather than exploratory. Jimmy was quite silent and expressionless and only began screaming and hitting out at others when someone attempted to interfere with his wanderings.

Medical and Neurological Analysis

No abnormalities were found on the physical examination or on various routine and specialized laboratory tests. Nor were abnormalities noted in reflex responses or in other areas of function evaluated on the neurological examination. However, an electroencephalogram demonstrated positive findings and was interpreted as "a moderately abnormal record." There were indications of both a generalized cerebral dysfunction and localized dysfunctions in the parietal and frontal areas of the brain. Specialized hearing tests indicated that Jimmy's auditory acuity was within the normal range.

Psychological and Learning Analysis

Jimmy was seen by Dr. S., a psychologist who had had a great deal of experience in evaluating nonverbal children. She noted that Jimmy formed eye contact with her, but this contact did not last long and did not result from her request that Jimmy look at her. However, he did sit down at a small table when Dr. S. asked him to, and he began looking at and manipulating the test materials. He also occasionally smiled in response to praise. Jimmy made sounds fairly frequently, often with what could be interpreted as signs of pleasure, demand, or protest.

The youngster's arm and body movements as he sat in the chair were fairly continuous although not extremely rapid. Gross and fine motor coordination generally appeared quite adequate. He tended to look away from the activity he was engaged in, although Dr. S. noted that it was sometimes possible to redirect his attention back to the test materials. Despite his fleeting attention, Jimmy demonstrated that he understood the concepts of shape, size, and color, and that he could function on some tasks at an age-appropriate level.

Jimmy was seen also by a person trained in special education. Dr. V. noted that the youngster used specific strategies to shut Dr. V. out from demanding that he perform on various tasks: Jimmy would look away from the table, push the test objects away, and get out of his chair. These strategies seemed attentive, planned, and very goal-directed. Jimmy appeared to exhibit a strong negativism and resistance to cooperate and interact with others, and these behaviors clearly would interfere with his performance level and his opportunities to learn new tasks. The youngster readily worked for a candy reinforcer when the task was an easy one that did not require him to communicate, but the reinforcer's effectiveness decreased significantly when increased demands were made on him to communicate and cooperate. However, Jimmy demonstrated some skills and intellectual functioning within the normal range for his age.

The consensus of those who had observed Jimmy for the three-week period on the ward and in the various testing situations was that he manifested many of the behaviors associated with autistic disorder. The parents were advised to allow Jimmy to remain at the hospital for at least three to four months. The children's unit was structured as a therapeutic milieu and Jimmy would have the opportunity to learn more appropriate social skills through the application of reinforcement techniques. Also, Jimmy could attend half-day sessions at a school for autistic children associated with the hospital. Mr. and Mrs. Peterson readily agreed to this recommendation, and both parents expressed the hope that Jimmy could be helped in some way to eventually function better in his home environment.

Hospital Treatment Progress

Jimmy was not placed on any medications to control his autistic behaviors. A cooperative program was initiated between the children's unit and the school for autistic children, and Jimmy spent the morning at the school and resided on the unit the rest of the time. The school worked with him on a one-to-one basis; the initial aim was to break through his negativism by shaping him to establish a close, affectionate relationship with his teacher. The academic tasks, such as teaching him to draw a line, fit toys together, or exchange named objects, were seen as vehicles for promoting cooperation and overcoming his initial negativistic response to those around him.

During the first week of the school program, Jimmy was allowed to wander around the room while carrying various objects, but his teacher would occasionally call him over to her to perform simple tasks. Once he had carried out these tasks, he was allowed to wander off again. The strategy was to teach him new behaviors through successive small steps, but to make this interference in his habitually isolated response pattern as unstressful as possible. The teacher also made efforts to increase his physical contact with her. She forcibly picked him up, swung him around, and held him as much as possible. His tolerance for the amount of time he would accept contact with her increased over the week.

The teacher also held Jimmy on her lap during the teaching periods and thus directed his attention to the work materials. When Jimmy focused his gaze on a task and then succeeded in carrying it out correctly, she hugged him and gave him lavish praise. Social approval and hugs were the sole reinforcers used. If Jimmy tried to get out of his teacher's lap during their short work periods, she forcibly constrained him by holding him, and remained holding him throughout the tantrum that ensued. In this manner, Jimmy learned that his tantrums would not result in his being allowed to continue his solitary wanderings. The teacher's comments and positive affect while hugging Jimmy were quite different in quality from the matter-of-fact manner in which she restrained him and said "no" when he was in the midst of a tantrum. Therefore, Jimmy eventually was able to learn to discriminate between various types of physical contact.

Over a period of several months, Jimmy made consistent progress in learning academic skills and in following directions. He also imitated and later repeated words he had learned, and smiled more frequently. His first move with persons was no longer to escape. He showed greater enjoyment in being with other persons, and eventually sought others out from time to time in order to play with them.

On the hospital ward, Jimmy was reinforced with praise for developing self-help skills and for cooperating in getting dressed. He was taught by means of active holding and social praise to stay at the dining room table with the other children. Also, the staff attendant assigned to work with him gradually taught and reinforced him with particularly favored foods for eating with a spoon and for eating a greater variety of foods. A toilet training program was initiated that was an expansion of the procedure reported on by Pumroy and Pumroy (1965). Jimmy's behavior was shaped so that he spent some time each day in the proximity of the toilet. During specified periods of time when he might be likely to urinate, he was given a piece of candy once every minute and praised whenever he was within one foot of the toilet. Several days later, he was given the candy and verbal praise for each minute he actually sat on the toilet, and eventually, only after urinating. Therefore, the goal of teaching Jimmy to urinate in the toilet was accomplished through small steps that were successive approximations of the target behavior.

Eventually, Jimmy spent less time in isolated activities such as wandering around the room or rocking in a chair. He more frequently sought out social interaction with the other children and adults, and he also initiated physical contact with adults, such as hand-holding or hugs. He exhibited a greater overt response to what was going on around him and began to establish more frequent and prolonged eye contact with others.

Placement and Follow-Up

Over the course of Jimmy's hospitalization, Mr. and Mrs. Peterson were given specific instructions on how to interact with him in ways similar to the methods used in the school and hospital. Near the time of the youngster's discharge, the teacher spent a weekend with Jimmy at the Petersons' home and demonstrated to them the specific techniques she had used to establish cooperation and reinforce language skills in the classroom. Arrangements also were made to enroll Jimmy in a special program in a school system near the Petersons' home, and the local teachers visited the school for autistic children and observed and practiced the procedures used there.

One year after discharge from the hospital, the parents and teachers reported that Jimmy was making slow but continued progress in speaking in sentences. They also indicated that he was more socially responsive than he previously had been, and easier to take care of. A follow-up visit by the hospital staff confirmed that although one could not consider Jimmy "normal," he clearly had made substantial progress in language skills and in becoming more positively oriented toward other persons.

Discussion

Jimmy's behavior resembled the kinds of behavior patterns that are considered part of the disorder of autism. The current revision of the *Diagnostic and Statistical Manual of the American Psychiatric Association* (DSM-III-R) (1987) classifies autistic disorder under the category of pervasive developmental disorders. Pervasive developmental disorders were listed in DSM-III (1980) under Axis I Clinical Syndromes, but were moved in DSM-III-R to the Axis II developmental disorders category. This modification is a recognition of the profound impairment in development that occurs in autistic disorders, and their usual lifelong manifestation.

The DSM-II distinction between infantile autism and childhood onset pervasive developmental disorder is no longer maintained. The diagnosis of autistic disorder is based on whether the behavior is abnormal for the person's developmental level, with onset in infancy or childhood. The diagnostic criteria are grouped in terms of a qualitative impairment or an absence of reciprocal social interaction (awareness of the existence or feelings of others, the seeking of comfort when distressed, engaging in social play, making peer friendships): verbal, nonverbal, and imaginative communication impairment; and markedly restricted repertoire of interests and activities (DSM-III-R, pp. 38–39). The diagnostic criteria therefore emphasize an early occurring, chronic disorder with significant deficits in virtually all areas of functioning. A distortion rather than a delay in the development of a number of basic psychological functions is seen.

Kanner (1943) employed the term "early infantile autism" to describe a group of children who were brought for evaluation because they appeared to be feebleminded. In a number of the cases, there had also been a question of whether the child suffered from auditory impairment. However, Kanner reported that the children's cognitive potentialities and hearing ability were not defective, but only masked by a basic disorder. This disorder was a disability, seen from the beginning of the child's life, in relating in the usual manner to other persons and situations. The child's behavior was described as governed by an obsessive desire to maintain a sameness that no one but the child could disrupt. Changes of routine or in the placement of objects often disturbed the child extremely and could result in a tantrum until the sameness was restored. It was also noted that the autistic child related to persons as objects rather than as human beings. If someone tried to take a block or other object away from the autistic child, he or she would struggle and become angry with the person's hand, rather than with the person, per se. Language, when present, was not used to convey meaning to other persons, although many of the youngsters were able to repeat certain words or phrases over and over, or echo words that another person was saying to the child (echolalia).

Kanner (1972) also observed that the autistic children he diagnosed and treated came from families with highly intelligent parents. A great deal of obsessiveness was noted in the family background. Kanner felt that very few parents of autistic children could be described as warmhearted, and the parents' marital relationship was seen as cold and formal. However, Kanner stated that one could not overlook the possibility of a constitutional predisposition to autism, although he strongly felt that the cold and prefectionist parental interaction patterns were more important causative factors.

In discussing severe emotional disorders of early childhood, Mahler (1952) made a distinction between early infantile autism and a pattern that she termed symbiotic infantile psychosis. She stated that the latter disturbance occurs at a somewhat later point in the child's development than the autistic syndrome. Mahler theorized that symbiotic infantile psychosis represented a desperate effort to avert the severe anxiety of mother-child separation. In both types of disorders, she pointed to the disturbed relationship between mother and child, rather than focusing on heredity or metabolic dysfunction as causative factors.

Ferster (1961) presented a learning theory analysis of the development of autism. He analyzed the kinds of behaviors the parent engaged in while interacting with the child, and the effect of the parent's behavior in shaping the child's behavior. The typical activities of the autistic child were viewed as the result of the child learning that these particular behaviors will bring parental attention, while a wider variety of behaviors will bring no reinforcement.

Ferster described the parents as exhibiting a prepotent behavioral repertoire. This was defined as a pattern in which the behaviors and activities of the parent are strongly dominant over most activities of the child. The parent is primarily engrossed in his or her own activities and spends as little time as possible interacting with the child. The parent's needs and interests therefore continually take precedence over those of the child. In this type of situation, the child gains parental attention primarily when he or she forcibly intrudes on the parent's repertoire. The child soon learns that the most effective way of intruding is by engaging in primitive, negative behaviors such as screaming and temper tantrums. When the child engages in quieter, more socially acceptable behaviors, the parent does not pay attention to the child. Positive behaviors therefore remain low on the child's response hierarchy or are extinguished entirely.

Lauretta Bender (1952) discussed the general syndrome of childhood schizophrenia and did not specify early infantile autism or symbiotic psychosis as qualitatively different types of disorders. She considered childhood schizophrenia as basically a biological disturbance, manifested by poor physiologic functioning in all organ systems. She stated that these youngsters revealed pathology at every level and in every area of integration and patterning within the central nervous system. Included were the vegetative, motor, perceptual, intellectual, emotional, and social areas of functioning.

An epidemiological study of children ages eight to ten carried out in Britain (Lotter, 1966; 1967) found a relatively greater incidence of neurological and other abnormalities in a group of youngsters with marked autistic behavior as compared with other groups of children. This finding has been pointed to in support of the theory of an organic etiology of autism. The overall ratio of boys to girls with autism in the Lotter study was 2.6 to 1.

Rutter and Lockyer (1967) and Rutter, Greenfeld, and Lockyer (1967) reported on a five-to-fifteen-year follow-up study of a group of children diagnosed as having "infantile psychosis." The majority of these youngsters manifested psychotic development in early infancy, and probably would have been labeled autistic if current criteria for the diagnosis of autism had been employed. Contrary to Lotter's findings, none of the psychotic children manifested strong signs of neurological impairment at the physical examination upon hospital admission. However, over a quarter of the children manifested a probable to a strong likelihood of brain damage at the follow-up. (The strength of these findings is tempered somewhat by the fact that Rutter and his colleagues conducted almost all of the physical examinations, and the possibility of inadvertent examiner bias in the diagnosis of organic difficulties cannot be ruled out.) In regard to social adjustment, the psychotic children at follow-up in the Rutter et al. study were functioning at a more adverse level than the control group of nonpsychotic, hospitalized children. All but 8 percent of the psychotic group were in some type of institutional or special setting. The investigators also found that the child's initial score on an intelligence test was the most important factor related to later favorable outcome. However, the opportunity to attend school, irrespective of initial level of disturbance, also was associated with a higher probability of receiving a good adjustment rating at adolescence.

The discrepancy between the studies by Lotter and by the Rutter group on the initial manifestation of neurological problems might have been due to a stricter diagnostic criterion for autism or infantile psychosis in the investigation by Rutter and his colleagues. However, the fact that so many of the youngsters in the Rutter et al. study later showed signs of brain damage suggests that some type of organic impairment is a significant factor in autism. Ornitz and Ritvo (1976) proposed a model of autism based on a hypothesis of a central nervous system dysfunction manifested at birth or shortly thereafter that causes perceptual inconstancy. This underlying neuropathophysiological process was viewed as affecting developmental rate, sensorimotor integration, cognition and language, and social development. Rutter (1974) also highlighted an impairment in linguistic function affecting cognitive skills as fundamental to the disorder of autism. The emotional and relational difficulties were seen as secondary to the basic linguistic impairment. Similarly, Fein, Humes, Lucci, and Waterhouse (1984) posited some type of central nervous system damage in autism in which the form and severity of the major autistic symptoms are dependent on the timing, locus, and severity of the damage.

Other biological pathways are suggested by the findings of Ritvo, Freeman, Mason-Brothers, Mo, and Ritvo (1985) of an extremely high concordance for autism in monozygotic twins (95.7%) whose genetic makeup is identical, and a lesser concordance in dyzygotic twins (23.5%)

whose genetic composition is only as similar as that occurring in any other sibling. These figures suggest the possibility of an abnormality in the intrauterine environment as well as some type of genetic transmission. Ritvo and others also identified a group of families with multiple incidences of autism, and proposed that this was caused by autosomal recessive inheritance (Rivto et al., 1985). It therefore seems possible that there can be multiple pathways to the development of autistic disorder; future research should help to clarify the etiology of this severe developmental disorder.

It is highly likely that the severe stress often evident in families with an autistic child is secondary to the difficulties in coping with the emotional and interpersonal problems these children manifest. This perspective spares the parents the unfortunate stigma popularized by some theories of the etiology of autism that suggest that they (and particularly the mother) are the cause of the child's severe disturbance.

Jimmy Peterson's life history illustrates many of the characteristics of autistic disorder viewed from an organic rather than a psychogenic perspective. In contrast to Kanner's descriptions of the parents of autistic children, numerous contacts with the Petersons suggested that they were warm and interested persons and had a genuine affection for both their children. Their older child had developed normally, was doing well in school, and apparently was comfortable with her peers and with adults. The parents reported that they had a good relationship with each other, and no unusual family crises occurred at the time Jimmy was born or in his early years. Both parents agreed that Jimmy had been a "special" child, different from birth on, and that he had never responded to physical contact or social stimuli in the way that their older child had. As Jimmy grew older, his lack of language development and possible cognitive deficits became more evident. As he matured, the gap grew wider between his intellectual and language performance and that of other children the same age. Although he gave evidence of some age-appropriate intellectual functioning, in most intellectual skills his performance was well below the norm for his age level.

Jimmy's poor language skills may partly have been due to deficits in the input and processing of sensory information. The focal abnormalities noted on the electroencephalogram also suggest the possibility of some specific type of cerebral dysfunction. This dysfunction could possibly be a contributing factor to the type of unevenness of performance noted in many autistic children. For example, some autistic youngsters demonstrate the ability to count, choose colors, or imitate words if their attention is focused on the task, but they have difficulty in spontaneously naming these colors or engaging in simple sentence conversations when their attention is not specifically directed to the task. The aversion to physical contact and interactions with other persons might also stem in part from an inability to integrate the various sources of incoming sensory stimulation.

These sources of multiple sensory input could be a combination of tactile, visual, auditory, and kinesthetic sensations. The difficulty in understanding one's environment and responding appropriately to it through verbal and nonverbal communications might reinforce a generalized withdrawal from that environment. The reinforcing properties of this withdrawal could account for the development of the autistic aloneness. Repetitive behaviors such as rocking or rhythmically spinning objects could acquire a strong reinforcing value if these activities are the few that the child can control. The hand flapping of autistic and some retarded children, often noted when they are frustrated, could also function as a learned response that reduces frustration or aversive arousal through the discharge of energy.

A social learning analysis of the behaviors manifested in autistic disorder can be reconciled with a biological theory if one views many of the emotional and social difficulties noted in autistic children as learned responses secondary to a basic central nervous system deficit. Thus, one may not know the specific etiology of the processes that initially caused the child to engage in temper tantrums, rhythmic rocking, and solitary play. A further unknown may be the specific processes that prevented the youngster from developing appropriate language skills. However, these maladaptive behaviors become further reinforced and increase in frequency through their effect on the environment. Engaging in a temper tantrum results in being left alone, and not speaking prevents one from going through the difficult and perhaps confusing process of learning how to talk and communicate through words and sentences. The longer the child develops without speech, the more established this pattern becomes. From a Piagetian viewpoint, the amount of practice in developing sensory images to process information determines the amount of cognitive development that occurs . Therefore, youngsters who have not acquired language skills by age five or six may be unable to "catch up" and develop complex language skills at a later time. The inability to make up this lost developmental time occurs because the youngsters never learned and practiced the cognitive processes necessary to formulate basic concepts.

One should remember that an effective treatment program need not explain the etiology of a disorder. Systematically used behavioral techniques could extinguish some of the autistic behaviors Jimmy manifested, and gradually increase his repertoire of prosocial behaviors. Jimmy's teacher and the ward personnel demonstrated and rewarded him for small steps of behavior change. This procedure led ultimately to the youngster's development of newly learned behavior patterns and proved quite effective in teaching Jimmy academic and self-help skills. A dramatic decrease in tantrums and an increase in his academic attainment resulted from the technique of holding him, waiting until his tantrum subsided, and then continuing with the demand that he perform a given task. In this manner, the adult did not reinforce him for his tantrum behavior by allowing him to be left alone or by giving up the demands for new learning. The patience and skill his teacher and the staff of the children's unit demonstrated in gradually establishing a relationship with him resulted in Jimmy's eventually gaining greater reinforcement for interacting with others than for being left alone. This dramatic behavior change was initially accomplished by forcibly intruding on his isolation, not allowing him to withdraw, and then giving him a great deal of social reinforcement for interacting with others. Gradually, physical contact with persons became associated with other reinforcing events, and the aversive properties of approaching people and being hugged extinguished over time.

An important part of the treatment program was to teach the parents and the local school personnel who would be working with Jimmy the specific techniques that had been employed to change his behavior. This approach is consistent with the developmental therapy program established by Schopler and colleagues (Schopler, 1974; Schopler & Reichler, 1971) in which parents of autistic children were taught how to function as co-therapists for their child both in the clinic and home environment. The rationale of this program is that autistic children can be at different developmental levels for different skills and abilities. Thus, careful diagnosis of developmental levels is important, followed by a comprehensive treatment program. The clinic personnel teach parents special education procedures, and with training the parents can eventually implement these procedures in their home. The program philosophy is therefore quite different from a "curing" psychotherapy model.

Lovaas (1977) has documented a program for teaching behavioral and language skills to autistic children that uses systematic behavior modification techniques. Trained personnel carry out these procedures in institutional settings where the reinforcement contingencies can be closely controlled. It is important to note that the follow-up results indicated that maintenance of the treatment effects varied among the children. Those who were sent back to families or institutions that did not follow through with the behavior modification program reverted to their pretreatment autistic behaviors (Lovaas, Koegel, Simmons, & Long, 1973).

Lovaas (1987) reported on a first-grade follow-up of a group of autistic children participating in a behavioral intervention treatment program since they were approximately three-and-a-half years of age. The treatment program was implemented by staff and parents during most of the child's waking hours. Almost half of the youngsters treated in this extremely intensive program were categorized as recovered. However, the remainder showed only minimal improvement, possibly reflecting different etiologies including the loci of brain dysfunction in the recovered and nonrecovered groups.

In Jimmy's case, the importance of continuing with the same methods of teaching him both at home and at school was stressed, which is consistent with the research findings just reviewed. These methods included reinforcing social behaviors, ignoring negative ones, and forcibly intruding on his isolation. It did not seem likely that the progress he had made at the hospital and special school would generalize or be maintained in the natural environment without continuing these techniques at home.

Social learning processes appear unlikely to have caused Jimmy's autistic disorder. However, the systematic application of the techniques of reinforcement, imitation learning, and procedures for the extinction of negative behaviors clearly helped Jimmy to function in a more verbally communicative and prosocial manner. With intensive effort from persons in his home environment, it is hoped that the youngster's slow but continuous progress will be sustained.

References

American Psychiatric Association (1980). *Diagnostic and statistical manual of mental disorders* (3rd ed.) (DSM-III). Washington, DC: Author.

American Psychiatric Association (1987). *Diagnostic and statistical manual of mental disorders* (3rd ed., rev.) (DSM-III-R). Washington, DC: Author.

Bender, L. (1952). *Child psychiatric techniques.* Springfield, IL: Thomas.

Fein, D., Humes, M., Lucci, D., & Waterhouse, L. (1984). The question of left hemisphere dysfunction in infantile autism. *Psychological Bulletin, 95,* 258–281.

Ferster, C. B. (1961). Positive reinforcement and behavioral deficits of autistic children. *Child Development, 32,* 437–456.

Kanner, L. (1943). Autistic disturbances of affective contact. *Nervous Child, 2,* 217–250.

Kanner, L. (1972). *Child psychiatry* (4th ed.). Springfield, IL: Thomas.

Leon, G. R. (1971). Case report. The use of a structured mother-child interaction and projective material in studying parent influence on child behavior problems. *Journal of Clinical Psychology, 27,* 413–416.

Leon, G. R., & Morrow, V. (1972). Differing patterns of maternal behavior control and their association with child behavior problems of an active or passive nature. *Journal Supplement Abstract Service, 2,* 136–137.

Lotter, V. (1966). Epidemiology of autistic conditions in young children. I. Prevalence. *Social Psychiatry, 1,* 124–137.

Lotter, V. (1967). Epidemiology of autistic conditions in young children. II. Some characteristics of the parents and children. *Social Psychiatry, 1,* 163–173.

Lovaas, O. I. (1977). *The autistic child: Language development through behavior modification.* New York: Irvington Publishers.

Lovaas, O. I. (1987). Behavioral treatment and normal educational and intellectual functioning in young autistic children. *Journal of Consulting and Clinical Psychology, 55,* 3–9.

Lovaas, O. I., Koegel, R., Simmons, J. Q., & Long, J. S. (1973). Some generalization and follow-up measures on autistic children in behavior therapy. *Journal of Applied Behavior Analysis, 6,* 131–166.

Mahler, M. S. (1952). On child psychosis and schizophrenia: Autistic and symbiotic infantile psychosis. *Psychoanalytic Study of the Child, 7,* 286–305.

Ornitz, E. M., & Ritvo, E. R. (1976). The syndrome of autism: A critical review. *American Journal of Psychiatry, 133,* 609–621.

Pomroy, D., & Pumroy, S. (1965). The systematic observation and reinforcement technique in toilet training. *Psychological Reports, 16,* 467–471.

Ritvo, E. R., Freeman, B. J., Mason-Brothers, A., Mo, A., & Ritvo, A. M. (1985). Concordance for the syndrome of autism in 40 pairs of afflicted twins. *American Journal of Psychiatry, 142,* 74–77.

Ritvo, E. R., Spence, M. A., Freeman, B. J., Mason-Brothers, A., Mo., A., & Marazita, M. L. (1985). Evidence for autosomal recessive inheritance in 46 families with multiple incidences of autism. *American Journal of Psychiatry, 142,* 187–192.

Rutter, M., (1974). The development of autism. *Psychological Medicine, 4,* 147–163.

Rutter, M., Greenfeld, D., & Lockyer, L. (1967). A five-to-fifteen-year follow-up study of infantile psychosis: II. Social and behavioural outcome. *British Journal of Psychiatry, 113,* 1183–1199.

Rutter, M., & Lockyer, L. (1967). A five-to-fifteen-year follow-up study of infantile psychosis: I. Description of sample. *British Journal of Psychiatry, 113,* 1169–1182.

Schopler, E. (1974). Changes of direction with psychotic children. In A. Davids (Ed.), *Child personality and psychopathology: Current topics* (205–236). New York: Wiley.

Schopler, E., & Reichler, R. J. (1971). Parents as cotherapists in the treatment of psychotic children. *Journal of Autism and Childhood Schizophrenia, 1*, 87–102.

2

Attention-Deficit Hyperactivity Disorder—The Interaction of Perceptual-Motor and Social Processes

Beth Goldberg was five-and-a-half years old when her parents brought her to a local guidance clinic for evaluation. The parents complained of difficulty in disciplining the child, and now that the youngster was enrolled in kindergarten, the teacher was also having disciplinary problems. The kindergarten teacher reported to the parents that Beth was easily distracted, inattentive, and hyperactive. The teacher also noticed a number of visual-motor difficulties that suggested a possible perceptual problem. At the teacher's suggestion, the parents made an appointment at the guidance clinic.

The Goldberg family was white and of lower-middle-class background. At the time of evaluation, the father was employed as the manager of a service station. The family owned a small three-bedroom home, where Beth shared a room with her four-year-old sister. The youngest member of the family was a brother, who at the time was 18 months old.

Developmental History

Mrs. Goldberg reported that her pregnancy with Beth was uneventful and that she felt quite good during this time. The period of labor and delivery, however, was extremely difficult. The labor lasted approximately 20 hours, and forceps were used to deliver the child. When Beth was born, the umbilical cord was wrapped around her neck, and the obstetrician's report indicated that the youngster was slightly blue in color, indicating anoxia (lack of oxygen). The infant was placed under intensive care for the first 48 hours of her life. No other symptoms occurred and the parents were able to bring Beth home from the hospital on the fifth day. Mrs. Goldberg stated that there were no unusual circumstances during the pregnancy and birth of the other two children.

A report from the pediatrician noted that the youngster had shown continual developmental progress, but at a slower-than-average rate. Beth was not able to sit unaided until she was nine months old, and she began crawling at 13 months of age. The onset of walking was at 19 months, also somewhat later than average. Beth spoke single words at 20 months and did not speak in sentences until she was approximately two years and nine months old. At the time of evaluation, her speech was occasionally difficult to understand. Beth was bottle fed until 13 months of age, and according to her mother, toilet training was completed with great difficulty when the child was three years old. Mrs. Goldberg indicated that Beth still wet her bed occasionally at night.

When Beth was two years old, there were four different episodes when she fell on her head. These events occurred over a two-month period, and she reportedly landed on her brow each time. On the first occasion, she fell out of a shopping cart at the supermarket, and the other times she fell downstairs or off a chair at home. Beth did not lose consciousness, nor did she have any long-term symptoms after these falls. She was taken to her pediatrician when she fell out of the shopping cart, and the pediatrician reported no evidence of concussion. Beth has not had any episodes of high fever, convulsions, or severe illness.

Social History

Beth was the result of a planned pregnancy. Her parents indicated that they had been hoping for a boy, but were no more than momentarily disappointed with the birth of a daughter. Their major concern immediately after the youngster's birth was whether or not she had been harmed by the difficult labor and delivery. When Beth responded well in the hospital, and the parents were able to take her home at the usual time, the parents were reassured that she was unharmed. The pediatrician felt that Beth had overcome the difficulties experienced at birth, and he saw no evidence of impairment at that time.

As Beth grew older, her development was somewhat slower than average, but was not grossly retarded. The parents were not unduly concerned, because there was continuing evidence of developmental progress. Since Beth was the first born, there were no other children to compare her with for the first year and a half of her life. As the eldest, Beth had always been ahead of her siblings in overall progress.

Mrs. Goldberg reported that Karen, who is one-and-a-half years younger than Beth, appeared to be catching up with Beth in ability. Karen had begun to recognize and copy letters, and was able to catch a ball, tie her shoes, and build objects with blocks at least as well as Beth.

The parents related that they were extremely pleased when their son Harmon was born, because they had greatly desired to have a boy. The youngster was one-and-a-half at the time of the interview, and the parents stated that he was a special delight. They indicated that they tended to focus a great deal of attention on him, perhaps at times to the exclusion of the two older daughters.

Mrs. Goldberg felt that her chief problem with Beth was that her daughter would not cooperate with her. She stated that it was very difficult to get Beth to follow any instructions, and spankings and shouting appeared to have no effect. Mrs. Goldberg reported that Beth had frequent temper tantrums characterized by screaming, kicking her feet, and occasionally holding her breath. The mother felt that these episodes occurred primarily when she insisted that Beth do something the youngster did not want to do, such as pick up her toys, put her coat on by herself, or refrain from fighting with one of the other children. Mrs. Goldberg's response to Beth's tantrums was to threaten to spank her, or yell at her to stop. Beth usually ignored her mother's threats, so eventually she did receive a spanking.

The mother indicated that she became very exasperated because Beth was so active and constantly ran around the house. When Beth played outside, Mrs. Goldberg said that she had to be constantly alert as to Beth's whereabouts, because she never played in one place for any length of time. Mrs. Goldberg complained of Beth's inability to sustain play activity, whether inside the house or outside, for more than a few minutes at a time. According to the mother, Beth quickly tired of whatever activity she was involved in, and would then begin doing something else. As a result, Beth constantly scattered toys about which she refused to pick up.

Mr. Goldberg indicated regret that he could not spend more time at home with his family than he did. His job required long working hours, and many times when he was short of help, he worked seven days a week. When he got home, he was often too tired to interact with the children for any length of time. The parents stated that their marital relationship was harmonious, although Mr. Goldberg's long working hours left little opportunity to do things together. Both parents agreed that the primary responsibility for disciplining the children rested with the mother. Mr. Goldberg said that he reprimanded or spanked Beth occasionally if his wife indicated that Beth had been particularly difficult and destructive with some toys or household objects.

Mrs. Goldberg felt that most of her interactions with Beth were unpleasant. She said that because Beth was so active, the youngster was constantly getting into trouble. Therefore, the mother was continually required to discipline her so that she did not get completely out of control. Mrs. Goldberg also indicated a constant fear that Beth would be kid-napped, because Beth was just as friendly to strangers as to people she knew. Beth did not appear shy or inhibited in the presence of persons she did not know, but would start talking to anyone.

Mrs. Goldberg explained that a great deal of friction existed between Beth and her sister Karen. Karen was beginning to become more asser-tive, and there were frequent fights between the two girls. These disputes were usually about toys that both children wanted to play with or differ-ent television programs that each wanted to watch. Karen would not follow Beth's directions and Beth would then resort to hitting Karen. Karen's customary response was to come crying to her mother. Mrs. Goldberg usually handled the situation by intervening and letting Karen have her way, assuming that Beth was older and therefore should be more responsible. Both girls were punished if they interfered with their broth-er's activities or disturbed him when he was sleeping. Mrs. Goldberg felt that, on the whole, Karen was much more likely than Beth to mind her, and Karen seemed to enjoy playing with Harmon more than Beth did.

Although a number of children in the neighborhood were Beth's age, Beth usually played alone. She tended to play with other youngsters for short periods of time, but then would often get into a fight with one of them. Beth's response to the dispute would be to wander off by herself and engage in some other activity.

School Progress

Beth had been attending kindergarten for four months before the clinic evaluation. Her teacher noticed that the child was having trouble performing tasks that most five-year-olds were able to do quite easily. For example, Beth found it extremely difficult to cut out figures from a sheet of paper and paste them in a given manner on another piece of paper. The youngster's drawing skills were also well below her age level, as was her ability to build objects with blocks or copy letters or numbers with some degree of accuracy. When the teacher tried to help Beth after she performed poorly on a task, Beth usually walked away.

The teacher reported that Beth was overactive, constantly distracted, and unable to maintain a single activity for an extended period of time. She also noted that Beth tended to run into or over objects that were in her way. The teacher suggested that a psychological evaluation might gain more information about the nature of the youngster's difficulties at school. The teacher thought that placing Beth in a special class in first grade might be advisable, but that decision would not be made until the outcome of the evaluation was known.

Both parents were quite concerned about the problems their daughter was having in kindergarten and immediately followed the teacher's suggestion that Beth be taken for a psychological evaluation. The parents also took Beth for an eye examination, and the ophthalmologist indicated that Beth's vision was normal for her age.

Psychological Evaluation

Beth was an active, neatly dressed youngster with brown hair and eyes, who appeared to be somewhat small for her age. She separated easily from her mother and walked with the psychologist to the testing room. Dr. S. offered Beth his hand as the two of them walked down the corridor, and she readily held his hand and talked to him. The youngster did not ask any questions about where her mother would be while she was being seen.

Upon entering the testing room, Beth immediately began to pick up objects lying on the shelf and started to look at the materials in some of the boxes. When Dr. S. asked Beth to sit in a chair next to the table she sat down for a moment, but then got up and came over to stand next to the examiner. The psychologist again asked Beth to go back to her seat, so they could begin the first of the activities they would be working on together. Beth complied with his request.

There were two testing sessions with Dr. S., and on both occasions Beth tended to manifest a short attention span. She quickly lost interest in one task and began to ask questions about something else. She was so easily distracted that any noise extraneous to the testing room commanded her immediate interest and attention. Subsequent to the distraction, the examiner had difficulty getting Beth to return her attention to the task that she was working on. The youngster also tended to get up and wander around the room quite frequently, and a number of times asked to leave the room to get some water or to go to the bathroom. Her speech was generally intelligible.

Dr. S. conversed with Beth and gave her a number of tests in order to gain more information about her difficulties. Some of the hypotheses he wished to evaluate were the possibility of mental retardation, neurological impairment, maturational lag, or problems resulting from social-behavioral factors.

The results of an intelligence test indicated that Beth was functioning at a mental age level of four years, one month. This was approximately a year-and-a-half below her chronological age, and technically placed her at a borderline level of functioning. However, her performance revealed a great deal of scatter—that is, she failed some items that were easy for her age, while she passed other, more difficult items. Beth performed at her age level on the vocabulary subtest and on questions dealing with the ability to form verbal concepts. However, her performance was much weaker on those items involving perceptual or motor skills. Beth had trouble with such tasks as stringing beads in a particular pattern or order, recognizing geometric figures, and remembering and being able to describe objects that were no longer in front of her.

The youngster also manifested an inability to visualize objects in space and execute tasks involving fine motor coordination. For example, when Beth was asked to draw some pictures of various persons, she was unable to draw a closed circle for the head, and she drew arms and legs that were joined at inappropriate places to the body. She wrote her name with the letter "B" reversed, and she wrote the letter "A" upside down. Dr. S. noted that Beth's gross motor coordination in tasks such as walking and reaching for objects was adequate for her age, but she consistently had difficulty when fine motor skills were called for. Her performance on these tasks was below her age level. An example of the problem with fine motor coordination was Beth's inability to place a small doll on a toy chair without the doll falling off.

Beth's response to the Tasks of Emotional Development (TED) cards revealed expressions of sibling rivalry, and also feelings of worthlessness because of a perceived lack of ability to do the tasks expected of her. The youngster pictured the mother on the cards as always angry with the child for not being able to do what she demanded.

In light of the youngster's case history of hyperactivity, distractibility, poor attention span, and visual motor problems, she was diagnosed as suffering from an attention-deficit hyperactivity disorder. Mental retardation and maturational lag were ruled out because Beth's disability was not consistent in all areas of functioning and she possessed verbal comprehension commensurate with her age level. Her emotional difficulties seemed in large part a reaction to her frustration at being unable to perform certain tasks as well as the persons around her expected. The negativistic behavior that the parents and teacher complained of was probably due to an inability to comprehend instructions, as well as fear of failure.

Neurological Examination

A neurological consultation was obtained at the time of the clinic evaluation. The neurologist reported that Beth's electroencephalogram (EEG) was normal for her age level. There was no evidence of generalized irregularities in brain functioning nor of any abnormality localized in a specific area of the brain. Reflex development and motor coordination were below age level, but were not grossly abnormal. The neurologist noted the difficulty in fine motor coordination and the perceptual problems, and on this basis, suggested some type of cerebral dysfunction.

The Observed Interaction

Beth and her mother entered the playroom and Mrs. Goldberg listened as the psychologist described the interaction procedure. Beth immediately began to explore the room and enthusiastically commented on the toys she found. Her exclamations did not appear to be directed to either her mother or Dr. S. After several minutes, Mrs. Goldberg firmly told Beth to be quiet so that she could hear what Dr. S. was saying. Beth continued to handle the toys in the room, but did not speak as loudly as before.

The youngster spent the entire free play period wandering from one toy or game to the next, and she did not play with any particular object for longer than a few minutes. Her play activity took on a pattern of looking at the pieces of a game such as a checker set, and then moving the pieces around in the box. With each succeeding motion, the pieces banged together harder and harder, until eventually some fell on the floor. Beth then left this game and walked over to look at another object. The youngster briefly handled some puppets and then later a dart gun, but only played with these toys by holding them in her hand or banging them on the table. Beth punched the inflated clown several times and laughed as the clown moved back and forth. However, unless she stood quite close to it Beth had difficulty aiming accurately at the clown and hitting it.

Virtually no verbal communication between mother and child took place during the free play period. Beth laughed and made comments throughout the time interval, but these comments did not seem to be directed to her mother. Mrs. Goldberg did not react verbally to what Beth was saying, and the youngster did not ask her mother any questions. Mrs. Goldberg sat in a chair next to the table and silently watched what Beth was doing. When Beth's exclamations or play activity became too loud, Mrs. Goldberg said, "shh," or "You're making too much noise," and Beth responded by lowering her voice level for a while.

Mrs. Goldberg called Beth over to the table when the free play period ended. Beth complied, listened to her mother's instructions for filling out the questionnaire, and then got up from the table and began playing with a toy telephone. Mrs. Goldberg again told Beth to sit down; the youngster returned to her chair for a moment but then got up again. Mrs. Goldberg repeated her request that Beth sit down, and Beth said "no." The mother got up from her chair, took the child by the hand, and brought her back to the table. She then asked Beth for an answer to the first questionnaire item. Beth replied, and while Mrs. Goldberg was writing down the answer, the youngster got up and looked in the sink. Mrs. Goldberg did not ask Beth to sit down again while they were working on the question- naire, but directed the remaining questions wherever Beth happened to be at the moment. Beth answered the questions asked of her, and the few times she said "I don't know," her mother accepted this answer and wrote it down.

Beth sat down at her mother's request when the latter put the picture puzzle on the table. Mrs. Goldberg explained to Beth that the two of them had to solve the puzzle together. Beth held some of the pieces in her hand and pushed other pieces around on the table, but did not attempt to join any of the parts. Her mother did not repeat the instructions to Beth, nor did she demonstrate how the pieces should fit together. Mrs. Goldberg began working on the puzzle herself, and did not say anything when Beth left the table. The mother continued working alone until the puzzle was completed.

Mrs. Goldberg then got up from the table and asked Beth to come to the cabinet with her to help with the basket puzzle. Beth went over to the cabinet, and her mother handed her the wire basket and told her to hold it steady. Beth held the basket approximately four minutes, but she did not hold her arms still and the basket moved somewhat. Mrs. Goldberg indicated several times that Beth was not holding the basket steady enough, but these instructions did not produce any change. The mother then helped Beth to brace the basket by holding it with one hand while she strung the rods through the mesh, but she was unsuccessful in steadying the basket by this procedure. Beth began to complain that the basket was too heavy for her, and eventually Mrs. Goldberg said "All right. I'll do it here," and put the basket on the table and completed the task in this manner. She did not say anything to Beth when she was finished, but sat down in a chair and without comment, waited for the examiner to return.

The interaction procedure indicated that Mrs. Goldberg tended to communicate with her daughter primarily when the latter was engaged in loud or disruptive activities. Mrs. Goldberg did not make much effort to teach Beth how to do the various tasks, and she carried out the joint procedures herself when Beth's attention became focused on some other object in the room. Beth was not encouraged or reinforced for cooperating with her mother.

Course of Therapy

Dr. S. met with the parents and explained that the results of the psychological evaluation and the information received from the various consultants pointed to the possibility of a cerebral dysfunction, resulting in an attention-deficit hyperactivity disorder. The parents were informed that this condition could have occurred as a result of the difficult labor and delivery, although many other youngsters with problems like Beth's did not have a history of any unusual problems or head injuries.

Dr. S. was careful to point out that the psychological and other test findings did not imply that Beth would be unable to understand classroom material or make progress in school. The test results did indicate, however, that she would have difficulty with visual-motor skills such as those involved in eye-hand coordination, and there would be problems in areas requiring fine motor control. Most important, the parents would need help in learning to recognize the behavior that resulted from perceptual-motor dysfunction, and not expect Beth to behave at a level at which she was incapable. Dr. S. also suggested that the parents could benefit from guidance in how to help Beth use her abilities, and in how to deal with her behavior problems.

Dr. S. recommended that on entering first grade, Beth be placed in a class for children with learning disabilities so she could receive special instruction geared to her perceptual problems. Mrs. Goldberg and Beth were also offered the opportunity to receive therapy at the clinic, and the nature of the therapy was described.

Mr. and Mrs. Goldberg were quite upset to hear Beth's problems described in terms of cerebral dysfunction. Mrs. Goldberg was particularly shocked to find out that what she had been viewing solely as a behavior problem had a physical basis. The parents were somewhat reassured when Dr. S. repeated that Beth's difficulties were not of a completely incapacitating nature, that she was not mentally retarded, and that she would be able to make progress in school. The parents agreed to the recommendation that Beth be placed in a special class the following year, and they also arranged for the mother and child to participate in the therapy program.

Beth and her mother were introduced to a unique form of treatment called filial therapy. This method of therapy, devised by Dr. Bernard G. Guerney, Jr. (Guerney, 1964; Guerney, 1976; Stover & Guerney, 1969), involves having the mother perform play therapy with her own child. A group of mothers who will be participating in filial therapy are initially taught the technique by observing a trained professional. The professional therapist engages in play therapy with one of the children from the group of participants, while all of the mothers observe behind a one-way mirror. The therapist then discusses with the group the specific methods that were used and emphasizes that the mother must allow the child to lead in the play. The child is free to do whatever he or she wants to in the play sessions except for a few carefully defined limits. For example, the child is not allowed to hit or hurt the parent or stab the inflated doll with a sharp instrument.

An important process in filial therapy is that the mother, as therapist, accept whatever feelings the child wishes to express through play. The child is thus allowed to express positive as well as negative feelings, and the mother learns to accept and reflect these emotions. In this manner, the child will begin to trust the parent more, and will feel that the parent is more sensitive to and has more trust in the child.

The mothers learn the technique of reflection of feelings through teaching sessions, by repeatedly observing the professional therapist, and then by taking turns performing play therapy with their child while the others watch. The observers have the opportunity to provide suggestions and comments immediately after the practice sessions. When the technique is learned, the therapy is carried out by the mother once a week in a designated place in the home, using a standard set of toys and equipment. The mothers also continue to have weekly group meetings where they observe one of the members and her child in a play session. Following the observation, the mothers meet with the group therapist to discuss their observations and to bring up any problems they may be having with their children.

Filial therapy has been shown to be effective in improving mother-child relationships (Sywulak, 1977); the improvement was maintained over a three-year interval in a significant number of pairs evaluated at follow-up (Sensué, 1981). This procedure has been particularly helpful for mothers who have difficulty communicating with their youngsters, and who find it hard to express positive emotions to them. Research findings indicate an increase in ratings of maternal empathy after the mothers have been involved in filial therapy for a period of time (Guerney, Stover, & De Meritt, 1968).

When Beth was evaluated at the clinic, a filial therapy group was just being formed for youngsters with hyperactivity and perceptual-motor problems. Beth and her mother appeared to be good candidates for the program, since Mrs. Goldberg had such great difficulty in expressing or communicating positive feelings toward her daughter. Mrs. Goldberg and Beth particpated in the program for 14 months.

Mrs. Goldberg initially stated that she felt awkward and self-conscious engaging in play therapy with Beth, but eventually she was able to become more sensitive to and accepting of her daughter's feelings. Mrs. Goldberg's comments in the group sessions showed that she had a greater understanding of how Beth felt when stressful episodes occurred at home or at school.

Beth reportedly looked forward to the weekly play sessions where she could have her mother's undivided attention. The youngster was able to play out feelings of frustration and impotence that occurred when she was expected to perform tasks or behave in ways that were beyond her capacity. She also began to show evidence of an enhanced self-concept, in the sense of a greater feeling of adequacy or ability to master the environment. The higher self-esteem probably occurred because she was able to gain parental approval and later self-reinforcement for engaging in activities in which she was able to perform well.

A great deal of the group discussion centered on problem behaviors that occurred in the home. The therapist helped the mothers to focus on differentiating between the behaviors that a given child could be expected to perform and behavioral expectations that were beyond the child's capability. The relationship of the child to other children in the family was also discussed, and numerous examples of friction among siblings were brought up for group comment.

Along with the ongoing filial therapy program, the therapist outlined behavior modification techniques the parent could use in dealing with some of the child's problem behaviors. The addition of reinforcement techniques was an adaptation of the filial therapy procedure specifically for youngsters with cerebral dysfunction. It is important to note that many problems that might have an organic component, such as hyperactivity, were modified through the use of rewards and social approval for less active behavior.

The mothers were able to give each other social support in trying new behavior modification techniques, and being with others who had similar types of problems was helpful to them. The mothers learned from each other that many of the behavior problems secondary to cerebral dysfunction were modifiable through the systematic use of reinforcement procedures.

Therapy with the Goldberg family was terminated by mutual agreement after 14 months. At that time, Mrs. Goldberg was much more consistent and loving in her interactions with Beth, and Beth was manifesting markedly fewer behavior problems at home. The youngster was progressing well in a class for children with learning disabilities, and the teacher reported no particular behavior problems at school.

Periodic phone calls to the family over the next several years indicated that Beth was continuing to make good progress in her special class, and there were no unusual behavior difficulties at home.

Discussion

This case illustrates two important points. First, parental expectations may be unrealistic in light of a child's abilities, and second, behaviors that may have a cerebral dysfunction component can be modified by changing the parent-child interactions. In the case presented, the parents learned that some of the performance expectations they had for their daughter were unrealistically high. Yet within this broad framework, the child was able to make continued academic progress, and she was able to adhere to specific standards of behavior set up by the parents.

Disorders involving a marked hyperactivity component have been conceptualized and categorized in a number of ways. The term "minimal brain damage" has often been used to describe youngsters with problems of hyperactivity, on the assumption that some subtle type of brain damage exists that simply is not apparent on medical and psychological tests. However, this diagnosis is problematic because many of the commonly accepted indicators of cerebral damage are also found in individuals who do not manifest organic pathology. For example, an abnormal electroencephalogram could be a sign of cerebral dysfunction, but generalized abnormal brain activity may also be found in children with behavioral problems and no brain damage (Klinkerfuss, Langa, Weinberg, & O'Leary,

1965; Werry, 1968). A prolonged labor and a difficult delivery do not automatically mean that the child will suffer brain damage. Many children go through a complicated birth without manifesting any long-term aftereffects.

Beth's perceptual-motor difficulties were not obvious enough to suggest she suffered from an organic disorder. The DSM-III-R (1987) classification of attention-deficit hyperactivity disorder (ADHD) emphasizes behavioral aspects rather than positing unverifiable brain damage. This diagnostic category seems most appropriate in describing Beth's problem behaviors, that is, a poor attention span, excessive physical activity, and impulsive, nonreflective behavior. The diagnostic criteria for ADHD include behaviors such as fidgeting, difficulty remaining seated, distractibility, difficulty sustaining attention on task or play activities, and interrupting or intruding on others; an onset before age seven; and a duration of at least six months. The focus is on the kinds of overt behaviors exhibited both at home and at school. The primary disfunction in ADHD is the attention deficit.

Loney (1980) pointed out that a characteristic of this disorder is its unpredictability, that is, that hyperactive children will not exhibit these behaviors in a consistent, cross-situational manner. Therefore, these youngsters may occasionally be able to pay attention to various tasks. They also may show differences in the amount of on-task behavior exhibited at school, at home, or in a clinical diagnostic situation.

There has been recent speculation about the role of sugar ingestion and food additives in influencing the behavior of hyperactive children. However, a carefully controlled study comparing the effects of drinks with sugar and with comparable sweetness placebo drinks on the classroom and play behavior of attention-deficit hyperactive boys failed to find any differences (Milich & Pelham, 1986).

Pharmacological treatment for attention-deficit disorders has been used for a number of years. Various stimulant medications have been prescribed based on the observation that central nervous system (CNS) stimulants have a "paradoxical" or calming effect on hyperactive children. However, the same effect occurs in nonhyperactive children; that is, there is a greater focusing of attention on the task at hand, an enhancement of cognition, and lesser distractibility to competing stimuli (Rapoport et al., 1978; Weingartner et al., 1980). A review of treatment outcome studies indicates that drug treatment has not resulted in an improvement in long-term adolescent outcome (Weiss et al., 1975). The use of medications to treat the problem behaviors that fall in the attention-deficit disorder category may lead parents, teachers, and others to develop an attitude that the child's behavior problems are treatable through medications. Such an attribution will not encourage parents or teachers to become active in modifying the child's problem behaviors in a more prosocial direction.

The long-term status of ADHD children can be problematic. Satterfield, Hoppe, and Schell (1982) followed up attention-deficit hyperactive boys over an eight-year period. Most of the boys had received stimulant drug treatment. The researchers found that by late adolescence, 25 percent of the group had been institutionalized for delinquent behavior. The investigators questioned whether stimulant medication is helpful since it may convince the parents and others that the hyperactive child is receiving adequate treatment, while in reality the behavioral problems the youngster is manifesting are not being addressed. Studies following hyperactive children into adulthood have found that while the adolescent period is a difficult one, the majority exhibit an acceptable although not necessarily untroubled adjustment as adults (Wallender & Hubert, 1985). This improvement seems related to leaving the demands of the structured academic setting.

Strategies for modifying the behavior of children with ADHD can be developed that do not rely exclusively on the use of medication. When meeting with the parents, the clinician can point to the specific perceptual-motor, family, and interpersonal difficulties that were noted during an evaluation. Identifying the child's specific problems and developing educational and behavioral techniques to deal with them would clearly benefit both the child and the parents.

Beth's case includes a number of circumstances that could have led to some type of perceptual dysfunction. First, the difficult labor and associated anoxia would alert one to the possibility of future problems. The four falls when Beth was approximately two years old were most likely a result of an already present visual-motor problem, rather than the cause of that difficulty. The falls occurred at an age when the youngster was still learning to walk. This "accident-proneness" probably reflected the difficulty in synthesizing visual and motor information that was consistently seen throughout Beth's development.

Beth's indiscriminate friendliness to friends or strangers may also reflect her perceptual problems. Just as she had difficulty discriminating between a six-sided and eight-sided figure, it may also be that she was unable to visually differentiate, at first glance, the persons she knew from those she did not know.

Beth manifested a phenomenon commonly seen in children with attention-deficit disorder. She was able to perform well in certain but not all areas of functioning. However, Beth's verbal ability was adequate for her age level in spite of the fact that it was occasionally difficult to understand a given word that she was saying.

Children with learning disabilities (irrespective of the etiology) are often under great pressure for achievement because the parents may not realize that the youngster is experiencing any problems. The mother may view the youngster's difficulties as stemming from the fact that the child "won't mind," and she responds to the child on this basis. Therefore, the child may be punished for being too noisy or destructive or for not finishing a chore, when in fact the child has extreme difficulty performing that task. The parents thus may shout at, criticize, or spank the child for something that is not within the child's capacity to carry out.

Further, other siblings may ridicule the youngster for clumsiness or for constantly getting into trouble. The child then becomes more and more frustrated, and begins to feel that he or she is "bad," or that no matter what the child does, he or she will be criticized for that action. The child may then respond by having a temper tantrum that becomes more severe the longer it lasts, because of the youngster's difficulty in controlling or inhibiting a behavior once it begins. The same type of phenomenon (disinhibition) can be seen in the child with substantiated brain damage who gradually becomes wilder and more destructive while playing with some toys or games.

A youngster who encounters problems accomplishing tasks might have particular difficulty if he or she has a younger sibling close in age. The other child may be rapidly catching up in ability to the impaired child, and the latter may then be unfavorably compared to the younger sibling.

In evaluating the results of the filial therapy program, improvement could be seen in a number of areas. Irrespective of the benefits derived from allowing Beth to express her feelings in play, the technique also allowed the interpersonal relationship between mother and child to become more positive and rewarding. The mother spent a period of time each week giving her undivided attention to her daughter's play activities, and the child began to relate to the mother in a manner other than by having tantrums and arguments. The mother in turn began to respond to the child with more positive affect, and the interaction between them became more enjoyable. The mother also became more sensitive to the child's feelings and more empathic with her. These attitudes were not specific to the play sessions, but from the mother's report generalized to events that occurred during the rest of the week. The entire emotional tone of the mother-child interactions gradually changed with therapy.

The mothers' group sessions also proved to be beneficial. The participants learned that other persons had similar problems, and thus were able to receive social support from each other. The mothers were also taught behavior modification techniques that they could apply to their children's problem behaviors. The successful use of these procedures again changed the interpersonal relationship with the child from a punitive and critical one to one of reward and praise. Associated with this change, the home environment became a setting where standards of behavior were clearly defined and realistically attainable.

Beth showed good progress in her disabilities class and was able to learn quite well once specialized techniques were used to compensate for her perceptual problems. It is extremely important that the child experiences frequent success and praise. The child's feelings of mastery and self-image as a worthwhile, competent person depend on the individual's life experiences and influence the approach to future learning situations.

One cannot accurately predict that the intellectual progress of an impaired child will rise to a given point and no higher. The parents and the school personnel must deal directly with the intellectual and behavioral difficulties these children are experiencing, but in so doing, they do not have to condemn these youngsters to an inferior status. On the contrary, it is possible to give these children the opportunity to reach greater levels of development than was ever previously expected of those with attentional problems and learning disabilities.

References

American Psychiatric Association (1987). *Diagnostic and statistical manual of mental disorders* (3rd ed., rev.) (DSM-III-R). Washington, DC: Author.

Guerney, B. G., Jr. (1964). Filial therapy: Description and rationale. *Journal of Consulting Psychology, 28,* 304–310.

Guerney, B. G., Jr. (1976). Filial therapy used as a treatment for disturbed children. *Evaluation, 3,* 34–35.

Guerney, B. G., Jr., Stover, L., & De Meritt, S. A. (1968). Measurement of empathy in parent-child interaction. *Journal of Genetic Psychology, 112,* 49–55.

Klinkerfuss, G. H., Langa, P. H., Weinberg, W. A., & O'Leary, J. L. (1965). Electroencephalographic abnormalities of children with hyperkinetic behavior. *Neurology, 15,* 883–891.

Loney, J. (1980). Hyperkinesis comes of age: What do we know and where should we go? *American Journal of Orthopsychiatry, 50,* 28–42.

Milich, R., & Pelham, W. E. (1986). Effects of sugar ingestion on the classroom and playgroup behavior of attention deficit disordered boys. *Journal of Consulting and Clinical Psychology, 54,* 714–718.

Rapoport, J. L., Buchsbaum, M. S., Zahn, T. P., Weingartner, H., Ludlow, C., & Mikkelsen, E. J. (1978). Dextroamphetamine: Cognitive and behavioral effects in normal prepubertal boys. *Science, 199,* 560–563.

Rosenthal, R. H., & Allen, T. W. (1978). An examination of attention, arousal, and learning dysfunctions of hyperkinetic children. *Psychological Bulletin, 85,* 689–715.

Satterfield, J. H., Hoppe, C. M., & Schell, A. M. (1982). A prospective study of delinquency in 110 adolescent boys with attention deficit disorder and 88 normal adolescent boys. *American Journal of Psychiatry, 139,* 795–798.

Sensué, M. B. (1981). *Filial therapy follow-up study: Effects on parental acceptance and child adjustment.* Unpublished doctoral dissertation, The Pennsylvania State University.

Stover, L., & Guerney, B. G., Jr. (1969). The efficacy of training procedures for mothers in filial therapy. In B. G. Guerney, Jr. (Ed.), *Psychotherapeutic agents: New roles for nonprofessionals, parents, and teachers* (534–544). New York: Holt, Rinehart, & Winston.

Sywulak, A. E. (1977). *The effect of filial therapy on parental acceptance and child adjustment.* Unpublished doctoral dissertation, The Pennsylvania State University.

Wallender, J. L., & Hubert, N. C. (1985). Long-term prognosis for hyperactive children. In B. B. Lahey & A. E. Kazdin (Eds.), *Advances in clinical child psychology* (Vol. 8, pp. 113–147). New York: Plenum Press.

Weingartner, H., Rapoport, J. L., Buchsbaum, M. S., Bunney, W. E., Jr., Ebert, M. H., Mikkelsen, E. J., & Caine, E. D. (1980). Cognitive processes in normal and hyperactive children and their response to amphetamine treatment. *Journal of Abnormal Psychology, 89,* 25–37.

Weiss, G., Kruger, E., Danielson, U., & Elmann, M. (1975). Effect of long-term treatment of hyperactive children with methylphenidate. *Canadian Medical Association Journal, 112,* 159–165.

Werry, J. S. (1968). Studies on the hyperactive child. *Archives of General Psychiatry, 19,* 9–16.

3

Elimination Disorder and Noncompliance— The Case of Carl Moore

Carl Moore was seven years old and in the second grade when he and his parents were initially seen at a family counseling center. They were referred to the clinic by a local physician because of problems with Carl's toilet habits: wetting his pants every day and each night, and soiling three to four times a week. The parents also reported that they felt the youngster tended to act in an effeminate manner, and that he was extremely negativistic and refused to comply with any of their requests.

Carl appeared for the initial evaluation dressed in a suit and tie, and his brown hair was neatly combed. Nothing in his mannerisms, gait, or tone of voice indicated the effeminate behavior of which his parents complained.

The family was white and of upper-middle-class background. The father owned a prosperous retail store, and the Moore family lived in a large home in the suburbs.

Developmental Background

Carl was the third of five children. At the time the family was seen, Carl was 7 years old, his two older brothers, Douglas and Frank, were 13 and 12, respectively. Carl's two younger sisters were Susan, age 4, and Cathy, 1½.

Mrs. Moore described all of her pregnancies as difficult, but particularly so when she was pregnant with Carl. On her obstetrician's orders, she frequently had to remain in bed for up to a week at a time because of uterine bleeding. Although this had happened an average of two or three times with the other children, Mrs. Moore estimated that she had spent a total of at least four weeks in bed during her pregnancy with Carl. No difficulties were reported, however, during Carl's delivery and birth.

Mrs. Moore stated that after Carl's birth, she had felt tired and depressed, particularly after arguments with her husband. Both she and her husband had wanted a girl and were very disappointed when Carl was born. Mrs. Moore said that she had been more disappointed than her husband because she greatly desired to have a daughter to counteract the "male emphasis" in her home.

Carl's general developmental progress appeared normal. Mrs. Moore reported that he was a good baby and had no special problems. He walked and spoke simple words at 12 months of age. He was bottle fed, then began to drink from a cup when he was approximately 13 months old.

The mother indicated that she began toilet training Carl when he was between 13 and 14 months old. She followed the same procedure with all of her children: she would place the youngster on a potty several times a day, stay in the room with the child when possible and read stories to him or her until either elimination occurred or the child got up from the potty and refused to sit any longer. Carl was able to remain dry during the daytime when he was about two-and-a-half years old. He was also able to control his bowels at this time and to use the potty for elimination. Mrs. Moore reported that by three years of age, Carl could remain dry throughout the night.

When Carl was three years old, Susan was born. Although there was a transitory problem at this time with Carl occasionally wetting his pants during the daytime, this pattern did not persist. Mrs. Moore said that she was too busy with Susan to make a fuss the few times Carl had an "accident." She would tell him "no, no" and help him change his pants, without too much additional comment. She did not tell Mr. Moore about the wetting episodes, because they were infrequent and soon stopped entirely.

Carl's toilet habits reportedly remained good until Mrs. Moore started toilet training the youngest child, Cathy, about six months before coming to the clinic. According to Mrs. Moore, Carl quite suddenly started wetting his pants every day and every night during sleep. He also began having bowel movements in his pants approximately three times a week. Two episodes of wetting occurred at school, but all of the remaining times the wetting and soiling occurred when Carl was at home or outside playing. Carl showed no apparent embarrassment or discomfort and tended to ignore the situation or deny that elimination had occurred. When confronted by his mother or siblings, he frequently stated that he did not realize that he had eliminated in his pants. Mrs. Moore generally cleaned up after Carl, rather than ask him to do it for himself. Both parents tended to react to the situation by shouting at Carl and ridiculing him by calling him a baby. Often both mother and father spanked Carl in response to a wetting or soiling incident.

Carl was taken to an urologist and hospitalized for two days for tests to determine whether there might be a physical basis to his elimination difficulties. All of the tests were negative and the urologist suggested that the child be referred for psychological evaluation.

Social History

The father and mother both described their marital situation as one of frequent discord. Mr. Moore, who was in his late 30s, reported that at times his wife was openly antagonistic to him. He stated that she often tended to "put down" his accomplishments, irrespective of whether they related to his successful business or to something he had made around the house. He felt that Mrs. Moore was unwilling to support him in any of his efforts at work or in disciplining the children.

Mrs. Moore was also in her late 30s when the family visited the counseling center. She stated that she felt resentful of her husband's being so seldom at home, and that when he was present, he tended to be autocratic with her and with the children. She also reported that Mr. Moore would issue commands that he expected the family to comply with immediately, and would shout at his wife or spank the children if his orders were not carried out at once. Mrs. Moore felt that she had to take her children's side in their disputes with the father, because she judged his demands and his frequent use of physical punishment to be unreasonable.

The parents very rarely went out together on social occasions. They had few friends, and neither had relatives in the immediate vicinity.

Both parents indicated that Carl seemed more of a problem than the other children. Mrs. Moore said that until the past year, Carl had frequently provoked fights with his older brothers. These arguments usually ended with either Douglas or Frank hitting Carl, and Carl then coming to the mother in tears. Mrs. Moore usually did not intervene, but rather told the boys to settle their disputes among themselves. She reported that it was very difficult to get Carl to do the things she asked of him. Until recently, when she told him to pick up his toys or get his jacket on to go outside, he usually said "no," and ran out of the room.

Within the year before the initial clinic visit, Carl's behavior pattern gradually changed. Carl did not interact with his brothers as often as he had previously. He also lessened his defiant behavior in relation to maternal requests. Mrs. Moore related that when she asked him to do something now, Carl's usual response was one of noncompliance rather than overt opposition. When asked to make his bed or straighten up the family room, Carl never said "no," but he somehow never got around to doing it either. He would continue to say "in a minute" or would disappear to some other part of the house. Eventually, Mrs. Moore ended up doing the job herself, or occasionally she asked one of the older boys to do the chore instead. Mrs. Moore would often complain about Carl's behavior to the father, but then would step in to protect Carl when his father began spanking him.

Mrs. Moore felt that Douglas and Frank were on the whole more cooperative than Carl. She did report, however, that at times Douglas and Frank were defiant of her requests. The mother responded to this by threatening to tell their father when he got home. If Mr. Moore found out about the episode, he would then administer physical punishment to either Douglas or Frank. Mrs. Moore did not tend to intercede in their punishment as much as she did in Carl's.

The mother stated that dealing with Douglas and Frank was easier than with Carl because at least she knew where she stood with the two older boys. If she asked Douglas or Frank to do something they did not want to do, they would just tell her "no," instead of saying nothing and disappearing, as was Carl's pattern. The two older boys, however, usually tended to comply with the mother's requests. Douglas's and Frank's chief area of conflict in interpersonal relationships appeared to be their aggressive interactions with Carl.

Susan and Cathy seemed to have a much more positive relationship with their parents. Both Mr. and Mrs. Moore described four-year-old Susan as "not too much of a problem." The mother expressed satisfaction that she had given birth to a daughter, after having three boys in a row. Mr. Moore also stated that he was pleased to have a daughter. Because Susan was so much easier to care for after the difficulties with the boys and particularly Carl, the parents were also pleased with the birth of their youngest daughter, Cathy.

Susan tended to comply with the mother's requests and received a great deal of praise from Mrs. Moore for acting like a "good girl," rather than noisy or rowdy like the boys. Mr. and Mrs. Moore frequently commented on how cute and ladylike Susan acted. The mother reported that she rarely had to yell at Susan to get her to obey, and Mr. Moore could remember only two incidents when he had spanked her. Both situations, as Mr. Moore described them, involved episodes in which Susan began hitting her younger sister, Cathy. The mother corroborated these events. She stated that she had witnessed the situations and had interceded at the time the dispute took place and had made Susan stop. The mother did not administer a spanking but waited and told the events to her husband who then spanked Susan.

Cathy was one-and-a-half, "into everything" in the house, and needed a great deal of supervision because she was so active. Mrs. Moore frequently asked Carl to watch Cathy to see that she did not get into trouble. Carl seemed to enjoy being with Cathy and Susan more than with his older brothers.

Mrs. Moore began toilet training Cathy six months before the clinic visit. She would place Cathy on the potty, and then sometimes read to her for 15 or 20 minutes in hopes that she would eliminate while her mother interested her in a story. Although Cathy was active at other times, she sat quietly on the potty while Mrs. Moore stayed and read to her. As soon as Mrs. Moore left the room, Cathy would also get up and walk out of the bathroom. Toilet training had not as yet been accomplished.

Carl's brothers presently refused to play with Carl because he "acted like a sissy or a girl," and because he wasn't interested in sports or rough and competitive games. Carl enjoyed playing house with his sister Susan, and frequently assumed the role of mother or female teacher in their games of make-believe. Carl did not have any male friends at school or in the neighborhood. His only friend was a neighborhood girl a few months older than he.

During the period when Carl began to have problems with elimination, his brothers were quite hostile to him. They tended to ridicule him until he started to cry, or else they refused to interact with him in any manner. The parents did not usually respond to the teasing, except occasionally to agree with what the brothers were saying. Susan also began to make fun of Carl and call him "stupid" and "baby," and played with him much less than she used to. The only family member with whom Carl seemed to have a warm relationship was one-and-a-half-year-old Cathy. Although he occasionally teased her, on the whole he appeared to enjoy playing with her. Carl and Cathy played together with blocks and dolls, and he also would gently push her on a small bike or help her ride on a rocking horse.

The effeminate behavior that the parents complained of seemed related primarily to Carl's choice of female playmates and his preference for quiet fantasy games, particularly those in which he could play a feminine role. Mrs. Moore tended to respond with amusement to Carl's feminine-role play activity, although she also stated that Carl was acting like a sissy. The mother encouraged Carl to play with Cathy because this gave her more free time, since Cathy was so active and in need of almost continuous supervision. Mr. Moore usually responded to Carl's play activity with ridicule, much as Douglas and Frank did. However, Mr. Moore did not tend to encourage Carl to play more active or competitive games, and Carl rarely went with his father to any sporting events. Occasionally, Mr. Moore would take Douglas and Frank to a baseball game, but when he asked Carl if he wanted to go too, Carl would always say "no." Mr. Moore did not attempt to persuade Carl to change his mind. As the elimination problem continued, Mr. Moore stopped asking Carl to accompany him anywhere, although he still took the older boys with him from time to time.

Psychological Evaluation

To obtain more information about the nature of his difficulties, Carl was given a battery of psychological tests. He was seen by a male psychologist who introduced himself to Carl and his mother in the waiting room. The youngster accompanied the examiner to the testing room, but only after he had been told exactly where his mother would be while he was being tested. Carl did not attempt to converse with the psychologist either while in the corridor or in the testing room. He answered the examiner's questions in a very brief manner and seldom looked directly at him. Carl spoke softly and did not attempt to explore the room or ask questions about the various testing materials. There were no indications of effeminate behavior.

Carl's performance on an intelligence test indicated that his overall intellectual functioning was in the bright normal range. There was some discrepancy between the relatively higher scores he gained on the subscales measuring verbal ability and abstract reasoning, and the relatively lower scores he received on the subscales measuring coordination and the ability to use concepts dealing with spatial relationships. His relatively higher performance in the verbal area probably reflected an interest and ability pattern involving school work, reading, and fantasy play, rather than interests and abilities in manipulating tools or building objects.

Carl was asked to make up stories from cards in the Tasks of Emotional Development (TED) series. Each of these cards shows a scene involving peers or family members in some type of interaction. The cards are moderately ambiguous in that an individual can give a number of different descriptions for what appears to be happening in the card scene. The traditional rationale for using cards of this type is that when confronted with an ambiguous situation for which there are no clear-cut right or wrong answers, the individual will "project" his or her own needs and problems into the responses given to the test stimuli (Murray, 1933). The cards can also be interpreted as providing information about current social interaction patterns.

Carl did not reply as rapidly to the cards as he had to the intelligence test material. He repeatedly asked if he could switch to other tasks, and he gave quite short descriptions to a number of cards presented to him. He also indicated that he could not think of anything to say on three of the cards presented. Several of the story themes elicited from Carl involved passive noncompliant behavior directed toward the parents. Other stories centered on rivalry among siblings for parental affection and attention.

The passive noncompliant interactions that Carl related on some of the card stories tended to corroborate the type of behavior his mother had complained about in her interview with the social worker. Carl told a story about a child being asked by his mother to clean his room. The child continually told his mother "later," and never actually carried out this chore. This story closely resembled a real-life incident his mother had related.

The stories Carl gave were quite sparse and matter-of-fact in light of his bright normal intellectual ability and his relative superiority in the verbal area. The psychologist concluded that Carl was inhibited in expressing any type of emotion, and that the youngster was uncomfortable in situations where he was not sure exactly what was expected of him. At these times, Carl apparently tried to respond in as minimal a fashion as possible.

The Observed Interaction

Mrs. Moore and Carl entered the playroom together, and both listened as the psychologist explained the procedure for the structured interaction.

During the ten-minute free play period, Mrs. Moore sat in a chair and watched Carl's play activities. Carl looked about the room and picked up a toy gun. He held it for a moment, then put it down and started looking through a box containing small toys. The youngster occasionally picked up a play object such as an animal puppet or toy accordian and showed it to his mother, commenting "look at this," or "this is neat." Mrs. Moore's response was a short "hmm." She tended to ignore the child's presence, and communication between the two was quite limited. Only a few times during the free play period did she converse with Carl. In one instance, she told him to speak more quietly when he started to comment in a loud voice about his success in shooting darts from a dart gun. Mrs. Moore also told Carl he was becoming too noisy when he began hitting an inflated clown and saying "pow" with each hit. Carl did not play with the dollhouse or with any of the dolls in the room.

At the signal that the free period was over, Carl and his mother began working on the questionnaire. Mrs. Moore asked each question in a matter-of-fact tone of voice, and wrote down Carl's responses. A number of times she disagreed with an answer Carl gave. For example, in response to the question "What do you usually do if you are the first one up in the morning?" Carl said, "Play downstairs, until everyone else is up." Mrs. Moore said, "No, you don't. You start making noise and wake everybody up." She then proceeded to write down what *she* said rather than what Carl had said.

After completing the questionnaire, mother and child worked together on a jigsaw puzzle. Although instructed to work together cooperatively, Mrs. Moore set about doing the puzzle by herself. Carl literally had to grab pieces of the puzzle out of his mother's hands in order to complete the part of the puzzle he was working on. When finished, Mrs. Moore commented approvingly on her own performance, but ignored the work her son had done.

The final activity was the basket puzzle. To finish this task successfully, the child has to hold a wire basket completely steady while the mother threads some rods through the mesh and bolts them in place. Carl held the basket reasonably steady, but complained a number of times that he was getting tired of just standing there. Mrs. Moore ignored these comments and firmly told Carl to hold the basket up when Carl changed position while standing. Mrs. Moore again expressed satisfaction about her own performance when the task was finished, but failed to comment on her son's role in helping her.

In general, Mrs. Moore tended to ignore any questions Carl asked her, or said, "I don't know," irrespective of whether these questions pertained to the play materials, activities mentioned on the questionnaire, or clinic procedures. The mother manifested either neutral or negative affect in her interactions with Carl, and Carl in turn tended to exhibit a pattern of passive complaints rather than open defiance of his mother's commands.

Course of Psychotherapy

Mr. and Mrs. Moore were seen together in counseling sessions once a week. Carl was also seen weekly in play therapy with a male therapist. The choice of a male therapist for Carl was based on the notion that he needed a warm and accepting male figure with whom to identify.

Carl had participated in 19 play therapy sessions when treatment was recessed for the summer vacation. At the end of this time period, the therapist felt that Carl had made substantial progress in becoming more open and expressive in his play activities and in his relationship with the therapist. The therapist reported that Carl was able to handle competition more adequately by the end of the year; he no longer insisted on winning every game played. The youngster continued to express to the therapist his liking for school because in this situation he knew that there was a definite right or wrong answer. Carl felt that in his relationships with people, he was not sure how to behave much of the time.

An initial counseling plan had involved helping the parents set up a behavior modification program for dealing with Carl's elimination problems. However, the parents reported some difficulty in observing and tallying specific behaviors, and the behavior modification procedure was temporarily suspended. The Moores tended to spend more time talking about their own personal and marital problems than about their children's problems. Their therapist encouraged this under the assumption that many of Carl's difficulties derived from his parents' interpersonal difficulties. At the end of the first year of treatment, the parents reported that Carl still soiled and wet his pants and that they were still unable to change his negativistic behavior. The parents seemed to accept the observation made early in therapy that Carl's problem was not one of effeminacy as much as one of difficulty in engaging in competitive activity. They were told that these problems would be dealt with in play therapy. The Moores never again brought up the issue of effeminacy as a problem in and of itself.

Carl and his parents returned for a second year of therapy. The same social worker continued to see the parents, while a female therapist now saw Carl weekly in play therapy. The play therapy sessions still revolved around the theme of competition, with Carl beginning to express a concern about accidents happening, and how one cannot always control the things that happen in life. Carl's relationship with the female therapist was quite mixed. He frequently insisted to his parents that he did not want to come to the clinic, although once there, he appeared to enjoy the sessions.

During the second year of therapy, the parents were given more specific instructions about how to use behavior modification procedures to lessen the frequency of soiling and wetting. This problem decreased markedly once positive reinforcement was systematically used whenever elimination occurred in the toilet. The parents also focused more specifically on their reactions to Carl's negative behavior. They began to give him more social approval and attention for positive behaviors, rather than berate him for acting in a nonassertive manner or allow him to get involved in some other activity before he completed a job asked of him. However, the bulk of the sessions with the parents continued to be a discussion of their own personal difficulties.

After two years of treatment, the Moores felt that some progress had been made in helping Carl with his problems. They decided that they would like to try to deal with the family situation without outside help. The social worker and psychologist concurred, and therapy was terminated at this point.

Discussion

Carl's parents brought him to a family counseling center because of several kinds of concerns—toileting problems, negativistic behavior, and effeminate interests and activities. DSM-III-R (1987) classifies toileting problems under elimination disorders, subcategories of functional encopresis, and functional enuresis. The specification of a primary type of disorder indicates that there was never a prolonged period of continence; a secondary type designation is made if there was a prior period of continence lasting one year or longer. The term "functional" points to a psychological rather than organic cause of these problems. The amount of impairment is a function of the effects of these toileting problems on the child's self-esteem and interpersonal relationships.

In some children with functional encopresis, the soiling behavior has been conceptualized as a power struggle between the parent and child, and a hostile assertion of the child's will (Bemporad, 1978). Because severe stress can also provoke loss of bowel or bladder control, some therapists feel that when severe family problems are evident, it is necessary to deal with these issues before attempting to modify the elimination problems (O'Dougherty, 1983). Behaviorally oriented clinicians suggest that faulty learning experiences may be the cause of functional encopretic behavior, and the attention-getting value of this behavior can reinforce and maintain the problem (Doleys, 1989). Therefore, a close evaluation of the specific reason that a particular child soils is necessary in order to teach that child the appropriate toileting behaviors. Comprehensive behavioral programs that provide instruction and then reinforcement, contingent on the child detecting the need to defecate, learning how to disrobe, and engaging in appropriate defecation in the toilet, have proven effective.

Negativistic behavior patterns can occur as a normal developmental process. Parental standards or criteria of appropriate behavior by a child may vary. Thus, parents will differ in their labeling of particular behaviors as noncompliance or argumentativeness, and families will also differ in whether they consider these behaviors a problem.

Carl's negativistic behavior fit within the DSM-III (1980) criteria for oppositional disorder. However, his behavior pattern was not consistent with the revised and more stringent DSM-III-R criteria for oppositional defiant disorder, which requires a more confrontive oppositional pattern. It therefore is interesting to observe that behaviors that in 1980 were designated as a mental disorder are not a mental disorder in 1987. Serious problems remain in many of the child and adolescent DSM-III and DSM-III-R categories listed as a mental disorder. Cultural, social, and developmental phenomena are not adequately attended to (Garmezy, 1978), and clear psychoeducational problems such as reading or arithmetic difficulties are designated in DSM-III-R as mental disorders within the Axis II developmental disorders category.

The parental complaint that Carl behaved in an effeminate manner can be analyzed in relation to a social labeling process. Carl manifested an interest pattern that involved a preference for quiet, noncompetitive games, an enjoyment of playing house (at times playing the part of the mother), and a preference for female rather than male companions. Most parents would probably tolerate these behaviors for a time in a younger boy. They would also not become too concerned if these play behaviors occurred infrequently, perhaps in a social context where the youngster could not find anyone else in the neighborhood to play with other than his sisters or female peers. However, at some point related to the child's age and the pervasiveness of this behavior in many different social situations, the parents, older siblings, and perhaps a teacher as well, apply the label "effeminate" or "sissyish" to this behavior. The behavior is then considered abnormal. Ullmann and Krasner (1969) have defined abnormal behavior as a function of the behavior itself, the social context in which the particular behavior occurs, and the presence of a societal agent who observes the behavior and performs the labeling.

An interesting issue to pursue is whether Carl's play interests reflected an attempt to resolve the Oedipus complex by assuming a feminine identification, or whether Carl enjoyed quiet play activities with girls because he had found this type of behavior reinforcing in the past. The Oedipus complex is a Freudian concept suggesting that the boy between the ages of three and six is torn by sexual strivings for the mother and intense hostility and fear of the father. The father is seen as a strong and threatening competitor for the mother's love, and therefore someone who can harm the youngster if he continues to strive for the mother's affection. Castration anxiety results from this perception of the father's power and aggressive intent.

A psychoanalytic analysis of Carl's difficulties suggests that because the father was so competitive and castrating in his interactions with his son, Carl was unable to resolve the Oedipus complex by identifying with the father-aggressor. As a result, he was not able to achieve a masculine identification. The youngster found it safer to stop competing with the father for the mother's love, and he therefore assumed a feminine, noncompetitive behavior pattern through identifying with the inconsistently protective mother.

A social learning analysis of the same situation would explore the particular pattens of interaction that occurred in Carl's life experiences, in order to find out why playing with girls in noncompetitive situations was such a highly reinforcing activity. From Carl's social history, we learned that Carl's two older brothers were quite active and fairly aggressive in their interactions with him. Carl attempted to model his behavior after that of his brothers, but his natural temperament might have been more quiet and passive. When Carl tried to act in a more assertive or aggressive manner, this behavior was not reinforced because his brothers' greater physical strength enabled them to maintain a dominant role. When Carl tried to compete with them, they taunted him and called him "sissy," or if he cried when they hit him, they called him "cry baby."

Frank and Douglas showed discrimination learning in their aggressive behavior toward different family members. They learned that if they were defiant of parental requests they would be punished, but if they aggressed against Carl nothing would happen. Carl, on the other hand, was punished by his brothers and received no support from his mother when he interacted aggressively with Frank and Douglas. Carl was also unsuccessful in acting aggressively with other boys his own age. Further, if he aggressed against Cathy or Susan, his father punished him. The discrimination training that Carl received was that he would not be rewarded for acting in an aggressive manner, but that he would receive attention from others when he behaved in a nonaggressive manner.

Carl did not experience a consistently warm or supportive relationship with either of his parents. Mrs. Moore tended to intercede when her husband began spanking Carl, after she had complained about Carl's behavior. From Carl's point of view, his mother was therefore a source of both punishment and gratification. The Observed Interaction showed that the mother also interacted in either an indifferent or competitive manner with Carl. She did not allow him the satisfaction of mastering the puzzle they were working on together, nor did she praise him or show an interest in any of his activities in the playroom.

Carl's relationship with his father was also quite mixed. Mr. Moore spent very little time at home with his children when Carl was growing up. His primary role seemed to be that of punisher for the children's daily transgressions. Mrs. Moore set her husband up in this role by presenting him with a chronicle of the children's misdeeds upon his arrival at home, and expecting that he would deal with these problems by physically punishing the wrongdoers. The mother therefore transformed the father's arrival home into an extremely aversive event for the children. Mr. Moore concurred with this arrangement, and as a result, his presence frequently was an unpleasant experience for the children.

In contrast to his own situation, Carl was able to observe the parents' more positive behavior in relation to his younger sisters. His sister Susan was praised for acting like a "good girl" and the parents gave her a great deal of social approval for showing traditional feminine interests and for acting in a nonaggressive manner. When Carl played quiet games with his sister, he did not get into any difficulties with his mother, and therefore avoided being punished by the father. His mother also encouraged him to keep his youngest sister amused. It was only after this behavioral pattern had become established for some time that the parents labeled Carl's behavior as "effeminate," "sissyish," or "babyish." It is clear, however, that Carl was avoiding punishment and gaining attention by acting in this way.

The question arises as to whether or not Carl's "effeminate" behavior should have been modified. The definition of what is acceptable masculine and feminine behavior in a given society is strongly determined by that society's sex-role stereotypes. In our culture, the stereotype of masculine behavior does not include an acceptance of boys showing interest in dolls, playing house, or acting in a submissive manner. This type of behavior, however, does conform to the traditional stereotype of appropriate feminine behavior.

The concept of psychological androgeny (Bem, 1974) postulates that well-adjusted individuals can exhibit both traditionally masculine and feminine sex-role behaviors. The individual then engages in the behaviors that would be most appropriate for a particular situation, irrespective of whether these behaviors are stereotypically masculine or feminine. A goal in therapy would be to teach and encourage a youngster to feel comfortable in behaving in ways that do not always conform to rigid sex-role stereotypes. However, this communication is clearly based on the therapist's value judgment that it is acceptable to behave in ways other than those society has defined as appropriate for one's sex (London, 1964).

The judgment of the professionals dealing with the Moore family was that it was not their function to change Carl's behavior to conform to a masculine sexual stereotype that does not allow for growth and free expression (Friedan, 1963; Greer, 1971; Schaffer, 1980). Rather, it seemed more appropriate to help Carl obtain greater flexibility in his relationships with others, by teaching him the social skills necessary to interact with male peers in the more traditional male-oriented games. However, it seemed important to encourage him to feel that he was not a sissy if he also played with girls. Because acting in a submissive, nonassertive manner in all social situations is not helpful for personality development, it was felt that Carl should be reinforced for acting in a more assertive manner. The counseling sessions with the parents that related to Carl's play interests did not focus on changing "effeminate" behavior, but dealt with how to help provide Carl with alternative ways of behaving.

Carl's elimination problems appeared when his mother started toilet training his youngest sister. Although nocturnal enuresis is not uncommon in seven-year-olds, daytime wetting and bowel incontinence at this age are more infrequent. Carl was able to observe that his sister, during the process of her toilet training, was gaining a great deal of attention from the mother. Mrs. Moore read stories to Cathy and entertained her as long as she remained on the potty. The mother was expressing a great deal of interest in her daughter's eliminative functions, and this occurred at a time when Carl was receiving very little social approval for any of his behavior. Carl's incontinence at the time of Cathy's toilet training served the function of diverting a great deal of attention to him. Negative attention was more reinforcing than just being ignored by the family. The fact that the elimination problems continued for almost a year-and-a-half suggests that Carl was able to gain very little positive reinforcement or social approval at home for engaging in other types of behaviors. A dramatic decrease in incontinence occurred only when the parents consistently began a behavior modification program aimed at rewarding Carl for eliminating in the appropriate place. Most important, they also learned to give him social approval for positive behaviors that had previously gone unnoticed.

The negativism that the parents complained about when they brought Carl for evaluation was related to the nonassertive behavioral pattern the youngster adopted. When his mother asked him to make his bed and he said "no!" he was inviting punishment. If he continued to respond "in a minute" each time his mother asked, quite often nothing would happen. In the counseling sessions, the parents began to learn how to set limits so they were not reinforcing noncompliance, and at the same time, they were also taught to give Carl social approval for acting in a positive manner.

The method of treatment used in this case needs to be examined. The author does not agree that play therapy in a clinic setting is the treatment of choice for youngsters with behavioral-emotional difficulties. The process of a therapist seeing a child once a week and then returning him or her to an essentially unchanged home environment appears to be an ineffective treatment plan. Even though the parents were also being seen, the sessions with the parents during the first year of treatment were devoted primarily to their own marital problems, not to how their marital problems affected their interrelationships with their youngsters.

In the author's opinion, a more effective treatment strategy would have involved not seeing the child at all, but working intensively with the parents, who could then have been helped to understand the reinforcement contingencies operating in the home, that is, which behaviors they were reinforcing through attention and social approval and how these reinforcement patterns shaped the types of behaviors in which their children were engaging. By dealing with the parents, one might have avoided the remission of elimination problems that occurred when Carl found out that the play therapy was to be discontinued. A number of studies with parents of noncompliant children have shown that the parent can be an effectve therapist in modifying the problem behaviors of the child (Forehand et al., 1979; McBurnett, Hobbs, & Lahey, 1989; Patterson & Fleishman, 1979; Wahler, 1976).

Many times parents receiving counseling for their children will bring up episodes from their own past or from their present life situation. For therapy to be most effective, the therapist should help the parents to relate these episodes to current problems with their child. The focus of the sessions is then on the child's behavioral difficulties. The therapist is in a position to suggest to the parents alternative ways of responding, and the therapist can provide encouragement and approval to the parents for changing their behavior with the child and with each other. In Carl's case, as the parents began to notice and provide approval for the more socially acceptable behaviors that he engaged in, he began to be more likeable to them. They in turn were able to respond to him in a more loving way than they had previously, and the parents also began to be more aware of the feelings and behaviors of one another. The entire emotional tone of the interactions began to change, and the parents themselves, with the therapist's help, were able to begin modifying the problem behaviors of their child.

Ideally, the role of the therapist vis à vis the parents should be one of an educator, rather than a curer (Guerney, Stollak, & Guerney, 1971). Hopefully, the lessons that the parents learn on how to handle problem behaviors in one child will generalize to their relationships with their other children. In order to accomplish this goal, it is important for the therapist to continue to focus on the role of the parents in the development of behavioral difficulties in the child, and on how the parents can modify the child's problem behavior. A model of the therapist as a teacher, rather than a curer of the sick, seems most appropriate to this conception of the therapeutic process.

References

American Psychiatric Association (1980). *Diagnostic and statistical manual of mental disorders* (3rd ed.) (DSM-III). Washington, DC: Author.

American Psychiatric Association (1987). *Diagnostic and statistical manual of mental disorders* (3rd ed., rev.) (DSM-III-R). Washington, DC: Author.

Bem, S. (1974). The measurement of psychological androgyny. *Journal of Consulting and Clinical Psychology, 42,* 155–162.

Bemporad, J. P. (1978). Encopresis. In B. B. Wolman, J. Egan, & A. O. Ross (Eds.), *Handbook of treatment of mental disorders in childhood and adolescence.* Englewood Cliffs, NJ: Prentice-Hall.

Doleys, D. M. (1989). Enuresis and encopresis. In T. H. Ollendick & M. Hersen (Eds.), *Handbook of child psychopathology,* (2nd ed.) (pp. 291–314). New York: Plenum Press.

Forehand, R., Sturgis, E. T., McMahon, R., Aguar, D., Green, K., Wells, K. C., & Breiner, J. (1979). Parent behavioral training to modify child noncompliance: Treatment generalization across time and from home to school. *Behavior Modification, 3,* 3–25.

Friedan, B. (1963). *The feminine mystique.* New York: Dell.

Garmezy, N. (1978). DSM-III: Never mind the psychologists, is it good for the children? *The Clinical Psychologist, 31,* 4–16.

Greer, G. (1971). *The female eunuch.* New York: McGraw-Hill.

Guerney, B., Jr. Stollak, G., & Guerney, L. (1971). The practicing psychologist as educator—an alternative to the medical practitioner model. *Professional Psychology, 2,* 276–282.

London, P. (1964). *The modes and morals of psychotherapy.* New York: Holt, Rinehart, & Winston.

McBurnett, K., Hobbs, S. A., & Lahey, B. B. (1983). Behavioral treatment. In T. H. Ollendick and M. Hersen (Eds.), *Handbook of child psychopathology* (2nd ed.) (pp. 439–471). New York: Plenum Press.

Murray, H. A. (1933). The effect of fear upon estimates of the maliciousness of adult personalities. *Journal of Social Psychology, 4,* 310–329.

O'Dougherty, M. M. (1983). *Counseling the chronically ill child. Psychological impact and intervention.* Lexington, MA: Lewis Publishing.

Patterson, G. R., & Fleishman, M. J. (1979). Maintenance of treatment effects: Some considerations concerning family systems and follow-up data. *Behavior Therapy, 10,* 168–185.

Schaffer, K. F. (1980). *Sex-role issues in mental health.* Reading, MA: Addison-Wesley.

Ullmann, L. P., & Krasner, L. (1969). *A psychological approach to abnormal behavior.* Englewood Cliffs, NJ: Prentice-Hall.

Wahler, R. G. (1976). Deviant child behavior within the family: Developmental speculations and behavior change strategies. In H. Leitenberg (Ed.), *Handbook of behavior modification and behavior therapy.* Englewood Cliffs, NJ: Prentice-Hall.

4

Conduct Disorder in Association with a Disadvantaged Environment

Oswald Williams was 11 years old when his mother brought him to a community guidance center. The family was black and at the lowest socioeconomic level. The mother was a 36-year-old widow who lived with her eight children in a public housing project. The family had been on welfare for the past five years. A welfare worker in the district where the family lived referred Mrs. Williams to the center.

Mrs. Williams was primarily interested in an evaluation of her son's intelligence. She questioned the accuracy of his placement in a special class for children of borderline or retarded intelligence, where he had remained since the second grade. Oswald also had difficulties related to his frequently unprovoked aggressive behavior both at school and at home. The aggressive behavior occurred in interactions with peers and teachers, as well as with his mother and siblings.

Oswald appeared for the initial interview in faded, neatly pressed trousers and shirt. He seemed to be somewhat small for 11 years of age. He sat close to his mother in the waiting room, but separated readily from her when asked to go with the psychologist for the testing session.

Developmental Background

Oswald was the fourth child in a family of five boys and four girls. Two years previously an older brother had died in an accident at the age of 15. At the time the family was seen, the eldest sister was 15, his brother Percy was 13, and Oswald was 11. The younger siblings included two brothers, ages 10 and 4, and three sisters, ages 8, 7, and 5.

Oswald was born prematurely during his mother's eighth month of pregnancy. The delivery progressed without complications and the youngster was placed in an incubator for three weeks. Oswald weighed four pounds at birth, and was released from the hospital in his mother's care five weeks after he was born. His weight at that time was approximately five pounds, four ounces.

Mrs. Williams reported that Oswald was the only one of her children who was born prematurely. The other children were all born full term and had fairly uneventful infancies. Oswald, however, required a great deal of extra care as an infant. Because he was born prematurely and was quite small when brought home, Oswald was often hungry and required food every two or three hours the first three months of his life.

Oswald's early life was accompanied by a number of illnesses. At four months of age he was hospitalized with a diagnosis of meningitis, and was released from the hospital after a one month stay with no apparent aftereffects. He contracted pneumonia before the age of two and was treated at home. Mrs. Williams noted that Oswald had always been more susceptible to colds than had the other children.

The mother reported that Oswald began to walk unaided at 18 months, which is slightly later than average, although within normal limits. He began to speak words when he was two years old, and according to the mother began stuttering at three years of age when he stopped sucking his thumb. Oswald continued to have episodes of stuttering and his speech was always unclear. The stuttering became more pronounced when he was involved in emotionally charged situations. Toilet training was started at about one-and-a-half years of age and completed a year later. However, Mrs. Williams related that Oswald continued to wet his bed occasionally until he was nine years old.

The youngster had always been somewhat small for his age and on the slender side, although he ate regularly, and according to his mother, enjoyed his food.

School History

Oswald entered first grade when he was six years old. In May of that school year he was referred to the special education department because of "partial lack of communication and reading impairment." The youngster was given the Stanford-Binet intelligence test, which is individually administered. On the basis of his performance on this test, his intellectual functioning was considered to be at the retarded level (I.Q. below 70). At the start of the next school year, he was placed in a special class for educable youngsters—that is, those children judged to be able to profit from classroom instruction presented at a slower rate than usual.

In light of Oswald's premature birth and multiple childhood illnesses, the teacher at the school referred him to a neurologist. An electroencephalogram was given to determine whether there were any signs of neurological impairment. The results were inconclusive, and the neurologist diagnosed the youngster as mildly retarded.

Subsequent intellectual evaluations with other tests during Oswald's second year of school resulted in his being classified in the category of borderline intelligence (I.Q. 70-80). Oswald has continued in a special class throughout his school career.

Social History

The Williams family suffered an extremely traumatic event two years before visiting the guidance center. Mr. Williams and the eldest son were riding in an automobile that another car crashed into, and both father and son were killed. Mrs. Williams related that she and the children were stricken with grief and shock for a number of months, and only with great difficulty accustomed themselves to getting along without the father and eldest brother.

Mrs. Williams described her husband as a loving and devoted father, and a strict disciplinarian. He had been employed as a laborer but was frequently out of work because jobs were in short supply in the area where they lived. Mrs. Williams was used to having her husband make most of the family decisions, and found it extremely difficult to take over the entire burden of family responsibility after her husband's death.

Mrs. Williams indicated that even before the deaths occurred, she was quite anxious and concerned about her children's whereabouts and activities. After the accident, this concern deepened, and Mrs. Williams tried to know where each child was at every moment. She stated that if one of the children was even five minutes late getting home from school, she became acutely anxious and set out on foot to look for that child. She also reported that when she went out to the supermarket or to a church activity, she called home every 10 or 15 minutes to make sure the children were all right and that they were home and still being supervised by the eldest daughter. Mrs. Williams rarely went out in the evening until she recently began working.

Part of this mother's concern about her children's activities was of a long-standing and quite realistic nature. The Williams family lived in a low-income public housing project in an area where robberies and violent crimes occurred frequently and drug pushers and addicts were in abundance on the streets. Mrs. Williams's anxiety about the children walking alone in the daytime or in the evening appeared well-founded in light of the environmental hazards prevalent in the area where they lived.

The family's income level had always been marginal. When the family grew in size, they were often on welfare to supplement the father's earnings. Until her husband's death, Mrs. Williams had stayed home and cared for the youngsters. After therapy began, she started working several evenings a week as a cleaning woman in an office building.

Mrs. Williams reported that she tended to rely on her husband to set limits and take the initiative in disciplining the children. She stated that Mr. Williams was also concerned about where the children were, and would spank them if they were late in getting home or if they did not obey him. Since the father was periodically unemployed and home all day, he was able to supervise the children's activities quite closely. Mr. Williams had administered physical punishment frequently, but Mrs. Williams indicated that he had never been abusive with the children and, therefore, they respected him. Mrs. Williams tended to yell at the children when they disobeyed her, and threatened to tell the father about the children's misbehavior. The mother felt that the children were equitably disciplined, and it did not appear to her that any one child was singled out for a greater amount of punishment.

After the father's death, Mrs. Williams continued to discipline the children primarily by shouting at them. She stated that she constantly had to yell at the children, and that they tended to ignore her. She felt that the children were in control of her emotions, because they could get her very anxious or very angry in a moment's time, depending on what they were doing. Mrs. Williams reported that lately she had to resort to physical punishment more often in order to get the children to mind her. Spankings seemed to be effective in getting the younger children to comply. However, she was worried about whether in the future she would be able to control the older children, particularly the boys. Mrs. Williams felt that when Percy and Oswald got older and larger, they would not continue to allow their mother to hit them. She was afraid that eventually they would begin to strike her back, and then she would have absolutely no control over them.

Mrs. Williams was also worried about her eldest daughter's behavior. Janice was 15 years old and her mother constantly worried that she was keeping company with a crowd of friends who would have a bad influence on her. The school reported that Janice was absent from time to time, and Mrs. Williams feared that her daughter might be tempted to begin shoplifting, or that she might get into some difficulty related to sexual activity.

Mrs. Williams had recently formed a friendship with a man who lived with his mother in the same housing project that she lived in. He was in his early forties and had never been married. Mr. Adams visited the Williams family and spent the night there on the weekends. Mrs. Williams felt that the children enjoyed Mr. Adams's visits. She had given her friend permission to discipline the children, and occasionally he spanked one of them for misbehavior. Mrs. Williams said that the children were more likely to obey Mr. Adams than her, and she was grateful that she could rely on him to help her with the children.

From the mother's report, it appeared that Oswald and his siblings were experiencing a great deal of friction in their relationships at home and at school. Mrs. Williams continually and ineffectually shouted at the children or hit them, and the children quite frequently fought among themselves. Oswald and his ten-year-old brother Leroy were constantly fighting because Leroy wore Oswald's clothes without asking Oswald's permission. Leroy was one year younger, but taller than Oswald. Their verbal disputes quickly turned into punching matches that necessitated intervention by Mrs. Williams or one of the older siblings. Mrs. Williams tended to respond to these episodes by yelling at the boys. The boys would ignore her, and quite frequently the fighting would erupt again.

Oswald also fought with his 13-year-old brother Percy, but their disputes did not result in drawn-out fights. Percy was quite a bit larger than Oswald, and after Percy hit Oswald a few times, Oswald would back off and the fight then ended. Oswald fought with his younger brothers and sisters also, and hit them when they got into arguments with him. However, Oswald occasionally played games with his younger sisters, and when he did argue with them, he did not punch them as hard as he did Percy and Leroy.

Since the family lived together in a four-room apartment, the children were quite frequently in each other's way, and fighting often ensued. When Oswald's brothers and sisters got angry at him, they often teased him by mimicking his stuttering. This made Oswald even angrier and he tried to hit whoever was imitating him. When he began shouting at the child with whom he was fighting, he stammered even more.

Mrs. Williams left Janice in charge of the children when she was out of the house. Oswald was not likely to listen to Janice, but he usually did not go outside without her permission.

Oswald spent a great deal of time watching television, and did not play very often with the neighborhood children. This was partly a result of his mother's attempts to keep the children home after school or outside under her supervision. Also, the neighborhood children made fun of Oswald when he began to stutter, and because Oswald was small for his age, his attempts to beat up the boys who were teasing him were usually unsuccessful.

At school, Oswald, Percy, and Janice were in frequent trouble with the teacher and were often sent to the principal's office because of disciplinary problems. Shortly before coming to the guidance center, Janice, Percy, and Oswald were all suspended at the same time from their respective classes. The suspensions occurred because of similar complaints of not listening to the teacher, walking out of the classroom, and in Percy and Oswald's case, fighting with other boys while class was in session.

Oswald's teacher sent a report to the guidance center stating that the youngster encountered frequent difficulty in class because he did not comply with the teacher's requests. For example, Oswald refused to obey the teacher when asked to return to his seat after he got up and grabbed something that belonged to another child. He continued doing whatever activity he was engaged in at the moment. The teacher stated that he had often observed Oswald engage in unprovoked physical or verbal aggression against one of his classmates, and that lately the severity of problems had increased. Recently, Oswald lit matches in class, and when he took some papers and attempted to start a fire in the hallway, he was suspended from school for two weeks. This episode had occurred two months before the visit to the guidance center. In addition, Oswald had been suspended several times for periods of from three days to two weeks, for turning over chairs in class, fighting with other youngsters, and refusing to wait in the principal's office.

Despite these behavior problems, Oswald had made some progress in class. He had learned to read at a beginning second-grade level and could do simple arithmetic problems. However, the teacher reported that Oswald stuttered when emotionally aroused. He also tended to stutter when the teacher asked him a question in class to which he did not know the answer.

Psychological Evaluation

A female psychologist interviewed and tested Oswald. When she came to the waiting room to meet Oswald, he quickly got up without glancing at his mother, and followed the examiner to the testing room. Oswald was very quiet and did not initiate any conversation. He sat in a chair throughout the testing session, and was very cooperative. He briefly answered the questions asked of him, and stuttered only when the topic turned to the difficulties he was experiencing with his siblings, and the disciplinary problems he was having at school.

At times understanding the youngster was difficult. He frequently substituted one sound for another, such as the *f* sound in place of the *th*, and the *d* sound in place of the *t*. These substitutions were consistent, so that the examiner was able to understand the youngster's speech pattern after listening to him for a while.

Oswald was given a battery of tests administered over two testing sessions. The particular tests were chosen to enable the psychologist to gain information about the youngster's current intellectual and academic functioning, and about areas of behavioral or emotional problems. Oswald was also given a number of tests of perceptual-motor functioning, to ascertain any evidence of neurological impairment.

At age 11, Oswald's performance on the intelligence test was consistent with the scores he had received on tests given five years earlier. The youngster scored in the range of borderline intelligence. He did slightly better on tasks involving spatial concepts than on those dealing with abstract verbal skills. An assessment of reading and arithmetic ability, which indicated that Oswald was performing at a beginning second grade level, was consistent with what one would expect in terms of his age and intellectual functioning.

The test results did not indicate any signs of neurological impairment or brain damage. Oswald was able to perform tasks measuring visual motor ability, visual memory, and auditory discrimination at a level commensurate with his overall intellectual functioning.

The youngster was given a number of cards from the TED series and was asked to make up a story about the scene depicted on each card. His responses suggested mixed feelings about the desire to be assertive and independent, and the wish to be dependent and seek the mother's protection. A conflict of this nature is quite typical for youngsters who are close to adolescence.

The maternal figure that Oswald described in the stories was a woman who frequently resorted to physical punishment to get her child to obey. The youngster made numerous references in his stories to a boy who gets "beat up" by the mother for some transgression such as breaking a window, not cleaning his room, or not doing his homework. The mother, however, was also pictured as a person who genuinely cared about her son, even though the boy was described as physically hurting after some of the punishments the mother administered. Adult males were generally described as passive figures showing little influence in the boy's life.

Another theme of the projective stories was the fear of physical harm from peers. The boy in the pictures was described as playing ball or games with other youngsters, but many times the boy was fearful that something would happen and he would get beat up. Oswald also described some calamity or accident suddenly befalling a group of children playing together.

The Observed Interaction

Mrs. Williams and Oswald entered the playroom with the psychologist and were given the procedure instructions for the Observed Interaction. During the free play period, Mrs. Williams sat rather stiffly in a chair while Oswald walked around and explored the room. Mrs. Williams appeared somewhat uncomfortable in the surroundings; she frequently told Oswald to hush when he spoke in a moderately loud tone of voice, and she picked up the procedure card a number of times and re-read the instructions for the interaction. Oswald rarely conversed with his mother during this period. He spent most of his time shooting darts at the ceiling and walls or hitting the inflated clown. Oswald expressed a great deal of glee when a dart hit a ceiling light, and his mother responded to this by telling him to stop shooting at the light or he might break something. The frequency of shooting darts gradually increased over the course of the free play period, and the verbal accompaniment to each shot also became louder. Oswald showed an increase in the intensity of pummeling and jumping on the clown as the session progressed, and he began to ignore his mother's pleas to play quietly.

Mrs. Williams called Oswald over to the table when it was time to work on the questionnaire. This task took a long time to complete as Oswald did not remain seated for very long; he got up a number of times and played with objects in the room. Mrs. Williams had to ask him several times to come back and sit down before he eventually did so. The mother had difficulty reading some of the questions and deciding with Oswald on an appropriate response.

Mother and child initially worked on the jigsaw puzzle together. After several minutes, Oswald left the table and began to wander about the room, ignoring his mother's requests to come back and work on the task. Following a number of unsuccessful efforts to get Oswald to work with her, Mrs. Williams slowly and methodically finished the puzzle by herself.

Oswald cooperated with his mother for several minutes on the last task, the basket puzzle. However, he soon began to complain that he was tired of just standing there and holding the basket. His mother rather sharply told him that he had better stand there and hold the basket if he knew what was good for him. Oswald responded by holding the basket more steadily until the task was finished, but he still complained about being tired just standing there.

The youngster gave evidence of a short attention span during the interaction, and he also showed a gradual increase in verbal and motor activity as he became more engrossed in play activity. As the interaction session progressed, he tended to ignore his mother's attempts to get him to cooperate, until she spoke firmly to him and conveyed a threat of punishment. Mrs. Williams did not attempt to teach Oswald how to perform the various tasks.

Course of Psychotherapy

The social worker who interviewed Mrs. Williams and the psychologist who saw Oswald met jointly with the mother. They told her that on the basis of the tests given, it appeared that Oswald was in an appropriate school placement. The tests did not indicate a higher intellectual potential. For the youngster to make the most satisfactory progress, they recommended he be kept in a special education class, and not be put in a regular class. The slower pace of the special class seemed better suited to his intellectual functioning. They also discussed with Mrs. Williams Oswald's orientation toward physical punishment. They suggested that both she and the youngster could benefit by coming regularly to the center for therapy. Mrs. Williams agreed, and a male therapist was chosen for Oswald in an effort to give the youngster a nonpunishing male figure to model his behavior after. Mrs. Williams also came for weekly sessions with a male social worker. These sessions were oriented around teaching the mother adequate skills for dealing with her children's behavioral difficulties.

The mother was also told that speech therapy would help Oswald. He would be less likely to get into fights based on taunts about his speech if he had help in controlling his stuttering and modifying his unclear speech pattern. Mrs. Williams agreed to this suggestion, and numerous efforts were made over a five-month period to enroll Oswald in a speech therapy class. Because the family had no funds for private help, the only places contacted were public agencies. This proved to be an exercise in frustration, as the few facilities available, including Oswald's school, consistently reported that either their enrollments were filled, or no staff person was free to take on an extra case. In spite of repeated efforts by the center staff, it was impossible to place the youngster in a speech therapy class.

The psychotherapy sessions with Oswald generally centered around an attempt to build a friendship with the boy. In the more structured testing session with a woman, Oswald's speech was fairly understandable except when personal topics were discussed. In contrast, the male therapist had extreme difficulty in conversing with the youngster. Oswald did not initiate any conversation, and minimally answered the therapist's questions or comments. Oswald also tended to stutter a great deal when conversing with the therapist, and the latter found it extremely difficult to understand the boy. The therapy sessions were therefore oriented around building up a relationship through nonverbal means, and Oswald appeared to enjoy coming to the guidance center. He played cards, checkers, or darts with the therapist, went for walks with him, and the two of them routinely stopped off at the snack bar for a soft drink.

Mrs. Williams met weekly with the social worker. She expressed a desire to receive counseling, but cancelled her appointments or else just failed to appear on an average of one out of four sessions. On the occasions when she failed to come, Oswald missed his counseling session also.

Mrs. Williams was able to bring up issues for discussion with the therapist. She freely expressed her frustrations in trying to discipline so large a family and her fears that some harm would befall her children. The therapist attempted to get the mother to see that physical punishment and shouting were ineffective means of dealing with her children. He explored with her specific incidents that had occurred at home, and using these incidents, pointed out how she rarely gave approval or attention for positive behaviors, but instead tended to focus primarily on her children's disruptive behaviors.

Mrs. Williams complained of feeling constantly anxious and upset; she would express these feelings by yelling at the children. The therapist suggested that Mrs. Williams spend some time out of the house engaged in activities that did not include the children. Mrs. Williams began to go to some church activities occasionally. With the therapist's support, she was able to limit her calls home to once an hour, instead of telephoning every 15 minutes, as she had previously done.

Mrs. Williams desired to provide her family with more comforts than she could obtain from the welfare checks she received, and she was encouraged to obtain a part-time job. Although she preferred to work during the day, the only job she could find was as a cleaning woman several evenings a week. Mrs. Williams reported that after she started working, she felt more relaxed than she had in a long time. She was pleased that she was able, from time to time, to get away from her difficulties with her children. The therapist continued to confront the mother with the ineffectiveness of her attempts to discipline the children, and he used examples from some of the events that occurred in the Observed Interaction. He also urged her to actively change her customary modes of interacting with the children. His suggestions were based on the principle of giving social approval for positive behaviors, instead of attention primarily for negative behaviors.

Even though Oswald appeared to have a pleasant relationship with his therapist, the youngster was getting into more and more difficulty at school and had been suspended a number of times. It was decided that setting up a systematic program to modify his behavior in the school setting would be useful. With the concurrence of the mother and teacher, Oswald's therapist met with the teacher and worked out a behavior modification program. The program involved the teacher rewarding Oswald with a token worth one penny each time he worked quietly at his seat for a 15-minute period. Oswald would then take the tokens home to his mother and she would cash them for him.

Both the mother and teacher agreed that this approach was workable and Mrs. Williams was told that she could discuss the progress of the procedure during her therapy session the following week. However, Mrs. Williams called and cancelled her next two appointments, and then stopped calling the center entirely. Letters sent to her were not answered The program in the school could not be carried out without the mother's cooperation, and because the family ceased contacting the guidance center, it was not possible to continue to intervene in the school situation.

Discussion

Conforming to the 1987 DSM-III-R diagnostic scheme, Oswald would be viewed as exhibiting a conduct disorder, solitary aggressive type. The criteria for this diagnosis include the following: starting physical fights, cruelty to animals, skipping school, stealing, running away from home, lying, engaging in fire setting, and deliberately destroying others' property. The solitary, aggressive type initiates aggressive physical behavior as a solitary rather than group or gang activity. The age of onset of this disorder is usually before puberty, and personality characteristics that are commonly exhibited include low self-esteem, the projection of an image of toughness, and poor frustration tolerance. According to DSM-III-R, academic achievement is often below what one would expect in terms of age and intelligence level.

Engaging in a persistent pattern of aggressive behavior is an indicator of poor later adjustment. Robins (1966) carried out a follow-up study of persons who had been referred to a child guidance clinic 30 years previously. She found that those most likely to exhibit antisocial or psychotic behaviors as adults were males who had been referred initially because of problems of theft or aggression embedded within a general antisocial behavior pattern. Further, Loney (1980) concluded from an analysis of the long-term outcome of hyperactive children that childhood aggression, rather than hyperactive behavior, is associated with adjustment problems and delinquent behavior in adolescence. These findings are particularly sobering in light of research indicating a stability of aggressive behavior over a several year period for child and adolescent boys and girls (Moskowitz, Ledingham, & Schwartzman, 1985).

Treatment progress for the Williams family was quite variable. Both Oswald and his mother came to the guidance center for weekly sessions over a period of five months. However, Oswald had extreme difficulty in communicating with his therapist, and this dearth of conversation served the function of diverting attention away from a discussion of his behavioral difficulties. Mrs. Williams terminated the visits when the therapist began pressing her to make some specific changes in her behavior at home with the children.

Mrs. Williams spent a great deal of time in therapy complaining about the problems she was having. When the therapist encouraged and instructed her in how to take active steps to change her interactions with the children, she did not follow through. It may be that once she found some interests outside of the home and felt less anxious, her motivation for changing her behavior with the children lessened. Even though Oswald's difficulties at school were becoming increasingly more serious, his behavior at home was no worse than usual. Mrs. Williams appeared to have adapted herself to a great deal of fighting and shouting in the home, and may have been relieved that it was no worse.

It seems important at this point to review briefly some of the research that has been done on the attitudes of individuals from the lower socioeconomic class toward receiving help for emotional problems. A number of studies have also been done on the nature of mental health services to the poor, and the attitudes of the professionals delivering these services. This information may help provide for a more meaningful discussion of whether alternative procedures might have been more effective in aiding the Williams family.

Hollingshead and Redlich (1958) and Sue (1988) reported that persons of lower socioeconomic status and ethnic minority clients were more likely to frame emotional problems in physical rather than psychological terms. These individuals were therefore more likely to seek and receive some sort of somatic therapy such as pills or treatments, rather than verbal psychotherapy. In the Williams case, their appearance at a guidance clinic was related primarily to a desire to reevaluate Oswald's school placement, rather than seek help for emotional problems.

Our mental health services to the poor and racial and ethnic minorities have been quite limited and relatively ineffective. The sobering studies by Hollingshead and Redlich, and the Midtown Manhattan Study (Srole, Langner, Michael, Opler, & Rennie, 1962) clearly showed a preponderance of severe emotional disorders in individuals of the lower socioeconomic strata, many of whom are members of minority groups. There were very few mental health services available to prevent or treat problems other than by providing custodial care. The poor are a high-risk, underserved group.

The community mental health movement gained momentum in the early 1960s with the allocation of federal funds to develop community mental health centers in neighborhoods in which the poort resided. Related programs were initiated to train primariy-care professionals such as nurses, teachers, or police to intervene with problem individuals and families in response to specific difficulties (Levine & Perkins, 1987). The President's Commission on Mental Health (1978), however, concluded that there continues to be a lack of adequate mental health services to underserved populations including racial and ethnic minority groups. Concerns continue to be expressed tha the primarily Caucasian mental health professionals who provide services to ethnically diverse populations are not sensitive to the linguistic and cultural differences of their clients (Malgady, Rogler, & Costantino, 1987; Rogler, Malgady, Costantino, & Blumenthal, 1987). This lack of cultural sensitivity may result in inappropriate diagnosis and ineffective treatment programs.

Other research has indicated that not only do lower-class clients feel uncomfortable in expressing themselves verbally to a middle-class therapist (Hollingshead and Redlich), but the therapist may also feel ill at ease, less empathic, and less optimistic about the success of psychotherapy with persons whose life experiences have been markedly different from his or her own (Strupp & Williams, 1960; Wilcox, 1971). Lorion (1973) found that lower socioeconomic status persons were accepted less often in psychotherapy, were more likely to be assigned to an inexperienced therapist, and were more likely to drop out of treatment. On the other hand, poor people who persist in psychotherapy appear to have as good a treatment outcome as persons of higher socioeconomic levels (Jones, 1982; Lerner, 1972; Sue, 1988). Greater cultural sensitivity by therapists may therefore be an important means of keeping persons in treatment long enough for positive change to occur.

Mrs. Oswald was a person overwhelmed by personal and absolutely realistic environmental stresses. The death of her husband and eldest son left her in a situation where, in her middle 30s, she was faced with the primary responsibility of caring for and providing guidance to eight children. Further, she was living in a dangerous neighborhood where her children were constantly prone to some sort of harmful influence. To compound this situation even further, Oswald functioned in school at a borderline level of intelligence and was taunted for his slowness and his speech problems. The school that he attended did not provide him with speech therapy, and had large numbers of children in one classroom. The teacher was apparently unable to deal with the disciplinary problems that ensued except by suspending the offending child from school. This, of course, put the child back out on the street, and caused him to get even further behind in school. The family also clearly needed a continually present stepfather, who could provide a good role model for the youngsters, help institute firm discipline, and share in the raising of the children.

One may legitimately ask, "What can really be done to help this mother?" The answer is not easy, and labeling the mother as unmotivated for treatment is perhaps unfair. Mrs. Williams may have felt it useless to continue coming to receive help for one problem, when all of the other problems facing this family were so overwhelming and difficult to solve. As long as Oswald was not behaving any worse at home and Mrs. Williams was feeling less anxious, perhaps she felt that this was the best she could hope for.

A mental health aide with knowledge about the resources in that community might have been able to suggest more practical help, such as where to get a larger place to live so that the children were not constantly together and irritating one another. Perhaps Mrs. Williams could have undergone some special job training in order to find work during the daytime, or someone could have worked more consistently with the school to alleviate some of Oswald's difficulties there. However, the problems of the adverse environmental circumstances this family was forced to live in are not an issue that can be solved by one mental health professional or one agency. The problem is one for our entire society (Albee, 1986).

The genesis of Oswald's aggressive behavior pattern can be understood in part as an attempt to imitate or model the type of behavior that he had observed to be successful in his environment. The youngsters who were able to fight and defend themselves did not tend to get beaten up by others. According to a writer who grew up in Harlem (Brown, 1965), one of the ways of attaining status in the local community and in school was by being able to fight. Also, if one was more aggressive than the other children, then one could strike first and thereby prevent others from taking one's money or possessions.

In Oswald's home, a similar situation occurred. His mother was ineffectual in her attempts to prevent fighting, so each child's place in the pecking order was determined by whom he or she could beat up. The only way that Oswald could stop his brothers and sisters from teasing him or taking things that belonged to him was to fight with them. Further, all of the children observed their father engaging in a great deal of physical punishment. After his death, Mrs. Williams increased her frequency of resorting to physical punishment. However, hitting the children further modeled aggressive behavior. Although physical punishment had an immediate suppressive effect on aggression, it did not lessen the probability that the child would again act aggressively at a future time. Mrs. Williams did not use deprivation of privileges as a punishment. This procedure might have been more effective because the child learns that the penalties or consequences for various negative behaviors last over a longer duration than the time period involved in getting a spanking. Mrs. Williams also did not tend to comment on or give approval for more socially appropriate behaviors. Because she tended to respond to the children primarily when they engaged in disruptive behaviors, they were not motivated to behave in more prosocial ways. As an aggressive interaction pattern becomes more pronounced, the child experiences increasing problems in family and peer relationships, a reduced ability to deal with social expectations, and a decrease in positive mood.

Research with relatively younger conduct problem children demonstrated that less time was spent with their mothers in positive shared activities and more time was spent in conflict interactions than was seen in pairs of nonproblem children and their mothers (Gardner, 1987). Futher, a study of the peer interactions of conduct disordered and well-adjusted adolescents found less social competence and positive affect in the conduct disordered group (Panella & Henggler, 1986).

There may be a reciprocal relationship between a lack of role models for learning harmonious relationships, and the continued engagement in aversive interactions with family and peers. The aggressive behavior itself may drive other people away who otherwise could have been models for more prosocial behavior.

Oswald's aggressive behavior in school partly served the function of diverting attention from his poor academic performance and his speech problems. Perhaps Oswald could have received a greater feeling of competence and academic mastery if he had been taught with a programmed text, so that he could learn in small, easy steps, with a frequent experience of success. Further, there might have been a diminishment of aggressive behavior at school if the behavior modification program had been structured so that the reinforcement was provided directly by the teacher rather than the mother.

Behavioral intervention in the classroom has moved from a primary emphasis on modifying disruptive behavior to a concern with the separate issue of enhancing academic performance. Points of concern include the selection of the appropriate target behaviors to reinforce (McBurnett, Hobbs, & Lahey, 1989), and the loss of intrinsic interest in tasks for which one receives external rewards (Reiss & Sushinsky, 1975). More recent cognitive-behavioral treatment programs have attempted to increase academic performance through enhancing the ability to learn. Instead of reinforcing changes in classroom behaviors, reinforcement is provided for learning specific skills in reading, writing, arithmetic, memorization methods, and self-control procedures to decrease impulsive and disruptive behaviors (Wong, 1985). However, the generalization of training beyond the specific tasks for which the youngster is reinforced is an area in which more progress needs to be made.

Once a child is labeled as deficient in intelligence and is put in a special class, he or she learns less and less each year in comparison to what a child in a regular class learns. After five or six years in a situation like this, it is virtually impossible for a child to catch up. Irrespective of any speculation about whether Oswald was categorized fairly when he first entered school, at the time Oswald was evaluated at the center, he clearly needed remedial education of some type.

Oswald's borderline intellectual functioning and lack of reinforcement in the school setting might increase the likelihood of his developing a more defined aggressive pattern as he grows up. A longitudinal study has indicated an association between low I.Q. and delinquent involvement even after socioeconomic status has been controlled for (Moffitt, Gabrielli,

Mednick, & Schulsinger, 1981). These investigators suggested that less intelligent children may engage in delinquent behavior to compensate for the lack of rewards associated with their school performance. In Oswald's case, making the school experience meaningful and nonaversive for him seems particularly important for his vocational as well as interpersonal future.

From the standpoint of therapy, it may be too harsh to say that the Williams case was a failure, but it certainly was not a success. The mental health field has just begun to grapple with the problem of reaching the disadvantaged members of our society who are faced with a multitude of problems, many of them outside their own personal control. Let us hope that eventually we will be able to reach these people, and that they will have better control over their own destiny.

References

Albee, G. W. (1986). Toward a just society. Lessons from observations on the primary prevention of psychopathology. *American Psychologist, 41,* 891–898.

American Psychiatric Association (1987). *Diagnostic and statistical manual of mental disorders* (3rd ed., rev.) (DSM-III-R). Washington, DC: Author.

Brown, C. (1965). *Manchild in the promised land.* New York: Macmillan.

Gardner, F. E. M. (1987). Positive interaction between mothers and conduct-problem children: Is there training for harmony as well as fighting? *Journal of Abnormal Child Psychology, 15,* 283–293.

Hollingshead, A. B., & Redlich, F. C. (1958). *Social class and mental illness.* New York: Wiley.

Jones, E. E. (1982). Psychotherapists' impressions of treatment outcome as a function of race. *Journal of Clinical Psychology, 38,* 722–731.

Lerner, B. (1972). *Therapy in the ghetto.* Baltimore: Johns Hopkins University Press.

Levine, M., & Perkins, D. V. (1987). Principles of community psychology: Perspective and applications. New York: Oxford University Press.

Loney, J. (1980). Hyperkinesis comes of age: What do we know and where should we go? *American Journal of Orthopsychiatry, 50,* 28–42.

Lorion, R. R. (1973). Socioeconomic status and traditional treatment approaches reconsidered. *Psychological Bulletin, 79,* 263–270.

McBurnett, Hobbs, S. A., & Lahey, B. B. (1983). Behavioral treatment. In T. H. Ollendick & M. Hersen (Eds.), *Handbook of child psychopathology* (2nd ed.) (pp. 439–471). New York: Plenum Press.

Malgady, R. G., Rogler, L. H., & Constantino, G. (1987). Ethnocultural and linguistic bias in mental health evaluation of Hispanics. *American Psychologist, 42*, 228–234.

Moffitt, T. E., Gabrielli, W. F., Mednick, S. A., & Schulsinger, F. (1981). Socioeconomic status, IQ, and delinquency. *Journal of Abnormal Psychology, 49*, 152–156.

Moskowitz, D. S., Ledingham, J. E., & Schwartzman, A. E. (1985). Stability and change in aggression and withdrawal in middle childhood and early adolescence. *Journal of Abnormal Psychology, 94*, 30–41.

Panella, D., & Henggler, S. W. (1986). Peer interactions of conduct-disordered, anxious-withdrawn, and well-adjusted black adolescents. *Journal of Abnormal Child Psychology, 14*, 1–11.

President's Commission on Mental Health (1978). *Report to the President.* Washington, DC: Government Printing Office.

Reiss, S., & Sushinsky, L. W. (1975). Overjustification, competing responses, and the acquisition of intrinsic interest. *Journal of Personality and Social Psychology, 31*, 1116–1125.

Robins, L. N. (1966). *Deviant children grown up.* Baltimore: Williams & Wilkins.

Rogler, L. H., Malgady, R. G., Costantino, G., & Blumental, R. (1987). What do culturally sensitive mental health services mean? *American Psychologist, 42*, 565–570.

Srole, L., Langner, T., Michael, S., Opler, M., & Rennie T. (1962). *Mental health in the metropolis: The midtown Manhattan study* (Vol. 1). New York: McGraw-Hill.

Strupp, H. H., & Williams, J. V. (1960). Some determinants of clinical evaluations of different psychiatrists. *Archives of General Psychiatry, 2*, 434–440.

Sue, S. (1988). Psychotherapeutic services for ethnic minorities. Two decades of research findings. *American Psychologist, 43*, 301–308.

Wilcox, R. C. (1971). *The psychological consequences of being a Black American.* New York: Wiley.

Wong, B. Y. L. (1985). Issues in cognitive-behavioral interventions in academic skill areas. *Journal of Abnormal Child Psychology, 13*, 425–442.

II

Adolescent and Adult Disorders

5

Phobic Behavior in a College Student— An "Irrational" Fear of Spiders

Joyce Ryan phoned for an appointment at a university counseling center because she had become increasingly upset and embarrassed about her long-standing fear of spiders. She indicated that her only problem was this fear and that she was baffled by the panic reaction that ensued when she saw a spider.

When Joyce came to the counseling center for evaluation, she was a 20-year-old college junior, majoring in English literature. She lived in a dormitory on the school campus and saw her family during vacation periods and occasionally on weekends.

Social History

Joyce was the middle child in a family of three children. Her older sister, Barbara, was 24 years old and had been married for two years at the time Joyce was seen. A younger brother, Ted, 17, was a senior in high school.

Joyce was raised in a comfortable, white, middle-class environment. Her father had earned an M.S. in chemistry, and worked for a large chemical concern. Mrs. Ryan was a housewife, with interests centering primarily around home activities. Barbara always received higher grades in school than Joyce, and Joyce felt that her older sister had been continually held up as an example for her to emulate. However, even though Joyce was an above-average student, she never was able to match her sister's academic performance.

When Joyce was growing up, her relationship with her sister and brother was one of frequent discord. She and Barbara fought continually, and Barbara usually won the dispute because she was older. Joyce described an incident that occurred when she was 10 or 11. Joyce had dressed up in some of Barbara's clothes and when her sister saw her, she became very angry and began ridiculing Joyce, calling her "stupid" and "baby." Joyce in turn began to kick Barbara, and Barbara tried to remove the blouse and hair band that Joyce had on, which belonged to Barbara. In the process, the blouse got torn and Barbara then went crying to her mother. Mrs. Ryan was downstairs, and although she had heard the dispute, she had not attempted to intervene. Instead, she complained to her husband about the episode when he got home, and Joyce then got a spanking from her father. Barbara was not punished, and Joyce felt this was unfair. She said that if Barbara had asked her to give the items back instead of calling her names, she would have given them back to her.

Joyce related that she was never able to get along well with her sister, and even though Barbara was now married, she still did not feel very close to her. Joyce did not experience a close emotional bond with her brother Ted, either. Because Ted was three years younger, Joyce felt that they never had much in common. Ted always seemed to be the "pesty little brother" who was constantly disturbing her things, just as she was always involved with Barbara's possessions. When they were younger, she and Ted often ended a dispute by punching each other. Mrs. Ryan usually did not intervene, and if Mr. Ryan heard about or observed the fight, he tended to encourage Ted to defend himself, but did not interfere in any other way.

Joyce felt that her parents had a reasonably happy marital relationship. Mr. Ryan made the decisions in the family, and he generally assumed a protective role toward his wife. Mrs. Ryan looked to her husband for advice and guidance on many daily situations. Mr. Ryan appeared to be interested in matters involving the home and children, and willing to take the time to consider the situation and express an opinion.

Mr. Ryan was often involved with job-related activities and frequently brought work home in the evenings. Although Mr. Ryan took an interest in his daughters, he interacted more with Ted than with the two girls. He bought Ted a chemistry set when the latter was quite young and encouraged him in this area. Ted learned a great deal about chemistry from his father, and Mr. Ryan was quite pleased that his son was planning to major in chemistry in college.

Joyce indicated that it had always been difficult for her to confide in either of her parents, despite the fact that she knew they meant well. Mrs. Ryan never seemed able to give Joyce any advice. When Joyce brought up problems about peer interactions or difficulties at school, Mrs. Ryan's usual response was "Don't worry. It'll work out all right." Mr. Ryan always seemed preoccupied with other matters, and Joyce did not seek out her father for advice.

In a number of areas, Mrs. Ryan did not set for her children an example of competent behavior. She tended to defer most of the decision making to her husband, and she also referred the children to him if they had any questions about their homework assignments. Further, she was afraid of insects, and if there was an insect in the house, she usually called on either Barbara or Ted to get rid of it. Mr. Ryan tended to express amusement at his wife's fears and joked about these events.

Joyce could not relate any specific event as being the origin of her fear of spiders. She said that she remembered neighborhood children teasing her because of this fear and that several times some of the neighborhood boys had caught a spider to tease and scare her. She felt, however, that her fear occurred prior to these childhood teasing episodes. For as long as she could remember, she felt uneasy when there was a crawling spider or some other insect nearby. If she saw a spider in the same room that she was in, she would run out and get someone to remove it. When younger, she often began to cry when confronted with a spider. At the time of evaluation, she reported that she still became panic-stricken when she saw a spider.

Present Status

Joyce felt that her current level of functioning was quite satisfactory except for her unexplainable fear of spiders. She was baffled by the intense anxiety she experienced at the sight of a spider and troubled because the anxiety would not subside until she got away from the phobic stimulus. Although the most intense anxiety response occurred in relation to spiders, Joyce became quite anxious when she saw other insects as well. Joyce recognized that she was reacting with extreme anxiety to something that would not harm her, but she said that she could not control her anxiety response.

The client also described a number of current habit patterns that could be categorized as obsessive in nature. She reported that she worried a great deal about pending examinations and had recurring doubts about whether she would be able to answer the questions asked on the exam. She realized that these thoughts were not very realistic because she generally studied a great deal and did quite well on exams. Nonetheless, these doubts still bothered her. Joyce also found it difficult to make decisions, ranging from which of two dresses to buy, to what major to follow in college. She tended to ruminate among a number of alternative possibilities, and usually was able to come to a decision only when some other person intervened and suggested a choice to her.

Joyce described her present relationship with her family as an ambivalent one. She said that she missed her parents and siblings when she was away at school. However, when she was home, she frequently became moody over seemingly trivial events, and then preferred to stay in her room. Her parents recognized these moods and generally did not attempt to interact with her during these episodes. When Joyce's affective state changed, she would then come out of her room. Neither she nor her parents made any mention of the incident, nor did anyone try to find out what had precipitated the emotional occurrence.

On the whole, Joyce felt that college life was a pleasant experience. She had a good academic record, though her cumulative grade point average was not as high as Barbara's had been. Joyce found it difficult to make friends, but she did have one close girl friend that she met at school, and the two were roommates. Joyce said that she was able to confide in her roommate when she was troubled with various school or family problems. Her friend had initially made the suggestion that Joyce contact the counseling center, and Joyce went along with this suggestion.

Joyce had not dated very often in college until ten months previously, when she met her present boyfriend. Larry also came from a white, middle-class environment, and they met on campus. They soon began to go out together quite frequently, and they had an understanding that neither would date anyone else. Larry was the first boy with whom Joyce had had a sexual relationship, and she felt somewhat anxious about how her parents would respond if they found out. Although from time to time they discussed the possibility of eventually getting married, both felt that they were not ready to take this step within the near future. Both Larry and Joyce were uncertain about what they wanted to do after graduation.

Joyce reported that she was embarrassed by her panic reaction at seeing a spider when she was with her boyfriend. However, he appeared to think it was cute and enjoyed playing the role of defending Joyce from the insect.

Psychological Evaluation

Joyce, an attractive young woman, appeared for the initial interview dressed in the standard campus attire of jeans and a shirt. Joyce sat in a chair in the waiting room, with her hands tightly clasped together. She immediately jumped up from her chair when Dr. K. appeared. Joyce responded briefly to his comments as they walked down the corridor to an interview room, but the client did not initiate any questions or conversation.

During the interview Joyce described her problems and current life situation. At times, the psychologist asked specific questions or directed the conversation to other topics in order to gain more detailed information about the difficulties Joyce was experiencing. Joyce was quite emphatic in stating that her major interpersonal problem was her fear reaction to spiders, and she wanted psychological assistance primarily for solving that particular problem.

Dr. K. administered a selected group of subtests from an intelligence test to gain a general estimate of intellectual functioning. They were also used as a rough screening device for a possible thought disorder. Joyce was also given the Thematic Apperception Test (TAT). Many of the cards on this test show an individual in either a solitary or interpersonal situation. The card scenes are rather vague, so that each person tends to give a somewhat different story of the events depicted on the cards.

Joyce also was asked to complete a number of self-administered inventories, including the Fear Inventory (Wolpe & Lazarus, 1966), and the Minnesota Multiphasic Personality Inventory (MMPI). The Fear Inventory was originally designed to measure the intensity of fear in various situations. The information gained can then be used to construct anxiety hierarchies for systematic desensitization therapy.

Joyce's verbal comments and her performance on the various tests suggested that she approached the testing situation with extreme uncertainty. She frequently qualified her responses with comments such as "this may not be right, but . . . ," or "I'm not sure, but I think." She also tended to give long and overly detailed answers or descriptions, and showed a meticulous concern for small details on the figures that she drew.

The client scored in the superior intellectual range. There was no evidence on any of the tests of thought disturbance or poor reality testing suggestive of psychotic functioning. The responses generally indicated an extremely anxious individual who centered much thought and activity on a concern with insects. The area of greatest fear was in situations with crawling insects or spiders.

Several themes emerged from the responses given by the client on the TAT. Joyce described a number of family situations suggestive of sibling rivalry, or of a child attempting to get parental attention. Social situations with peers were described as being uncomfortable because of lack of certainty about how to interact with others, particularly when expressing one's feelings. As a result, both positive and negative emotions were kept to oneself and not communicated.

The responses to the personality inventory and the profile drawn from these responses corroborated the other test findings. The client's profile indicated a phobic and excessively indecisive individual, who experienced difficulty in communicating with others.

Course of Therapy

Joyce appeared to be reasonably comfortable in her present social environment even though relating to other persons caused her some difficulty. The psychological test results were consistent on the whole with the client's stated treatment goal of receiving help for her fear of spiders. The behavior therapy technique of systematic desensitization therefore seemed to be well suited for treating the client's phobic behavior.

Joyce readily accepted the recommendation of desensitization treatment and agreed to come to the counseling center twice a week for half-hour sessions. Dr. K. made it clear that if Joyce felt the need to discuss other problems, these issues could be brought up after each desensitization session.

The therapist determined that Joyce was amenable to systematic desensitization by testing whether she had the ability to visualize scenes clearly, and whether the anxiety-provoking scenes eventually used in treatment generated anxiety when visualized without relaxation. Joyce was given relaxation training during the initial treatment sessions and was asked to practice this technique at home each day. The client and therapist also devoted the early therapy sessions to constructing an anxiety hierarchy. An anxiety hierarchy is a list of scenes centered on a common anxiety-provoking theme. The scenes are ordered according to the client's report of the amount of anxiety she judged each scene to evoke.

Dr. K. and Joyce worked very closely on establishing a hierarchy centered on the theme of a fear of spiders. The client was instructed to list a number of scenes and then compare the amount of anxiety the imagination of each scene generated. The final list reflected a step-by-step progression in the amount of anxiety the client judged each scene to evoke.

The client stated that her fear of other insects was similar to, although somewhat weaker than, her fear of spiders. Since the anxiety hierarchy was constructed specific to the theme of a fear of spiders, an evaluation was to be made later to ascertain whether spider desensitization also generalized to other insects. If generalization did not occur, separate hierarchies would then be constructed for other insects.

The anxiety hierarchy eventually arrived at was the following, presented in a descending order of anxiety arousal:

1. Spider crawling on client's arm
2. Spider touching client's arm
3. Spider next to client's arm
4. Spider approaching client's arm on arm rest
5. Client watching spider near arm rest
6. Spider crawling up arm rest
7. Spider standing still at chair leg
8. Spider crawling toward chair client is sitting on
9. Spider moving around at far end of room
10. Spider standing still at far end of room
11. Spider crawling around in next room
12. Spider standing still in next room

Once the hierarchy was constructed, the actual desensitization sessions commenced. Dr. K. instructed Joyce to relax and imagine the last scene on the hierarchy. After about eight seconds, the client was instructed to terminate visualization. Joyce was then asked whether she had experienced any anxiety while visualizing the scene; she reported that she felt mildly anxious. The therapist then instructed the client to relax again and to visualize the same scene for a number of seconds. This procedure continued until the client was able to picture the scene without anxiety arousal. At this point, the therapist and client worked on the next scene on the hierarchy. Each new session started with the last scene mastered at the previous session. This scene was repeatedly visualized under relaxation, until the client was able to picture the scene without feeling anxious. Only then did the client proceed to the next item.

After each desensitization session, Joyce usually brought up other personal problems that she wanted to talk over with Dr. K. The latter pointed out to the client typical behavior patterns Joyce used in interacting with others, and also discussed the consequences of her behavior on those around her. Joyce was given support and social reinforcement for changing the interaction patterns that were creating problems for her, such as her relationship with her family and her difficulty in expressing her feelings.

Joyce progressed through all of the items on the hierarchy in a three-month period. She reported that the desensitization had also generalized, so that she no longer had an anxiety reaction to any type of insect. Joyce was quite pleased with the results of the therapy program. The alleviation of the fear of confronting spiders was associated with a lessening of other anxieties and doubts. Joyce reported that she was now able to approach social situations from a positive viewpoint, instead of a feeling of apprehension about whether she would see a spider and have a panic reaction.

Follow-up information was obtained one year after the completion of systematic desensitization therapy. The client indicated that there had been no recurrence of her phobic reaction to spiders and other insects, nor had any other phobic symptoms developed. She reported that she felt more at ease in interpersonal relationships than she had felt prior to therapy. Joyce was doing well academically and she still maintained a close relationship with her boyfriend.

Discussion

Freud (1938) postulated that phobias are mechanisms constituted by the unconscious to prevent anxiety from breaking out. The DSM-II (1968) diagnostic criteria for phobias also emphasized unconscious processes. However, the DSM-III (1980) and DSM-III-R (1987) classification criteria for phobias are behaviorally or symptom oriented. According to DSM-III-R, a simple phobia is classified under the general category of anxiety disorders. Simple phobias are distinguished from two other categories of phobias, agoraphobia (a fear of public places from which escape might be difficult) and social phobia (a persistent fear of situations in which one might be scrutinized by other people). The diagnostic criteria for simple phobia include a persistent fear of a particular object or situation, and during some phase of the disorder, an immediate anxiety response upon exposure to the phobic stimulus. Further criteria are as follows: the phobic stimulus is avoided, or endured with extreme anxiety, the fear or avoidance behavior with regard to the phobic stimulus significantly interferes with the individual's usual activities and relationships with others, or there is significant distress about having the fear. The individual also recognizes that the fear is unreasonable or excessive. Simple phobias are diagnosed more often in females. The most common simple phobias involve animals or insects.

In a two-process theory of avoidance learning, Mowrer (1947) formulated a learning theory-based model of phobic reactions that is consonant with more recent conceptions of phobic disorders such as those of Eysenck

(1983). Mowrer proposed that classical conditioning is the first process that takes place in avoidance learning; that is, a conditioned emotional response (fear) becomes associated with a previously neutral stimulus (the phobic object). The second step in avoidance learning is a process of instrumental conditioning. The person learns that there is a reduction in the conditioned emotional response when the particular object is avoided. Over time, the avoidance (phobic) behavior becomes a highly overlearned response because of the negative reinforcement derived from fear reduction each time escape or avoidance occurs. Eventually, the individual learns to avoid the phobic object even before the onset of the conditioned emotional response. However, the avoidance response does not extinguish because the person does not stay in the phobic situation long enough for the conditioned emotional response to dissipate.

Over the past several years, greater attention has been placed on the specification of cognitive factors in understanding the development of phobic disorders and in providing an additional direction for treatment. Beck (1976) wrote that many phobic individuals are afraid not only of particular situations or objects, but also of their perception of what will happen to them when confronted with what they fear. Beck posited that the crucial anxiety provoker in agoraphobia is the individual's fear of losing control and panicking in public. Thus, agoraphobics *fear the fear* they expect to experience in public crowds.

Foa and Kozak (1985) defined anxiety disorders in terms of three dimensions: anticipated harm, external fear cues, and avoidance behaviors. The anticipated harm is due to an erroneous evaluation of the phobic object, while avoidance behaviors preclude the learning of new information about the phobic object which could result in anxiety reduction.

Lang (1985) formulated an information processing model of anxiety and anxiety disorders that also moves beyond an emphasis on the external stimuli that elicit avoidance behaviors, to an examination of the components of fear and anxiety. In phobic disorders, information about the feared object is explicit (i.e., one can recognize what the feared object is), imagery is focused on this object, and the response pattern centers around active avoidance. The increased heart rate evident as phobics move closer to the feared object suggests a physiological preparation for flight, and this physiological response occurs when there is imagery about and confrontation with the feared object. The psychophysiological anxiety responses are represented in memory, and become part of the cognitive fear structure that can result in escape or avoidance behaviors if the phobic object is present.

The role of genetic factors in the development of various anxiety disorders including phobias has also been considered. Research has indicated that animals can be bred to be high or low in emotional arousal (Hall,

1951). Some individuals may have a greater predisposition to respond to stressors with anxiety if they have inherited a greater degree of autonomic lability or anxiety readiness (Lacey, 1967). Noyes, Clancy, Crowe, Hoenk, and Slymen (1978) found an increased prevalence of anxiety neurosis among close relatives of persons diagnosed as anxiety neurotic or exhibiting related anxiety disorders. A later study found that the relatives of agoraphobic patients exhibited a higher proportion of agoraphobia in comparison with other types of anxiety disorders (Noyes, Clarkson, Crowe, Yates, & McChesney, 1987). One explanation for these findings is the possibility that there is an inherited tendency toward autonomic reactivity, particularly anxiety arousal. This inherited tendency then interacts with various learning influences.

Implosive therapy (Stampfl & Levis, 1967) was inspired by learning theory conceptions of the nature of anxiety. This technique was based on the assumption that the phobic reaction would extinguish if the person forced himself or herself to imagine the phobic situation intensely and allowed the full extent of anxiety to occur rapidly. As in Mowrer's theory, it was assumed that extinction would result when the individual experienced the anxiety without any actual negative consequences.

Systematic desensitization treatment (Wolpe, 1969) also was based on the rationale of having the client directly experience the anxiety associated with the phobic situation. However, in systematic desensitization the client is exposed to only small amounts of anxiety at a time, while simultaneously engaging in relaxation procedures. Wolpe posited that the essential treatment process in systematic desensitization is one of reciprocal inhibition or counterconditioning. Through gradual scene visualization, relaxation responses become conditioned or paired to the cues that previously elicited anxiety responses. Thus, relaxation serves as an inhibitor of anxiety.

Controlled treatment outcome studies comparing the efficacy in eliminating simple phobias of anxiety exposure through scene visualization versus *in vivo* (real-life) exposure to the fear stimulus have found that *in vivo* exposure is more effective than fantasy exposure (Foa & Kozak, 1985; Franks & Wilson, 1980; Mathews, 1978). Foa, Steketee, and Grayson (1985) suggested that *in vivo* presentations have greater efficacy in activating the strongly coherent fear structure (defined as physiological and subjective feelings of anxiety) that is the characteristic of simple phobias. *In vivo* treatment also may be more effective than other procedures in disconfirming expectations of harm (Foa & Kozak, 1985).

Research by Marks and colleagues (Marks, 1983) demonstrated that *in vivo* exposure to the phobic stimulus was effective in reducing fear and anxiety, irrespective of whether the *in vivo* exposure was gradual or involved high-anxiety evocation. An interesting direction in phobia treatment that is consistent with the emphasis on cognitive and self-control strategies for anxiety management (Goldfried, 1979), is the use of self-exposure homework (Greist, Marks, Berlin, Gournay, & Noshirvani, 1980).

The modeling or observational learning formulation of Bandura and Walters (1963) is another learning-based approach to understanding and treating phobic disorders. They proposed that one of the ways in which phobic behavior can be learned is through exposure to another person who exhibits a fear or avoidance response. Treatment outcome research has demonstrated that the phobic individual will exhibit an extinction of particular fears if approach behaviors to the feared objects are modeled by adults and peers (Bandura, Blanchard, & Ritter, 1969; Blanchard, 1970). Bandura (1977) has further proposed that the changes that occur in a particular treatment regimen are due to the creation and strengthening of expectations of personal effectiveness. Thus, the cognitive component contributing to the success of a modeling, *in vivo,* or any other treatment program is this attitude of self-efficacy—that is, the belief that one will be able to deal with and overcome one's phobic or other problem behavior patterns. Consistent with this notion, Williams and Watson (1985) found that phobics with low self-efficacy attitudes about their ability to manage their fear when exposed to the feared situation showed greater avoidance behavior than those with high self-efficacy attitudes.

In analyzing the origin of Joyce's phobic reaction, it is evident that she had ample opportunity to observe her mother engage in phobic behavior toward insects. Mrs. Ryan modeled this fear reaction and exhibited anxiety reduction when the aversive stimulus was removed. Joyce was reinforced for imitating her mother by the maternal solicitude she received when expressing fears similar to those her mother exhibited. Mr. Ryan socially reinforced phobic behavior in both his wife and daughter by amusedly indulging their fears and playing the role of protector.

Mr. Ryan did not provide social approval to Ted for engaging in phobic behavior, probably because specific fears are considered more in keeping with feminine role stereotypes and are therefore reinforced more with girls. A boy engaging in the same type of behavior is labeled a "sissy," or seen as manifesting effeminate behavior. According to Joyce's account of her childhood, Ted was not given attention for exhibiting a fear of spiders, and he did not imitate this behavior. For Ted, social approval was contingent on engaging in a number of behaviors considered more in keeping with the male role, such as an interest in chemistry.

An interesting issue is why Joyce developed a phobia while her sister Barbara, also female and also observing the mother, did not. It seems likely that Barbara had a larger behavioral repertoire from which to gain social reinforcement than Joyce. We know that Barbara was older and therefore had more skills than Joyce. She was also more assertive and got better grades in school. These skills would therefore broaden the behaviors available to Barbara for social reinforcement. Joyce, being younger, could not match her sister's accomplishments at the same moment in time when Barbara performed these activities. She was therefore continuously presented with a model who was achieving at a level that Joyce could not match. However, one of the ways that Joyce was able to gain attention was by expressing a fear of insects.

Although Joyce did not remember experiencing an anxiety provoking event associated with spiders, it does not necessarily follow that she was repressing a traumatic episode. A synthesis of the principles of avoidance and observational learning theories can provide an alternative explanation for the client's behavior. Through observing her mother's fear of spiders, Joyce learned not only the phobic behavior, but the emotional response as well. She therefore developed an anxiety response when confronted with the phobic object, and the conditioned emotional response subsided only when she engaged in avoidance or escape behavior. Irrespective of whether the avoidance learning occurred directly or through observation, the functional relationship between avoidance behavior and anxiety reduction appears to be the same. In Joyce's case, the phobic problem persisted until adulthood primarily because the anxiety reduction associated with escape or avoidance prevented extinction from taking place. The factor of social reinforcement through the attention she received within her family situation was important as well. It also is possible that Joyce inherited a high level of anxiety readiness through a strongly arousable physiological system.

Overcoming the phobia did not result in the appearance of a new symptom, nor were there any indications of a deterioration of behavioral functioning. On the contrary, the alleviation of the phobia resulted in greater feelings of self-confidence. Joyce no longer found it necessary to approach each social situation with a plan about what to do in case she encountered a spider or other insect. Because of Joyce's phobic disorder, a great number of interpersonal situations had become anxiety provoking to her. After going through the desensitization process, she experienced a marked lessening of feelings of anxiety and an increase in self-efficacy that allowed her to interact in a more competent manner with other people.

In addition to a fear of spiders, Joyce also exhibited many obsessive-compulsive patterns. After treatment, Joyce reported that the obsessive ruminations involved in decision making had lessened also. The greater feelings of self-confidence associated with successful mastery of the phobic problem had apparently made it easier for Joyce to feel more confident in other areas of functioning.

Joyce stated during the initial evaluation that she wanted help primarily with her fear of insects. This comment could have been interpreted as a sign of defensiveness suggesting that she would be a poor therapeutic risk. On the other hand, the client was communicating a desire to be treated primarily for the situation that was causing her the most discomfort. She perhaps made a quite realistic appraisal that her other problems were within her present coping ability. When the symptom causing her the most discomfort was removed through behavior therapy, Joyce was then able to quite accurately report an improvement in interpersonal functioning.

The difficulties the client described in communicating with others and in interacting with her parents were not explored at great length during the therapy sessions. The student might perhaps ask, "Was this client really helped in therapy?" The response to this question is in large part a value judgment. From a psychodynamic, insight-oriented point of view, the evaluation of the success of therapy would most likely be primarily negative. The client was still faced with a number of personal difficulties, the underlying cause of the disorder had not been dealt with, and she had not achieved insight into the reasons for her behavior.

A behaviorally oriented therapist, on the other hand, would probably view this case as a success. The therapy had achieved its goal of extinguishing the phobic behavior, and there was also a general improvement in interpersonal functioning. Symptom substitution had not occurred, and although the client continued to have a number of "hang-ups," she also experienced much greater satisfaction in her life situation. Further, the treatment had been accomplished fairly quickly and at much less expense to the client than verbal psychotherapy.

A total restructuring of personality did not occur during treatment, nor did the client have the opportunity to bring up repressed childhood memories. A question worth pondering is whether these latter procedures are necessary to help persons with psychological problems. Because symptom-oriented therapies have more limited goals, these methods of treatment may result in improved functioning in a shorter period of time. Clearly, it was not necessary for Joyce to explore her childhood memories deeply in order to be helped to function more adequately at the present time.

References

American Psychiatric Association. (1968). *Diagnostic and statistical manual of mental disorders.* (2nd ed.) (DSM-II). Washington, DC: Author.

American Psychiatric Association. (1980). *Diagnostic and statistical manual of mental disorders* (3rd ed.) (DSM-III). Washington, DC: Author.

American Psychiatric Association. (1987). *Diagnostic and statistical manual of mental disorders* (3rd ed., rev.) (DSM-III-R). Washington, DC: Author.

Bandura, A. (1977). Self-efficacy: Towards a unifying theory of behavioral change. *Psychological Review, 84,* 191–215.

Bandura, A., Blanchard, E. B., & Ritter, B. (1969). The relative efficacy of desensitization and modeling approaches for inducing behavioral, affective, and attitudinal change. *Journal of Personality and Social Psychology, 13,* 173–199.

Bandura, A., & Walters, R. H. (1963). *Social learning and personality development.* New York: Holt, Rinehart, & Winston.

Beck, A. T. (1976). *Cognitive therapy and the emotional disorders.* New York: International Universities Press.

Blanchard, E. B. (1970). The relative contributions of modeling, information influences, and physical contact in the extinction of phobic behavior. *Journal of Abnormal Psychology, 76,* 55–61.

Eysenck, H. J. (1983). Classical conditioning and extinction. The general model for the treatment of neurotic disorders. In M. Rosenbaum, C. M. Franks, & Y. Jaffe (Eds.), *Perspectives on behavior therapy in the eighties* (pp. 77–98). New York: Springer Publishing.

Foa, E. B., & Kozak, M. J. (1985). Treatment of anxiety disorders: Implications for psychopathology. In A. H. Tuma & Jack D. Maser (Eds.), *Anxiety and the anxiety disorders* (pp. 421–452). Hillsdale, NJ: Lawrence Erlbaum Associates.

Foa, E. B., Steketee, G., & Grayson, J. B. (1985). Imaginal and *in-vivo* exposure: A comparison with obsessive-compulsive checkers. *Behavior Therapy, 16,* 292–302.

Franks, C. M., & Wilson, G. T. (1980). *Annual review of behavior therapy. Theory and practice: 1979* (Vol. 7). New York: Brunner/Mazel.

Freud, S. (1938). *The basic writings of Sigmund Freud.* New York: Modern Library.

Goldfried, M. R. (1979). Anxiety reduction through cognitive-behavioral intervention. In P. C. Kendall & S. D. Hollon (Eds.), *Cognitive-behavioral interventions. Theory, research, and procedures* (pp. 117–152). New York: Academic Press.

Griest, J., Marks, I. M., Berlin, F., Gournay, K., & Noshirvani, H. (1980). Avoidance vs. confrontation of fear. *Behavior Therapy, 11,* 1–14.

Hall, C. S. (1951). The genetics of behavior. In S. S. Stevens (Eds.), *Handbook of experimental psychology* (pp. 304–329). New York: Wiley.

Lacey, J. I. (1967). Somatic response patterning and stress: Some revisions of activation theory. In M. H. Appley & R. Trumball (Eds.), *Psychological stress*. New York: McGraw-Hill.

Lang, P. J. (1985). The cognitive psychophysiology of emotion: Fear and anxiety. In A. H. Tuma & Jack D. Maser (Eds.), *Anxiety and the anxiety disorders* (pp. 131–170). Hillsdale, NJ: Lawrence Erlbaum Associates.

Marks, I. (1983). Behavioral concepts and treatment of neuroses. In M. Rosenbaum, C. M. Franks, & Y. Jaffe (Eds.), *Perspectives on behavior therapy in the eighties* (pp. 112–137). New York: Springer Publishing.

Mathews, A. M. (1978). Fear reduction research and clinical phobias. *Psychological Bulletin, 85,* 390–404.

Mowrer, O. H. (1947). On the dual nature of learning—a reinterpretation of "conditioning" and "problem solving." *Harvard Educational Review, 17,* 102–148.

Noyes, R., Clancy, J., Crowe, R., Hoenk, P. R., & Slymen, D. J. (1978). The familial prevalence of anxiety neurosis. *Archives of General Psychiatry, 35,* 1057–1059.

Noyes, R., Clarkson, C., Crowe, R. R., Yates, W. R., & McChesney, C. M. (1987). A family study of generalized anxiety disorder. *American Journal of Psychiatry, 144,* 1019–1024.

Stampfl, T. G., & Levis, D. J. (1967). Essentials of implosive therapy: A learning theory-based psychodynamic behavioral therapy. *Journal of Abnormal Psychology, 72,* 496–503.

Williams, S. L., & Watson, N. (1985). Perceived danger and perceived self-efficacy as cognitive determinants of acrophobic behavior. *Behavior Therapy, 16,* 136–146.

Wolpe, J. (1969). *The practice of behavior therapy.* New York: Pergamon Press.

Wolpe, J., & Lazarus, A. A. (1966). *Behavior therapy techniques: A guide to the treatment of neuroses.* Oxford: Pergamon Press.

6

A Life of Compulsive Rituals— The Case of Ruth Langley

Ruth Langley was 30 years old when she sought the help of a behavior therapist. Since childhood she had been treated by a succession of therapists who had used other treatment methods. The client had read about some recent developments in the field of behavior modification, and after a period of indecision, she made an appointment to see Dr. M.

Ruth was extremely thin. She sat rigidly in her chair, with her hands tightly folded, and she maintained an expressionless gaze and tone of voice. She revealed that a long-standing feeling of contamination compelled her to carry out numerous cleansing activities each day. She stated that she became intensely uncomfortable if she noticed any dirt on her person or in her immediate environment, and she responded to this feeling by thoroughly washing her hands and arms. If she detected some dirt in her house, she was compelled to scrub her apartment completely and methodically, as well as shower in a rigidly specified manner. The client reported that she also felt contaminated after using the bathroom and doing housework or cooking, and again, she was compelled to wash herself thoroughly.

Ruth complained that her life was extremely restricted because most of her time was spent in some type of behavior she felt driven to carry out. In addition, each ritual activity was becoming more involved and time-consuming. At the time of the interview, she was washing her hands at least three or four times an hour, showering six or seven times a day, and thoroughly cleaning her apartment at least twice a day.

The client was white and came from a Protestant, upper-class background. Ruth was unmarried and she lived alone in a studio apartment. She had an independent income that provided her with comfortable financial support, and she spent her free time painting. However, she had done very little art work over the past few years, because her time had been so occupied with the performance of the various ritualistic behaviors.

Childhood Background

The client indicated that her parents had an extremely superficial marital relationship. Mr. Langley was often away on extended trips, and her parents pursued their own separate interests. They usually interacted with each other in a polite and formal manner, although Ruth said that occasionally she had heard them arguing. When Mr. Langley was at home, he sometimes invited friends of the family over for dinner. However, Ruth felt that her mother did not really enjoy being with other people, and Mrs. Langley also seemed more at ease when her husband was not at home.

Ruth described her mother as a cold and distant person, who was always involved primarily with her own interests. The client felt that her mother preferred the company of her horses and dogs to human companionship. Mrs. Langley typically spent most of her time alone, and only on rare occasions did she attend a social function. Ruth could not recall her mother ever hugging or kissing her, and Mrs. Langley tended to be very critical of Ruth when they were together. Mrs. Langley has been in some form of psychotherapy ever since Ruth could remember.

Ruth said that she was always very excited and happy when her father was at home. They laughed and had fun together, and they often spent some time horseback riding. She always felt keenly disappointed when he abruptly departed after being home for just a few days, even though he typically left in this manner and would then be gone for an indefinite period.

Ruth was an only child, and she grew up in the care of a succession of governesses. She described her family's large house as a very quiet and lonely place, with no other children close by for her to play with. As a child, she sometimes sought out the companionship of persons on the household staff, but the employees tended to relate to her in a very formal manner.

Ruth stated that the persons who took care of her consistently discouraged her from running around in spontaneous play, and they always made sure that she was immaculately clean. Mrs. Langley was highly critical of Ruth and her caretakers if her daughter was less than perfectly well-groomed. The client said that her father was not as concerned about her appearance around the house, but if company was present, he too expected her to look impeccably neat.

School History

Ruth attended private day schools throughout her school career. She generally did not participate in games or play activities at school, and she particularly tried to avoid any kind of physical contact with the other children. She indicated that she was concerned that she would get dirty if she got too involved in play activities.

Ruth did not have any friends during adolescence, nor did she attend social functions at school. The behavior rituals she engaged in were quite noticeable by this time, and her classmates often ridiculed her because she repeatedly washed her hands in a specified manner, or walked around the school grounds in a precise and unvarying pattern.

The client received adequate grades in school and she excelled in her art courses. She enjoyed painting, and her teachers and the other students often made favorable comments about her work. Ruth stated that she was more comfortable while she was painting than at any other time in her daily existence.

Symptom History

Ruth had engaged in ritual behaviors for as long as she could remember. She recalled that her caretakers encouraged her to perform these behaviors, so she would keep clean and be occupied in some type of activity. By the time she was four or five years old, she had already developed a complex play sequence that involved putting all of her dolls in exactly assigned postures. She would raise a particular doll's arm to a certain angle and would then point its legs in a given direction. She then placed each of her many dolls in other specified positions. When all of the dolls were arranged, she moved each of them in turn to another part of her room, where she established a different pattern of doll placement and position. She repeated this sequence four or five times, organizing each placement somewhat differently from the previous one. She also repeated in order certain words and phrases, such as "good doll," "bad doll," as she engaged in this play activity. Ruth remembered that she became extremely uneasy if she was interrupted in the middle of the doll-placing ritual, and she continued to feel uncomfortable until she was able to complete the entire sequence.

Ruth indicated that she experienced a strong feeling of satisfaction when she carried out the minute details of the ritual she was engaged in, and as she grew older, she developed many other stereotyped patterns of behavior. Before going to bed, she went through a set procedure of placing her pillow, blankets, and various objects in her room in particular spots, and she repeated specific phrases as she carried out this activity. When she got up in the morning, she arranged her pillow and blankets in yet other positions and moved the objects in her room to other assigned places. If she did not complete the ritual each day in exactly the same manner, she experienced intense anxiety until she was able to do so.

Since childhood, Ruth had also engaged in complicated ritual activities related to procedures of cleanliness. She washed herself several times each day according to a set pattern. If it seemed as if she had soiled her clothing in any way, she repeated the washing sequence and changed her clothes as soon as possible. In the course of her activities at school and at home, it was often necessary to touch books or objects that she considered unclean. As a result, she was repeatedly compelled to wash her hands, with the thoroughness of the procedure depending on what she had been in contact with.

Ruth was ten years old when she was first taken to a mental health professional. Her teacher had indicated to her that the time and attention she devoted to repetitive behaviors were interfering with her classroom performance. Ruth presumed that the school personnel had also advised Mrs. Langley that Ruth needed professional evaluation, because she was taken to a therapist soon after Mrs. Langley attended a conference at school. Ruth has periodically been in some form of therapy ever since, initially in play therapy, and as she grew older, in some form of verbal psychotherapy. However, the ritual behavior did not lessen, despite these therapeutic efforts.

Present Functioning

Following her graduation from high school, Ruth occupied herself by painting and taking art courses. She said that she did not feel particularly close to anyone her own age, and she did not participate in social activities with either men or women. When she did converse with others, the topic of conversation usually centered on the subject of art. Ruth indicated that she did not feel comfortable discussing other topics.

The client moved into her own apartment when she was 21 years old, and since that time, she saw her family only infrequently. She enjoyed living alone because it enabled her to arrange her living space as she liked, without worrying that someone else would disturb her room arrangement or bring dirt into the room. Further, she was now free to buy and prepare only those foods that she considered healthful and free of contaminants.

Ruth stated that she was not bothered by all types of uncleanliness and disorder. She categorized aspects of her environment as "good dirt" and "bad dirt," and she did not engage in rituals in response to "good dirt." For example, she did not experience a compulsion to clean herself if she became spotted while painting, and there was no feeling of contamination when she ate foods she regarded as healthful.

For the past two years an almost constant feeling of contamination compelled Ruth to increase the extent of her compulsive behavior. However, she could not associate any particular event with the increasing severity of her ritualistic behaviors. At the time of evaluation, Ruth engaged in a complicated and especially thorough procedure of washing her hands after urinating or defecating. She scrubbed each finger in order, and she carefully washed between her fingers. She then washed both sides of her hands and eventually scrubbed her arms. She carried out this procedure with soap, and then repeated the sequence with a strong disinfectant. Following these steps, she dried her hands with a large number of disposable paper towels. Next, she thoroughly scrubbed the toilet and sink in a specific manner, and then repeated the hand-washing procedure. If she still felt contaminated, the ritual included taking a shower as well, according to a set sequence. The client also washed herself in this stereotyped manner after cooking and housecleaning, but she varied the thoroughness of the process according to how dirty she felt.

Ruth stated that she felt frustrated and tired most of the time, because of the amount of effort involved in these rituals. She experienced a great deal of pain in her hands because the outer layer of skin was virtually rubbed off. Nonetheless, she felt compelled to wash her hands thoroughly and clean her apartment repeatedly each time she felt that she or her environment was contaminated in some way.

Although Ruth was in extreme discomfort because of the burden of these compulsions, she could not rest until she went through all of her daily rituals. She was forced to awaken at four in the morning and work for a minimum of six hours, just to get through her personal and household chores for the morning. However, she generally repeated part of the cleaning sequence at least four additional times a day.

Ruth revealed that she had engaged in masturbation since she was a child, and the frequency of this behavior had increased over the past few years. She felt that she was doing something harmful and disgusting, but she could not prevent herself from engaging in this practice. Because she then felt unclean she was forced to take a shower, thoroughly scrub her hands, and change her pajamas and bed linens. Since she usually masturbated when she went to bed, these elaborate rituals continually interrupted her nightly rest.

Psychological Evaluation

Ruth was asked to complete a number of self-administered psychological inventories. She took an unusually long time to fill out the test material, and she indicated that it was often difficult for her to decide on the most accurate answer.

The Minnesota Multiphasic Personality Inventory (MMPI) results indicated an above normal elevation of the scales measuring anxiety, obsessive-compulsive characteristics, and unusual thought processes. These findings suggested that the client sometimes engaged in cognitive processes and behavior that were quite deviant from the societal norm. There were also indications that she occasionally had difficulty distinguishing between reality and fantasy, because she was confused by unusual thoughts.

Ruth rated a series of items on the Fear Inventory (Wolpe & Lazarus, 1966) according to the degree of fear elicited by each situation or object. She indicated extreme discomfort in interpersonal situations in which there was the possibility of an aggressive encounter. For example, she rated the following items as elicitors of strong fear: "one person bullying another," "tough-looking people," "angry people," and "the sight of fighting." Ruth also expressed a strong fear of "large crowds," "losing control," and "looking foolish," circumstances that in some way might draw attention to her. The client further indicated specific fears of dirt, mice, and spiders.

The test results therefore suggested that Ruth was hampered in her daily functioning by severe anxiety in social situations, as well as in situations related to dirt or uncleanliness. She seemed to fear that she would become anxious in interpersonal situations and lose control of herself. The compulsive, ritualistic behavior appeared to function as a means of preventing this loss of control.

Course of Therapy

Dr. M. indicated to Ruth that she believed in the client's sincerity in wanting to change her behavior, because of Ruth's continuing efforts to seek professional help. The therapist further stated she did not believe that Ruth enjoyed suffering, but felt that Ruth had been unable to find an effective means of eliminating her compulsive behavior patterns.

Dr. M. employed the techniques of modeling and *in vivo* flooding exposure to modify Ruth's fear of contamination, and the client was given relaxation training over a number of sessions. Ruth then observed and carried out a series of tasks aimed at the extinction of her fear of urine contamination. The therapist asked Ruth to go to the bathroom and bring back a sample of her urine. Next, Dr. M. instructed Ruth to sit in an easy chair in a state of relaxation, and while she relaxed, the therapist diluted one drop of urine into each of five large buckets of water. Dr. M. then directed Ruth to continue in a relaxed state, while the therapist immersed her own hands in one of the buckets. Ruth was told that it was only necessary for her to watch the therapist and she would not be asked to imitate Dr. M.'s behavior until she felt completely ready to do so. The therapist repeated the hand immersion procedure in each of the other buckets, and she again instructed Ruth to maintain a state of relaxation.

During the third therapy session, Ruth was able to imitate the therapist's behavior, and she immersed her hands in a bucket of water containing one drop of urine. During subsequent sessions, stronger concentrations of urine were added, and again Ruth was able to proceed with the hand immersion tasks after she had practiced relaxation for several minutes.

When Ruth had mastered the contact with urine without becoming anxious and feeling unclean, she was desensitized to other feared contaminants, such as perspiration and mucous. The client reported that in the home environment the rituals resulting from contact with these substances were greatly reduced following the *in vivo* desensitization procedures with the therapist.

Since the ritualistic behaviors took up so much of the client's daily activities, the beginning treatment sessions dealt almost exclusively with this problem. When there was progress in eliminating a particular behavior sequence, such as showering after handwashing, Dr. M. and Ruth began to work on reducing other segments of the stereotyped behaviors. Ruth was asked to designate which of the remaining rituals would be easiest to give up, and she was then given a daily homework assignment relevant to that ritual. These assignments took the form of directions to flush the toilet one time less after use, or to expend one roll less of paper towels each day for drying her hands. As a result, Ruth gradually began to give up increasingly greater portions of her compulsive behaviors.

The client reported her progress to the therapist, and the latter gave her strong approval and support for the successful completion of these tasks. As her relationship with the therapist strengthened, Dr. M. repeatedly told Ruth that she did not have to engage in these compulsive behaviors and, with practice, she would not feel anxious when she refrained from performing a particular ritual.

The therapist also instructed Ruth to record all of the activities she engaged in on one particular day each week. She was also asked to make a notation of the thinking associated with her various activities during that day. The records thus provided information about the environmental stimuli that elicited ritualistic behavior, and also furnished details about the few relationships that Ruth had with other people. The information on the records also served as a gauge of progress in therapy. Dr. M. used the client's activity record to point out to her the cold and formal way she interacted with other persons. Part of each session was devoted to a behavioral analysis of the effect of Ruth's behavior on other persons, and how the behavior of others influenced her interactions.

After the client had been in treatment for ten months, Dr. M. suggested that Ruth participate in group therapy sessions in addition to individual therapy. Because Ruth had made progress in eliminating a great many of her ritualistic behaviors, it now seemed appropriate to provide her with the opportunity to practice social interactions in a supervised group setting. Ruth would then have the opportunity to gain social approval for relating to others without engaging in stereotyped behaviors.

Ruth continued to make progress in narrowing the frequency and the scope of her compulsive rituals. She reported a marked reduction in the number of objects in the environment that elicited a feeling of contamination. She also showed an improvement in interacting with other people, due to the reduction in the time spent in ritualistic behaviors and the concomitant acquisition and practice of more effective social skills. She was now able to converse with others about topics other than art, and for the first time in many years, she sometimes initiated a conversation.

Discussion

Obsessive-compulsive disorder (or neurosis) is described in DSM-III-R (1987) as "recurrent obsessions or compulsions sufficiently severe to cause marked distress, be time-consuming, or significantly interfere with the person's normal routine, occupational functioning, or usual social activities or relationships with others" (p. 245). Obsessions are recurrent, persistent impulses, images, or ideas that are experienced as intrusive and senseless, and that the individual recognizes are a product of his or her own mind. The person attempts to suppress or neutralize these thoughts or impulses by engaging in some other thought, or carrying out some particular type of activity. According to DSM-III-R, the most common obsessions involve thoughts of violence, contamination, and doubt.

Compulsions are repetitive, intentional, and often stereotyped behaviors that are carried out in response to an obsession. The person may recognize that the behavior is excessive, and he or she does not gain pleasure from carrying out this activity. Engaging in the ritual behaviors results in a release of tensions even though the person realizes that the behavior is unreasonable or excessive. Obsessions and compulsions are time-consuming, cause significant distress, and seriously interfere with the individual's usual activities.

An intensive study of persons with an obsessive-compulsive disorder indicated that most developed marked symptoms during adolescence or early adulthood (Rasmussen & Tsuang, 1986). A chronic waxing and waning course was evident, with stress related exacerbations of symptoms. A substantial number of parents of persons with an obsessive-compulsive disorder also exhibited obsessive-compulsive symptoms or the full-blown disorder. It is unclear whether the parents provided a model of symptoms that the offspring then imitated, whether there is a genetic influence, or a combination of both processes.

The obsessive-compulsive individual has been characterized as a cold, intellectualizing, and rigid person who has difficulty reacting to others in a spontaneous manner (English & Finch, 1954). The individual approaches social interactions and problem situations from an intellectual point of view, devoid of affect. The obsessive-compulsive person may also exhibit a behavior pattern marked by excessive cleanliness, extreme orderliness, and tendencies toward stinginess.

According to psychoanalytic theory, obsessive-compulsive neurosis is a disorder that stems from difficulties encountered in childhood, particularly during the anal stage of development (English & Finch). It was postulated that the parents of the obsessive-compulsive individual were unduly harsh and demanding during the toilet training period, and because of the parents' punitiveness, the child developed unresolved feelings of intense hostility. The function of the thoughts and rituals was to undo and neutralize unacceptable aggressive and sexual id impulses. During adulthood, the neurosis was manifested by these obsessions and compulsions, which continued to serve as defense mechanisms for keeping the primitive id impulses concealed even from oneself.

Cameron (1963) analyzed from a psychodynamic point of view a case of a young woman's obsessive-compulsive handwashing. He pointed out a familiar theme in obsessive-compulsive disorders: intense emotional ambivalence, preoccupation with contamination, and the use of defensive countermeasures—that is, the handwashing behavior. Cameron felt that an important feature of the case he described was the combination of intense love and hatred that was centered on the mother and father. Incomplete or defective repression caused an overuse of the defense mechanism known as reaction formation, that is, the individual acted too clean or good, in order to deal with unconscious impulses to soil or to be evil. The purifying hand washing ritual was therefore interpreted as an attempt to undo the harmful thoughts directed to other persons. The extremely painful nature of the continual hand washing was viewed as a retaliatory self-punishment for having evil thoughts and impulses.

Maher's (1966) analysis of the obsessive-compulsive behavior pattern falls within a social learning framework. He characterized the obsessive-compulsive individual's rituals as reparation or atonement behaviors. He noted that after a child commits a transgression, the parents generally demand that the child perform a reparative response such as saying "I'm sorry." The child may be deprived of parental forgiveness and affection until the desired reparative response occurs, while the performance of the atoning response will be reinforced by renewed parental approval.

When the parents set unrealistically high standards of behavior, the child will very likely commit numerous transgressions. If the parents reinforce the child for making a reparative response after each designated offense, these atoning responses will occur with great frequency and they will also result in anxiety reduction. Therefore, rigid parents, through the high standards they set, may create a situation in which they frequently reinforce the child for making a reparative response.

The sequence of punishment, anxiety, and specific reparative behaviors thus becomes established through numerous repetitions. These responses may show stimulus generalization and eventually occur in circumstances unrelated to the original learning experiences, or in situations in which the individual is merely expecting punishment. Certain types of obsessive thoughts can function in the same manner as reparative responses and also result in anxiety reduction. Maher wrote that the hand washing compulsion need not necessarily be viewed as symbolic of the cleansing of guilt. This behavior can be interpreted simply as an over-learned anxiety reducer associated with thoughts or actions that may have no logical connection to the hand washing act itself.

Some compulsive rituals can be viewed as reparative behaviors, such as repetitive hand washing or methodically placing the objects in one's room in a certain order. Other ritualistic behaviors may be responses that generalized from an initial reparative behavior. However, it also is possible that many obsessive-compulsive behaviors are the result of a chance pairing of a particular response and the occurrence of anxiety reduction. The response will become habitual if it continues to be reinforced by anxiety reduction.

The obsessive-compulsive behavior pattern may become intensified at critical points in the individual's life if that person has not learned alternate ways of coping with anxiety provoking situations. When confronted with additional environmental stresses, the obsessive-compulsive individual may exhibit an increase in overlearned ritualistic thoughts and behaviors, because in the past these activities resulted in anxiety reduction. A person who has never learned more flexible social skills will probably respond with anxiety to any change in the customary social environment; an increase in obsessive-compulsive behaviors will then result.

The development of the obsessive-compulsive personality pattern may also be related to a general pattern of parental inflexibility, rather than to specific practices involved in toilet training, as psychoanalytic theory states. Sears, Maccoby, and Levin (1957) found that mothers who were rigid in toilet training their children were also demanding and punitive in their general approach to socialization procedures. These mothers tended to suppress the child's aggressive behavior and they were extremely punitive when the child engaged in sex play. Parents equated sexuality and bowel habits as comprising a general area of modesty.

Exposing a child to rigid toilet training practices may therefore be one of a number of inflexible behaviors that play a role in shaping the obsessive-compulsive behavior pattern. A parent who provides strong social approval to his or her child for conforming to a rigid toilet training schedule may also be likely to reward the child for general cleanliness, the suppression of affect, and the absence of sexual exploration. The parent will then chastise and punish the child when these standards of appropriate behavior are not adhered to. The child will learn to conform to the parent's criteria of acceptable behavior, and eventually these criteria will become a self-standard. As the child grows older, he or she will have the further opportunity to observe the parent's rigid moral standards, and one or both parents will again provide social approval when the youngster imitates these values and behaviors.

An analysis of the parents' role in the development of behavior disorders in the child also should include an assessment of whether the child viewed the parents in a positive manner. The attention of a parent who interacts with a child in a generally warm and loving manner will be positively reinforcing. However, if a parent consistently responds to a child critically and harshly the child will be positively reinforced by receiving no attention from that parent.

Ruth Langley's mother attended to Ruth primarily by criticizing her when she was not meticulously clean. Therefore, receiving no attention from her mother was a positively reinforcing situation for Ruth. In addition, the persons taking care of her learned very quickly that if Ruth was neat and subdued in emotional expression, they also would escape Mrs. Langley's disapproval.

Thus, the household staff also provided strong approval to Ruth for behaving in a quiet and orderly manner. Mr. Langley was more affectionate and approving of Ruth's spontaneous behaviors, but he was seldom home. Thus, he was not a consistent source of approval in Ruth's life, nor was he a continuous model of more socially outgoing behavior.

Mrs. Langley's attitude toward toilet training procedures was no doubt just as rigid and disapproving as her attitude toward dirt in general. It is likely that she elicited a great deal of anxiety in Ruth and her caretakers when her inflexible socialization standards were not adhered to. Ruth began to expect disapproval for untidiness, and she found that the anxiety provoked by this expectation was reduced when she took pains to keep herself clean. Her concern for self-cleanliness generalized to a concern for cleanliness and orderliness in her total environment. Thus, her doll playing activities and bedtime rituals became methodical and stereotyped, and any deviation from this routine produced intense anxiety until the ritual could be completed in appropriate sequence.

It can therefore be seen that Ruth's compulsive behavior pattern did not result from rigid toilet training practices per se. Her disordered behavior was the consequence of a general adult disapproval of emotional expression and the reinforcement by these socializing agents of inflexible, ritualistic behaviors. Ruth's behavior rituals also served an important time-filling function because she was alone so much. Through trial and error, she found that performing time-consuming rituals gave her something to do that would not bring disapproval from the persons around her.

As Ruth grew older, her primary means of interacting with other persons was in relation to conversations about her paintings and art work.

She did not label paint smears on her person as "bad dirt," because she received attention and approval from persons at school and in her social milieu for this activity. She also received gratification from the process of creating a painting, and she continued to engage in this activity when time-consuming rituals did not encumber her.

Ruth's poor social skills became increasingly more apparent as she reached adulthood. She was unable to establish a lasting relationship with any one individual, and she learned to gratify her sexual needs through masturbation. The intensification of self-stimulatory behavior at this time period might have been due to the anxiety provoked by the realization that she was growing older and there was little prospect of any improvement in her life situation.

The client's behavior at the time of evaluation was highly abnormal in many respects. Although obsessive thought patterns were not prominent in her case, she experienced intense and discomforting anxiety when she was unable to carry out a ritualistic behavior immediately. The signs of unusual thought processes and behaviors displayed on the psychological tests may have been in large measure a reflection of the intense daily involvement in these compulsive rituals. As the extent and the time-consuming nature of the rituals diminished, it was probable that the abnormalities manifested on the test material would also diminish.

The client's obsessive-compulsive behavior was modified by behavior therapy techniques similar to those employed in the treatment of phobias. While the phobic individual typically learns to reduce anxiety by avoiding a situation or object, the obsessive-compulsive individual learns to reduce anxiety by thinking certain phrases or performing given acts.

Desensitization procedures have been described in the treatment of obsessive compulsive disorders (Walton & Mather, 1963). Walton and Mather employed *in vivo* desensitization procedures in treating a woman who was a compulsive hand washer. During the course of treatment, she was asked to carry out a series of tasks that were graded according to their potency to evoke hand washing behavior. This technique was similar to the *in vivo* desensitization procedures used in treating Ruth. Walton and Mather's client showed an extinction of anxiety and compulsive behavior in relation to dirt when the desensitization training was completed. The authors felt that an important variable in behavior change was the extinction of anxiety, irrespective of whether one is dealing with phobic or ritualistic behaviors.

Marks (1983) pointed out that in the treatment of phobias and compulsive rituals, emphasis has gradually shifted away from fantasy exposure methods, such as systematic desensitization, to *in vivo* exposure procedures. Long-term improvement has been demonstrated with *in vivo* exposure and self-imposed response prevention methods (e.g., Foa & Goldstein, 1978), and these techniques appear to have relatively greater long-term treatment effectiveness than fantasy procedures used alone. Consistent with the more recent emphasis on self-control strategies, Marks stated that it was essential that clients carry out self-exposure homework assignments in the natural environment—that is, in the home and work settings that evoke these behavior rituals.

Foa and Kozak (1985) formulated a model of obsessive-compulsive disorder that focuses on an information processing deficit. The particular deficit seen in these disorders is an impairment in the rules for making inferences about harm. Rituals are carried out to reduce the probability that harm will occur, and even though harm does not occur, these rituals are continually repeated because the person never really experiences a feeling of safety. This attitude about the causation of harm is in contrast to the inferences of the phobic who avoids harm by simply avoiding the phobic situation.

Foa and Kozak stated that *in vivo* exposure with response prevention (not engaging in the compulsive behavior) is the treatment of choice for obsessive-compulsive disorders. Exposure extinguishes the physiological and experiential aspects of fear, while response prevention allows for a disconfirmation of anticipated harm (Foa, Steketee, Grayson, Turner, & Latimer, 1984). The emotional processing that occurs with successful treatment by exposure to the feared situations appears to include fear activation, the habituation of fear within sessions, and finally, the habituation of fear between therapy sessions (Kozak, Foa, & Steketee, 1988).

The therapy procedures employed in modifying Ruth Langley's behavior resulted in the extinction of anxiety to feared contaminants. However, there was an additional, extremely important feature of her therapy program. She was guided in learning more socially useful skills for relating to other persons through participating in group therapy. Ruth was eventually able to learn how to communicate with others more effectively, and in a way that was more personally satisfying. Although Ruth had already modified a great many of her problem behaviors, it was evident that she would continue to benefit from additional therapy aimed at enhancing her interpersonal skills.

References

American Psychiatric Association (1987). *Diagnostic and statistical manual of mental disorders* (3rd ed., rev.) (DSM-III-R). Washington, DC: Author.

Cameron, N. (1963). *Personality development and psychopathology.* Boston: Houghton Mifflin.

English, O. S., & Finch, S. M. (1954). *Introduction to psychiatry.* New York: Norton.

Foa, E. B., & Goldstein, A. (1978). Continuous exposure and complete response prevention treatment of obsessive-compulsive neurosis. *Behavior Therapy, 9,* 821–829.

Foa, E. B., & Kozak, M. J. (1985). Treatment of anxiety disorders: Implications for psychopathology. In A. H. Tuma & J. P. Maser (Eds.), *Anxiety and the anxiety disorders* (pp. 421-452). Hillsdale, NJ: Lawrence Erlbaum Associates.

Foa, E. B., Steketee, G., Grayson, J. B., Turner, R. M., & Latimer, P. R. (1984). Deliberate exposure and blocking of obsessive-compulsive rituals: Immediate and long-term effects. *Behavior Therapy, 15,* 450-472.

Kozak, M. J., Foa, E. B., & Steketee, G. (1988). Process and outcome of exposure treatment with obsessive-compulsives: Psychophysiological indicators of emotional processing. *Behavior Therapy, 19,* 157–169.

Maher, B. A. (1966). *Principles of psychopathology.* New York: McGraw-Hill.

Marks, I. (1983). Behavioral concepts and treatment of neuroses. In M. Rosenbaum, C. M. Franks, & Y. Jaffe (Eds.), *Perspectives on behavior therapy in the eighties* (pp. 112–137). New York: Springer.

Rasmussen, S. A. & Tsuang, M. T. (1986). Clinical characteristics and family history in DSM-III obsessive-compulsive disorder. *American Journal of Psychiatry, 143,* 317-322.

Sears, R. R., Maccoby, E., & Levin, H. (1957). *Patterns of child rearing.* New York: Harper & Row.

Walton, D., & Mather, M. D. (1963). The application of learning principles to the treatment of obsessive-compulsive states in the acute and chronic phases of illness. *Behavior Research and Therapy, 1,* 163-174.

Wolpe, J., & Lazarus, A. A. (1966). *Behavior therapy techniques: A guide to the treatment of neuroses.* Oxford: Pergamon Press.

7

Post-traumatic Stress Disorder in a Concentration Camp Survivor

Isaac Kranowitz made an appointment in December, 1978, to see his family physician because of longstanding problems of dizziness, stiffness, occasional swelling of the joints in his fingers and knees due to arthritis, and complaints of a "sour stomach." The problems had intensified recently, and at his wife's and children's urging he agreed to go to his physician for a general physical examination.

Mr. Kranowitz was a 59-year-old Jewish man who was born in Poland. He had survived close to five years of forced labor in concentration camps during World War II, and had come to the United States in 1949. His wife likewise was a concentration camp survivor. They had two children—Marshall, 29 years old, and Riva, age 27, both of whom were married and had two children. Mr. Kranowitz was self-employed; he worked at home as a hatmaker and sold his goods to a number of local stores.

Mrs. Kranowitz accompanied her husband to his appointment at the physician's office. Both of them spoke fluent English with heavy, Eastern European accents. Mr. Kranowitz was relatively short (five feet six inches tall) and weighed 150 pounds. His facial expression could be described as subdued; he was alert and responsive, but he did not show extremes of emotion. He walked into and later out of the office very quietly, in a way that did not draw attention to his presence. He wore gray pants, a shirt and tie, and a gray sweater. Mrs. Kranowitz was 56 years old and had lightly curled brown hair. She was approximately five feet three inches tall, and weighed about 138 pounds. She was neatly dressed in a suit and smiled readily. Because she took care of the bookkeeping and other matters related to her husband's work as a hatmaker, she said that she was the "business lady" of the family.

Both Mr. and Mrs. Kranowitz participated in a local project about the Holocaust. The information concerning the past experiences of concentration camp survivors was obtained from this data source.

European History

Mr. Kranowitz was born in a small town, "actually a village," in Poland. He was an only child, but he had an extended family living close by. His family life was happy and comfortable. He had fond memories of his parents, aunts and uncles, and other relatives and friends who had lived in the same village. Mr. Kranowitz related that his father had been a tailor, and although the family lived frugally, there was always enough to eat.

Mr. Kranowitz and the other Jewish boys attended daily religious school in their *shtetle* (small town). In addition, all of the children went to a local school. However, Mr. Kranowitz stated that the strong anti-Semitism that existed made going to this school quite unpleasant. The Jewish children were the constant target of teasing and stone throwing by youngsters from the larger community. Mr. Kranowitz attended the community school only until he was ten years old because of the generally worsening anti-Semitic atmosphere. He continued going to the synagogue school (*yeshiva*) where he was taught by the Rabbi, and he also began to help his father; in the process he learned the tailoring trade.

The Jewish community was a close-knit one, for reasons of cultural tradition as well as self-survival. Mr. Kranowitz recalled quite vividly the times of general turmoil as he was growing up. He remembered at least three occasions in which there was a pogrom through the Jewish section of the village. Everyone in his family's section of the town tried to hide, but some were taken from their houses and killed, and the houses were burned.

When he was 20 years old, Mr. Kranowitz married a young Jewish woman from a village nearby. They lived in the same house as his parents, and a year later, in 1939, his wife gave birth to a daughter. Mr. Kranowitz related that when Poland fell to Germany in September of that year, life became extremely difficult, particularly for the Jewish community. In 1941, the Jews of Mr. Kranowitz's town were shipped to a ghetto that had been established within the Polish city of Lodz. Some months after the entire Kranowitz family was forced to move into the Lodz ghetto, Mr. Kranowitz was rounded up and shipped to a concentration camp in Poland. He spent four years in slave labor, working up to 12 hours a day in a steel factory located within the greater Auschwitz camp area. In 1944, he was shipped to Buchenwald, a concentration camp for men in Germany. He was liberated from this camp by the Americans in May, 1945.

Mr. Kranowitz revealed that it was difficult for him to fully convey to the interviewer the conditions and experiences of existing in the concentration camps. He said that upon arriving at Auschwitz, his first reaction was one of horror and shock. He found himself suddenly pushed from the train into a place where corpses were stacked outside the windows of his sleeping quarters, and he could smell the burning of bodies and see the smoke rising from the chimneys of the crematorium. He explained that the human mind simply could not understand or accept the sheer brutality and terror of this situation. The only way that he could respond was to become "like a stone."

Mr. Kranowitz stated that given the combination of the near-starvation food rations, the grinding, long hours of work in the factory, and the intense cold in the unheated barracks in winter, becoming emotionally numb was not difficult. He related an incident that, according to his recollection, occurred in late October. He and a large group of male prisoners were marched to a site about 40 kilometers from Auschwitz, to work for several weeks at another factory. The German guard gave him his overcoat to carry when the day became warm. Mr. Kranowitz carried the coat for what seemed like several hours. He eventually became extremely tired and asked a fellow inmate to carry the coat for a while. This other man agreed to. However, while they were marching, the other prisoner fell back in line. Suddenly, the guard came up to Mr. Kranowitz and asked for his coat back. Because Mr. Kranowitz could not immediately find the man who now had the coat, the guard pulled Mr. Kranowitz out of the line and put a pistol to his head. At that moment, Mr. Kranowitz said, he recognized that he probably was going to die. However, he said he felt absolutely nothing while this incident was happening. He was not frightened, and at the time he truly did not care whether he lived or died. Just then, the prisoner carrying the overcoat walked by. Instead of being killed, Mr. Kranowitz was knocked down, and the guard kicked him in the head and body while shouting to the other man to bring him his coat.

Mr. Kranowitz related that survival in the camps was often a series of daily decisions. The first decision, and the most difficult one, was whether to get up in the morning or not. Those who did not get out of their bunks at the start of the day were immediately shot. Mr. Kranowitz revealed that he had a special reason that helped him summon the strength to get out of his bunk each morning. Because a prisoner had so little individual identity in the camps, he resolved that he would not become just another corpse in the pile of bodies outside his window. Further, he strongly felt that if he gave up, others would give up as well. Despite his resolve, he also had moments of great despair when it would have been so much easier just to stop trying to survive each day.

He indicated that it was possible to know when a prisoner might die, even though they were all given barely enough food to keep them alive, and they all worked at physically exhausting jobs for 18 or more hours a day. The danger sign was when an inmate stopped talking to his comrades and lost interest in what was going on around him. Mr. Kranowitz said that usually within a day or two, this person would be found dead in his bunk when they were awakened in the morning.

Mr. Kranowitz said that often there were times when a prisoner had to make very quick decisions that were crucial for survival. For example, one day he had fashioned a sling for his left arm because he had injured his wrist while pulling a heavy metal container. Unexpectedly, the inmates in his section were called to line up. He noticed that the weaker prisoners were told to go to the left as they filed by the camp doctor, while the stronger prisoners were waved to the right. He quickly tore off the sling and as he passed the inspection point, he held his hand in a way that disguised the injury. He was then directed to the right. The prisoners on the left were soon after exterminated.

Mr. Kranowitz believed that the help of God as well as luck were important in survival. An example of luck was a situation when the guards suddenly, without warning, would begin firing their machine guns at prisoners in the yard. He said that one time he and a large group of inmates were standing in an open space near the barracks, when a guard opened fire. In the confusion, he managed to get underneath the body of someone who had just been killed; he lay very still until the shooting stopped. He commented that events like this showed that if you wanted to survive, it was important to think quickly but not get too excited. Whoever became angry or openly frightened drew the attention of the camp guards. That usually meant death.

Through the camp grapevine, Mr. Kranowitz heard that in the fall of 1942, his wife and infant daughter had been picked up one day on the streets of the ghetto, and sent to the gas chamber at Maidenek. His parents and some other relatives were also deported and died in the gas chamber. Over the course of the war, other family members were lined up and shot on the street in Lodz by the Germans. The prisoners actively sought news of their families from all recent internees or persons transferred from other camps. However, a prisoner who heard bad news merely continued with the daily routine and did not mention the dead person again. If that person's name came up, the close relative in the camp usually discussed that person in an ordinary, matter-of-fact way. He said that they were all too worn out to be strongly emotional.

The last year of incarceration was difficult and confusing. Information smuggled into the camp indicated that the Germans were suffering heavy losses and beginning to retreat from positions held at several advance points. In the camp at Auschwitz, anticipating the actions of the camp commander and the guards became difficult. Unexpectedly, Mr. Kranowitz and a large group of other prisoners were herded onto open cattle cars and shipped to the concentration camp at Buchenwald in eastern Germany where he spent his fifth year of internment.

This last year was terribly trying. The prisoners were given even less to eat than at Auschwitz. Their daily diet consisted of some watery soup made out of rutabagas, and a few small pieces of bread. Their strength was directed toward getting through the day and remaining as inconspicuous as possible, if only to survive and be able to tell the world about what had happened in the camps. Mr. Kranowitz said that this need to "bear witness" became an overriding mission. The inmates realized towards the end of the war that the Germans were trying to destroy the evidence that the concentration camps had existed and functioned as slave labor and death camps.

During this last year, the health of the surviving prisoners deteriorated further. Mr. Kranowitz said that already he was showing the symptoms of what was later diagnosed as arthritis. The pain and swelling in his joints were particularly bad during the severe winter months. At times he had no shoes or slippers and had to walk barefoot through the snow. Shortly before liberation, he developed typhus. He was placed in a corner of his barracks, and he said that he and others who were sick would have been exterminated if the camp commander and staff had not been distracted by the advancing Allied armies. The Germans were using railroad cars to send prisoners to Buchenwald from parts of Poland and Germany where the Allies were winning.

Mr. Kranowitz stated that when the Americans liberated the camp in May of 1945, his weight had dropped to about 80 pounds and he was too weak to get out of his bunk. He was fed and given nursing care with whatever supplies the Americans had with them. Arrangements were made for Mr. Kranowitz to be sent to an American-run hospital in Germany. He spent one year there recovering from the effects of the typhus infection, as well as the severe malnutrition, cold stress, and exhaustion he had experienced over the five-year period of incarceration. He indicated that in the camp he had not really paid much attention to many of his other physical injuries that resulted from beatings and blows to the head by the guards.

Mr. Kranowitz recalled his year in the hospital as a very difficult one. In addition to a great deal of numbness in his right leg, he suffered from a general loss of appetite, and when he ate he was bothered by gas and indigestion. He estimated that it took him about six years to get back to his preinternment weight. He said that he felt extremely alone and without any ties. The magnitude of the deaths of his wife, child, and other family members began to sink in when he was not so preoccupied with daily survival. Each time he heard some news confirming the death of still another relative or friend, he felt even more alone. However, he strongly believed that after having survived so much brutality and terror in the camps, he certainly was not going to give up and die at age 27.

After a year in the hospital, Mr. Kranowitz was transferred to a nursing home, where he spent four months recovering further. Finally, he was sent to a displaced persons (DP) camp in Germany, run by the United Nations.

The facilities in the DP camp were adequate. Mr. Kranowitz had occasional panicky thoughts about getting enough to eat, but in general he just followed the daily routine. He also talked with the other survivors, and they shared with each other the personal losses they had experienced. He was very happy to find a man from his village with whom he recounted the fate of people they had known. They also talked about the location, dates, and type of work they had been forced to carry out while in the concentration camps. However, a great deal of their conversation centered on the future. The fellow villager wanted to go to Palestine. He was waiting for arrangements to be made so he could be smuggled into the country; the British, who held the governing mandate on Palestine, were allowing only a small number of survivors to enter.

Mr. Kranowitz stated that shortly after coming to the DP camp, he met his present wife, Mollie. She also was from a small town in Poland and had survived four years of forced labor in concentration camps. She was 20 years old when she was sent to Auschwitz in 1942; later she was transferred to three other camps before being liberated in 1945 from Bergen-Belsen in Germany. During the war, all of her relatives, including four sisters and three brothers, either died in the concentration camps or were shot by the Nazis in the Polish ghettos of Lodz or Warsaw.

After liberation, Mollie was sent to the same DP camp to which Mr. Kranowitz eventually was transferred. Gradually and with proper nourishment, her strength returned. She indicated that she had suffered from diarrhea and gas pains for about two months after liberation, even when eating relatively small meals. By the third month of freedom, she was able to eat regular meals despite some continued physical discomfort. She estimated that her weight had increased in six months from about 75 pounds at liberation to 125 pounds.

Mr. Kranowitz recalled that he and Mrs. Kranowitz had known each other for about four months when they decided to get married. He observed that many of the survivors who met for the first time in the DP camps had married. The survivors shared a common life experience that other persons could never understand. Further, many of them had lost their entire families, and even those lucky enough to have some surviving relatives had suffered significant personal losses. The survivors were left with a terrible sense of loss and aloneness. They were still living in camps under foreign authority and trying to make some plans for their future lives. Some who had decided to go to the United States still had to wait for their turn to emigrate.

Mr. and Mrs. Kranowitz were married by a rabbi in the DP camp. Like most of the Jewish survivors from Eastern Europe, they spoke Yiddish with each other. The couple had gravitated toward each other because of a compatibility in age and the fact that they were originally from the same region of Poland. Mr. Kranowitz indicated that from the time they first met, his feeling towards his wife was one of comfort and security; she was a person to care about and who also cared for him. He said that "romance and flowers" were for the movies. What was really important to them was to have enough to eat, and eventually a family and a house to live in. They were both emotionally exhausted and just wanted some peace and contentment.

Mrs. Kranowitz became pregnant about three months after their marriage. Mr. Kranowitz said they both were extremely happy about this event, but they were also concerned about what effects the long years in the concentration camp might have on Mrs. Kranowitz's ability to carry the baby full term. He said that they tried not to get too excited about the prospect of having a child so they would not be disappointed if something happened. However, they began to feel more optimistic the closer the time came to full term. They readied their quarters in the camp for the birth of their child, and in May, 1948, Mrs. Kranowitz gave birth to a healthy baby boy. The infant was named Mendel after Mr. Kranowitz's father. Both parents felt pleased that they had started a new generation, and Mr. Kranowitz stated that taking care of their son lessened somewhat their sense of overwhelming loss.

In July of 1949, the Kranowitz family received a visa to enter the United States. They were relocated in a large eastern city through the auspices of a Jewish refugee relief organization. When the Kranowitz family arrived in this city, the local branch of the relief organization helped them find a place to live and assisted them financially in getting settled. Arrangements were made for Mr. Kranowitz to work in a small clothing factory.

Mr. Kranowitz indicated that his family's life in the United States was very good. The year after their arrival, a daughter was born. They named her Riva after Mrs. Kranowitz's mother, who had been put to death in a concentration camp gas chamber.

While working in the clothing factory, Mr. Kranowitz learned a specialization in hatmaking. He continued this trade at home in the evenings, and gradually built up a clientele of stores that bought hats directly from him. Mr. Kranowitz stated that after he had made hats "on the side" for several years, a number of store owners promised to continue buying as many of his products as he had to sell. He said that he felt relieved, though somewhat concerned financially, to give up his factory job and work at home full-time. His wife had encouraged him to work at a trade at home because working in a factory with other people made him too nervous. He did not like the noise of the factory, and he also did not like to have to talk to so many people every day. He said that he felt more comfortable working at home at his own speed, and being near his family.

The Kranowitz's social life revolved around their children and a club of concentration camp survivors that had formed in the city where they lived. Mr. Kranowitz said he felt uneasy being among people who were not camp survivors. He wondered what they thought about him because of the experiences he had been through.

Over the years, he and his wife had derived a great deal of pleasure in their children's progress in school and at college. Mr. Kranowitz said that both he and his wife spent their money very carefully so they would have enough saved for their children's education. Mendel (Americanized to Marshall) had been a good student all through school. His parents were very pleased and proud of his decision to become a doctor. He was accepted into medical school at a university in the city they lived in and was now completing his residency training in internal medicine. Marshall had married a Jewish girl he had met at college, and they were the parents of two children. Marshall's father-in-law promised to "help the kids out" financially until Marshall finished his medical training. Riva was also a college graduate and had a teaching degree. Mr. Kranowitz said that Riva had married "a nice boy" who was Jewish, and they also had two children.

Mr. Kranowitz was extremely happy that his children and their families all lived in the same city. He proudly pointed out that his children had never "bummed around," used drugs, or "were dirty with long hair" when they were in high school and college. He observed that he was satisfied knowing that his children had received the kind of education he had never been able to obtain because of his life experiences. He said that his wife also was pleased with how the children had turned out. They were "no millionaires," but were very content. In looking back, he thought that perhaps the strong anti-Semitism he had experienced while growing up in Poland had strengthened him to overcome later adversities in life.

Symptom History

Mr. Kranowitz went to Dr. M. at his wife's and family's urging. The physician was one that Mr. Kranowitz had gone to for a number of years. Mr. Kranowitz complained of several recent episodes of dizziness, and he was in obvious pain because of the arthritis that had troubled him since the concentration camp days. The pain from the swelling and stiffness in his joints was becoming progressively worse, especially in the last few years. He said that he continued to have indigestion problems and a "sour stomach," dating from the period when he was in the hospital after liberation.

While talking with Dr. M. about his present physical problems, Mr. Kranowitz confided that ever since he was in the concentration camp, he had been troubled by nightmares. This problem had become much worse recently, and the trouble he had sleeping made him feel quite nervous and jumpy. In a later conversation with Dr. M. and her husband, Mrs. Kranowitz confirmed that he seemed unusually restless at the present time. She said that "he can't sit still for two minutes," and that recently he had had vivid nightmares about the camps. However, both agreed that Mr. Kranowitz was stable and tough, and although these problems might bother him, he had never let them interfere with his daily activities. Mr. Kranowitz said that he did not like to talk about his wartime experiences, but occasionally "it just pours out of me." He said that he sometimes found himself thinking about events that had happened in the concentration camp, even when he tried not to.

Mr. and Mrs. Kranowitz agreed that they both had experienced a great many intense positive and negative feelings over the past few months. A television dramatization about the Holocaust had been shown for several nights, and they had watched the entire series. They said that numerous memories had been brought back to each of them. They had both felt sad and nervous and had difficulty sleeping. Some of their friends who were survivors also told them that the series had made them recall many of the terrible things that happened to them that they had not thought about in years. On the other hand, they had a strong feeling of satisfaction in having the entire United States get some information about experiences such as theirs, "finding out something" about what had happened during that time period.

Mr. and Mrs. Kranowitz said that they had told their children very little about their life in the concentration camp. However, during and after the television series, they shared with their children some of the things that had happened to them. Mrs. Kranowitz said that for the first time, the whole family cried together a little bit about the Holocaust. She felt that sharing these feelings was good, even though both she and her husband found that at times so many memories returned that they had to try not to be overcome by them.

A thorough physical examination indicated that the dizziness Mr. Kranowitz complained of was not due to any type of heart problem. The symptoms the patient described suggested that he was hyperventilating. This was consistent with a previous medical evaluation following complaints of dizziness and several fainting episodes. A neurological screening examination revealed hyperresponsive reflexes, suggesting a hypervigilant, anxiety pattern. Although an EEG (electroencephalogram) taken on a previous visit was normal, Dr. M. felt that the dizziness that had troubled Mr. Kranowitz for so long might be due in part to an inner ear dysfunction caused by repeated blows to the head by the concentration camp guards. The "sour stomach" seemed part of an overresponsive autonomic nervous system pattern.

Dr. M. asked Mr. Kranowitz to complete an MMPI for a research project. Mr. Kranowitz was somewhat uncertain about whether he wanted to participate in a study, but eventually agreed to do so. The clinical profile showed scores on scales measuring anxiety and dysphoric mood that were somewhat higher than the normal range. Other relatively high scale scores indicated an alertness or vigilance to the actions of other persons and the ability to respond quickly in specific situations. (These personality or behavioral characteristics can be seen as quite adaptive for survival.) The overall MMPI profile configuration did not indicate significant psychological disturbance.

Dr. M. prescribed a different type of pain medication for the arthritis symptoms and told his patient to continue taking liquid antacid before meals to alleviate the gastric upsets. He asked Mr. Kranowitz if he wanted to take some pills for his "nerves" and to help him sleep better. However, Mr. Kranowitz said that he did not believe in taking too many pills and that he would be all right.

Mrs. Kranowitz laughingly told Dr. M. that for sure her son would be calling to get the full report, and Dr. M. said that he would be happy to talk to him. They all expressed relief that Mr. Kranowitz did not seem to have any serious physical problems other than the arthritis.

Discussion

The essential feature of a post-traumatic stress disorder is that symptoms develop after a psychologically traumatic life experience that is beyond the realm of usual experience. These events include episodes that took place in military combat, an assault, rape, torture, natural disasters such as earthquakes or floods, or accidental disasters including airplane crashes or large fires. This trauma would be expected to evoke symptoms of distress in all who experienced the same situation. The feelings at the time the event occurred are often significant helplessness, fear, and terror.

According to DSM-III-R (1987), the characteristics of post-traumatic stress disorder involve a persistent reexperiencing of the traumatic event through dreams, memories, or flashback experiences, or avoidance of all reminders of the event and a general numbing of responsiveness. Increased arousal also is present, such as difficulty falling or remaining asleep, irritability or anger outbursts, hypervigilance, an exaggerated startle response, or problems concentrating. Symptoms of depression or anxiety may be evident, and sometimes impulsive behavior can occur, such as life-style changes or unexplained absences. Delayed onset post-traumatic stress disorder is diagnosed if the symptoms first occurred at least six months after the traumatic event.

The long-term psychological status of concentration camp survivors has been a matter of much debate. Psychodynamically oriented clinicians such as Bettelheim (1943), Krystal (1968), and Niederland (1968) have described the status of survivors based on their own experience or the cases they treated. The psychological processes posited to be significant during incarceration were an identification with the aggressor and an extreme infantilization or regression in the inmates' behavior. Strong repression and retroflexion of aggressive impulses were also described. A survivor syndrome was postulated, which included symptoms such as chronic anxiety and dread of the future, depression, psychosomatic illness, restlessness, lack of affect, and difficulties in cognition and concentration. Essential features of this syndrome are survivor guilt and emotional blunting.

A number of investigators have questioned the existence of a specific "survivor syndrome." Eitinger (1965) found that many of the symptoms attributed to psychological processes were due to documented organic pathology associated with repeated blows to the head. Other causes of brain damage were infectious diseases and malnutrition. Matussek (1975) reported on a sample of 245 concentration camp survivors seeking indemnification, who were extensively evaluated approximately 15 years after liberation. A specific survivor syndrome was not found, although a significant number were suffering from physical or psychophysiological disorders. Psychological problems centered on feelings of resignation and despair, apathy and inhibition, and aggressive-irritable moodiness.

Gronvik and Lonnum (1962), Matussek, and Niederland found that one of the best predictors of post-war adjustment was premorbid history, that is, the individual's adjustment and the quality of family relationships before incarceration. An independent contributor, however, was the work stress in the camp. Men who performed extremely severe labor tended to be more passive and had greater difficulty adapting to an occupation after release from internment. Eitinger found a post-war chronic state of hopelessness and anchorlessness among a number of Israeli survivor immigrants, many of whom had no birthplace to go back to and no relatives left. They had emigrated to a country in which 75-80 percent of the citizens at that time were the sole surviving members of their families.

Des Pres (1976) explored the issue of "survivor guilt" in an interview study. He concluded that the will to bear witness was an overriding factor in survival. Further, the sardonic pride the survivors expressed in having succeeded in their long struggle to exist would seem to negate the notion of a chronic, overwhelming, and incapacitating sense of guilt at surviving. The significant depression many survivors no doubt felt upon liberation and for varying periods thereafter may have been a factor in theorizing about a universal syndrome of guilt. The symptoms of depression include the expression of guilt feelings and self-deprecating thoughts. Thus, the expression of guilt at surviving noted in some survivors may have been the result of depressive affect rather than the cause of that depression.

The emotional blunting described in survivors may be understood as a lack of marked overt responsiveness caused by the grinding stress of chronic physical exhaustion over a period of four to five years of slave labor. The happiness and contentment of many survivors who nonetheless exhibited quiet and subdued facial expressions does not suggest "emotional blunting" as a universal phenomenon (Leon, Butcher, Kleinman, Goldberg, & Almagor, 1981).

More recent investigations have assessed the psychological status of survivors 25–33 years after internment. Dor-Shav (1978) reported a constriction in perceptual-cognitive functioning in a group of survivors compared to a control group. However, studies by Leon et al. and Weinfeld, Sigal, and Eaton (1981) failed to find significant impairment in survivors studied from the general population. On the other hand, survivors were more likely than matched controls to have mild symptoms of impairment such as restlessness, somatic complaints, and a feeling of distance from other persons (Eaton, Sigal, & Weinfeld, 1982). The long-term adjustment of infant and child survivors seems variable; in follow-up interviews orphaned survivors expressed a tremendous sense of loss and aloneness (Moskovitz, 1983).

The psychological status of the children of concentration camp survivors has been a subject of recent interest, particularly because these offspring are now reaching adulthood. Children of survivors were compared with a matched group of first-generation Jews whose parents had emigrated from Europe just before World War II. No differences in psychological adjustment existed between the groups (Leon et al., 1981). However, many offspring of survivors commented on the impact their parents' experience had on them with regard to their psychological and social functioning (Epstein, 1979), although this impact was not necessarily a psychopathological one.

Some clinicians posited that children of survivors would have difficulty expressing aggression because of the recognition of what their survivor parent(s) had experienced. From childhood on, they did not behave in an aggressive manner because they did not want to upset their parents. A study using a projective test to measure externalization of aggression indicated a more internalizing characteristic in children of survivors (Nadler, Kav-Venaki, & Gleitman, 1985), and a small proportion of children of survivors felt that there were difficulties in family relationships (Sigal & Weinfeld, 1987). On the other hand, a large scale study found that children of survivors were not at increased risk for problems related to the control of aggression (Sigal & Weinfeld, 1985).

The research evidence therefore seems to indicate that a significant number of survivors do have an emotional and physical residual of their experiences that, if severe enough, can be labeled as a chronic post-traumatic stress disorder. These symptoms include the restlessness, nightmares, and recurrent memories that some survivors continue to experience. Physical problems due to autonomic hyperreactivity, such as hyperventilation and dizziness, "sour stomach," and heartburn, may be present. Chronic, low-intensity anxiety or "jumpiness," feelings of separateness, and dysphoric mood can be exhibited as well.

What seems most impressive in evaluating groups of survivors is that despite the extreme trauma they experienced, they are nonetheless able to cope with their present discomfort. They show substantial evidence of leading productive lives and raising children who also are productive. An important aspect of coping seems to be the reconstituting of family ties through marriage and having children. Another significant source of social support was the survivor clubs.

Both Mr. and Mrs. Kranowitz experienced life events that, fortunately, most of us simply cannot comprehend. The magnitude of the terror and stress, as well as of their losses, is overwhelming. Some individuals broke down physically and psychologically and did not survive, while others were killed at random. Some survivors have suffered serious psychiatric impairment at some point and have been hospitalized or are under some other type of care. The body of evidence suggests, however, that although many survivors suffer symptoms of impairment consistent with the criteria for a post-traumatic stress disorder, they have been able to cope with this residual of their experiences and do not suffer significant problems in functioning. It may also have been the case that the physically and psychologically fittest had the greatest likelihood of survival, and these are the persons who are continuing to cope at the present time.

Some individuals including Mr. Kranowitz continue to be troubled by nightmares, anxiety, and feelings of distance from persons who have not gone through what they have experienced. However, Mr. Kranowitz has been able to adapt to these problems by being self-employed and working at home. It is significant that he sought professional help primarily for physical problems related to arthritis, and to rule out heart disease. He did not consider the post-traumatic psychological residual a problem or symptoms that needed to be modified. Further, no evidence suggested that the family itself was isolated or psychologically disturbed. Mr. and Mrs. Kranowitz had survivor friends with whom they interacted, they took great pleasure in their children's accomplishments, and they enjoyed their grandchildren. Relationships between the Kranowitzes and their children appeared to be relatively harmonious. The aspiration level of this family was defined by both Mr. and Mrs. Kranowitz as being content with one's family and secure. Significant financial or occupational success was not an important aspect of their goals for themselves.

Mrs. Kranowitz did not seem to be troubled to the same degree by the stress reactions Mr. Kranowitz was still experiencing. Part of the reason for the relative absence of significant difficulties may be that she experienced a lesser degree of severe work stress than her husband. Further, she had been able to recuperate more quickly after liberation. Within six months (rather than six years as in Mr. Kranowitz's case) she had reached her pre-war weight level. Mr. Kranowitz, on the other hand, continued to have a number of physical problems dating from the camp experience and the long bout with typhus. On a psychological level, another of Mr. Kranowitz's predisposing factors for post-traumatic stress disorder was the loss of his first wife and child—a traumatic event with which Mrs. Kranowitz had not been confronted.

At the present time, medication for Mr. Kranowitz's arthritis and indigestion problems, and mild sedation for the sleep disturbances seem an appropriate treatment direction. The psychological symptoms of the stress disorder seem stabilized, although a transitory worsening of symptoms occurred with the airing of the television series on the Holocaust. However, the expectation is that Mr. Kranowitz will be able to cope with these difficulties as he has been able to cope with so many previous stressful circumstances.

References

American Psychiatric Association (1987). *Diagnostic and statistical manual of mental disorders* (3rd ed., rev.) (DSM-III-R). Washington, DC: Author.

Bettelheim, B. (1943). Individual and mass behavior in extreme situations. *Journal of Abnormal and Social Psychology, 38,* 417–452.

DesPres, T. (1976). *The survivor: An anatomy of life in the death camps.* New York: Pocket Books.

Dor-Shav, N. K. (1978). On the long-range effects of concentration camp internment of Nazi victims: 25 years later. *Journal of Consulting and Clinical Psychology, 46,* 1–11.

Eaton, W. W., Sigal, J. J., & Weinfeld, M. (1982). Impairment in Holocaust survivors after 33 years: Data from an unbiased community sample. *American Journal of Psychiatry, 139,* 773–777.

Eitinger, L. (1965). Concentration camp survivors in Norway and Israel. *Israeli Journal of Medical Science, 1,* 883–895.

Epstein, H. (1979). *Children of the Holocaust: Conversations with sons and daughters of survivors.* New York: Putnam.

Gronvik, O., & Lonnum, A. (1962). Neurological conditions in former concentration camp inmates. *Journal of Neuropsychiatry, 4,* 50–54.

Krystal, H. (1968). *Massive psychic trauma*. New York: International Universities Press.

Leon, G. R., Butcher, J. N., Kleinman, M., Goldberg, A., & Almagor, M. (1981). Survivors of the Holocaust and their children: Current status and adjustment. *Journal of Personality and Social Psychology, 41,* 503–516.

Matussek, P. (1975). *Internment in concentration camps and its consequences*. New York: Springer.

Moskovitz, S. (1983). *Love despite hate: Child survivors of the Holocaust and their adult lives*. New York: Schocken Books.

Nadler, A., Kav-Venaki, S., & Gleitman, B. (1985). Transgenerational effects of the Holocaust: Externalization of aggression in second generation of Holocaust survivors. *Journal of Consulting and Clinical Psychology, 53,* 365–369.

Niederland, W. G. (1968). Clinical observations of the survivor syndrome. *International Journal of Psychoanalysis, 49,* 313–316.

Sigal, J. J., & Weinfeld, M. (1985). Control of aggression in adult children of survivors of the Nazi persecution. *Journal of Abnormal Psychology, 94,* 556–564.

Sigal, J. J., & Weinfeld, M. (1987). Mutual involvement and alienation in families of Holocaust survivors. *Psychiatry, 50,* 280–288.

Weinfeld, M., Sigal, J. J., & Eaton, W. W. (1981). Long-term effects of the Holocaust on selected social attitudes and behaviors of survivors: A cautionary note. *Social Forces, 60,* 1–19.

Wilson, A., & Fromm, E. (1982). Aftermath of the concentration camp: The second generation. *Journal of American Academy of Psychoanalysis, 10,* 289–313.

8

Psychological Factors Affecting Physical Condition— A Gut Reaction to Environmental Stress

Edward Polowski was examined by a specialist in internal medicine, and then referred to a clinical psychologist for further evaluation. The patient complained of a long-standing problem of severe cramps and diarrhea whenever he ate highly seasoned foods or encountered any type of stressful situation. This problem was diagnosed as an irritable colon when the patient was a child. Since that time, he had been treated by a series of physicians, all of whom confirmed this diagnosis. The patient reported that the medications prescribed for him had varied in effectiveness, and he had recently been in severe discomfort.

Edward was 35 years old, married, and the father of a six-year-old boy and a two-year-old girl. He was a college graduate with a degree in library science and had been a librarian in the same city library since he graduated from college. Edward stated that he began having unusually severe gastrointestinal symptoms at the time that a new director was appointed to the library a number of months ago. Recently, he had been sexually impotent on occasion, and this problem also concerned him.

Childhood History

Edward was an only child. His parents were working-class first-generation Americans of Polish origin. Their formal education concluded at the grade school level, and both were employed in factories. Edward's father had worked on the night shift for many years, and throughout Edward's childhood, he had little contact with his father except on weekends. Edward portrayed Mr. Polowski as a well-meaning but gruff person who usually let his wife handle disciplinary matters. He occasionally spanked Edward for misbehaving, but if he intervened at all, it usually involved shouting at his son. If Edward continued to behave in a provocative manner, his father did not follow through with any further disciplinary action.

Mr. Polowski generally stayed around the house when he was not working, but from time to time he took his son to a sporting event. Edward said that he felt affection for his father, but they had never had common interests, nor had there been much communication between them.

Edward described his mother as a tender and affectionate person. She was usually quite cheerful, and she spent a great deal of time with her son when she was home. Mrs. Polowski was very pleased when Edward helped her with the household chores, and she was extremely solicitous to him when he was ill. Edward felt that his parents had a good marital relationship. They sometimes had loud arguments, but these incidents did not last for long, and there was no carry-over of negative feelings.

Edward attended Catholic parochial schools until he went to college, and his parents were very pleased with the good grades he received. He particularly enjoyed reading, preferring this activity to playing with other youngsters. If his parents got into a dispute with each other or with him, he habitually withdrew to his room and read.

Edward related that he had had numerous occurrences of intestinal difficulties ever since childhood. These episodes were associated with circumstances such as his mother or teacher insisting that he do something he did not want to do. He also became ill when he had to make a public appearance such as participating in his First Communion or in a play at school. His mother tended to be quite concerned about making him comfortable when he had intestinal symptoms, although she always told him that it was just a "nervous stomach." She said that she knew how he felt because she also was troubled with a "nervous stomach" when she was anxious or upset.

When Edward was nine years old, his mother took him to her physician because Edward was in severe discomfort. He was in the midst of an episode of cramps and diarrhea that lasted for about a week. The onset of the symptoms was associated with Edward's complaints that his new teacher was too strict and forced him to keep going over material he had already mastered. Edward stayed home from school during the latter part of that week, and the physician prescribed some medication that relieved a great deal of discomfort. Mrs. Polowski pleaded with the doctor to call the school principal and explain the reason for Edward's symptoms. This was done and Edward reported that his teacher became somewhat more flexible in relation to his school activities. Edward had other occurrences of cramps during that school year, but none as severe as the earlier occasion.

Edward also had periodic intestinal problems while he was growing up, but these attacks usually lasted for just a few hours at a time. In high school, he experienced another prolonged occurrence of intestinal symptoms during a final examination period. Edward generally received good grades in school, but he was always quite anxious before a test because he feared that he would not do well. He was very anxious during these particular examinations because he had received lower grades than he had expected on some of his previous tests. He therefore studied a great deal and ignored his mother's assurances that he would do well on the exams.

Edward began having intestinal symptoms during the examination period, and the symptoms did not subside, even with medication, until ten days later when he went to a physician. He was given a complete medical examination, including a number of special tests of the gastrointestinal tract. These tests revealed no structural defects or damage, and the problem was again diagnosed as chronic irritable colon. Edward was given a new medication to take when he felt that the symptoms were about to recur.

Early Adult Years

Edward lived at home while he attended a city college. The first friends he ever had were some students he met at college. He had always been shy and somewhat detached from others, and before college, he had never met anyone his age with whom he felt comfortable. Because of his interest in books, he decided to major in library science, and he eventually got to know some of the other students majoring in similar fields. There were relatively few males in most of Edward's classes, but he did meet two or three young men with whom he became friends. They sometimes went to movies or concerts, and occasionally they went out together with some women they knew from school.

Although Edward found it pleasant to be part of a group that included women, he was a senior in college before he decided to go out on a date. At that time, he met a person he was attracted to, and he eventually asked her out. Edward said that he enjoyed being with Mary, and they spent a great deal of time together over the next several months. Mary was also of the Catholic faith and they sometimes went to church together. Mrs. Polowski told Edward that Mary was a nice person, but Edward felt that his mother did not really encourage or discourage his friendship with Mary.

Edward had not had much sexual experience before he met Mary. He had begun masturbating before adolescence, but he felt this activity was sinful and would harm him. He recalled that he tried to control this urge as best he could, but he was not always successful. Edward's physical approach to Mary was tentative and unsure. Mary told him that she believed it was wrong to engage in premarital sexual activity, and Edward stated that he felt the same way, too. Edward said that they lost interest in each other after about five months, and they eventually drifted apart to other friendships.

Edward met Jean, a college sophomore, two months before he graduated. As Edward phrased it, "We got used to spending our time together." Jean had also been brought up in the Catholic faith, and she and Edward began to attend church together on Sundays. Jean's immediate family was quite large, and each time Edward went over to her house, a number of family members were there. Edward said that he did not feel at ease with Jean's family, but he made an effort to converse with whomever happened to be home.

After they had known each other for about a year, Edward and Jean decided to get married. They agreed that it would be best to postpone marriage until Edward was more financially secure in his position at the library. Edward said that both his and Jean's parents were pleased that they were going to get married, and they approved of the plan to wait until Edward and Jean had saved some money.

Jean told Edward that she felt they should wait until they were married before having any sexual relationship, and Edward said that he respected this wish. He related that his sexual relationship with his wife proceeded from a stage of mutual inexperience to one of satisfaction. However, he still felt that the sexual drive reflected the baser human instincts. Jean and Edward decided it would be best to delay having children for a few years, and they followed the rhythm method of birth control.

Edward reported that irritable colon symptoms had not troubled him greatly during college and when he first started to work at the library. He expected that he would have a "nervous stomach" during examination periods, and he took medication accordingly to keep these symptoms to a minimum. Jean knew of these problems so she tended to go out of her way to maintain Edward's good humor during these episodes. She watched the food he ate when they were together, and she encouraged him to rest rather than be with her. Edward also had some difficulty with intestinal symptoms during the period before their wedding. However, Edward recalled that he was able to function reasonably well, and he did not have to miss any of the social activities planned, as long as he took the prescribed medication.

Marital and Employment History

Edward stated that reading was one of the most gratifying activities he could think of. Jean had seemed pleased with his interest in books before their marriage, but her attitude later changed. She indicated to Edward that she had come to feel that he was using his constant reading as a means to avoid interacting with her and others. Especially after the children were born, Jean repeatedly told Edward that it was important for him to spend less time reading and more time with his family.

Edward said that because he was an only child, he had never really been with other children for any length of time when he was young. He revealed that he did not feel any more comfortable interacting with his own children than he had trying to relate to other youngsters during his childhood. He left disciplinary matters to his wife, and generally spent his time at home reading. Edward sometimes played ball with his son Matthew, but very infrequently, and only after his wife had asked him to do this for some time. His daughter Julie was two years old, and Edward commented that she was more verbal than Matthew had been at the same age. He occasionally interacted with Julie by teaching her to say new words.

Edward described his marriage as "reasonably good." Jean was on good terms with Edward's parents, and she and Edward's mother joined together in their efforts to prevent him from having episodes of intestinal difficulties. Edward said that Jean was a good homemaker, and she tried hard to please him. When they were first married, Jean did not seem to mind spending most of their evenings at home. She was very proud of the vocational advances Edward had made at the library, and she accepted his statements that he could not participate in various social events because the reading he did at home helped him with his work. They currently had some friends they saw from time to time, but they generally did not attend as many social activities as his wife would have liked.

Edward indicated that his relationship with his wife seemed to deteriorate after the children were born. He felt that he and Jean did not communicate with each other as much as they used to, and he recognized that many times he purposely withdrew from social interactions by reading. It appeared to Edward that his wife spent most of her time taking care of or nagging him about the children, and she did not seem as interested in his work as she used to. He realized that he did not talk with her about as many of the events that happened at work as he had previously. He also did not share his wife's belief that it was important for a father to interact with his children. He pointed out that his own father had spent very little time with him, but he cared for his father nonetheless and felt this lack of companionship had not hurt him.

Edward enjoyed working with books, and he found it gratifying to aid persons in finding the materials they were looking for. He eventually advanced to the position of head of the reference department, and two female librarians worked under his supervision. He stated that he had no difficulty interacting with them, and he generally ignored any attempt either of them made to influence the way he ran his department. Edward always avoided open confrontations. He typically listened without comment to what others said, then went ahead and did what he thought was best. He generally behaved this way with his wife also, whenever they had a difference of opinion on some matter.

Edward's vocational situation had been quite satisfactory until a number of months ago. A new library director had been hired, and Edward found getting along with this man extremely difficult. The director tended to issue statements to the library staff about policy changes without consulting with them first. Edward said that he was not able to ignore these orders and continue doing whatever he wanted to do, as he had with the previous administrator. Further, Edward felt that he should have been offered the director's position, and he found it especially difficult to take arbitrary orders from a man whom he felt was not as qualified as he was.

Over the past few years, Edward's intestinal difficulties had gradually become more severe and incapacitating, and there was a marked intensification of his problems during the previous year. The medication prescribed for him had been reasonably effective in controlling his symptoms, but lately he found it necessary to stay home in bed whenever he had an episode of bowel spasms. The intestinal cramps had become extremely painful, and he often had spells of diarrhea lasting for almost a week. These bouts came on suddenly, with little advance warning, and were generally associated with stressful events that had occurred at work or at home.

Edward stated that his wife continued to be very solicitous and helpful, encouraging him to rest at home when he was in discomfort. She went out of her way to see that the children or outside events did not disturb him. His mother also became greatly concerned when he was ill, and brought over special foods that she had found through her own experience were good for "settling your stomach."

Edward related that on a number of instances since his marriage he had been impotent. His wife was very understanding during these infrequent occurrences, and he noted that each of these occasions had been subsequent to a prolonged period of intestinal difficulties. During the past several months, the episodes of impotence had increased in frequency; at times he wanted to have sexual intercourse, but he was not sure whether he would be able to have an erection. He felt that his wife was also becoming more concerned about this problem, but she was purposely not saying anything for fear of making the situation worse.

To make sure that the irritable colon disorder had not developed into something more serious, Edward heeded the pleas of his wife and mother and made an appointment for a complete medical examination. He also hoped that the doctor would prescribe a stronger medication to control the distressing bowel symptoms. While in the process of the medical evaluation, Edward told the physician about the occasions of impotence.

Medical Evaluation

The physical examination and blood tests were all within normal limits. X-rays of the gastrointestinal tract revealed an irritability and hyperactivity of the bowel, but there were no indications of obstruction, ulcerations, or other organic changes.

The diagnosis of chronic irritable colon made at this time was consistent with earlier diagnoses of Edward's condition. His problem was viewed as psychophysiological in nature—that is, changes in bodily function were associated with emotional stress. The internist suggested that Edward seek psychotherapy to further explore the problems he was encountering in interpersonal relationships, and to learn more about the episodes of impotence. Edward was continued on antispasmodic medication.

Psychological Evaluation

Edward was tall and thin in appearance, and slightly balding. He was neatly dressed in a conservatively styled suit and tie. He met on two occasions with Dr. R., a male clinical psychologist. Edward readily answered the questions asked of him, but spoke of his problems in an impersonal, emotionless manner. It was apparent that Edward spent a great deal of time ruminating about his difficulties, and he indicated that he was aware of a relationship between stressors he experienced and the onset of his physical symptoms.

Edward was asked to complete the MMPI. He scored in a range that was higher than the population norm on the scale measuring an interest and concern with bodily processes. However, all of the other scale scores fell within normal limits, and his general response pattern indicated good reality testing. There were no suggestions of a thought disorder.

The client's responses on the Assertive Questionnaire (Lazarus, 1971) strongly indicated that he typically responded to interpersonal situations in a passive, nonassertive manner. This behavior pattern was exemplified by the client responding "no" to the following items: "If a friend betrays your confidence, do you tell him how you really feel?" "If someone keeps kicking the back of your chair in a movie, would you ask him to stop?"

Edward responded to the TAT cards in a highly formalized and intellectual manner. His perceptions and stories were very imaginative, but the responses functioned to draw attention to the structural details of the cards rather than deal with interpersonal relationships. For example, on one of the cards commonly described as an interaction between some women and a man plowing a field, Edward said that the scene was similar to a painting he had seen. He depicted the man as a symbol of an earth god. A response of this nature avoids dealing with any kind of emotional interaction, just as Edward's habitual response in his social milieu was to avoid emotional encounters.

The client's noninvolved, intellectualized response style was also evident on a sentence completion test. Edward responded with Biblical and other quotations to words such as "I," "A child," and "A mother." This is consistent with Edward's report that he engages in philosophical, rather than problem-solving introspection about his problems.

Some of the responses to the various tests suggested that Edward was ambivalent about sexual matters. His stories presented a dichotomy between love as a romantic, good, and noble emotion, and sex as a base and ignoble instinct. Strong religious overtones were associated with this distinction between sacred and profane love.

Course of Therapy

In addition to the prescribed medication, Dr. R. recommended that Edward engage in a behavior therapy program of assertion training (Wolpe & Lazarus, 1966). Dr. R. explained that Edward's interpersonal relationships would be more satisfactory if he learned to express his feelings and rights actively in a socially acceptable manner. There might also be an associated diminishment of the physical symptoms with assertion training. Edward agreed to these recommendations, and he participated in assertion training for approximately five months. (See Chapter 14 for another description of assertion training.)

Although medication is important in treating disorders in which psychological factors affect a physical condition, it also is essential for the individual to learn to respond to interpersonal events in a more flexible manner. Assertion training deals with specific situations in which the client is taught the difference between acting aggressively and assertively. In circumstances in which acting assertively could result in negative consequences, alternative behaviors are suggested and rehearsed.

During the initial therapy sessions, the client was encouraged to talk about any past events that had been particularly distressing. Through a discussion of these events, Dr. R. was able to point out the typical way that Edward interacted with other persons. It was quickly apparent that ever since childhood, Edward responded to aversive situations with physiological overactivation and passive withdrawal. As the therapy sessions progressed, Edward also became more aware of the relationship between his typical nonassertive behavior style and the negative behavior of others.

Edward brought up a recent situation that he still found extremely troubling. The library director had arbitrarily ordered some books for Edward's department without consulting him first. Edward was very upset by this action, but he said nothing to the director. He came home from work feeling extremely agitated and beset by intestinal cramps which became more severe as the evening progressed. He told his wife that he was not feeling well, but he did not tell her the details of the events at work. He ate very little at dinner, and soon afterwards, he went to his room and read in bed. Edward said that Jean made a special effort to keep the children out of the bedroom so they would not disturb him. Despite medication, the cramps continued sporadically the following day as well, and Edward said that he was forced to stay home from work that day because of his discomfort.

Dr. R. asked Edward to think of some other ways in which he could have interacted with the library director, which would have allowed him to express his opinions without provoking retaliatory behavior.

Eventually, a more assertive alternative was suggested and the ramifications of this new approach were discussed. Edward thought that he could have calmly but firmly told the director that it was a clearly acknowledged part of Edward's job to order books for his department. Since funds were available, the director should have given Edward the opportunity to submit his own purchase order.

Edward felt that his job would not have been in jeopardy if he had behaved in this manner. Therefore, a behavioral rehearsal took place, with Edward practicing the more assertive role, and the therapist playing the role of the library director. Next, Edward assumed the role of the library director, and observed the model of assertive behavior provided by the therapist's actions.

Edward eventually became more comfortable acting assertively, and he discussed with Dr. R. the changes in the behavior of others which resulted from the modification of his behavior. Edward showed greater awareness of how his typically detached behavior functioned to avoid family responsibilities and involvement with other persons, and he expressed a desire to change this behavior pattern. Dr. R. gave strong social approval to Edward for acting more assertively with his wife and for communicating both positive and negative feelings to her. Near the end of the course of therapy, Dr. R. felt that it would be beneficial to see Edward and Jean jointly for a number of sessions. Dr. R. discussed with them the contingencies between Edward's prolonged somatic distress and detachment and the strong reinforcement Jean's solicitude provided for this behavior.

As Edward began to act more assertively, he was very pleased to discover that the frequency and severity of the episodes of somatic distress gradually diminished. His physical condition generally improved as well, and he experienced enhanced gratification from interacting with his wife and children. Associated with these changes, the occasions of sexual impotence terminated. Although from time to time Edward still reacted to stressful situations with somatic difficulties, these episodes markedly lessened as he began to gain the necessary skills and be reinforced for acting in a more assertive manner.

Discussion

Disorders resulting from an interaction of psychological and physical processes have been categorized in previous diagnostic nomenclature systems as psychosomatic disorders, and then as psychophysiological disorders (DSM-II, 1968). The latter term was used to suggest the interactive nature of psychological conflict and somatic processes. This category was devised as a move away from the connotations of the term "psychosomatic"—that is, a duality or separateness of mind and body.

DSM-III-R (1987) uses the category psychological factors affecting physical condition. The assumption is that a wide range of stress factors (environmental, interpersonal, and intrapersonal) have an effect on bodily processes. These stress factors can affect the functioning of single organ systems, for example, the stomach, intestines, lungs, and bronchi—that are innervated by the autonomic nervous system and not fully under voluntary control. However, the DSM-III-R classification criteria also take into account research findings on the influence of stress on the development of physical illnesses. Thus, psychological factors can manifest an effect on disorders that have traditionally been viewed as entirely physical in nature, such as colds, sore throats, viruses, and stress-induced alterations of tumor growth (Sklar & Anisman, 1981).

The DSM-III-R diagnostic criteria for psychological factors affecting physical condition designate that environmental stimuli that are psychologically meaningful to the individual are related in time to the onset or exacerbation of a particular physical condition or disorder. The physical condition should have either obvious physical pathology, such as gastric ulcer or ulcerative colitis, or a clear pathophysiological process, as seen in migraine or tension headaches.

In the case of Edward Polowski, the specific physical condition or disorder would be listed as irritable bowel syndrome. An additional diagnosis would be made—sexual arousal disorder, male erectile disorder.

Cannon (1939) divided the basic biological patterns of reacting to stress into two major categories, the fight-flight and withdrawal-conservation patterns. These patterns were delineated on the basis of whether the primary site of activation is the sympathetic or parasympathetic portion of the autonomic nervous system. The fight-flight patterns represent a variety of active modes of coping with stress that involve sympathetic innervation. Startle movements, tremors, and altered respiration are some of the behavioral manifestations of these patterns. The withdrawal-conservation patterns involve a reduction of activity and a conservation of resources. These patterns result in a stimulation of gastrointestinal functions, which are primarily under parasympathetic control. Symptoms of diarrhea and intestinal discomfort are part of the withdrawal-conservation response process.

Engel (1963) employed Cannon's dual system of categorization in his explanation of various psychophysiologic dysfunctions. He also posited that an interaction existed between a particular type of emotional pattern and a somatic weakness or vulnerability. According to Engel, the emotions associated with the withdrawal-conservation patterns consist of a giving-up because of feelings of helplessness and hopelessness. In the case of irritable colon, the psychological stress is symbolically responded to as a need to rid one's body of a noxious situation or agent. The result is a defensive reaction involving intestinal over-activity.

Some evidence supports the notion of somatic vulnerability, if this concept is defined in terms of genetic or constitutional differences in autonomic response patterns. Richmond and Lustman (1955) demonstrated stable individual differences in the autonomic response patterns of newborn infants to environmental stress. In addition, Mirsky (1958) showed substantial differences in pepsinogen levels (related to ulcer formation) among newborn infants. If this differential autonomic response to stress continued throughout life, individuals could manifest vulnerabilities of different organ systems. Thus, an individual who characteristically responded to stressors with a rise in pepsinogen levels would manifest a sensitivity of different body systems than would an individual whose habitual response pattern involved activation of the cardiovascular system. Consistent with this notion are the findings of Weiner, Thaler, Reiser, and Mirsky (1957), who demonstrated that all army recruits developing ulcers after basic training came from a group classified at induction as having high pepsinogen levels.

Observational learning also may be important in the development of psychophysiological disorders. Berger (1962) demonstrated that the opportunity to observe a model responding emotionally to environmental stimuli resulted in a vicariously instigated emotional response in the observer. A child may thus learn to respond to aversive situations with intestinal symptoms, because of having repeatedly observed a parent respond in this manner to unpleasant events. The somatic response may then serve as a behavior that is reinforced by the attention of others and the opportunity to escape from the unpleasant situation.

Ullman and Krasner (1969) presented a variety of learning formulations of psychophysiological disorders. They cited evidence suggesting that certain behavioral roles have emotional concomitants that lead to physiological changes. If these physiological changes are of long duration, they may eventually result in structural damage. For example, both strong anger and fear are associated with a rise in systolic blood pressure (Ax, 1953). Therefore, a person who had consistently learned to interact with others in an angry or fearful manner may, over time, begin to show organic changes resulting from the chronically elevated blood pressure. In this particular case, hypertension is the result of a learned and consistently repeated way of reacting to specific situations.

Friedman and Rosenman (1974) postulated that individuals who manifest what they termed the "Type A" behavior pattern—that is, hostility, time-urgency, competitive achievement orientation—will be more prone to develop heart disease than individuals demonstrating a less aroused Type B behavior pattern. The concept of the Type A behavior pattern is based on the theory that learned behavior patterns can have a direct result on physiological functioning, placing the individual at risk for heart disease. A prospective study classified men as Type A or B who were initially free of heart disease at the start of the study. The findings demonstrated that Type A men were twice as likely to develop heart disease over an eight-and-a-half-year time period than were men initially classified as Type B (Rosenman, et al., 1975). However, other studies have not found the Type A behavior pattern to be a risk factor for the later development of coronary heart disease (e.g., Shekelle et al., 1985).

Because of the contradictory findings regarding the Type A behavior pattern and heart disease, other investigations have examined more specific components of the Type A pattern, particularly hostility. Again, the results of different prospective studies have not been consistent. Some have found a relationship between hostility score (as measured by the MMPI) and the later development of heart disease (Williams et al., 1980), while other studies did not find that hostility level predicted later coronary heart disease (Leon, Finn, Murray, & Bailey, 1988).

With regard to treatment of psychophysiological disorders, assertion training was an important component in Edward Polowski's treatment. Linehan (1979) pointed out that three content areas should be addressed in assertion training—the development of specific verbal and behavioral skills; the teaching of more adaptive cognitive skills (i.e., changing the person's unrealistic beliefs about the negative consequences of behaving in an assertive manner); and arousal management skills to counteract the disruptive effects of anxiety responses. The rationale of this multicomponent cognitive-behavioral program is that some persons may have the behavioral skills to act in an assertive manner in refusing the unreasonable requests of others, but because of faulty beliefs and anxiety arousal choose not to do so when it is appropriate.

Antispasmodic medication was an important component of Edward's treatment because the drugs blocked or lessened the intensity of the physiological response. A gradual decline in the strength of the gastrointestinal response to stress also occurred because of the learning of more adaptive coping behaviors. The physiological concomitants of the behaviors learned through assertion training were apparently antagonistic to the physiological components of the client's previous passive behaviors.

A study that assessed the interpersonal effects of positive assertion (openness in expressing positive feelings to others), and negative assertion (refusal of unreasonable requests) found that individuals who were able to engage in both types of assertion were viewed as more competent and likeable (St. Lawrence, Hansen, Cutts, Tisdelle, & Irish, 1985). These findings suggest that assertion training that focuses only on teaching refusal skills may not have as beneficial an impact on the client's interpersonal situation as training in a range of assertion skills.

People who respond to life stressors with physical dysfunction also may benefit from developing an array of coping methods that can be implemented as appropriate in a particular situation. A recent program for the treatment of the irritable bowel syndrome has reported promising findings using relaxation training, biofeedback, educational information, and training in coping strategies for dealing with stress (Neff & Blanchard, 1987). The use of a multicomponent strategy may prove effective in modifying physical as well as other types of detrimental responses to stressful life situations.

A number of investigations have studied the effect of life changes on the development of physical and mental diseases. One investigation assessed the retrospective reports of informants; a marked increase in life changes was reported in a group of men in the six-month period prior to suffering a heart attack (Rahe, Romo, Bennett, & Siltanen, 1974). However, life event and illness studies may be contaminated by the fact that life changes can be caused by the disease itself, and how one recalls past events may be influenced by current physiological distress.

More recent theory has examined the psychological and psysiological effects of daily "hassles" rather than discrete life events, that is, irritating experiences one confronts on a day-to-day basis (DeLongis, Coyne, Dakof, Folkman, & Lazarus, 1982; Lazarus & Folkman, 1984). These investigations have proposed that how one interprets the nature and seriousness of a threat (subjective appraisal) determines the intensity of the physiological response and the coping patterns the individual uses to deal with the stressor.

There is current interest in studying the role of stress on immune functioning, stemming from the general notion that psychological stress may predispose the body to many types of disorders, depending on the particular biological vulnerability of a given individual. A number of studies have demonstrated that stress related hormones affect the immune system through causing a decreased response of lymphocytes (white blood cells). The lowered ability of lymphocytes to produce antibodies and other chemicals that destroy foreign cells (Jemmott & Locke,

1984; Irwin, Daniels, Bloom, Smith, & Weiner, 1987) demonstrates a mechanism whereby stress can result in disease.

The importance of engaging in adaptive activity rather than remaining passive when confronted by stressful situations was highlighted by Gal and Lazarus (1975). Adaptive activity was seen as enhancing a sense of mastery and control, and discharging the energy generated by the physiological mobilization to threatening situations.

It is impossible to determine at this point whether or not Edward had exhibited a gastrointestinal response to stress from the time he was a newborn. However, it is apparent in Edward's case that modeling cues were important in the formation of the psychophysiological response. Edward reported that as a child, he observed his mother responding to stressful situations with intestinal dysfunction, and he was reinforced by his mother's attention and concern when he exhibited similar somatic difficulties.

Edward's social learning history illustrates how a person's behavior can be shaped by the lack of opportunity to learn the skills necessary for interacting with other persons. Edward led a fairly isolated existence from the period of early childhood until he went to college. He did not see his relatives very often, and before college, he rarely interacted with members of his peer group. His father worked on the night shift and spent a minimal amount of time with him during the weekends. Edward therefore had very little opportunity or encouragement to learn to act in a more socially outgoing and assertive manner.

Edward's mother reinforced passive and quiet behavior, and both of his parents were pleased that Edward took such a great interest in reading. His parents encouraged him in this activity, and Edward also received a great deal of attention from them when he complained of intestinal discomfort. Mr. and Mrs. Polowski rarely modeled or reinforced more assertive ways of behaving with others.

When they were first married, Edward's wife interacted with him in a manner similar to that of his mother. Jean made few demands on Edward, pampered him when he was ill, and reinforced him for his interest in reading. Jean apparently did not interact with her mother-in-law in a competitive manner, but instead, the two women formed a coalition aimed at catering to Edward's wishes and preventing him from being disturbed when he was ill.

Edward's habitual interaction style became less reinforcing when his children were born. He was no longer the center of his wife's and mother's attention. Caring for the children was time-consuming and fatiguing, and Matthew and Julie also demanded attention and concern. Edward found forming a positive relationship with his children extremely difficult. As a child, he had never learned the social skills necessary for interacting with his peers, and as a father, he was similarly unable to talk to or play with his children on their level. He interacted with Julie in a way that was consistent with his enjoyment of reading: he taught her to say new words.

Edward stated that many times he felt that his wife was imposing on him when she pressed him to relate to the children. The need to assume a behavioral role of responsibility and involvement with his family was quite aversive to Edward, and he avoided or escaped from his situation by withdrawing and reading. The bouts of irritable colon similarly allowed him to withdraw, and his discomfort served to divert his wife's attention away from the children and back to him.

With assertion training, Edward began to learn and practice more effective social skills for dealing with interpersonal problems. He gradually began to act more assertively, and establishing a more harmonious relationship with the new director reinforced this change of behavior. If there had been no reciprocal change in the director's behavior, Edward might have eventually been able to be assertive enough to look for a job at another library.

There was also an important change in Edward's relationship with his wife. Although Edward still obtained a great deal of pleasure from reading, he no longer used this activity as an escape from interacting with others. He began to communicate with Jean more than he had ever done previously, and this was gratifying for both of them. As his relationship with his wife improved, he also began to take a greater interest in household events, and this interest generalized to more frequent interactions with his children. When some event occurred at home that disturbed him, Edward learned to talk over his feelings and reactions with Jean, instead of withdrawing and reading.

Edward's new assertiveness required a change in Jean's habitual style of interacting with her husband. Rather than discouraging this assertiveness, Jean found it reinforcing to have her husband relate to her in a more interested and active manner. Through the joint therapy sessions, Jean was able to see how she was reinforcing Edward's noninvolved, sick behavior, and she subsequently began to modify her excessively solicitous interactions with him. With these modifications in their personal relationship and the lessening of the episodes of intestinal difficulties, the problem of sexual impotence was alleviated.

Edward's somatic reaction to stressful situations was a highly complex response, with physiological and learning components. However, it was possible for him to learn alternate ways of dealing with stressful situations. Edward acquired some of the skills necessary for positive interpersonal relationships, and he eventually learned to find these activities reinforcing. He also exhibited a change in self-concept in terms of developing a greater personal feeling of effectiveness in coping with the stresses in his everyday life. He no longer feared the consequences of acting in an assertive manner when appropriate. The new assertive behaviors may have been antagonistic to the physiologically stimulated gastrointestinal reaction. In time there was a marked reduction in the painful and inconvenient symptoms of irritable colon.

References

American Psychiatric Association (1968). *Diagnostic and statistical manual of mental disorders* (2nd ed.) (DSM-II). Washington, DC: Author.

American Psychiatric Association (1987). *Diagnostic and statistical manual of mental disorders* (3rd ed. rev.) (DSM-III-R). Washington, DC: Author.

Ax, A. (1953). The physiological differentiation between fear and anger in humans. *Psychosomatic Medicine, 15,* 433–442.

Berger, S. M. (1962). Conditioning through vicarious instigation. *Psychological Review, 69,* 450–466.

Cannon, W. B. (1939). *The wisdom of the body.* New York: Norton.

DeLongis, A., Coyne, J. C., Dakof, G., Folkman, S., & Lazarus, R. S. (1982). Relationships of daily hassles, uplifts, and major life events to health status. *Health Psychology, 1,* 119–136.

Engel, G. L. (1963). *Psychological development in health and disease.* Philadelphia: Saunders.

Friedman, M., & Rosenman, R. (1974). *Type A behavior and your heart.* New York: Knopf.

Gal, R., & Lazarus, R. S. (1975). The role of activity in anticipating and confronting stressful situations. *Journal of Human Stress, 1,* 4–20.

Irwin, M., Daniels, M., Bloom, E. T., Smith, T. L., & Weiner, H. (1987). Life events, depressive symptoms, and immune function. *American Journal of Psychiatry, 144,* 437–441.

Jemmott, J. B., III, & Locke, S. E. (1984). Psychosocial factors, immunologic mediation, and human susceptibility to infectious diseases: How much do we know? *Psychological Bulletin, 95,* 78–108.

Lazarus, A. A. (1971). *Behavior therapy and beyond.* New York: McGraw-Hill.

Lazarus, R. S., & Folkman, S. (1984). *Stress, appraisal, and coping.* New York: Springer Publishing.

Leon, G. R., Finn, S. E., Murray, D., & Bailey, J. M. (1988). The inability to predict cardiovascular disease from hostility scores or MMPI items related to Type A behavior. *Journal of Consulting and Clinical Psychology, 56*, 597–600.

Linehan, M. M. (1979). Structured cognitive-behavioral treatment of assertion problems. In P. C. Kendall, & S. D. Hollon (Eds.), *Cognitive-behavioral interventions. Theory, research, and procedures* (pp. 205–240) New York: Academic Press.

Mirsky, I. A. (1958). Physiologic, psychologic and social determinants in the etiology of duodenal ulcer. *American Journal of Digestive Diseases, 3*, 285–314.

Neff, D. F., & Blanchard, E. B. (1987). A multi-component treatment for irritable bowel syndrome. *Behavior Therapy, 18*, 70–83.

Rahe, R. R., Romo, M., Bennett, L., & Siltanen, P. (1974). Recent life changes, myocardial infraction, and abrupt coronary death. *Archives of Internal Medicine, 133*, 221–228.

Richmond, J. B., & Lustman, S. L. (1955). Autonomic function in the neonate: I. Implications for psychosomatic theory. *Psychosomatic Medicine, 17*, 269–275.

Rosenman, R. H., Brand, R. J., Jenkins, C. D. et al. (1975). Coronary heart disease in the Western Collaborative Group Study: Final follow-up experience of 8½ years. *Journal of the American Medical Association, 233*, 872–877.

St. Lawrence, J. S., Hansen, D. J., Cutts, T. F., Tisdelle, D. A., & Irish, J. D. (1985). Situational context: Effects on perceptions of assertive and unassertive behavior. *Behavior Therapy, 16*, 51–62.

Shekelle, R. B., Hulley, S. B., Neaton, J. D. et al. (1985). The MRFIT behavior pattern study. II. Type A behavior and incidence of coronary heart disease. *American Journal of Epidemiology, 22*, 559–570.

Sklar, L. S., & Anisman, H. (1981). Stress and cancer. *Psychological Bulletin, 89*, 369–406.

Ullmann, L. P., & Krasner, L. (1969). *A psychological approach to abnormal behavior.* Englewood Cliffs, NJ: Prentice-Hall.

Weiner, H., Thaler, M., Reiser, M. F., & Mirsky, I. A. (1957). Etiology of duodenal ulcer: I. Relation of specific psychological characteristics to rate of gastric secretion. *Psychosomatic Medicine, 17*, 1–10.

Williams, R. B., Haney, T. L., Lee, K. L., Kong, Y-H., Blumenthal, J. A., & Whalen, R. E. (1980). Type A behavior, hostility, and coronary atherosclerosis. *Psychosomatic Medicine, 42*, 539–549.

Wolpe, J., & Lazarus, A. A. (1966). *Behavior therapy techniques.* Oxford: Pergamon Press.

9

Sexual Abuse and Chronic Pelvic Pain— Somatoform Pain Disorder

Martha Stewart was referred to the psychiatric section of a large city hospital after she had undergone a thorough evaluation in the hospital's medical unit. Martha was 16 years old, and her chief complaints were severe pain in the lower abdomen and genital area, and chronic anxiety which had intensified during the past few months.

The client was white and of lower-class background. Her brother John was 18 and her sister Betty was 15 at the time of the evaluation. Martha's parents separated when she was 13 years old. Mrs. Stewart had worked part-time as a waitress for many years, and the family received welfare assistance to supplement their low income. Mr. Stewart was a carpenter by trade, but he had not worked for the past five years because of chronic and severe alcoholism.

Martha and her mother were seen by staff members of the hospital's psychiatric unit. A social worker interviewed Mrs. Stewart, and Martha was seen by a psychiatric resident and a psychologist.

Family History

Martha described her family life during the period when her father lived at home as "terrible" and "awful." Her earliest memories of her family were associated with incidents related to her father's drinking, and she vividly recalled occasions when Mr. Stewart began hitting his wife and the police had to be called. The client related that her father frequently stayed in the house, drank heavily, and became more and more abusive as he drank, until he eventually passed out.

Mr. Stewart's behavior became quite bizarre about six months before he left his family. At times while drinking, he would suddenly pick up any available object and throw it at whoever was close by, barely missing that person. He then laughed uproariously as the individual ran out of reach. On several occasions, Mr. Stewart reported that voices were bothering him, and he sometimes appeared to be carrying on a conversation with someone who was not physically present. On the other hand, Martha stated that when sober, Mr. Stewart was usually very quiet and mild and would help around the house.

Mrs. Stewart was extremely nonassertive with her husband. She did not comment on his drinking or make any effort to induce him to change his behavior. When he began to shout at or hit her, her usual response was to try to stay out of his way. It was generally a neighbor who called the police when Mr. Stewart became extremely belligerent.

Mr. Stewart was abusive toward the children also, and he frequently hit John forcefully with a belt. It was difficult to predict when these beatings would occur. Occasionally, when John did not comply with an order his father gave him, nothing happened. At other times and for no apparent reason, Mr. Stewart hit him. John would then run out of the house and stay out until his father drank enough to fall asleep.

Both Mrs. Stewart and Martha indicated that Mr. Stewart had sexually molested his two daughters on a number of occasions. All of these episodes occurred at times when Mr. Stewart had been drinking and Mrs. Stewart was away at work. Martha stated that she was about ten years old the first time her father "bothered her." She reported that he came into the bedroom she shared with Betty and proceeded to sexually molest her. At the same time, he threatened to hit her if she called for help from her brother, or told anyone about the incident. However, Martha later told her mother what had happened, and said that she pleaded with Mrs. Stewart to retaliate against her father in some way, and to protect her and her sister from a possible repetition of this behavior. Mrs. Stewart said that speaking with him would not help matters because she thought there was nothing she could do to prevent a similar incident from happening again.

Martha had observed Mr. Stewart molesting her sister Betty a number of times, too. She said she had told her mother about these events also and begged her to intervene but to no avail. Martha further related that on three or four occasions during the year before her father moved, when no one else was in the house, Mr. Stewart had forced her to "go all the way." She stated that she felt both angry and ashamed after each of these episodes, and was puzzled by the fact that she also felt very guilty. Martha did not tell her mother or Betty that her father had forced her to have sexual intercourse with him, and she never asked Betty the specific details about the extent to which he had molested her.

Mrs. Stewart told the social worker that she could have done nothing to prevent her daughters from being sexually abused, and further, she did not think that her husband's behavior was so unusual or harmful. It was apparent from Mrs. Stewart's comments that she did not ask questions about what took place at home on the evenings when she was working. She maintained a noninvolved attitude, and even when her daughters complained to her, she did not confront her husband about his behavior.

On his own initiative, Mr. Stewart moved into a rooming house in the same neighborhood. He told his wife that he did not want to be bothered with the family any more. Mr. Stewart was not employed at the time he moved out, and he lived on welfare assistance for a number of years. He continued to visit the family from time to time, and Mrs. Stewart said that she bore no hard feelings toward him. Martha reported that her father's physical condition had deteriorated as a result of his drinking behavior, and that he had frequently been hospitalized or arrested for drunkenness.

Martha indicated that she got along quite well with her sister and she felt there was a strong bond of mutual affection between them. However, the two girls rarely discussed their father or other family matters. They usually participated in social functions together and they had a number of mutual friends. Martha said that she and Betty did not get along with their brother John. He frequently started arguments and then began punching one of them. They found it difficult to defend themselves because John was bigger and stronger than they were. Martha indicated that she generally tried to be protective of her sister, but she appeared to be ineffective in preventing her brother from hitting Betty.

Mrs. Stewart also reported that John frequently acted in a physically aggressive manner. A number of teachers told her that her son was a severe behavior problem at school, and he was often sent to the principal's office as a disciplinary measure. When John was about ten, he was referred to a school psychologist for evaluation, and Mrs. Stewart said she was told that her son was emotionally disturbed. John was then placed in a special class, where he remained until he dropped out of school at age 16. John did not attempt to find a job, and he spent his time wandering around with a group of boys his age. He had not had any difficulties with the police, but Mrs. Stewart felt that this situation would not last for long. She noticed that John sometimes came home with small items that apparently were stolen from department stores. Mrs. Stewart said that she did not make an issue about where he got these items, because she felt helpless about what she could do to control John's behavior.

Social and Educational Background

Martha's parents had no friends, nor did they maintain ties with any of their relatives in the area. All of Martha's grandparents had been dead for some time, and she did not remember them.

Martha reported that she was quite active as a child, and she had always had a number of girl friends to play hopscotch and running games with. She indicated that she had played with girls exclusively, because boys were too rough and were constantly in trouble. As an example, she cited the difficulties in which her brother John and his friends were frequently involved.

Martha seemed to behave quite differently when she was at home compared with when she was with her friends. She stated that she was often tense and anxious at home, yet she behaved very exuberantly and was the "life of the party" when she was with her girl friends. She said that this alternating behavior style became more pronounced when she was around 13 years old and her friends began to be interested in boys. Mrs. Stewart also commented on Martha's changeable behavior, and said that she felt this was just Martha's nature. Martha reported that she began to smoke when she was about 14, and she smoked quite heavily when alone as well as when she was with her friends. She attributed the heavy smoking to her nerves.

Martha stated that because she enjoyed being with her girl friends, she spent as much time with them as she could. Their conversations were usually about favorite entertainers and boys they knew, or about teachers and events at school. The girls very rarely discussed personal matters, and Martha never mentioned her father. She said that she listened when her friends talked about sex, but she did not join in the conversation. She usually did not complain to her friends about the persistent pain and cramps she was having. Betty was also part of this peer group, and when she and Martha were in the house, they continued the conversations they had participated in with their friends.

Martha said that she and her girl friends occasionally went places together with a group of boys, but she never went out alone on a date. She indicated that she was very strict with the boys she was with and discouraged any sort of physical contact. She stated that she never let any boy hold her hand or put his arm around her; she wanted to wait until she was married before she had any further sexual experiences.

Mrs. Stewart reported that several months before the hospital visit, some neighbors had complained to the police that Martha and Betty were having a loud party while Mrs. Stewart was away at work. The group dispersed when they realized the police had been called, and the police did not pursue the matter further when they found out that everyone had gone. A neighbor told Mrs. Stewart that it sounded as if the group were drinking, and Mrs. Stewart discovered that the beds were in a state of disarray. Consistent with her behavior in the past, Mrs. Stewart did not ask the girls what had occurred nor did she say anything about the disordered house. Mrs. Stewart commented to the social worker that it was natural that teenage girls would get noisy at times. She made no other evaluation of the incident.

Martha also brought up this episode during one of her interviews, and she indicated great annoyance that the neighbors had called the police. She said that she and her friends had only been talking, although she recognized that their conversation might have gotten a bit loud and therefore disturbing to others. She firmly maintained that the neighbors were only trying to cause trouble and were not justified in calling the police. She stated emphatically that there were no drugs or liquor used at the party.

Martha revealed that she was not really interested in school, but she wanted to do better scholastically so she would graduate. She had been getting only marginal grades for the past few years, and at the time she was seen, she was failing all of her classes. Martha indicated that she did not do much homework and she was always behind in her school subjects. She stated that her "nervousness" and abdominal pains interfered with her ability to concentrate and study for examinations. She also stated that she did not think she was very smart, and this made her even more anxious when a test was pending.

Mrs. Stewart reported that she often woke up in the morning and found Martha sleeping in bed with her or on the floor beside the bed. Martha explained this behavior by saying that she always felt much better sleeping near her mother, and she had maintained this pattern ever since Mr. Stewart moved out of the house. Mrs. Stewart never commented on

Martha's sleep pattern, and she neither encouraged nor discouraged Martha from sleeping near her.

Present Status

Martha related that a number of conflicting emotions arose whenever she thought about her father's sexual assaults. She was extremely angry at him because of his sexual advances, but she also felt ashamed and guilty. She thought that if she had tried harder, she could have prevented him from molesting her. In addition, she told the interviewer about her concern that her mother would find out the full extent of what had happened. It appeared to Martha that none of her girl friends had undergone similar experiences, and she did not want any of them to find out about her father's behavior.

Martha said that she was often in extreme discomfort because of pain and cramps in the abdomen and genital area. Her menstrual cycle was quite irregular and she had a great deal of pain during her period. On numerous occasions over the past few years, Martha had been sent to the school nurse or had stayed home from school because of severe pain. She frequently cried at home because of her discomfort, and the pain intensified her feelings of nervousness. Her family was solicitous to her when she said she was in pain, and Betty often did some of Martha's share of the household chores when Martha complained of feeling ill.

It was difficult for Martha to locate precisely where the pain emanated from. The pain seemed to be a generalized sensation that spread out in waves inside her. It often felt like some outside force that had invaded her body and traveled inside her from place to place. Sometimes these sensations were pleasurable, but at other times the pain was so severe she felt unable to get out of bed. However, if she got involved in watching a program on television or if one of her friends called, the pain suddenly disappeared.

Martha was given a complete medical examination and underwent a number of special diagnostic procedures, but no physical basis for her reports of pain could be found. Previous medical examinations were also negative.

Martha indicated that she was quite puzzled about some events that had recently occurred. For amusement, she and her girl friends sometimes sat in a circle in a darkened room and stared at a candle burning in the center of the room. The girls told ghost stories or related frightening incidents, generally trying to scare each other. These occasions were marked by a great deal of giggling and by exclamations of fright and interest. Martha stated that they did not use drugs or alcohol during these games.

Martha reported that several months previously, when she and her friends were playing this game, she suddenly saw what appeared to be a spirit in the candle flame. This image was very clear to her, and she said that she sat transfixed at this vision, feeling awed and frightened by what she saw. The spirit looked like an older person, neither male nor female. It stared at her questioningly but did not say anything. Her friends noticed that Martha had suddenly become very quiet, and several asked her what was the matter. Martha said that the spirit disappeared when her friends started asking her questions. Martha denied that anything was wrong, and she did not share this experience with Betty or anyone else. She reported that she heard a constant ringing sound for several days after this episode, and she was quite frightened by the experience. However, she still did not tell anyone what was bothering her.

When her friends repeated the candle game about two weeks later, Martha again participated. She once more saw a spirit in the flame, but on this occasion, she immediately became quite frightened and asked that the game be stopped. She felt tense and anxious for several days after this second episode and indicated that she was again puzzled about why she had seen a spirit in the candle flame.

Psychological Evaluation

Martha was seen by a female psychologist for diagnostic evaluation. The client was neatly dressed and attractive. She sat at the edge of her chair, fidgeted with a button on her sleeve and smoked one cigarette after another. She answered questions promptly and spoke rapidly in a great rush of words. She spontaneously told about the sexual episodes with her father, but while talking about these incidents, she diverted her gaze from the examiner and looked down at her hands. Martha also mentioned her confusion about the spirits she had seen.

Martha scored in the average range of intelligence and gave evidence that she had the intellectual skills necessary to pass her courses at school. Some of her responses on the TAT projective cards indicated that she was intensely preoccupied with themes of victimization and sexual assault by men. The central figure in a number of her stories was a girl who was concerned about religious condemnation and maternal rejection. This concern was due to a violation of the rules for appropriate sexual behavior between members of a family. The tests further revealed a strong wish for and a mourning of lost innocence. The content of the stories on the projective cards was strikingly similar to the actual events of the client's life history as described to the interviewer.

A number of Martha's responses to the Rorschach inkblot test would be interpreted by psychodynamically oriented clinicians as a confusion or breakdown in reality testing. Some of the percepts were quite different from those given by the majority of persons taking the test, and the description of these percepts was quite personalized in nature. For example, on a card that is commonly interpreted as a bat or a butterfly, the client said, "It looks like someone who is hurt and calling for help. She's looking out of a dark room." One of the cards with an assortment of colors on it was seen as "the messed up insides of a person. She must of been in an accident. There's her blood smeared all over." This personalized nature of responding, usually interpreted as a lack of distancing between thoughts and objective stimuli, was not consistently seen on all of the test material. For the most part, Martha's responses suggested that she was able to function adequately in her social environment. However, the solutions she gave to many of her TAT stories suggested that she did not possess the skills necessary to effectively handle interpersonal problems. Her most frequent solution to various difficulties was to avoid thinking about these issues through withdrawal into fantasy, or by engaging in frequent social activities with other persons.

Recommendations for Treatment

Mrs. Stewart and Martha were seen individually to discuss the results of the psychological evaluation. Each was told that the consensus of the persons handling Martha's case was that she be seen in individual psychotherapy. Martha accepted this recommendation and agreed that it would be beneficial for her to have a chance to talk over her problems with someone. She strongly requested that she be seen by a female psychotherapist.

Mrs. Stewart also appeared to accept the advice that her daughter enter psychotherapy. However, she said that she did not understand how "talking" would change Martha's behavior, or why "nerve pills" would not be as effective. Mrs. Stewart had difficulty accepting the concept that problems at the present time could be related to past experiences. However, Mrs. Stewart agreed to follow the recommendation for psychological treatment. To prevent the possibility of further sexual abuse, she also agreed to the stipulation that Mr. Stewart not be allowed into the home.

Because the parents were separated and Mr. Stewart had not been actively involved with the family for some time, no efforts were made to interview him at the hospital as part of Martha's evaluation. Family therapy focused on preventing further sexual abuse also was not considered a viable option because of the severity and chronicity of Mr. Stewart's alcoholism, including numerous hospitalizations and arrests.

In view of the long waiting list for outpatient psychotherapy at the hospital, Martha was referred to a family counseling center nearby that handled many adolescent cases. A routine follow-up several months after Martha was seen at the hospital indicated that neither Mrs. Stewart nor Martha had contacted this agency.

Discussion

The chronic pelvic pain problems for which Martha sought medical attention fall within the DSM-III-R (1987) classification of somatoform pain disorder (referred to in DSM-III [1980] as psychogenic pain disorder). The individual is preoccupied with pain, but there are no physical findings or pathophysiological mechanisms to account for the pain or its level of intensity. The diagnostic criteria specify that the preoccupation with pain has been present for at least six months. If organic pathology is present, the pain complaints or resulting occupational or social impairment are highly in excess of what would be expected based on the physical findings.

According to DSM-III-R, individuals with somatoform pain disorder usually do not feel that there is a psychological contribution to their pain experiences, and for some individuals, the pain may have symbolic significance. Often, the pain appears suddenly following a physical trauma and increases in severity over time. This disorder is diagnosed more frequently in females, and symptoms of depression also may be present. In Martha's case, the pain she was experiencing seemed highly related to the genital sexual abuse she endured.

Martha's report of seeing a spirit in the candle flame was a visual illusion, that is, a misperception of sensory information. This illusion most likely was associated with an expectancy, within a setting with other suggestible adolescent girls who were telling "scary" stories, that something "spooky" might happen. Her response of anxiety and puzzlement may have been a partial recapitulation of earlier frightening experiences, that is, the sexual abuse by her father. Perhaps her psychological equilibrium was threatened by this new experience for which she had no explanation, and therefore she became anxious and concerned. The ringing in her ears after the first incident is an example of another physical or somatoform response to an emotionally upsetting experience.

Sexual abuse can have a life-long effect. Shapiro and Rosenfeld (1987) observed that children and adolescents exhibiting epileptic-like seizures for which no organic cause is evident have a higher frequency of sexual abuse history than seizure youngsters with clear organic pathology. A link between childhood sexual abuse and adult physical problems was demonstrated in a study comparing women seeking medical attention for pelvic pain, with a group of women seeking help for other gynecological problems (Walker et al., 1988). Patients with a variety of pelvic pain complaints were significantly more likely to have experienced childhood or adult sexual abuse; all of the women complaining of chronic pelvic pain had a history of severe sexual abuse as children. The latter group also were more likely to manifest an adult sexual dysfunction, major depression, or drug abuse. Other investigations with female psychiatric inpatients have reported a relationship between childhood sexual abuse and physical abuse, and the severity of adult psychiatric symptoms (Beck & Vander-Kolk, 1988; Bryer, Nelson, Miller, & Krol, 1988).

The kinds of sexual abuse that appear to be most damaging are experiences involving father figures, genital contact, and force (Browne & Finkelhor, 1986). The highest incidence of immediate psychological problems was found in the 7-to-13-year-old age group. The impact of sexual abuse also is seen in later interpersonal relationships, that is, problems in relating both to men and women, continuing parental problems, and difficulty in responding to their own children. Sexual abuse victims are at high risk of being raped at a later point in their lives (Russell, 1987); other investigators have reported later sexual promiscuity in incest victims.

The problems Martha was experiencing at the time of evaluation need to be viewed within the context of the extremely traumatic sexual abuse that continued over a three-year period. The pain in her pelvis and abdomen occurred in the area of her body violated in the sexual assaults. Her focus on her current pain experiences allowed her to avoid having to deal with the memories of the physical and psychological pain she endured during the abuse episodes. Martha may have been labeling a variety of normally occurring bodily processes such as mild bladder distention, premenstrual uterine contractions, or the genital manifestations of sexual arousal, as painful stimuli. The labeling of abdominal sensations as painful seems due to the close proximity of the abdominal and genital areas.

Incest often occurs in multiproblem families (Maisch, 1973; Meiselman, 1978). Frequent marital discord has been reported, including sexual rejection of the father by the mother, or an unsatisfying sexual relationship between the parents. Emotional problems may be evident in the parents, and frequently the father exhibited an alcohol problem and was unemployed (Lukianowicz, 1972; Virkkunen, 1974). Therefore he was at home a great deal, often while his wife was away. Several studies have reported that many parents who have committed incest were themselves sexually abused as children, and their childhood has been characterized as emotionally deprived and unstable (e.g., Gebhard, Gagnon, Pomeroy, & Christian, 1965).

Incest victims can be profoundly affected by the experiences they have undergone. Along with the traumatic effects of the forced sexual contact, the general attitude toward the mother and father may be significantly influenced. After the onset of the sexual abuse, the victim may experience confusion in distinguishing between parental love and affection and inappropriate sexual behavior (Finkelhor, 1979). The daughter's relationship with her mother may become quite confusing because disclosing the incest situation to the mother often results in expressions of disbelief by the mother, or the mother's discounting the significance of these sexual encounters.

Maisch (1973) found that 42 percent of the victims in his study spoke to their mothers about the incest, but these revelations did not result in the cessation of the incestuous activity. Thus, the incest situation can take on the character of a "family secret." The victim views the mother's passivity as her approval of this behavior pattern. Often, the victim may tell someone outside the family about the sexual abuse when she feels that the father might victimize a younger sister.

If sexual abuse occurs for the first time in middle childhood, the victim may experience psychosomatic problems, school problems, and fears. Adolescent onset incest victims have been reported to exhibit depression, suicide attempts, a sense of worthlessness, psychosomatic disorders, conduct problems, and sexual problems ranging from promiscuity to abstinence (Lewis & Sarrel, 1969; Maisch, 1973). The sexual encounters with the incest perpetrator may be particularly confusing if the victim becomes sexually aroused. Nonetheless, reports have shown that incest experiences are accompanied by an overwhelming sense of guilt; the victims view themselves as somehow responsible for the situation, and worry about hurting the mother or disrupting the family if legal action is taken. However, Meiselman reported that a majority of the incest daughters she studied several years after the termination of the incest continued to be angry at their mothers for having allowed them to be in a sexual situation with the father.

Martha was confused about her feelings not only toward her parents, but also concerning the incest experiences. She reported not feeling angry at her mother for failing to protect her from her father; instead she feared rejection by her mother, should the latter discover the details of the assaults. However, it seems likely that she also felt angry at her mother's passive acquiescence to the incest situation.

Martha's attitude towards her father as well as her view of sexuality in general were also ambivalent. Her father appeared to interact with family members in a relatively positive manner when he was sober. However, his drinking made him belligerent and physically and sexually abusive. The incest experience itself confused Martha. Although her primary response was one of fear and anger, the encounter also contained some positive elements. Martha had grown up in a family environment where parental reinforcement or attention occurred only infrequently. Her father's attention had some reinforcing value to her, and she might also have felt some sexual arousal. Martha's feelings that she could have stopped her father if she had tried hard enough might have had some element of fact.

Her mother interacted with her in a nonpunitive but distant manner and reinforced very little positive or negative behavior. For example, she took the time to bring Martha to the hospital for evaluation, but she did not appear to the interviewer to be greatly concerned about becoming involved in changing Martha's behavior. The behavior that Mrs. Stewart modeled consisted of a benign pattern of minimal emotional involvement with others, and Martha observed and engaged in this interaction pattern with her peers. The client related to others on a fairly superficial level. She could be talkative and the life of the party, but she did not develop the personal emotional involvement necessary to form a close friendship with another individual.

Despite Mrs. Stewart's minimal involvement with her daughter, she was still the major source of positive adult attention available to Martha. Martha learned that when she became anxious, her anxiety would be reduced if she left her bedroom and slept closer to her mother. Mrs. Stewart was not part of the general situation associated with the sexual abuse because the sexual assaults all took place when she was out of the house. Martha developed the habit of getting out of bed at night and sleeping in her mother's room or on the couch, away from the scene of the early frightening events.

Martha's most important source of interpersonal reinforcement was her sister, and she felt extremely protective towards Betty. Few alternative sources of social support were available to either girl when they were children, so their relationship with each other was quite important. The opportunity that Martha and Betty had to relate to each other provided them both with some of the skills necessary to interact with persons outside the family. However, in spite of the close emotional bond between them, they did not tell each other about many of their experiences.

The interaction patterns present in the Stewart family resulted in a very low probability of a positive relationship between John and his sisters. Martha generalized from her negative, anxiety provoking relationship with her father, and responded primarily in a negative manner to her brother. John, in turn, imitated many of the behaviors he observed in his father. He was very belligerent toward Martha and Betty, and he frequently punched them. John had little opportunity to observe positive male-female relationships, and he learned from his father's behavior that women were not highly valued. John did not respond to his mother in a positive manner either because of the attitude toward women he learned from his father's behavior, and because of the low frequency of Mrs. Stewart's interactions with him.

Because of Martha's personal history, the behaviors she expected from males were physical aggression and forced sexual activity. She learned to respond to her father's sexual assaults by passive submission, in order to avoid his threatened punishment and her mother's rejection if she found out. Despite her anxiety about sexual relationships, as she matures physically and more sexual demands are made on her, Martha may follow a pattern of passively submitting to others' advances. She therefore may engage in indiscriminate sexual activity if she accedes to demands by persons in whom she is not particularly interested. Martha never learned that interactions with men could occur in the absence of sexuality, and that affection and interest could be expressed in ways other than through sexual intercourse. Because there was no follow through on the recommendation for therapy, Martha may have difficulty overcoming her problems, particularly the pain complaints and sexual issues with which she will have to deal.

The fact that the therapy recommendation was not pursued points to the difficulty in persuading persons who feel that their problems are physical and require medical intervention, and who are unfamiliar with psychological services, to follow through with physchological treatment. The challenge of providing adequate mental health services to the poor is part of this complex problem.

References

American Psychiatric Association (1980). *Diagnostic and statistical manual of mental disorders* (3rd ed.) (DSM-III). Washington, DC: Author.

156 Adolescent and Adult Disorders

American Psychiatric Association (1987). *Diagnostic and statistical manual of mental disorders* (3rd ed., rev.) (DSM-III-R). Washington, DC: Author.

Beck, J. C., & vanderKolk, B. (1988). Reports of childhood incest and current behavior of chronically hospitalized psychotic women. *American Journal of Psychiatry, 144*, 1474–1476.

Browne, A., & Finkelhor, D. (1986). Impact of child sexual abuse: A review of the research. *Psychological Bulletin, 99*, 66–77.

Bryer, J. B., Nelson, B. A., Miller, J. B., & Krol, P. A. (1988). Childhood sexual and physical abuse as factors in adult psychiatric illness. *American Journal of Psychiatry, 144*, 1427–1430.

Finkelhor, D. (1979). *Sexually victimized children.* New York: Free Press.

Gebhard, P., Gagnon, J., Pomeroy, W., & Christian, C. (1965). *Sex offenders: An analysis of types.* New York: Harper & Row.

Lewis, M., & Sarrel, P. (1969). Some psychological aspects of seduction, incest, and rape in childhood. *Journal of the American Academy of Child Psychiatry, 8*, 606–619.

Lukianowicz, N. (1972). Incest: I. Paternal incest. II. Other types of incest. *British Journal of Psychiatry, 120*, 301–313.

Maisch, H. (1973). *Incest.* London: Andre Deutsch.

Meiselman, K. C. (1978). *Incest: A psychological study of causes and effects with treatment recommendations.* San Francisco: Jossey-Bass.

Russell, D. E. H. (1987). *The secret trauma: Incest in the lives of girls and women.* New York: Basic Books.

Shapiro, E. G., & Rosenfeld, A. A. (1987). *The somatizing child: Diagnosis and treatment of conversion and somatizing disorders.* New York: Springer-Verlag.

Virkkunen, M. (1974). Incest offenses and alcoholism. *Medicine, Science, and the Law, 14*, 124–128.

Walker, E., Katon, W., Harrop-Griffiths, J., Holm, L., Russo, J., & Hickok, L. R. (1988). Relationship of chronic pelvic pain to psychiatric diagnosis and childhood sexual abuse. *American Journal of Psychiatry, 145*, 75–80.

10

Antisocial Personality Disorder and Chronic Drug Abuse— The Trip Too Many

Dennis Bancroft was committed to a mental hospital for observation after he suddenly smashed a wine bottle and tried to strike his father with the jagged edge. The police were called for aid in taking Dennis to the emergency room of the psychiatric hospital. The attending physician did not feel that Dennis was under the influence of a drug at the time of the assault and he recommended that Dennis be hospitalized for an observation period.

Dennis was 23 years old when he was committed, and of white middle-class background. He had been attending a college near his home for the past seven months. The patient reported that he had tried a wide variety of drugs, but he indicated a preference for hallucinogenic drugs such as LSD, mescaline, and psilocybin. He indicated that he had experienced hallucinations on innumerable occasions, but only when he was under the influence of a psychedelic drug. He also revealed that he had used alcohol extensively since he was 15 years old.

Dennis was extremely angry with his parents for committing him to a mental hospital. He challenged their right to have him "put away" and he accused them of saying that he was crazy so they would not have to be bothered with him or embarrassed by his behavior.

Childhood History

Mr. Bancroft was an executive in a large engineering company. When Dennis was a child, the family moved quite frequently to different locations both in the United States and abroad. Until recently, the Bancrofts had rarely lived longer than three years in any one city. Dennis attended many different schools, so he did not have the opportunity to form long-term friendships with any youngsters his age. His only sibling was a brother Walter, who was ten years his senior. The family was of Catholic religious affiliation, but had never attended church regularly.

Mr. and Mrs. Bancroft were interviewed together by a social worker. Mrs. Bancroft stated that she definitely had not wanted a second child because of her vivid memories of the intensely painful and prolonged labor she had undergone during Walter's birth. Throughout her pregnancy with Dennis, she was extremely frightened that she would have to go through another unbearable ordeal, and she blamed her husband for the fact that she was pregnant.

Mrs. Bancroft said she was surprised that Dennis's delivery was not as painful as Walter's had been. However, she was disappointed that she had given birth to a second boy, because she felt that boys were too active and difficult to discipline. Mrs. Bancroft openly stated that she had never felt particularly close to Dennis, because he always acted in a sullen and unloving manner.

Mr. and Mrs. Bancroft both agreed that Dennis's behavior had been a severe problem to them since early childhood. As an infant, he had difficulty sleeping through the night, ate poorly, and frequently became distressed and cried. He usually did not seek out his parents or older brother to comfort him when upset. When he was just three years old, the other parents in the neighborhood would not allow their children to play with him because he was rough. He constantly hit and kicked his brother, even though Walter was ten years older than he. Mrs. Bancroft indicated that Walter usually tried to push Dennis away without hitting him, but occasionally Walter hit him back quite hard. This seemed to infuriate Dennis and caused him to fight back even more vigorously.

The parents stated that compelling Dennis to obey them had always been difficult. Dennis invariably ignored his mother's threats and scoldings and even when she spanked him, his behavior did not change. Mrs. Bancroft recounted an episode when Dennis, at four years of age, had run outside naked. She chased him down the block until she caught him, then she carried him home while he struggled and screamed. In the process, Mrs. Bancroft got kicked in the abdomen. She indicated that she was so angry with Dennis she could have killed him. She gave him a sound spanking, but the next day he was just as mean and difficult to handle as always.

Mrs. Bancroft felt that Dennis had a constant need to be the center of attention. Since his early childhood, he had tried to dominate social situations by talking constantly and running around the room. Further, he did not stay in the house when he was told to do so. Walter and his parents were continually looking for him even though he was supposed to be home. Dennis refused to go to sleep at a set hour, and ever since he was nine or ten years old, he could be heard walking around the house when the rest of the family was in bed.

The parents reported that Walter had always been more quiet and congenial than Dennis and he conformed more readily to parental discipline. Mrs. Bancroft said that it had always been easier for her to feel affection toward Walter. She was not constantly involved in arguments with him, and Walter was willing to help her discipline Dennis. Mrs. Bancroft sometimes asked Walter to hit Dennis when he misbehaved, and Walter always obeyed her request.

Dennis's parents agreed that Mrs. Bancroft assumed the responsibility for disciplining the children. Mrs. Bancroft told the social worker that she blamed her husband for Dennis's continuing behavior problems, because she felt that Mr. Bancroft had not been strict enough with Dennis. Mr. Bancroft in turn complained that when he came home in the evening, his wife always presented him with a list of Dennis's wrongdoings for that day. She expected him to deal with these problems immediately, and if he did not, she accused him of spoiling Dennis and a loud argument ensued.

Mr. Bancroft felt that it was important to talk and reason with children rather than react to every situation by shouting and hitting. He acknowledged that his approach to Dennis's misbehavior resulted in continuous disagreements with his wife. He indicated that he resented her attitude that he alone was at fault for Dennis's constant problems.

Both Mr. and Mrs. Bancroft used some type of external substance, reportedly to help them cope with the arguments they had about Dennis's behavior. Mrs. Bancroft indicated that her husband drank liquor to escape from dealing with family problems and his use of alcohol had already begun to affect his liver. She also stated that Mr. Bancroft sometimes became very hostile and verbally abusive while he was drinking; Mr. Bancroft agreed that this was so. However, he pointed out that his wife's heavy use of tranquilizers and sedatives was her own means of escaping from family difficulties.

School History

Dennis had experienced numerous academic and behavioral difficulties throughout his school career. On two occasions in elementary school, he failed the grade he was in. Both times, Mr. Bancroft went to the school and persuaded the principal to pass Dennis on to the next grade, arguing that Dennis would be even more of a problem if he were in a class where he was bigger and older than the other children. In addition, Mr. Bancroft promised to spend more time helping Dennis with his studies.

The school complained continually that Dennis had great difficulty getting along with female teachers, and he would not listen to their directions. When Dennis was in the eighth grade, his teacher reported that his reading was still at second-grade level. Reports from Dennis's high school teachers indicated that he disrupted his classes by laughing, wandering around the room, and picking fights with the other students.

Dennis rarely completed his homework assignments, and his standard comment was that he had already done the work in school. Mrs. Bancroft said that on many occasions she stood over Dennis and tried to force him to work at his desk, but to no avail. If Mr. Bancroft sat down and went over the assignments with him, he sometimes got his work done. However, Mr. Bancroft often ended up completing the homework assignment for Dennis.

Because the family moved so frequently, Dennis was often enrolled in schools where he was not known. Mr. Bancroft typically went to the school that Dennis was going to attend and succeeded in having Dennis placed in classes commensurate with his age, rather than with his academic skills. Mr. Bancroft also blocked any attempts to transfer Dennis to a class for emotionally disturbed youngsters.

Childhood Treatment History

Dennis was taken for evaluation to numerous psychiatrists, psychologists, and neurologists. The results of these consultations consistently indicated that Dennis was not suffering from any type of neurological disability. His hyperactive behavior was therefore considered to be psychogenic in nature.

Dennis was periodically in treatment with a psychologist or a psychiatrist throughout his childhood, but his parents reported that there was no change in his behavior. At one point, the Bancrofts and Dennis participated together in family therapy, but Mrs. Bancroft terminated these sessions after three months because she felt that they were not making any progress. The longest interval that Dennis remained in therapy with any one professional was four months. At some point with each new therapist, Dennis refused to continue in therapy and Mrs. Bancroft acceded to this refusal.

Adolescence

When he was 14 years old, Dennis stole a car and drove it home. As soon as his mother found out about the theft, she called the police and had him arrested. Dennis was held in police custody for several hours until his father came to the precinct station. Mr. Bancroft promised the police that he would see to it that a similar incident would not happen again and the case was dropped. However, Mr. Bancroft indicated that on a number of occasions in other cities, he was forced to intervene again because for one reason or another Dennis was in police custody.

Dennis had periodically run away from home from the time he was ten years old. At age 12, he was missing for over a week before the police located him. When he was found, he was staying with a farmer who had provided him with food and shelter. Again, his father talked with the juvenile authorities and persuaded them to drop the case and release Dennis in Mr. Bancroft's custody.

Dennis was sent to a military academy upon entering the ninth grade, because his parents hoped that he would benefit from the strict discipline. The Bancrofts revealed that Dennis was furious when he found out that he had been enrolled in the school and he promised that at the first opportunity, he would cause trouble and run away. Mr. Bancroft was eventually able to calm Dennis and talk him into attending the school on a trial basis. However, Dennis soon got into difficulty with the school administration because of smoking and drinking liquor on the premises. The parents also received a report that Dennis was found with a pocket knife that belonged to one of the other boys. Dennis ran away from the school after he was punished for stealing the pocket knife, and he was not found until several days later. He was then expelled from the academy and went back to the school in his neighborhood.

At age 16 Dennis dropped out of high school. He then spent his time with a group of older boys who drank together quite frequently and drove around in cars. Mr. Bancroft did not pressure Dennis to obtain a job after he left school, because he felt that Dennis should have a chance to "find himself."

Dennis was 18 years old when he told his father that he was getting bored with sitting around the house and he wanted to join the armed forces. Mr. Bancroft said that he was delighted with Dennis's decision and he accompanied him to the recruiting station. Mr. Bancroft spoke with the military personnel and persuaded them to approve his son for enlistment, despite Dennis's past difficulties in school and with the police.

After he had been in the service for three months, Dennis was confined to quarters following a bar fight with some other recruits. He attempted to slash his wrists with a piece of glass several hours after he was restricted. The suicide attempt was noticed almost immediately and Dennis was taken to the psychiatric ward of the base hospital. However, he slipped out of the hospital two weeks later when he was given permission to go to the canteen. Dennis was listed as AWOL for a period of one year.

Young Adulthood

Dennis was interviewed and tested when he was committed to the mental hospital. The rest of the details of the life history were provided by the patient during his interviews with the psychologist.

Dennis reported that he began smoking marijuana and experimenting with drugs when he was in high school. He sometimes used drugs and liquor at the same time, which made him act in a "pretty far out way." He indicated that his suicide attempt in the army occurred because of strong feelings of depression brought on by a combination of an alcohol and amphetamine hangover.

Dennis hitchhiked around the country during the year that he was AWOL. He was usually able to find someone to provide him with a place to sleep for a few nights, and when he tired of one location, he drifted somewhere else. He stated that he used drugs quite frequently during this time period. Whenever he was short of funds, he contacted his father, who always sent him some money. Dennis ignored Mr. Bancroft's pleas to come home and turn himself in to the military authorities. However, about a year after he left his unit, he rather impulsively hitched a ride and went to his parents' house.

Dennis stated that when he arrived home his parents were shocked by his appearance. His hair had grown quite long and the clothes he was wearing were dirty and torn. He also had lost about 20 pounds since the last time his parents had seen him. Dennis said that his mother was quite angry because he had just suddenly appeared at the door one day. Before she let him into the house, she made him wash and change in the basement and she insisted that he throw the clothes he had with him into the garbage can.

Mr. Bancroft talked Dennis into reporting to military headquarters and he also persuaded Dennis to have his hair cut before giving himself up. Promising that Dennis would seek psychiatric help, Mr. Bancroft then convinced the authorities to discharge Dennis from the service without any kind of disciplinary action.

However, soon after Dennis was discharged, he decided to move on to a larger city where the drug scene was more active. He said that he was not interested in or in need of psychiatric treatment. He felt that his mother was probably quite pleased when he decided to leave, because all she did was yell at him to find a job and stop lying around the house. Dennis felt that working at a meaningless job was society's means of controlling people and he wanted no part of that manipulation. Mr. Bancroft gave Dennis some money when he decided to leave and drove Dennis out to the highway so he could hitch a ride.

Dennis reported that he spent most of his money on drugs. He worked at odd jobs when he was in immediate need of funds, but he generally relied on his father to support him. Dennis was jailed for vagrancy on two occasions over the next few years. Each time he was arrested, his father sent him money for bail.

Dennis stated that he had probably tried every available drug except heroin. He had seen too many junkies during his travels and he was genuinely afraid of getting hooked. He indicated that he liked the "cool" feeling he experienced with cocaine, but he enjoyed the psychedelic drugs most of all.

Dennis had used LSD, mescaline, and psilocybin quite frequently over the past five years and had had innumerable hallucinatory experiences. He estimated that he had taken some type of hallucinogenic drug at least three hundred times. He indicated a feeling of excited anticipation before each trip and he commented on how beautiful many of the visual experiences were. Colors became very pronounced and vivid, and he sometimes perceived exquisitely beautiful spinning pinwheels of color. Shiny objects seemed to glitter and tree limbs appeared to move with a gentle, undulating motion. Occasionally, objects became blurred and wavy, like heat rising off a blacktop road. Dennis described visual illusions in which persons or objects in the center of the visual field looked disproportionately large and round, while those at the edge of the visual field seemed smaller or stretched out. He further stated that the persons he was with seemed more beautiful and loving when he was under the influence of an hallucinogenic drug.

Dennis indicated that he enjoyed the special social communion that came from living with persons who were also involved in the drug scene. He said that he was more relaxed and he could relate better to others when he was under the influence of a drug. He also revealed that he had had intercourse for the first time while he was under the influence of marijuana, and his sexual pleasure was always enhanced if he was "stoned" at the time.

Dennis reported that over the course of his experimentation with hallucinatory drugs, he had had approximately ten or fifteen bad trips. He indicated that it was impossible to predict when a bad trip would occur. These episodes were extremely nightmarish; the world and the people in it seemed very grotesque and threatening. Dennis said that his usual response to these fearful visions was to become panic-stricken and run from place to place. He often struck out at anyone who tried to come near him, and occasionally he injured himself. After a bad trip it usually took a day or two before he was able to feel relatively calm. However, he said that he disregarded the memories of these frightening and sometimes violent hallucinatory experiences the next time he obtained some drugs. In addition, he continued to drink whisky fairly often, a practice maintained since adolescence.

Dennis sometimes felt extremely depressed and let down after an hallucinatory episode, irrespective of whether the experience had been pleasant or unpleasant. However, he continually sought out more opportunities to use drugs because there was always the potentially beautiful trip to look forward to.

Current Situation

After five years of drifting from place to place, Dennis began to tire of wandering around. Every time he came home for a short while, his father pleaded with him to continue his education, and eventually, Dennis agreed to try to get into a college near his home.

Mr. Bancroft accompanied his son to the school and arranged for Dennis to take a high school equivalency examination. Dennis received a borderline score on the examination, but his father talked with the dean of admissions and the school eventually agreed to admit Dennis on a probationary basis. Mr. Bancroft paid the tuition fees and provided money for Dennis to rent a room on campus. Dennis entered college in 1965.

Dennis said that he had had no difficulty becoming acquainted with some students who were interested in taking drugs, and he associated primarily with these persons. He met a young woman who was part of this group and they spent a great deal of time together. Janet was intensely interested in social problems and her conversations with Dennis stimulated him to become more sensitive to political and social issues.

Janet belonged to a student organization whose avowed philosophy was the revolutionary overthrow of the present form of government. Dennis became quite active in this organization because he felt that helping to change the social system gave him a purpose in life. He said that he pictured himself as a social prophet and a reformer, and he stated a personal belief that one should be able to do as one pleases, as long as one's actions do not hurt others. However, he revealed that he had helped to plan the bombing of a building, although the group later abandoned these plans. The members of the organization also precipitated a strike action that forced the college to close down for several days.

Dennis indicated that although drug use was not a regular part of the organization's activities, the group members sometimes smoked marijuana together after meetings. Janet and Dennis usually associated with a different group of persons when they wanted to take drugs. However, Janet gradually started to lose interest in drugs, and she told Dennis that she did not like the fact that his entire life revolved around drug use. As Janet became involved in a greater variety of activities with other persons, she and Dennis spent less time together.

Dennis reported that his classes were not particularly interesting or relevant to his life, and he generally did not attend lectures. His grades were very poor at the end of the first semester and he was placed on academic probation. Dennis failed to appear for any of his second semester midterms. A short time thereafter, he was committed to the mental hospital.

Admission History

The patient stated emphatically that he was not under the influence of any kind of drug when he attacked his father. The two of them had been drinking together at home and the next thing he knew, he had smashed a bottle and tried to hit Mr. Bancroft with the jagged edge. He recalled struggling with his father while the latter shouted for Dennis's brother to come and help him. Walter, who had never married, happened to be home and he managed to force Dennis to drop the bottle. Dennis said that he did not understand why he had tried to injure his father. He was puzzled by the combination of angry and panicked emotions he had felt at the time of the struggle.

Dennis was enraged because Mr. Bancroft committed him to a mental institution for observation. He repeatedly stated that no one had the right to deprive another person of his freedom. The patient said that he despised his father and had never been able to respect him. He emphasized that he was not mentally ill and he viewed the attack on his father as the sort of unexplainable event that happens in the life of every normal person.

Dennis claimed that his parents were putting him away so they would not have to bother with him. He insisted that he was not dangerous and he did not need to be protected from himself and others, as his father had indicated. Dennis did not feel that his use of drugs had in any way changed his personality or caused him to behave unusually. He denied experiencing hallucinations or delusions except when he was under the influence of psychedelic drugs.

A staff physician tried to explain to Dennis that he was being hospitalized for an observation period in order to gain a clearer picture of his behavior patterns. Dennis, however, maintained that there was nothing wrong with him and that he was being forced into the hospital against his will. During the admission procedures, Dennis was told that his long hair would have to be cut for health and sanitary reasons. He refused consent and despite his vehement protests, he was forcibly restrained while an attendant cut his hair.

Psychological Evaluation

A psychology intern administered a battery of tests to Dennis while he was hospitalized. The intern was in his late 20s and was able to establish good rapport with the patient. Dennis behaved in a subdued and cooperative manner, but at times his emotional expression was not congruent with the topic of conversation. He sometimes smiled fleetingly while he described an unhappy circumstance, and he maintained a neutral expression as he described how angry he was at having been committed. Dennis spoke freely about his past life and his drug experiences. He provided details about the effects of the drugs he had experimented with and he gave information about the frequency with which he had taken various drugs.

Dennis's test scores indicated that he was able to function in the average range of intelligence. His responses further suggested the capability to perform at a superior level in certain areas of verbal ability. However, his performance was consistently poor on a number of tests measuring perceptual-motor functioning and memory.

The numerous errors Dennis made on the tasks involving the visual processing of information and visual-motor coordination raised the question of whether he might have suffered some subtle brain damage as a result of the long-term use of psychedelic drugs. However, the data supporting this inference were largely circumstantial in nature—that is, the signs of cortical impairment were primarily visual dysfunctions, and the most characteristic perceptual changes occurring with hallucinogenic drugs are also primarily in the visual sphere.

On the Rorschach test the patient showed evidence of thought disturbances that are generally considered to be psychotic in nature. His responses to the projective test stimuli were highly unusual and bizarre, and he verbalized peculiar thoughts that seemed to intrude on him while he was engaged in the testing activities. There were indications of feelings of confusion, difficulties in concentrating, and an intense depressive affect. His TAT responses suggested a tendency to react to interpersonal relationships in a suspicious and aggressive manner. There was no indication of any plans or strivings for future goals.

The patient gave evidence of a long-standing thought and behavioral disturbance, with a probable deterioration in functioning due to the chronic use of drugs. Thus, his marginal state of functioning became more deviant as a result of drug abuse.

Hospitalization Record

When Dennis's parents visited him the day after his admission to the hospital, he became very agitated and destructive. He threw a chair at his father and blamed him for the fact that his hair had been cut against his will. Mrs. Bancroft commented that he looked much better with shorter hair and Dennis then directed a verbal tirade at his mother as well. Eventually, a staff member suggested that it might be best if the parents left so Dennis could calm down. The patient was given a sedative after his parents' departure and he went to sleep.

Dennis behaved in a depressed manner during the entire six weeks he spent in the hospital. He slept a great deal during the day and he interacted only minimally with the other patients. When he did converse with others, he expressed his belief that his parents were to blame for all of his problems. He also said that the only hope for the world was in starting a new society, free from the false values of the present social system.

Dennis received no treatment other than mild sedation. Six weeks after his admission, he was released in his father's custody, with the understanding that outpatient psychiatric care had been arranged.

There was no follow-up information regarding Dennis Bancroft.

Discussion

Dennis's case history reflects an array of DSM-III-R (1987) diagnoses at different points in his life. His childhood problems suggest co-occurring diagnoses of attention-deficit hyperactivity disorder, and conduct disorder, solitary aggressive type. (See Chapters 2 and 4 for diagnostic criteria for these disorders.) The pervasive difficulties he exhibited from adolescence on are consistent with the diagnoses of psychoactive substance use, hallucinogen dependence, and alcohol abuse. (Psychoactive refers to substances that modify mood and behavior.)

At the time of hospital admission, the diagnosis of psychoactive substance use, polysubstance dependence probably was most accurate, with an antisocial personality disorder as a co-existing, long-term disorder upon which the polysubstance dependence was superimposed. The category of polysubstance dependence requires that the individual has repeatedly used at least three categories of psychoactive substances for a minimum of a six-month period, but no single one of these substances has predominated.

The diagnosis of antisocial personality disorder is designated for persons at least 18 years of age who have a history of conduct disorder before the age of 15. Additional criteria for the diagnosis of antisocial personality disorder include the presence of four of a relatively large list of behavior patterns: the inability to sustain consistent work behavior, repeatedly engaging in acts that are grounds for arrest, irritability and aggression, repeated failure to honor financial obligations, impulsive failure to plan ahead, no regard for the truth, recklessness regarding own or others' personal safety, the inability to function as a responsible parent, no sustained monogamous relationship for more than a year, and lacking in remorse.

According to DSM-III-R, persons with an antisocial personality disorder tend to use drugs and engage in sexual activities earlier than their peers. Signs of tension, depression, inability to tolerate boredom, and other indications of personal distress often are evident. Antisocial individuals are more likely than persons in the general population to die by violent means. Lack of consistent parental discipline appears to increase the probability that youngsters with conduct disorder will develop an antisocial personality disorder later in life.

The specific reason for hospitalizing Dennis was his attack on his father after they had been drinking together. The etiology of this attack is unclear, but it might have been related to metabolic changes in the absorption of alcohol due to a chronic drug and alcohol use pattern. These changes may have potentiated (made more potent) the amount of alcohol actually ingested. Therefore, the physical assault could have been triggered by a lesser amount of alcohol than might have been necessary in a person who did not have a chronic substance abuse history.

DSM-III-R lists a category of alcohol idiosyncratic intoxication under organic mental disorders that includes maladaptive behavioral changes such as disinhibition of aggressive impulses. However, only additional time could tell whether Dennis's aggressive attack on his father while drinking was an isolated event, or the beginning of some type of organically induced change in function during alcohol ingestion. Unfortunately, the absence of post-hospitalization information precludes one from understanding the specific etiology of the attack.

The drugs that Dennis used most frequently were LSD, mescaline, and psilocybin. The effects of mescaline and psilocybin are similar to those of LSD. Each of these drugs has a psychedelic (mind expanding) and a psychotomimetic (mimicking a psychosis) effect (Bridger, Barr, Gibbons, & Gorelick, 1978). Rapid tolerance develops to the physiological and psychological effects of LSD and mescaline, and cross-tolerance between these drugs occurs as well. Psilocybin shows cross-tolerance only with LSD. The psychotomimetic effects of these drugs include transitory hallucinations, although they are generally visual in nature while schizophrenic hallucinations are typically auditory. However, chronic drug use can induce a subsequent schizophrenic or other psychotic reaction even in persons with no evidence of thought disorder prior to drug use (Bridger et al.). Premorbid personality disturbances, high levels of drug use, and stress appear to increase the risk of a drug-induced psychosis. It is unclear whether mescaline and psilocybin also can precipitate subsequent psychotic reactions.

Amphetamine-induced psychoses (a drug that Dennis also used) are similar to other types of toxic psychoses, and include symptoms of delirium and general confusion. Visual hallucinations also may be present, and the above described reactions may occur after a single extremely high dose (Snyder, 1974). Some individuals who gradually consume large amounts of amphetamine over a several day period may develop an amphetamine psychosis characterized by persecutory and other delusions typical of paranoid schizophrenia. Visual and auditory hallucinations may be present as well. Stereotyped compulsive behavior may be evident such as pacing back and forth, grimacing, and taking objects apart and sorting them. It is therefore clear that the risk of chronic deleterious consequences from the use of hallucinogenic and amphetamine drugs as well as alcohol are escalated considerably with a pattern of polydrug use.

The behavioral effects of a single dose of psilocybin can be observed for a period of approximately four hours after drug ingestion, while the influence of LSD and mescaline is often noticeable for eight to twelve hours after the drug is taken (Barber, 1970).

Some of the initial effects of LSD ingestion are trembling, dizziness, and difficulties in breathing. These symptoms appear to be due to the stimulation of the sympathetic nervous system (Barber). Another consistently reported effect is a change in body image—that is, the body or a limb feels heavier or lighter than usual, or feels as if it had changed shape in some way. Alterations in tactile sensitivity have also been frequently noted—for example, the texture of clothing, the skin, or various objects seems to feel different than usual (Hoffer & Osmond, 1967).

The most vivid and characteristic perceptual changes associated with LSD intake are visual in nature and result in alterations in colors or in the size and form of objects. Hoffer and Osmond stated that subjects whose eyes were closed often described varied patterns of light and color. A distortion in three-dimensional space also was commonly indicated. There also seems to be a greater awareness of emotions and features of the environment that are usually below a conscious level of experience (Snyder, 1980). However, the nature of the psychedelic experience is importantly related to the dosage level of the drug, and the reported symptoms increase in magnitude as the potency of the drug is elevated.

The setting in which LSD is taken is also of importance. In a group setting with familiar persons, many individuals become talkative and report a feeling of elation. However, if the person is in an unfamiliar setting and is somewhat anxious before drug use, a negative, extremely frightening reaction may ensue even with low or moderate doses of LSD. Many individuals have reported a vivid memory of the perceptual and emotional changes that occurred during hallucinogenic drug use (Hoffer & Osmond). Linton, Langs, and Paul (1964) found a high degree of recall of the drug experience on the day following LSD intake. However, many of the subjects who reported a feeling of loss of control during the LSD trip did not recall this feeling accurately on the following day. Katz, Waskow, and Olsson (1968) found that a number of subjects indicated an unusual change of mood after LSD intake. Some individuals reported that they experienced opposing emotions that existed simultaneously or almost simultaneously, and they could not say why they felt both so elated and so hostile at that particular moment. The Katz group concluded that this particular "ambivalent" state produced by LSD ingestion could be an extremely bizarre and upsetting experience for many individuals.

Barber presented evidence suggesting that the naive user who becomes frightened by the effects of LSD or manifests a prolonged adverse reaction has a generalized difficulty in tolerating strangeness and ambiguity. Under the influence of LSD, the person may fear that he or she is becoming insane and that the perceptual changes being experienced will continue indefinitely. Barr, Langs, Holt, Goldberger, and Klein (1972) found that superficially well-adjusted persons who were experiencing a great deal of inner turmoil and conflict responded to the effects of LSD by becoming extremely anxious and fearful that they were going crazy. For the experienced LSD user, bad trips apparently occur when the individual takes an unusually large amount of the drug. Since LSD is so potent, a very small increase in dosage level seems to produce an extremely negative and frightening psychedelic experience.

Barber reviewed a number of studies of individuals who manifested long-term adverse reactions following LSD use. It was evident that the great majority of these individuals had a history of psychiatric problems long before they used drugs. The current disturbance seemed due to an interaction of chronic psychological conflicts and current environmental stresses. Many persons who are hospitalized because of psychotic reactions associated with LSD use report the indiscriminate use of a wide variety of drugs. Therefore, the adverse reactions occurring in these individuals cannot be attributed solely to the action of LSD.

Flashback experiences have been reported by some individuals subsequent to LSD use. Flashback episodes seem to occur more often in high frequency LSD users, particularly when the individual is under stress. However, Smith (1969) found that some persons reported a flashback experience up to three years after an LSD trip, even though there was no further use of the drug during this time interval. Louria (1971) reported that the unpleasant aspects of a trip seemed to dominate the reported hallucinatory recurrences.

Polydrug users and heroin addicts seeking treatment have been compared through MMPI testing to ascertain whether a particular personality configuration is common to each of these groups (Penk, Woodward, Robinowitz, & Parr, 1980). The findings did not indicate a personality type specific to a particular pattern of substance abuse, and both groups exhibited significant levels of psychological disturbance.

The role of the chronic ingestion of drugs in exacerbating psychological problems and in causing neurological deterioration has been assessed in a retrospective study of Adolph Hitler. Heston and Heston (1979) extensively interviewed persons who had worked for Hitler, and also inspected the medical records and the papers of persons close to Hitler during the period of 1923 to 1945. They documented an extensive abuse of amphetamines by Hitler, particularly during World War II. Heston and Heston pointed out that many of the increasingly bizarre behavior characteristics that Hitler exhibited during this time period were consistent with the toxic effects of amphetamines. These symptoms included irrational rages, hyperactivity, risk taking, repeated jaw-gnawing movements, biting at the skin, and limb tremors. Hitler's role in the Nazi era cannot be "explained away" by the behaviors just noted, but the documented evidence suggests a high likelihood that some behavioral characteristics that were evident, and the various neurological and other organic changes that were documented, were due to amphetamine toxicity.

The life events of Dennis Bancroft suggest that numerous temperamental, interpersonal, as well as substance toxicity factors influenced the development of his difficulties. His early history indicates that his temperamental pattern, usually considered a biological characteristic, was difficult. This pattern may be of prognostic significance because of findings of some consistency in temperament from childhood to early adulthood (Thomas & Chess, 1984). Those of difficult temperament in childhood were somewhat more likely to manifest adult adjustment problems than those with an easy temperament. However, temperamental characteristics do not occur in a vacuum, but interact with and have an effect on family and other environmental influences.

Dennis's family situation was problematic in part because of his parents' use of alcohol and drugs. West and Prinz (1987) found that parental alcoholism can be a significant source of stress for children in that family, and is associated with an increased incidence of various forms of psychopathology in the children. Other factors also are important in adolescent drug use. Age at first use, frequency of marijuana, alcohol, and cigarette use, and the amount of spending money available were predictive of current and subsequent hard drug use in adolescents (Mills & Noyes, 1984). Dennis's early initiation into the use of drugs coupled with available funds to buy these substances influenced his path to chronic drug use.

From an interpersonal perspective, there is little evidence that Dennis was given approval for socially acceptable behavior by anyone in his social milieu. There are few indications that he was ever able to establish a lasting and satisfying relationship with another person. His mother's attitude toward him was severely rejecting even before he was born, and she constantly criticized him irrespective of the behaviors he was engaging in. Dennis's efforts to approach her nonaggressively were probably met with continual rebuff. In addition, she encouraged her other son to act aggressively toward Dennis, and she regularly berated her husband for not punishing Dennis severely enough for his alleged misbehaviors.

Mr. Bancroft's response to Dennis's behavior also reinforced his son's aggressive and antisocial activities. He did not punish Dennis for negative behaviors, even when some type of disciplinary measure seemed justified. Mr. Bancroft tended to minimize his son's misdeeds, perhaps in response to his wife's over-reaction to these same activities. Mr. Bancroft was extremely successful in preventing Dennis from facing the usual consequences of his actions. Ever since Dennis was a child, his father had made excuses for him or supplied money to get him out of trouble. Mr. Bancroft interceded at school, with the police, and with the military authorities.

Dennis had little opportunity to observe his parents engaging in positive social behaviors. Mr. Bancroft generally related to his wife in a passive and compliant manner, but he became belligerent and abusive when he was drinking. Mrs. Bancroft continually belittled her husband and criticized his behavior. Both of Dennis's parents modeled the use of external substances as a means of producing mood changes. Mrs. Bancroft was a conspicuous user of tranquilizers and sleeping pills and Mr. Bancroft's heavy drinking was causing serious liver complications.

Dennis imitated his father's pattern of excessive drinking and he may have used alcohol to reduce the unpleasant emotional arousal generated by interactions with persons in authority. Consuming liquor with persons his age was also reinforcing, because he gained their companionship while they were drinking together. Dennis also began experimenting with drugs in the context of peer group social activities. Drugs, even more than alcohol, were a gratifying escape from the unpleasant realities of his life existence. Further, the use of illegal substances gave him the gratification of knowing that he was defying the rules set by adults.

Dennis became acceptable to a particular peer group because he used drugs, and as a result of this acceptance, a new way of life opened up to him. As a member of the drug subculture, he was able to hitchhike across the country and find food and shelter with persons he had never met before. This type of existence was additionally gratifying because Mr. Bancroft supplied Dennis with the funds for his wanderings without requiring Dennis to get a job or go to school.

Dennis's enlistment in the armed forces was consistent with his learned pattern of escaping from environmental problems. Joining the service allowed him to remove himself physically from his social milieu, just as using drugs provided him with a psychological flight from his everyday existence. Dennis quickly became acquainted with persons in his unit who were also drug users and he associated primarily with these individuals. However, the overall rules and restrictions of military life were too strict and confining for him. He responded to this situation as he had to so many pressures and unpleasant circumstances in the past—he tried to leave the scene of his difficulties. First he attempted suicide; then he went AWOL.

Dennis attempted suicide when he was experiencing strong feelings of depression following drug and alcohol use. This gesture was another example of the extremely maladaptive way that he had learned to deal with environmental pressures. Whether or not Dennis fully intended to kill himself, the attempt may have had reinforcing consequences for him because he gained the attention and concern of the military personnel. Dennis's decision to run away from these surroundings may have occurred when the hospital routine became dull and the staff was no longer as attentive. Therefore, he again physically removed himself from an unsatisfying situation. Further, he repeated a long-established pattern of terminating treatment. Many previous experiences had taught Dennis that his father would reinforce this escape-from-pressure pattern by using his influence to prevent the negative consequences.

After five years of drifting, Dennis apparently became satiated with wandering. Therefore, he accepted his father's offer to provide the means for him to go to college and live on campus. Dennis was further attracted to college life because he knew that he would have money for drugs and he would have the opportunity to relate to persons who also found it gratifying to use these substances.

When Dennis entered college, Janet acquainted him with the activities of the student organization to which she belonged, and he found that the philosophy of this group coincided with his own feelings of anger and discontent. However, Dennis's personal formulation of revolutionary ideals seemed highly determined by his extremely aversive family experiences and his subsequent difficulties with other agents of society. As Janet became more involved in this political organization and less involved in taking drugs, her relationship with Dennis deteriorated. Although Dennis was enthusiastic about discussing social injustices and participating in strike actions, his strongest reinforcement came from the use of drugs. Polydrug use apparently took precedence over all of his other activities and relationships.

When Dennis was committed to the hospital, he manifested a number of symptoms generally considered to be psychotic in nature. He had just engaged in unprovoked, highly aggressive behavior; he showed a confusion in thought processes; and at times he manifested intensely depressed affect. Since Dennis had an extensive history of highly disturbed behavior, it does not seem likely that his current difficulties in functioning could be attributed solely to the use of psychedelic drugs.

Nonetheless, the continued use of these substances over a five-year period undoubtedly exacerbated interpersonal problems already in existence. Some of the reported short-term side effects of the hallucinogenic drugs are confused thought processes and various mood changes. Since Dennis frequently used these drugs and suffered from alterations in thought and mood, these side effects may have contributed to his difficulty in relating to other persons. In addition, the sudden attack on his father possibly might have been provoked by a flashback of an earlier unpleasant hallucination involving Mr. Bancroft.

At this point in our scientific knowledge about hallucinogenic drugs, one can only speculate about the intriguing question of whether Dennis suffered brain damage as a result of prolonged drug abuse. Repeated psychological and neurological evaluations during childhood failed to reveal any definite signs of cerebral dysfunction. However, Dennis's adult evaluation indicated a number of perceptual problems that may possibly have been the result of drug use, or perhaps the result of the combination of drug and alcohol use. Further research is obviously needed before this issue can be fully resolved.

An extremely troubling factor in this case is Dennis's loss of liberty and his civil rights through the process of being involuntarily committed to a mental hospital. As Szasz noted:

> The committed patient suffers a serious loss of civil rights. In many jurisdictions he is automatically considered legally incompetent: he cannot vote, make valid contracts, marry, divorce, and so forth.... The committed person is incarcerated against his will, must suffer invasions of his person and body, cannot communicate freely with the outside world, usually loses his license to operate a motor vehicle, and suffers many other indignities as well. (1963, pp. 40-41)

Szasz pointed out that the legal justification for commitment generally centers around a judgment that the person is psychotic or is otherwise mentally ill, but does not understand his or her condition or the need for treatment. A further criterion is whether one is considered dangerous to oneself or others. However, Szasz felt that the social disturbance created by the individual's behavior may be a crucial factor in determining whether an individual is committed or not. He also stated that another important consideration is the social role of the deviant person, in comparison with the individuals who judge that a particular person should be removed from society.

In Dennis's case, the behavior that provoked commitment was obviously dangerous to another person. Dennis's attack on his father was apparently the first known episode of behavior that was dangerous to others, where commitment on this basis could be legally justified. The psychiatrist and the judge evaluated the attack on Mr. Bancroft in the context of Dennis's continuing history of behavior problems. The fact that Dennis had used drugs for a long period of time was also taken into consideration. This information apparently was sufficient for the professionals in authority to determine that commitment for an observation period was in order. Dennis's hospitalization was clearly involuntary, and since he was admitted for observation, he received no treatment except for the administration of sedatives. Dennis quickly learned that he had no civil rights when he was physically restrained and had his hair cut against his will.

One is faced with the dilemma of how to simultaneously preserve Dennis's civil rights and protect other members of society. The possibility exists that at a future time Dennis might engage in further outbursts of aggressive behavior, either with or without alcohol or drug use. However, commitment in a mental hospital is not a realistic or humane solution to his behavior problems. Although Dennis may never be more than a marginal member of society, one cannot lock up everyone who has the potential for harming oneself or others.

A residential group setting may be a promising treatment approach for individuals with drug problems. Many of these persons share with Dennis a history of noncompliance to authority, and their peer relationships have centered around the use of drugs. In settings in which there is strong peer pressure to completely abstain from using drugs and alcohol, conforming to these group norms can provide significant social reinforcement. Other group members also may serve as models of drug-free functioning. However, an individual must learn to find this group experience more reinforcing than the gratification derived from using drugs. Whether Dennis Bancroft ever reached this point remains an open question.

References

American Psychiatric Association (1987). *Diagnostic and statistical manual of mental disorders* (3rd ed., rev.) (DSM-III-R). Washington, DC: Author.

Barber, T. X. (1970). *LSD, marijuana, yoga, and hypnosis.* Chicago: Aldine.

Barr, H. L., Langs, R. J., Holt, R. R., Goldberger, L., & Klein, G. S. (1972). *LSD: Personality and experience.* New York: Wiley.

Bridger, W. H., Barr, G. A., Gibbons, J. L., & Gorelick, D. A. (1978). Dual effects of LSD, mescaline, and DMT. In R. C. Stillman & R. E.

Willette (Eds.), *The psychopharmacology of hallucinogens* (pp. 150-180). New York: Pergamon Press.

Heston, L. L., & Heston, R. (1979). *The medical casebook of Adolph Hitler*. New York: Stein & Day.

Hoffer, A., & Osmond, H. (1967). *The hallucinogens*. New York: Academic Press.

Katz, M. M., Waskow, I. E., & Olsson, J. (1968). Characterizing the psychological state produced by LSD. *Journal of Abnormal Psychology, 73*, 1-14.

Linton, H. B., Langs, R. J., & Paul, I. H. (1964). Retrospective alterations of the LSD-25 experience. *Journal of Nervous and Mental Disease, 138*, 409-423.

Louria, D. B. (1971). *Overcoming drugs*. New York: McGraw-Hill.

Mills, C. J., & Noyes, H. L. (1984). Patterns and correlates of initial and subsequent drug use among adolescents. *Journal of Consulting and Clinical Psychology, 52*, 231-243.

Penk, W. E., Woodward, W. A., Robinowitz, R., & Parr, W. C. (1980). An MMPI comparison of polydrug and heroin abusers. *Journal of Abnormal Psychology, 89*, 299-302.

Smith, A. E. W. (1969). *The drug users*. Wheaton, IL: Harold Shaw Publishers.

Snyder, S. H. (1974). *Madness and the brain*. New York: McGraw-Hill.

Snyder, S. H. (1980). *Biological aspects of mental disorder*. New York: Oxford University Press.

Szasz, T. S. (1963). *Law, liberty, and psychiatry*. New York: Macmillan.

Thomas, A., & Chess, S. (1984). Genesis and evolution of behavioral disorders: From infancy to early adult life. *American Journal of Psychiatry, 141*, 1-9.

West, M. O., & Prinz, R. J. (1987). Parental alcoholism and childhood psychopathology. *Psychological Bulletin, 102*, 204-218.

11

The Development of Anorexia Nervosa— "I Just Want to Lose a Few More Pounds"

Janet Caldwell was 14 years old and in the eighth grade. She was five feet, two inches tall and weighed 62 pounds at the time of her admission to the psychiatric unit of a local general hospital. Janet began dieting at the age of 12 when she weighed 110 pounds and was chided by her family and friends for being "pudgy." She continued to restrict her food intake over a two-year period, and as she grew thinner, her parents became increasingly more concerned about her eating behavior. She was hospitalized after outpatient treatment by the Caldwell's family physician proved ineffective in arresting her continuous weight loss.

Janet was the middle child in a family of three children. At the time of admission, her older sister was 17 and a senior in high school, and her brother was 12. Her parents were of Protestant, middle-class background, and the family attended church regularly. Mr. Caldwell said that his work as an engineer kept him quite busy, but he tried to spend as much time with his family as he could spare from his heavy work load. Mr. and Mrs.

Caldwell described their marriage and family life as reasonably happy, although they were quite concerned about the intractability of Janet's weight loss and her inability to resume a more normal eating pattern.

Family Background

Janet was initially interviewed at the hospital by a psychiatry resident. She was extremely emaciated, and her skin was stretched tight over the bony skeleton of her face and arms. She spoke rapidly with a clipped, staccato intonation, and she frequently shifted position in her chair. Janet characterized her family as one in which high performance expectations were the rule. Each of the children was strongly encouraged to do as well as he or she could at school. Mr. Caldwell frequently pointed out to them that he usually brought papers home from his office to work on in the evening because he felt that it was also important for him to do the best possible job he could in any activity in which he was involved.

Janet indicated that she got along fairly well with her brother and sister. She said that she sometimes fought with her sister about whose turn it was to perform certain chores around the house, but these disputes were not too frequent or severe. Each of the girls had her own room and circle of friends. However, they generally shared confidences about persons they liked and social activities they were involved in. Both of them enjoyed listening to and talking about the rock music they played on the stereo. Janet said that her younger brother was a nuisance and very untidy, and she sometimes felt annoyed because her parents pampered him and seemed to shower a great deal of attention on him. However, she stated that she usually tried to avoid arguing with her brother and did not interact with him very frequently.

Janet described her mother as more involved with the children in day-to-day matters than her father was. She was firm in disciplinary matters, although a bit more flexible than her father. Typically, Mrs. Caldwell talked and pleaded with the children when she wanted them to change their behavior in some way, while Mr. Caldwell tended to be more stern and more likely to issue directives that he expected the children to obey immediately. Janet indicated that she and her siblings generally did not disobey their father. However, if possible, they went to their mother first for permission to engage in various activities with friends, since she was somewhat more likely to say yes to their requests than their father was.

The expression of emotions such as anger, fear, or unhappiness was not encouraged at the Caldwell home, and the children were told by their parents that they were being childish if they verbalized strong feelings of any kind. The usual parental approach to dealing with emotional issues was to sit down and spend a great deal of time talking about the precipitating events that led up to a particular emotional feeling or outburst. However, expressing strong feelings was considered a sign of immaturity. The parents did not provide their children with sexual information nor were sexual issues discussed in the home.

Social History

It had always been fairly easy for Janet to make friends. She usually went out with a circle of three or four girlfriends with whom she had become particularly close over the past few years. She reported that she was quite active and enjoyed participating in sports and other activities with her friends. She also attended school and church functions at which boys her age were present, but she had not gone to any activity with just one boy. As her weight loss became quite severe, she and her peers tended to withdraw from interactions with each other.

Janet achieved an "A" average in school over the two years prior to hospitalization. She indicated that she always got good grades in school, even when her weight loss was quite severe. However, she had to work hard and spend a great deal of time studying in order to do well in school. She frequently became anxious before examinations because she was afraid that she would not do as well as others expected her to, and she would try to cope with these feelings by studying even harder. Nonetheless, she indicated that she has willingly put in the effort to get good grades and she felt gratified by her academic achievement.

A separate interview with the parents confirmed the information Janet had communicated.

Symptom History

Mrs. Caldwell indicated that nothing unusual occurred during her pregnancy with Janet, and delivery and birth were also quite normal. The mother recalled that Janet's development proceeded at about the same rate as had the development of the other children in the family. As a child, Janet had had no problems related to appetite or eating patterns. Both Mr. and Mrs. Caldwell said that they had been somewhat surprised when Janet became slightly overweight at puberty, around the time when she began menstruating. They recalled that the family had mildly teased Janet about her weight, but stopped doing this when it appeared their comments were upsetting her.

Janet also felt that her weight problem began at the time of puberty. She said that her family and friends had supported her efforts to achieve a ten-pound weight loss when she first began dieting at age 12. Janet did not go on any special kind of diet. Instead, she restricted her food intake at meals, generally cut down on carbohydrates and protein intake, tended to eat a lot of salads, and completely stopped snacking between meals. At first, she was quite pleased with her progressive weight reduction, and she was able to ignore her feelings of hunger by remembering the weight loss goal she had set for herself. However, each time she lost the number of pounds she had set as her goal, she decided to lose just a few more pounds. Therefore she continued to set new weight loss goals for herself. In this manner, her weight dropped from 110 pounds to 88 pounds during the first year of her weight loss regimen.

Janet felt that, in her second year of dieting, her weight loss had continued beyond her control. Her menstrual periods had stopped shortly after she began dieting, and this cessation coincided with the point at which she began to lose weight quite rapidly. However, since her menses had occurred on only two or three occasions, she was not concerned about the cessation of her periods until the past year when her weight loss and change in appearance had become quite noticeable. Janet stated that she began to feel ugly and scared by her continuing weight loss during the last year. The stares she received from her classmates and from strangers also bothered her. She became convinced that something inside of her would not let her gain weight, and she often felt disgusted with herself and quite anxious after eating even a small portion of food.

Janet commented that although there had been occasions over the past few years when she had been fairly "down" or unhappy she still felt driven to keep active and move around a great deal, just as she felt driven to keep on dieting. As a result, she frequently went for walks, ran errands for her family, and spent a great deal of time cleaning her room and keeping it in a meticulously neat and unaltered arrangement.

When Janet's weight loss continued beyond the first year, her parents insisted that she see their family physician, and Mrs. Caldwell accompanied Janet to her appointment. Their family practitioner was quite alarmed at Janet's appearance, and prescribed a high-calorie diet. Janet said that her mother spent a great deal of time pleading with her to eat, and Mrs. Caldwell planned various types of meals that she thought would appeal to Janet. Mrs. Caldwell also talked a great deal to Janet about the importance of good nutrition. Mr. Caldwell, on the other hand, became quite impatient with these discussions and tended to order Janet to eat. Janet would attempt to eat something, but become tearful and run out of the room because she felt as if she simply could not swallow the food she had been ordered to eat. The youngster said that she often responded to her parents' entreaties that she eat by telling them that she indeed had eaten. She often listed foods that she said she had consumed but which in fact she had flushed down the toilet. She estimated that she was eating only about 400 calories a day.

Mrs. Caldwell indicated that Janet had appeared quiet and withdrawn, in contrast to her generally active and cheerful disposition, at the time she began dieting. The mother recalled that Janet was having difficulties with her girlfriends during that period, and Janet had mentioned that it seemed as if her friends were making excuses to avoid coming over when she invited them. Janet became very critical of her girlfriends, and Mrs. Caldwell felt that Janet behaved in an argumentative and stubborn manner with them. On occasions when Janet knew that some friends were coming over to the house, she drew up ahead of time a detailed plan of activities for them that encompassed the entire time period they had planned to spend at her house. She then became angry and uncomfortable if the girls did not want to engage in these activities or did not wish to do so in the order and for the amount of time Janet had planned. In general, Janet seemed less spontaneous and talked less with her family and others than she had during any previous period that her parents could recall.

At the time of her first appointment with the family physician, Janet said she recognized that her weight loss was too severe, but it was impossible for her to eat more. Despite her parents' and physician's entreaties and threats over the next few months, she continued to lose weight and eventually dropped to 62 pounds. Janet and her family then agreed with their physician that Janet should be hospitalized for treatment in an inpatient setting.

Psychological Evaluation

Janet was administered the Minnesota Multiphasic Personality Inventory (MMPI), and a number of projective tests. No signs of thought disturbance or severe emotional disorder were manifested on any of these measures. All of the scale scores on the MMPI were within normal limits, although reflecting a tendency toward sexual immaturity, concerns about one's body, a denial of problems, and a relatively high reported activity level. The projective tests suggested conflicts about dependence versus autonomy—that is, ambivalent feelings about growing up and achieving independence from one's parents and family. Another prevalent theme that emerged was suggestive of depression—for example, stories on the Thematic Apperception Test (TAT) about sadness, rejection, and unhappy and unsatisfying interpersonal relationships. Janet manifested a process of denial and undoing in her stories on the TAT cards. She frequently related a story that suggested an unhappy ending but, in the last sentence of her description, arbitrarily said that everything was going to turn out all right. She also told stories with stated unhappy endings and then changed the story resolution at the last moment to a happy one.

The psychological processes of denial and undoing were consistent with her behavioral tendencies to change or undo her weight status through dieting and physical activity. Denial also was a means of minimizing the threat to her health posed by her severe weight loss. However, although denial and undoing were evident in Janet's responses to the test stimuli and in her behavior, it is unlikely that these particular characteristics are sufficient to explain the etiology of her eating disorder. Further, the conflicts Janet expressed in relation to independence and separation from one's family are quite typical of the ambivalent struggles exhibited by adolescent youngsters and also were not indicative of serious personality disturbance.

Course of Hospital Treatment

Soon after admission to the hospital, Janet was placed on a behavior modification program aimed at changing her eating behavior. Before hospitalization, a contract was set up in which Janet signed a consent form signifying her agreement to participate in a program in which she had to gain at least one-half pound per day in order to earn and accumulate points for specified privileges. At first, the privileges consisted of time outside her room, which was barren except for a bed, table, and chair. Janet was weighed each morning, and if she did not meet the minimal weight gain requirement for that day, she remained alone in her room with the door closed until she was weighed again the following morning. On the days when Janet did not meet her weight gain requirement, the staff made no comments as they placed Janet's meals in her room on a tray. The tray was removed 45 minutes later, again without staff comment. This program had been described in detail to Janet's parents and their written consent was also obtained prior to Janet's admission to the hospital.

Janet ate her meals alone in her room during the initial stage of hospitalization. However, she was allowed to eat in the dining room with the other patients after she had made progress in gaining weight. As a result of sustained weight gain, Janet was able to earn points for privileges on and off the ward such as exercise activities, movies, outings, and other social events. A female therapist also saw Janet in individual therapy several times a week throughout Janet's hospitalization. These sessions were not held on days when Janet failed to meet her minimal weight requirement. Janet and Dr. C. talked about Janet's typically dependent, passively manipulative, or overly conscientious way of relating to other persons. Alternative, more socially flexible ways of interacting with others were discussed and sometimes role-played. These sessions also included an exploration of fairly typical adolescent concerns about sexuality, being able to express one's feelings openly, and asserting oneself without attempting to control other persons.

Janet manifested a continuous increase in weight during the first few weeks she was in the hospital. At this point, family therapy sessions were held with Dr. C. and included all the members of the Caldwell family. These sessions explored each family member's responses to Janet's eating behavior. The methods they could use to ignore non-eating were evaluated as well. The therapy sessions also focused on how important it was for each person in the family to be more open in expressing his or her feelings and concerns, and more receptive to the feelings and interests of other family members. There also was an exploration of possible areas in which the children could comfortably behave in a more independent manner as they grew older.

Janet remained in the hospital for ten weeks. She continued to make fairly steady progress in gaining weight over the course of hospitalization, and she weighed 93 pounds at the time of her discharge. There were only five occasions over the ten-week period when she had failed to earn a point for minimum weight gain. Janet stated at the time of her discharge that she now felt happier and more self-confident than she had in a long time, and she felt more comfortable when she ate. Although she admitted that she was concerned that she not gain too much weight, she felt that she would be able to maintain the improvement in her eating behavior that had occurred with treatment.

Ethical Issues of Treatment

Before instituting any type of treatment involving possibly aversive procedures, it is extremely important for ethical and moral reasons that the patient understand and freely consent to that particular treatment program. The establishment of objective review boards and patient's advocates to ensure the rights of persons committed to institutions resulted from various civil rights developments. Ethical and legal consid-erations make it important that a treatment program involving aversive procedures is evaluated and approved by a knowledgeable group that is not involved in the patients' day-to-day care.

Treatment professionals in hospitals and other institutional settings therefore have been obliged to become more sensitive to the issues of patients' rights, including not only the patient's right to treatment (Wyatt & Stickney, 1971; cited in Mental Health Law Project, 1973), but his or her right to refuse treatment (Cohen, 1971). The regulation of the use of aversive and nonvoluntary treatment procedures currently is being dis-cussed in many states. A change in the laws regarding the appointment of guardians to sign treatment consent, and the development of more stringent guidelines for involuntary commitment are under considera-tion. Although these issues are not completely resolved, the attempts to ensure the full rights of persons in hospitals and institutions is clearly a positive development.

Follow-Up

Janet was seen periodically by Dr. C. over the next year-and-a-half, and family therapy sessions also were conducted occasionally. An initial prob-lem during the first few weeks at home was that Janet again began losing weight. Therefore, Janet and her parents came in for a counseling session aimed at setting up a specific contract and token system that could be carried out at home. The use of a contract system for weight gain in the natural environment proved quite effective, and the contract contingency arrangements were gradually withdrawn as Janet's eating behavior stabil-ized at home and she neared an appropriate weight for her age. However, an important part of the treatment strategy was to prevent the possibility of continued weight gain until the point of obesity. Therefore, at a speci-fied point in the program, Janet was given encouragement and approval by the family and therapist for controlling food intake and weight level instead of continuing to consume large quantities of food. The therapist, in conjunction with Janet and her parents, carefully monitored and ad-justed the specifics of the contract conditions. Dr. C. also explored with Janet any difficulties the latter might be experiencing in family and social relationships.

Janet reached and maintained a normal weight level and also reported that she was happy in her peer relationships and was doing well in school. She had a number of comfortable relationships with boys her own age, and she attended dances and other social activities with her friends. However, she no longer felt the pressure to keep doing something every minute of the day. Janet's menstrual periods returned, and she did not exhibit anxiety or unusual conflicts in discussing sexual matters. Mr. and Mrs. Caldwell confirmed Janet's account of her improved and satisfying peer relationships, and indicated that Janet's food consumption only infrequently was a problem. They felt that Janet sometimes tested the limits of their control over her activities, but they did not feel that this behavior was unusual or different from the behavior of their other children. The parents indicated that the general family atmosphere seemed more positive and relaxed.

The prognosis appears good that Janet will be able to maintain a normal eating pattern. Favorable factors in her history were the fact that she came to a decision that she wanted help with her eating problem, and that she felt ugly and ashamed of her appearance and was bothered by the stares of other persons. She also did not manifest the self-induced vomiting and periodic eating binges often found in persons who exhibit a recurrence of the anorexic pattern. The social contacts she made after release from the hospital were a further positive sign.

Discussion

Anorexia nervosa is classified as an eating disorder under disorders usually first evident in infancy, childhood, or adolescence. The criteria include "refusal to maintain body weight over a minimal normal weight for age and height, e.g., weight loss leading to . . . body weight 15% below that expected" (DSM-III-R, 1987, p. 67). Other criteria are an intense fear of weight gain or becoming fat even though underweight, a disturbance in the way in which one's shape and weight is experienced, and in females, amenorrhea (the absence of menstrual periods) for at least three consecutive cycles. If self-induced vomiting or other means of purging are engaged in, the diagnosis of bulimia nervosa also may be appropriate.

Anorexia nervosa is a serious disturbance involving many aspects of physiological as well as psychological functioning. It occurs primarily in adolescent and young adult females. Of those diagnosed as anorexic, approximately 5 to 10 percent are males. A greater degree of overall psychological disturbance has been reported in male anorexics. A survey of treatment outcome studies indicates a long-term recovery rate from anorexia nervosa averaging approximately 40 percent, with an additional 30 percent classified as improved in terms of weight and other criteria.

However, continued significant impairment has been noted in 20 percent, and the mortality rate averages about 9 percent (Garfinkel & Garner, 1982). Weight recovery and the return of menstruation at follow-up was associated with fewer psychological problems (Szmukler & Russell, 1986). Many anorexics at follow-up continue to exhibit significant preoccupations about weight, disordered eating habits, depression, and social anxiety.

A characteristic of most anorexics is their desire for an extremely thin appearance. A strong need for thinness, rather than a diminishment or cessation of hunger, appears to be an important aspect of this disorder. Persons diagnosed as suffering from anorexia nervosa often maintain an avid interest in food and do not experience a true loss of hunger and appetite (Bemis, 1978). In anorexia nervosa, a strong fear of gaining weight or taking in food is coupled with a relentless pursuit of thinness. The experience of mastery over oneself and others through not eating and in this way controlling body shape seems a powerful reinforcer in the development and maintenance of this disorder.

The anorexic manifests severely disordered eating patterns. Food intake can be quite restricted and may average only 200–500 calories per day. Some anorexics, particularly those with a higher pre-illness weight level and a family history of obesity, also may engage in periods of uncontrolled eating. These binge episodes are usually followed by self-induced vomiting, and/or the use of laxatives and diuretics. These methods of purgation also may occur after other periods in which the individual feels that she or he has consumed too much food. Recent studies indicate similar long-term outcome in bulimic and restricting subtypes of anorexia nervosa (Szmukler & Russell; Toner, Garfinkel, & Garner, 1986).

The clinical literature typically has described the personality and behavioral characteristics of anorexic individuals before the onset of severe weight loss as conscientious, overachieving, obsessive-compulsive, perfectionistic, and shy. These characteristics, however, are found to a greater degree in the restricter than the bulimic subtype. Bulimic anorexics are more likely than restricters to exhibit a range of impulse control problems such as substance abuse, stealing, and school truancy. The former also reported a greater amount of sexual experience, but an inability to enjoy sexual activity (Garfinkel & Garner).

Questions about a possible relationship between eating disorders and depression have generated a great deal of interest. A number of studies of psychopathology in family members of anorexics have found higher rates of depression, substance abuse, and eating disorders in the relatives of those with eating disorders than in comparison groups (e.g., Strober, Morrell, Burroughs, Salkin, & Jacobs, 1985). The relatively higher rate of depression in the families of anorexics occurs primarily in anorexics who also are manifesting symptoms of depression. The findings of a family history of eating disorders and other forms of psychopathology in some anorexics suggests a subgroup in which genetic factors might interact with environmental factors in the predisposition to eating and other disorders.

Anorexics have been described as extremely manipulative in relation to their eating behavior and their avoidance of gaining weight, and they can often exert a tremendous amount of control over their families or hospital personnel. Persons easily become entangled in frustrating efforts to prepare foods the anorexic says that he or she would like to eat, or become involved in persuading or cajoling the individual to eat the food that has already been prepared. It is not uncommon for anorexics to lie about the amount of food they have eaten or hide food they tell others they had consumed. The marked hyperactivity noted in many anorexic individuals serves to burn calories and thus avoid weight gain, and also may serve as a distraction from feelings of hunger.

Anorexics display a number of the symptoms—for example, tension, irritability, emotional lability, sexual disinterest, and preoccupation with and dreams of food—similar to those observed in persons participating in studies of semistarvation (Schiele & Brozek, 1948). Some have proposed complex psychoanalytic explanations for these and other symptoms of anorexia nervosa (Waller, Kaufman, & Deutsch, 1940). However, many of the behaviors observed can be accounted for by the severe nutritional deprivation the person is undergoing.

Hilde Bruch (1970a, b) has posited that primary anorexia nervosa is caused by deficient ego development with a body image disturbance manifested by a lack of a sense of ownership of one's body. Bruch felt that this poor body identity was caused by the mother responding to all of the infant and young child's needs in the same manner, that is, by the giving of food. Therefore, the child grows up being unable to distinguish between feelings of hunger and emotional feelings because the caregiver's response has always been the same, that is, the provision of food. Bruch (1978) later emphasized the anorexic's need for autonomy and control which can only be met in her particular family through the refusal to eat. Based on her clinical experience, Bruch proposed that conflicts about maturity also are important in the development of this disorder. The anorexic deals with these conflicts by not eating and therefore looking much younger than her age.

Consistent with Bruch's statements about the importance of conflicts about maturity, sexuality concerns and negative feelings about social skills have been demonstrated empirically to be more predominant in anorexic as compared with normal weight high school groups (Leon, Lucas, Colligan, Ferdinande, & Kamp, 1985). Further, those anorexics who had the most negative views about sexuality at hospital admission showed relatively poor functioning at follow-up (Leon, Lucas, Ferdinande, Mangelsdorf, & Colligan, 1987).

The amenorrhea that occurs in anorexic females with weight loss has been a subject of some interest. Amenorrhea usually is caused by the individual possessing a lower amount of adipose tissue than the critical amount necessary for menstruation to occur. Because cessation of menstruation often precedes significant weight loss (Halmi, Goldberg, Eckert, Casper, & Davis, 1977), the stress of dieting and other psychological factors may be more important initially in producing the amenorrhea than the loss of adipose (fat) tissue. Psychological factors also have been shown to be important in the resumption of menstruation at expected weight levels (Falk & Halmi, 1982). Whether anorexics exhibit a physiological susceptibility to stress that is manifested in bodily symptoms such as amenorrhea and continued weight loss is an interesting subject that awaits further research.

Early behavioral formulations of anorexia nervosa centered on an analysis of environmental reinforcement patterns and avoidance behavior in regard to food intake (Blinder, Freeman, & Stunkard, 1970; Leitenberg, Agras, & Thomson, 1968). These analyses served as a rationale for the operant conditioning token reinforcement programs that were developed to treat anorexics. However, the efficacy of focusing treatment so specifically on the modification of the eating patterns was questioned (Leon, 1983) in light of the number of treated anorexics who developed bulimia patterns at some point after treatment. It seems crucial to deal with the anorexic's psychological, interpersonal, and family concerns, as well as the eating behavior, per se.

Recent treatment programs have involved a combination of a generally supportive hospital environment, dietary reeducation, and a controlled weight gain that patient and therapist agree upon. Further, a variety of psychotherapy, group therapy, and occupational therapy procedures have been concurrently implemented during hospitalization (Garner, 1986).

Garner and Bemis (1982) have described a cognitive-behavioral model of psychotherapy based on the cognitive therapy principles for treating depression outlined by Beck (1976). The anorexic learns to identify and modify faulty thinking patterns and erroneous beliefs, including dichotomous (all-or-none) reasoning, personalization, and superstitious thinking (belief in a cause-and-effect relationship between unrelated events). Although this approach is of interest in the treatment of anorexia nervosa, controlled treatment studies with long-term outcome assessment have not as yet been published.

The obsessive-compulsive, perfectionist, and intellectually striving behavior patterns that Janet manifested before and during her period of severe weight loss are similar to the premorbid histories of many individuals diagnosed as anorexic of the restricter subtype. Few specific precipitating factors were noted at the onset of the weight loss other than a concern about being overweight, some mild teasing by family and peers, and the encouragement of these persons to begin dieting. The episodic depression and aloofness Janet exhibited during the period of symptom onset were not atypical of the fluctuations in mood that many youngsters experience at the time of puberty. However, her growing concern about dieting and losing weight became an overriding issue that eventually dominated her life. It is therefore not surprising that her peers grew less interested in interacting with her as her energies became more centered on the desire for thinness and as her physical appearance began to change markedly with weight loss. The scheduling of her friends' activities when they visited her seems to be one aspect of the generalized obsessive behavior pattern she manifested at that time, and further served to alienate her peers. Janet's typically high activity level also increased in intensity with her efforts at dieting and might have served as a distraction from thoughts of food and conflicts about eating.

The anorexic individual gains an extremely powerful hold over family interactions because the severe weight loss poses a critical health problem. Therefore, Janet's parents and other family members easily became enmeshed in a struggle over persuading her to eat. It would seem inevitable that Mr. and Mrs. Caldwell would eventually begin differing with each other about the techniques they should use to induce Janet to stop dieting and start eating regularly. Further, this added attention to and controversy over her eating behavior contributed to Janet's control over her family and provided a further reinforcement for her lack of eating.

An interesting issue in Janet's case is that during the second year of her weight loss she did not gain a great deal of reinforcement from being thin. Her physical appearance appalled her and she wanted to stop losing weight, but she was unable to start eating normally. She felt that something inside of her was preventing her from consuming food. Psychological testing indicated adequate reality testing. No evidence of the severity and bizarreness of thought disturbance seen in schizophrenic disorders could explain her feelings of disgust in relation to food.

Janet's difficulty in terminating her dieting behavior could have been the result of a strong learned association between food consumption and severe anxiety about gaining weight, with anxiety reduction occurring through the avoidance of food intake. By restricting the consumption of food, Janet received self-reinforcement through the belief that she was able to control her body and her life in general by not giving in to her strong feelings of hunger. Her increasingly emaciated reflection in the mirror, as well as the attention she received from her family and others pleading with her to eat, further confirmed and reinforced this feeling of control.

At the point when Janet became frightened by her continuing weight loss, she was unable to resume a normal eating pattern without professional intervention. This inability may have been due to a combination of physiological and habit pattern changes that had occurred through starvation. In the controlled hospital environment, Janet was able to learn again to respond to cues of hunger with food intake. She also had to relearn the habit of eating relatively larger quantities of food, and to practice doing so without being overwhelmed by feelings of anxiety. The current state of knowledge about anorexia nervosa is not comprehensive enough to specify precisely why Janet eventually became frightened about her weight loss and decided she wanted to change this pattern while other anorexics continue to want to lose weight despite severe starvation. However, Janet's stated desire to stop her self-starvation pattern seems a positive sign for favorable long-term treatment outcome.

Janet consented to a treatment program in which the consequences for not eating apparently were more aversive than eating—that is, restriction to a barren and uninteresting room on the days that she did not gain weight. Janet progressed extremely well on the behavior modification program designed for her. The reinforcement derived from being allowed outside her room, and the associated privileges on and off the ward proved potent enough to maintain her eating behavior. Over the course of treatment, different behaviors in relation to food were established. These new eating patterns became self-reinforcing because of their association both with certain hospital privileges and progress in therapy. A further reinforcement might have been the greater feeling of well-being she experienced as her health improved with weight gain.

The individual and family sessions with Dr. C. seemed extremely helpful in dealing with Janet's interpersonal relationships and in preparing the family for her return from the hospital. Family counseling enabled Janet and her siblings to explore many aspects of their relationships with each other and their parents. Further, the entire family felt a part of the treatment process. In Janet's case, the additional step of closely monitoring and adjusting the contract procedures after she returned home was important in maintaining her improved eating patterns in the natural environment. The eventual reinforcement of balanced and controlled eating behavior, rather than eating as much as possible was effectively accomplished at home because the Caldwells were familiar with the process of monitoring and reinforcing specific behavior patterns. However, the close monitoring of eating habits and the use of a family contract procedure, while helpful for Janet, have not proven to be an effective treatment maintenance procedure for many anorexics. The need to move beyond contract procedures to more natural sources of support in the social environment has been a general concern in the evolution of behavior therapy procedures.

Recent reports indicate that an increasing number of people have been hospitalized with a diagnosis of anorexia nervosa, and that these admissions are predominantly of Caucasian, adolescent females (Jones, Fox, Babagian, & Hutton, 1980; Willi & Grossman, 1983). Studies with ninth grade and high school populations demonstrated that adolescent females already are dissatisfied with their body appearance and engage in dieting (Leon, Perry, Mangelsdorf, & Tell, in press).

The American preoccupation with slimness has been pointed to as a significant element in the increased incidence of anorexia nervosa (Bruch, 1973) and, indeed, the factor that many cases have in common is the youngster's desire to lose weight in order to overcome a perceived state of obesity. Whether this is a particularly American phenomenon or a phenomenon of affluence interacting with the body image ideals of various cultures can be debated. A dissatisfaction with body appearance during adolescence is fairly common in both sexes in our culture. However, the intense preoccupation with and anxiety about physical appearance that many adolescent females exhibit seems to be strongly influenced by the phenomenon of sex-role stereotyping (Leon & Finn, 1984). In many cultures, including the American one, female status is often equated solely with physical beauty, defined in part as a slim body appearance. Although recently there has been more of a tendency to provide social approval to adolescent females for academic and other accomplishments than was previously the case (Kaplan & Bean, 1976), interpersonal attraction is still strongly related to physical appearance. The incidence of cases of anorexia nervosa might not diminish until there is a significant change in the inordinate amount of social reinforcement that adolescent females receive for physical attractiveness, and until other kinds of attributes also are strongly reinforced by the social milieu. Further, it would seem necessary to develop prevention efforts through public education in order to teach people to recognize the first signs of anorexia nervosa. Intervening at this early stage might help to reduce the number of people suffering from this devastating disorder.

References

American Psychiatric Association (1987). *Diagnostic and statistical manual of mental disorders* (3rd ed., rev.) (DSM-III-R). Washington, DC: Author.

Beck, A. T. (1976). *Cognitive therapy and the emotional disorders.* New York: International Universities Press.

Bemis, K. M. (1978). Current approaches to the etiology and treatment of anorexia nervosa. *Psychological Bulletin, 85,* 593–617.

Blinder, B. J., Freeman, D. M. A., & Stunkard, A. J. (1970). Behavioral therapy of anorexia nervosa: Effectiveness of activity as a reinforcer of weight gain. *American Journal of Psychiatry, 126,* 1093–1098.

Bruch, H. (1970a). Instinct and interpersonal experience. *Comprehensive Psychiatry, 11,* 495–506.

Bruch, H. (1970b). Eating disorders in adolescence. *Proceedings of the American Psychopathological Association, 59,* 181–202.

Bruch, H. (1973). *Eating disorders: Obesity, anorexia nervosa and the person within.* New York: Basic Books.

Bruch, H. (1978). *The golden cage.* Cambridge, MA: Harvard University Press.

Cohen, D. (1971). Constitutional law—civil commitment: A patient involuntarily committed to a state mental institution who has not been adjudicated incompetent may refuse treatment based on his First Amendment right of free exercise of religion. *Brooklyn Law Review, 38,* 211–222.

Falk, J. R., & Halmi, K. A. (1982). Amenorrhea in anorexia nervosa: Examination of the critical body weight hypothesis. *Biological Psychiatry, 17,* 799–806.

Garfinkel, P. E., & Garner, D. M. (1982). *Anorexia nervosa: A multidimensional perspective.* New York: Brunner/Mazel.

Garner, D. M. (1986). Cognitive therapy for anorexia nervosa. In K. D. Brownell & J. P. Foreyt, *Handbook of eating disorders* (pp. 301–327). New York: Basic Books.

Garner, D. M., & Bemis, K. (1982). A cognitive-behavioral approach to anorexia nervosa. *Cognitive therapy and research, 6,* 123–150.

Halmi, K. A., Goldberg, S. C., Eckert, E., Casper, R., & Davis, J. M. (1977). Pretreatment evaluation in anorexia nervosa. In R. A. Vigersky (Ed.), *Anorexia nervosa* (pp. 43–54). New York: Raven Press.

Jones, D. J., Fox, M. M., Babagian, H. M., & Hutton, H. E. (1980). Epidemiology of anorexia nervosa in Monroe County, New York: 1960–1976. *Psychosomatic Medicine, 42,* 551–558.

Kaplan, A. G., & Bean, J. P. (Eds.). (1976). *Beyond sex-role stereotypes: Readings toward a psychology of androgyny.* Boston: Little, Brown.

Leitenberg, H., Agras, W. S., & Thomson, L. E. (1968). A sequential analysis of the effect of selective positive reinforcement in modifying anorexia nervosa. *Behavior Research and Therapy, 6,* 211–218.

Leon, G. R. (1983). Anorexia nervosa: The question of treatment emphasis. In M. Rosenbaum, C. M. Franks, Y. Jaffe (Eds.), *Perspectives on behavior therapy in the eighties* (pp. 363–377). New York: Springer.

Leon, G. R., & Finn, S. (1984). Sex-role stereotypes and the development of eating disorders. In C. S. Widom (Ed.), *Sex roles and psychopathology* (pp. 317–337). New York: Plenum Press.

Leon, G. R., Lucas, A. R., Colligan, R. C., Ferdinande, R. J., & Kamp, J. (1985). Body image, sexual attitudes, and family interaction patterns. *Journal of Abnormal Child Psychology, 13,* 245–258.

Leon, G. R., Lucas, A. R., Ferdinande, R. F., Mangelsdorf, C., & Colligan, R. C. (1987). Attitudes about sexuality and other psychological characteristics as predictors of follow-up status in anorexia nervosa. *International Journal of Eating Disorders, 6,* 477–484.

Leon, G. R., Perry, C. L., Mangelsdorf, C., & Tell, G. J. (in press). Adolescent nutritional and psychological patterns and risk for the development of an eating disorder. *Journal of Youth and Adolescence.*

Mental Health Law Project. (1973). *Basic rights of the mentally handicapped.* Washington, DC.

Schiele, B. C., & Brozek, J. (1948). Experimental neurosis resulting from semi-starvation in man. *Psychosomatic Medicine, 10,* 31–50.

Strober, M., Morrell, W., Burroughs, J., Salkin, B., & Jacobs, C. (1985). A controlled family study of anorexia nervosa. *Journal of Psychiatric Research, 19,* 239–246.

Szmukler, G. I., & Russell, G. F. M. (1986). Outcome and prognosis of anorexia nervosa. In K. D. Brownell & J. P. Foreyt, (Eds.) *Handbook of eating disorders* (pp. 283–300). New York: Basic Books.

Toner, B. B., Garfinkel, P. E., & Garner, D. M. (1986). Long-term follow-up of anorexia nervosa. *Psychosomatic Medicine, 48,* 520–529.

Waller, J. V., Kaufman, M. R., & Deutsch, F. (1940). Anorexia nervosa: A psychosomatic entity. *Psychosomatic Medicine, 2,* 3–16.

Willi, J., & Grossman, S. (1983). Epidemiology of anorexia nervosa in a defined region of Switzerland. *American Journal of Psychiatry, 140,* 564–567.

12

Bulimia and Athletics—
The Need to Maintain a
Low Body Weight

Ginny Nelson was referred by her gymnastics coach to the university counseling center because she was exhibiting a pattern of binge eating followed by vomiting. These behaviors had become obvious to some of Ginny's teammates who lived in the same dormitory and had shared their concerns with their coach. Ginny was a 21-year-old college junior who was five feet three inches tall and weighed 110 pounds. She agreed to make an appointment at the student counseling center after Ms. Colwin, her coach, talked to a psychologist at the center. The psychologist confirmed that the kinds of binging-purging behaviors Ginny was engaging in could be detrimental to her both psychologically and physically. Ms. Colwin then convinced Ginny to receive professional guidance regarding her eating patterns.

Ginny reluctantly agreed to contact the student counseling center. She told Ms. Colwin that she realized her food consumption patterns might not be usual, but she was not entirely sure that these practices were detrimental to her health. However, at the urging of Ms. Colwin and her teammates in the dormitory, she eventually called for an appointment.

Ginny arrived on time for her interview at the counseling center. She was neatly dressed in pants, short-sleeved blouse, and running shoes. Her short, brown hair was styled and combed, and she wore light eye makeup and lipstick. The first impression of the psychologist, Dr. R., was that Ginny looked somewhat pale and drawn, and her facial expression suggested that she was anxious.

After Ginny and Dr. R. had talked for awhile, Ginny indicated concern that she was losing control over her eating habits, and she now felt relieved that others had pressured her to come to the center. She was particularly worried because over the last three weeks, she had engaged in binge episodes almost every day; she always vomited after a binge. Until recently, she felt that she could control the binging and purging, and she also believed that the purging helped her maintain her weight at a competitive level for athletics. However, since the gymnastics season was over and she was not currently involved in another school sport, she was not exercising as vigorously as she did during training. Thus, she was gradually gaining weight even though she regularly vomited after a binge episode.

Ginny revealed that she always felt guilty and disgusted with herself after she binged and vomited. She also had to deal with a lot of other negative feelings because she had done poorly in gymnastics during the past season. According to Ginny, these bad feelings about previous binges and other matters tended to trigger still more binge-vomiting episodes. Because she recognized that these cycles were becoming more frequent, she decided to seek the help others were urging her to obtain.

Family Background

Ginny was the second youngest in a family of four children. She had an older brother, Wally, age 27, who worked as a computer technician in another city. At the time she was seen, her older sister Leslie was 24 years old and working in a boutique; her 19-year-old brother Tom was attending a local community college. Ginny's father managed a discount store in the growing midwestern city where they lived. Her mother worked part-time as a cashier at a local supermarket. The Nelson family had a number of relatives in the area whom they saw occasionally. However, the only one with whom they maintained close ties was Mrs. Nelson's mother, who lived in a low-cost senior citizens' apartment building not too far away.

Ginny indicated that her father had had a drinking problem for a number of years. To Ginny's knowledge, he did not drink at work, but usually drank in the evenings and on weekends. He apparently functioned adequately enough at his job to avoid the pressures that might compel him to seek treatment. Mrs. Nelson occasionally fought with her husband about his drinking, particularly when she found an empty liquor bottle in the garbage can in the morning. Ginny said that her father got very angry if anyone commented about his drinking, and he denied that he drank too much. Ginny stated that not talking to her father about his drinking behavior made things easier all the way around.

Mrs. Nelson liked to paint with water colors in her free time, and she also enjoyed cooking. Ginny indicated that her mother always seemed to be dieting, and she tried every new diet or "magical cure" for weight reduction. However, she never succeeded in keeping her weight at a lower level. Her mother weighed approximately 140 pounds and was about five feet four inches tall. Ginny stated that her mother frequently used diet pills along with various "crash" diets to help her lose weight.

Ginny revealed that her mother often overate when she was upset. When Ginny was in junior high school, the family went through a period of stress during which her mother's weight increased 30 pounds above its usual level. Mrs. Nelson went on a strict, low-calorie diet that she followed very closely. Eventually, she lost much of the added weight she had put on. However, Ginny said that her mother continued to go through periods of eating too much, followed by strict dieting. She also stated that her mother was never satisfied with her weight, no matter what she weighed.

Ginny related to Dr. R. that her home life had always been full of conflicts. She felt it a relief to be living in the college dormitory on the athletic scholarship she had received for being on the gymnastics team. Her parents fought about almost anything that came up; when Ginny was 12 years old her father had moved out of the house for about two months. (This was when her mother had gained 30 pounds.) She recalled that her parents had argued constantly about Mr. Nelson's drinking and about where he was going in the evenings. One Sunday he simply packed his clothes and moved out in a fit of anger. The period of separation had been extremely difficult, both financially and emotionally. Mr. Nelson eventually decided to come back home; his wife told the children they would just have to put up with his behavior because it was too difficult to manage without his full financial help. According to Ginny, though, her parents' relationship continued to be one of frequent friction and occasionally heated arguments.

Ginny indicated that she often argued with her parents about silly things. Her entire family seemed stubborn, and no one wanted to give in to the other person's wishes. She felt that the only time things went smoothly between her and her parents was when she was involved in activities related to school sports.

Ginny stated that she usually got along fairly well with her older brother Wally. However, he and Mr. Nelson had always fought a great deal, and after Wally graduated from high school he got a job and moved out of the house. Wally attended school part-time and eventually earned certification as a computer technician. The company he worked for opened a new plant in another city two years previously, and he voluntarily transferred to this new plant. A year ago Wally married a woman he met after he moved. Ginny said the entire family went to the wedding, but she has not seen Wally or his wife since then.

Ginny and her older sister got along reasonably well. Leslie had been working at various jobs since high school. She currently shared an apartment with two other people and worked full-time. Ginny indicated that after a few months Leslie usually got tired of the people she was living with; she would then move back home. Typically, after several weeks at home she would make other living arrangements. Her parents came to expect this pattern and did not argue with her about moving in and out. For about ten months during the previous year, Leslie had lived with a boyfriend. Mr. and Mrs. Nelson had more or less ignored their living together. When their relationship ended Leslie moved to still another place.

Ginny described her brother Tom as "lazy and spoiled" and said she fought a lot with him. He was taking a part-time course load in college, and Ginny stated that he was perfectly content to work just enough to pay for his tuition, and to study just enough to squeeze by. She said that Tom drank too much and he was also too fat. He often had "pig-out" periods when he ate large quantities of cookies, candy, and various "junk" foods. Ginny doubted that Tom engaged in vomiting or any other means of purging after a bout of overeating.

School and Social History

Ginny told Dr. R. that she had always enjoyed the camaraderie of her teammates and the members of other athletic teams, and she generally attended parties with her peers on the various teams. At these parties she and her friends drank beer and smoked pot, but they were careful not to overindulge, particularly when they were in training. During the summer she and her friends would occasionally drink to the point of being dizzy and "hungover" the next day, but she did not feel that she had a drinking problem, and, she repeated, she never drank to excess during the athletic season.

Ginny did relatively well in her school subjects, but her greatest enjoyment was the athletic and other extracurricular activities she participated in with her friends. She had worked hard practicing and training for gymnastics ever since junior high school, when her physical education teacher told her that she had an aptitude for this sport. Ginny and her friends also participated on the track and diving teams, but she said she did best in gymnastics, and in high school and college focused most of her athletic activities in that area.

Ginny made the state finals in several gymnastics events during her junior year in high school. Winning the state championship in her division for vaulting and floor events during her senior year was extremely exciting, and her parents, who attended as many of her meets as possible, were very proud of her. She was even more excited when she was offered one of the few athletic scholarships for women at the university in the city where she lived.

During her freshman year of college, Ginny met Scott, a young man from another city who was on the cross-country running team. They started going out together, and for about six months neither dated anyone else. Ginny had had sexual relationships with two different boys in high school, but Scott was the first person that she cared deeply about. However, after they had gone out together for several months, both began to lose interest in having an exclusive relationship with each other. Eventually they went their separate ways. Ginny has had periodic sexual relationships with other young men at college, but at the time she was seen at the counseling center, she was not interested in anyone in particular.

Weight and Dieting History

The tremendous amount of energy Ginny expended on athletic training served to keep her weight within 105 and 108 pounds. However, Ginny's high school and college coaches consistently told her and her teammates that they would be better athletes if they kept their weight as low as possible. Ginny felt that extremely strict "crash" dieting both at the start of training and during competition was generally encouraged.

Ginny stated that during high school, maintaining her weight was usually easy. Because she was involved in sports throughout the school year, she practiced very vigorously every day, and she exercised on a fairly continuous basis. However, she also began to go through periods of four or five days during which she would have several binge episodes, usually in response to some type of emotional upset.

While in high school, Ginny followed her mother's pattern of dieting by severely restricting her food intake. She also used over-the-counter diet pills to make dieting easier. However, she indicated that trying to lose weight in this manner made her feel extremely hungry and irritable. When she was in training, it was easier to work off "nerves" and tension as well as lose weight by exercising. During the summer months when she was not so physically active, overeating and weight gain became more of a problem. Because she was home more during the summer, she also had more frequent and upsetting fights with her parents. Ginny said that she noticed in high school that she was developing a more intense pattern of "pigging out" on food whenever she became upset.

In college, Ginny worked hard in athletics and struggled to keep her weight at about 105 pounds. Performing well in competitive events during her freshman and sophomore years pleased her tremendously. She noticed, however, that her periods of overeating when under stress were becoming more of a problem, and recognized that part of the stress she was experiencing was caused by trying to maintain her weight.

Eventually, the episodes of overeating began to take on a different quality. In the summer between her sophomore and junior years in college, Ginny began to experience occasions when she felt driven to eat whatever food was available. She became frightened that she was out of control and would not be able to stop eating. Afterwards, she felt guilty and disgusted with herself for having eaten so much. Also, her loss of control over food intake confused her, and she worried that the next time she felt the urge to overeat she would again lose control. She also began inducing vomiting after some binge episodes, but at this point she did not regularly vomit after a binge. At home she disguised her vomiting by closing the bathroom door and running the water in the sink.

The binge episodes followed by vomiting increased significantly during her junior year in college, and she gradually put on about five pounds despite intensive physical training. The junior-year gymnastics season had been a poor one for her. She did not place in any meets that season, and her poor performance disappointed and embarrassed her. After the season, she did not exercise regularly. The binge episodes and periodic vomiting continued, and her weight increased to 128 pounds. She felt quite desperate and tried to keep her daily food intake at about 1000 calories through strict dieting and using diet pills. However, restricting her food intake was not successful, and she had numerous episodes of binge eating often followed by vomiting.

Ginny revealed that her feelings about herself were tied in with how she performed as a gymnast. The attention she received from her family and friends when she excelled in athletics still gave her a great deal of pleasure, and the scholarship she received allowed her some financial independence. She felt that her poor performance during the past season was related to her difficulty maintaining an optimum weight. After the season was over, Ginny tried to hide her worsening eating problem from her family, friends, and gymnastics coach.

Ginny had recently begun to induce vomiting every time she engaged in a binge. She had initially accomplished this by putting her finger down her throat to make herself gag. However, after several months she could vomit simply by moving her throat muscles. She related a recent episode in which she had engaged in a binge. She had been feeling extremely irritated and "bummed out" because she was behind in her studies and final exams were approaching. While reading her course assignments in her room at the dormitory, she realized very clearly how far behind she had actually fallen. As she studied, she became increasingly more irritated and scared that she would fail the examination. Eventually, she felt so uncomfortable that she left her room, went out, and bought several boxes of donuts, cookies, candy, and popcorn. She returned to her dormitory room and closed the door quietly so the other students would not know she was in. In approximately one hour, she ate all of the food she had purchased. She said that she felt out of control, as if she would have kept on eating as long as a morsel of food was available. After she consumed the food, she forced herself to vomit.

Ginny indicated that her menstrual cycle, although generally quite irregular, had become more so over the past months. She had had only one menstrual period lasting three days during the previous six months. She told Dr. R. that she felt her whole body was "messed up." She stated that the more she talked to Dr. R., the more she realized she needed help.

Psychological and Behavioral Evaluation

Ginny completed the MMPI and several other psychological inventories. Dr. R. also asked her to monitor her eating patterns, emotional states, and life events on a daily basis for a period of one week. The MMPI clinical profile showed evidence of significant anxiety, depression, and feelings of confusion or alienation from other persons. These feelings and attitudes were superimposed on a more basic characteristic of persistent impulsive behavior followed by feelings of guilt and anxiety. Problems associated with acting before one has thought through the consequences of an activity would be consistent with this impulsivity pattern.

The MMPI scoring configuration also indicated a tendency toward some type of substance abuse problem. The impulsivity and substance abuse potential noted on the test results seemed consistent with the bulimic behavior Ginny was engaging in, with food as the substance that was being abused. However, Ginny's profile pattern also suggested an acutely distressed individual who might be at an optimum point for benefitting from treatment.

Ginny completed the Family Environment Scale (Moos, 1974), an inventory that assesses the client's view of the general atmosphere and interaction patterns within the family. Her response pattern suggested an enmeshed but chaotic family environment in which the various members were very aware of each other's activities, and in which there was little encouragement for acting independently. However, because the family system was not viewed as structured or well-organized, the individuals within the family would occasionally find it difficult to know what was expected of them.

Ginny's daily food and activity records, self-monitored over a seven-day period, indicated an erratic meal-time pattern. Although she generally awakened at about 8:30 AM, her daily records showed that she never ate before 11:30 AM. On some days, she did not eat again until 5 PM, while on others she ate again around 4:30 PM and then in the evening around 8:30 to 10 PM.

The foods that Ginny recorded eating, irrespective of which meal it was, were bagels with cream cheese, popcorn, granola bars, peanut M & M's, candy bars, potato chips, donuts, and sugar-free beverages. The only significant source of protein she recorded eating was some scrambled eggs on Day 4. Ginny indicated feeling anxiety, restlessness, and irritability before eating; she did not record her emotional state after food consumption. Ginny's food intake on Day 5 consisted of a bagel with cream cheese, an oatmeal cookie, and a can of diet soft drink at 11:30 AM. At 4 PM, she had two vodka sours, one glass of rosé wine, three beers, and two medium bowls of popcorn. She recorded feeling content before the drinking episode, and did not record her feelings afterwards.

The client recorded three binge episodes over the seven-day period, and each binge was followed by vomiting. The feelings before the binge at 10:30 PM on Day 2 were recorded as "fat and irritable." The following food was eaten: one baked potato with sour cream and butter, one package of peanut M & M's, a "large amount" of chips and sour cream, one large strawberry croissant with whipped cream, a medium-size salad with dressing, and two cans of Tab. She recorded feeling disgusted and guilty after this episode.

Course of Therapy

Ginny agreed to participate in a ten-week group therapy program that Dr. R. was offering for women with eating disorders. The program was based on a cognitive-behavioral approach focusing on the irrational beliefs persons held about their eating behavior (Ellis, 1962). The therapist also examined the beliefs participants had concerning the possibility of controlling their weight and eating (Phelan, 1984).

A common erroneous belief clients in the group sessions expressed was that they would gain a significant amount of weight by eating just one donut or one cookie. This belief frequently resulted in a full-blown binge episode. Clients reported their assumption that as long as they had taken in a significant number of calories through eating one cookie, they had "blown it" anyway and might just as well keep on eating. Marlatt (1979) termed this phenomenon the "abstinence violation effect," while Herman and Polivy (1975) described the mechanism of a binge as counterregulatory behavior in restrained eaters.

Further components of the cognitive-behavioral therapy program Ginny participated in were the daily monitoring of food intake, including binges and vomiting episodes, the emotional and social circumstances in which eating occurred, and the cognitions or evaluations about these particular circumstances. The goal was to specify problem areas at home or at work that the clients might judge they had dealt with inappropriately, that upset them, and that resulted in eating. Thus, the clients could perceive that these negative evaluations may result in emotional states such as anger or frustration, or other cognitions such as, "I'm worthless. I can't do anything right." These thoughts and feelings may then serve as the antecedents of a binge episode.

The group discussions involved suggestions by the therapist and other group members regarding more effective ways to deal with problem situations. The particular client then had the opportunity to try out these alternative behaviors during the week and report back to the group at the next session. Assertion training, other types of role playing, and various stress management techniques were taught during the sessions as relevant to a client's problems with binge eating. The clients were also encouraged to engage in regular exercise as a means of alleviating stress and as a general physical fitness strategy. In addition, they discussed the sex-role stereotyping that pushed women to define their self-worth in terms of their physical appearance, and the unrealistically low societal standards of ideal weight for women.

The group members were eventually able to specify their unrealistic ideas about food and their weight status, and how self-defeating these beliefs were. Dr. R. worked with each client in developing a plan for regular, nutritionally balanced meals. The clients were also told that most likely some relapses would occur. Dr. R. instructed them to think of strategies to regain control over their eating if they had a "slip" and engaged in an eating binge. A realistic goal was set for each person to reduce the number of binge-vomiting episodes by the end of treatment.

Dr. R. stressed a crucial procedure to help the client avoid feeling out of control when in the process of a binge. This involved planning out ahead of time the behaviors that would be effective in quickly reasserting control after a binge had started. For example, for some clients feelings of anxiety might be a significant cue in a sequence resulting in a full-blown binge. The next link in the binging process might then be the consuming of cookies, donuts, or other foods that the bulimic has labeled as forbidden. Control over food intake could be implemented by instructing the client to leave the room containing the "forbidden" foods when he or she feels anxious. Another self-control method might be a cognitive one, such as "self-talk" in which one reminds oneself that there is a difference between eating one cookie when anxious or depressed and engaging in an uncontrolled binge. This strategy is equally relevant when the person is not anxious. Dr. R. also strongly encouraged the clients to refrain from purging, no matter how much they had eaten, thus disrupting this aspect of the behavioral chain.

In the group sessions Ginny came to understand the tremendous amount of self-esteem and the feelings of personal worth that she had equated with doing well in athletics. The role of her family and friends in perpetuating this attitude was also pointed out. Ginny came to realize that her evaluation of herself as worthless because she did poorly in competition was translated into a dissatisfaction with her body. She then acted upon the belief that achieving a low body weight would solve most of her problems.

Ginny made continuous progress in dealing more effectively with the situations that caused her to feel anxious, angry, and depressed. She also focused on her personal beliefs and behaviors in relation to the binge episode itself, and the attitude that once she started to binge she could not stop herself until she ate as much as possible and then vomited. Over the treatment period Ginny succeeded in reducing the number of binges she engaged in, and did not report any episodes of drinking to excess. At the end of treatment, she had not binged in two weeks, and her eating patterns were generally more regularized.

Dr. R. asked Ginny to come in for an individual follow-up session six months after treatment. At that time, Ginny weighed 113 pounds, exercised regularly but not to excess, and reported that over the six-month period she had had four binge episodes, all followed by vomiting. However, on the whole she felt she was continuing to make progress in controlling her eating behavior, and she felt more comfortable about her life in general. She also had been able to discuss with her parents her problem of bulimia and the progress she had made in treatment. She felt that her parents supported her decision to seek help for a personal problem, and they accepted the more assertive way she interacted with them. She stated that she was not drinking excessively or using drugs, and she was preparing for the start of her senior year of gymnastic competition. She indicated that her self-worth was not tied so strongly to doing well in gymnastics as had been the case before treatment. She had become involved in other school activities and was looking forward to finishing the requirements for a teaching degree in physical education.

Discussion

The DSM-III-R (1987) criteria for bulimia nervosa include: "recurrent episodes of binge eating (rapid consumption of a large amount of food in a discrete period of time); a feeling of lack of control over eating behavior during the eating binges; self-induced vomiting, use of laxatives or diuretics, strict dieting or fasting, or vigorous exercise in order to prevent weight gain; and persistent overconcern with body shape and weight" (p. 67). To meet the criteria for diagnosis, there is a requirement of two binge eating episodes a week for at least three months. Binges often are terminated by sleep, social interruption, abdominal pain, or self-induced vomiting; self-deprecation and depressed mood commonly follow a binge episode.

Binge eating is a disturbance seen in a number of eating disorders. Eating binges can be part of the symptom pattern of obese persons (who generally do not purge), persons of borderline or normal weight, and persons with the bulimia subtype of anorexia nervosa. Further, some anorexics who did not engage in a binging pattern before treatment develop binging-purging patterns by the time of the follow-up. Generally, the anorexics who exhibited bulimia patterns post-treatment maintained a borderline weight level (Schwartz & Thompson, 1981).

The prevalence of binge eating problems appears to be substantial. Surveys of female college student and young adult populations using

DSM-III (1980) criteria for bulimia found prevalence rates ranging from 4 to 13 percent (Gray & Ford, 1985). However, when the more stringent DSM-III-R criteria were applied requiring vomiting or other forms of purgation over an extended period of time, the prevalance figures fell to approximately 1–3 percent (Pyle, Halvorson, Neuman, & Mitchell, 1986). The majority of persons identified or treated for bulimia-purging and other eating disorders are Caucasian females (Halmi, Falk, & Schwartz, 1981; Johnson, Stuckey, Lewis, & Schwartz, 1982; Russell, 1979).

A number of studies have demonstrated a significant dissatisfaction with current body weight and a high frequency of dieting among Caucasian female high school students (Dwyer, Feldman, Seltzer, & Mayer, 1969; Leon, Perry, Mangelsdorf, & Tell, in press). Further, a sample of college students demonstrated significant sex differences in attitudes toward present body weight (Leon, Carroll, Chernyk, & Finn, 1985). A substantial proportion of the normal-weight female students indicated a desire for a lower weight level, while a significant proportion of the normal-weight males indicated they were pleased with their current weight level or wished to weigh more.

There were also sex differences among the subgroup that reported binge eating in the Leon group (1985) study. The description of the episodes of excessive eating among the females was similar to the binging descriptions of a clinically diagnosed group of female bulimics. In both groups the binge episodes were usually precipitated by negative affect; the individual felt driven to eat and out of control. Further, the female college bingers, like the clinical group women, reported feeling guilty and disgusted with themselves after binging.

The male overeaters often reported a quite different pattern of excessive food intake. A significant number of the males indicated that overeating was followed by feelings of happiness. The negative emotional arousal precipitant of the binge and the out-of-control feelings were not as evident.

There have been some interesting findings related to a substance abuse and a more generalized impulse control problem in bulimia. A substantial number of bulimics have indicated past or current excessive alcohol or drug use, and reported that close family members have also engaged in substance abuse patterns (Bulik, 1987; Leon et al., 1985; Pyle, Mitchell, & Eckert, 1981). Further, compared with other groups, a significantly greater number of bulimics reported engaging in stealing, truancy, and a high frequency of sexual activity.

The act of vomiting after binge eating has an aspect of impulsivity or lack of internal control. The individual is using an artificial, external means to be rid of a problem situation—that is, the food just consumed.

The control is exerted after the problem behavior has occurred rather than before, as in a self-control strategy. The physical removal of the problem (the food just consumed) therefore can become a highly reinforcing activity. Of interest are the findings of Abraham and Beumont (1982) that persons who induced vomiting following a binge were less likely to feel anxious and tense after the episode than those who did not vomit or purge. However, with the development of a chronic vomiting pattern, this anxiety reduction may be of short duration.

The question of whether eating disorders are a variant of an underlying mood disorder is a subject of considerable debate. In some individuals, a coexistence of bulimia nervosa and a mood disorder is evident. Overt depression, subjective feelings of gloom, thoughts of suicide, and successful and unsuccessful suicide attempts have been reported (e.g., Abraham and Beumont; Russell). Bulimics with depression also have a high prevalence of mood disorders in family members (Strober, Morrell, Burroughs, Salkin, & Jacobs, 1985). On the other hand, depressive affect can result from the stresses of the binging-purging cycles and the frightening experience of being out of control. In the latter case, the depressed mood may be secondary to the effects of the bulimic disorder.

A relationship between eating disorders and mood disorders in some individuals is suggested by findings that a subgroup of bulimics treated with antidepressant medication showed a marked improvement in symptoms (Pope, Hudson, Jonas, & Yurgelun-Todd, 1983). Further, some depressives and bulimics exhibit a similar pattern of abnormal physiological response on a test of neuroendocrine functioning involving cortisol suppression, the dexamethasone suppression test (Hudson, Laffer, & Pope, 1982). However, weight loss itself may cause cortisol suppression abnormalities similar to that seen in some depressives. The research thus far suggests that some bulimics may be suffering from a co-existing depressive disorder, but a substantial number of bulimics do not exhibit this relationship.

Family history studies have demonstrated problems of substance abuse and depression in some family members of bulimics (Bulik, 1987; Strober et al., 1985). Bulimic individuals often perceive their families as chaotic, lacking in nurturance, and rejecting of them (Humphrey, 1986; Johnson & Flach, 1985). These findings point to a stressful family environment that may place a particular youngster at risk for the later development of an eating disorder.

In Ginny's personal and family history, one can see a relationship between her eating disorder and life experiences. In the Nelson family substance abuse was modeled by the father's problem drinking behavior, in which Ginny's younger brother Tom eventually engaged though to a lesser extent. Ginny's mother expressed a continuing concern about her own weight status, and her chronic use of diet pills and restrictive diets modeled artificial, externally imposed solutions to one's problem eating behaviors. Neither parent stressed adaptive, self-control behaviors.

In the chaotic, conflict-ridden family environment that Ginny grew up in, Ginny incorporated an athletic performance criterion for her evaluation of herself. Her concern about her body weight was therefore multiply determined—through societal and peer group standards of ideal body weight for females, through her parents' influences in modeling alcohol abuse and diet pill use, and through their providing positive attention to her primarily for athletic accomplishments. An additional maladaptive influence was her various coaches' pressures on her to achieve and maintain an unrealistically low body weight, and thus their unwitting encouragement of the development of an eating disorder. Engaging in athletic activities also was overdetermined. Ginny indicated that she had dealt with family and personal stresses in junior and senior high school by participating in athletics to avoid thinking about her personal difficulties.

Ginny had inadequate skills for dealing with interpersonal problems and negative feelings. She did not deal with the possibility that she might already have reached her peak performance potential in gymnastics; or that perhaps there were other reasons for her disappointing performance than her body weight. Further, Ginny was probably attempting to maintain her weight below a physiologically comfortable level, and it was difficult for her to weigh as little as she wanted without experiencing upsurges of hunger and negative affect. The hunger and negative emotions also served to trigger binge episodes, which inevitably were followed by vomiting. The entire cycle then repeated itself several days later.

Ginny's transition from periods of overeating to engaging in behaviors that met the criteria for binge episodes involved the subjective experience of uncontrollable urges to eat, and the frightening feeling of a loss of control over food consumption (Halmi, Falk, & Schwartz, 1981). Ginny seemed to benefit from the self-control training she received in the group sessions. She learned behaviors that helped her avoid binging as well as behaviors to help her terminate food consumption before there was a loss of control. Attention to the development of more nutritionally balanced and regularized eating patterns was also helpful.

Multidimensional programs for the treatment of bulimia including nutrition education, behavioral management of food intake, and group and individual psychotherapy have been described (Johnson & Connors, 1987). Cognitive-behavioral approaches also have been reported (Fairburn, 1981). However, as in the treatment of anorexia nervosa, comprehensive outcome studies have not been conducted and the long-term efficacy of these various treatment programs remains to be demonstrated.

A significant aspect of the treatment process was to enable Ginny and the other members of her treatment group to deal with maladaptive cognitions and emotions in ways other than eating. The group process also involved a consideration of the unrealistic beliefs women have about the components of femininity. The constant need to please others and the definition of a pleasing body as "being as thin as possible" were explored (Boskind-Lodahl, 1976). A significant fact that Ginny learned through treatment was that she could maintain her weight at a realistic level when she stopped the binging-vomiting behaviors.

Ginny was fortunate in having teammates and a coach who became aware of the problems associated with binging and purging and were concerned about the evidence of these behaviors in Ginny. The effectiveness of the cognitive-behavioral program Ginny participated in may have been partially due to Ginny's relatively young age and the fact that she had not been engaging in the bulimia-purging pattern for a long time.

Although Ginny's overall status at follow-up was good, the future remains uncertain. Both her family history and the results of the psychological testing suggest the potential for future alcohol or other substance abuse problems. Further, Ginny recorded an instance of excessive alcohol use on her food and activity report before she started treatment, although it was unclear how often such episodes occurred. However, though Ginny may be at higher than average risk for other types of substance abuse disorders or a recurrence of an eating disorder, she did make substantial progress in treatment. If her social milieu is supportive of her changed interpersonal behavior patterns, and if Ginny can maintain a self-image based on factors other than doing well in athletics, one can be reasonably optimistic about her future adjustment.

References

Abraham, S. F., & Beumont, P. J. V. (1982). How patients describe bulimia or binge eating. *Psychological Medicine, 12,* 625–635.

American Psychiatric Association (1980). *Diagnostic and statistical manual of mental disorders* (3rd ed.) (DSM-III). Washington, DC: Author.

American Psychiatric Association (1987). *Diagnostic and statistical manual of mental disorders* (3rd ed., rev.) (DSM-III-R). Washington, DC: Author.

Boskind-Lodahl, M. (1976). Cinderella's stepsisters: A feminist perspective on anorexia nervosa and bulimia. *Signs: Journal of Women in Culture and Society, 2,* 342–356.

Bulik, C. M. (1987). Drug and alcohol abuse by bulimic women and their families. *American Journal of Psychiatry, 144,* 1604–1606.

Dwyer, J. T., Feldman, J. J., Seltzer, C. C., & Mayer, J. (1969). Body image in adolescents: Attitudes toward weight and perception of appearance. *American Journal of Clinical Nutrition, 20,* 1045–1056.

Ellis, A. (1962). *Reason and emotion in psychotherapy.* New York: Lyle Stuart.

Fairburn, C. (1981). A cognitive behavioral approach to the treatment of bulimia. *Psychological Medicine, 11,* 707–711.

Gray, J. J., & Ford, K. (1985). The incidence of bulimia in a college sample. *International Journal of Eating Disorders, 4,* 201–210.

Halmi, K. A., Falk, J. R., & Schwartz, E. (1981). Binge-eating and vomiting: A survey of a college population. *Psychological Medicine, 11,* 697–706.

Herman, C. P., & Polivy, J. (1975). Anxiety, restraint, and eating behavior. *Journal of Abnormal Psychology, 84,* 666–672.

Hudson, J. I., Laffer, P. S., & Pope, H. G., Jr. (1982). Bulimia related to affective disorder by family history and response to the dexamethasone suppression test. *American Journal of Psychiatry, 139,* 685–687.

Humphrey, L. L. (1986). Structural analysis of parent-child relationships in eating disorders. *Journal of Abnormal Psychology, 95,* 395–402.

Johnson, C. L., & Connors, M. E. (1987). *The etiology and treatment of bulimia nervosa.* New York: Basic Books.

Johnson, C. L., & Flach, A. (1985). Family characteristics of 105 patients with bulimia. *American Journal of Psychiatry, 142,* 1321–1324.

Johnson, C. L., Stuckey, M. K., Lewis, L. D., & Schwartz, D. M. (1982). Bulimia: A descriptive survey of 316 cases. *International Journal of Eating Disorders, 2,* 3–16.

Leon, G. R., Carroll, K., Chernyk, B., & Finn, S. (1985). Binge eating and associated habit patterns within college student and identified bulimic populations. *International Journal of Eating Disorders, 4,* 43–57.

Leon, G. R., Perry, C. L., Mangelsdorf, C., & Tell, G. J. (in press). Adolescent nutritional and psychological patterns and risk for the development of an eating disorder. *Journal of Youth and Adolescence.*

Marlatt, G. A. (1979). Alcohol use and problem drinking: A cognitive-behavioral analysis. In P. C. Kendall & S. D. Hollon (Eds.), *Cognitive-behavioral interventions: Theory, research, and procedures* (pp. 319–355). New York: Academic Press.

Moos, R. (1974). *Combined preliminary manual: Family, work, and group environment scales.* Palo Alto, CA: Consulting Psychologists Press.

Phelan, P. W. (1984). *Behavioral, attitudinal, and affective correlates of bulimia: Implications for treatment.* Unpublished doctoral dissertation, University of Minnesota.

Pope, H. G., Jr., Hudson, J. I, Jonas, J. M., & Yurgelun-Todd, M. S. (1983). Bulimia treated with imipramine: A placebo-controlled, double-blind study. *American Journal of Psychiatry, 140,* 554–558.

Pyle, R. L., Halvorson, P. A., Neuman, P. A., & Mitchell, J. E. (1986). The increasing prevalence of bulimia in freshman college students. *International Journal of Eating Disorders, 5,* 631–647.

Pyle, R. L., Mitchell, J. E., & Eckert, E. D. (1981). Bulimia: A report of 34 cases. *Journal of Clinical Psychiatry, 42,* 60–64.

Russell, G. (1979). Bulimia nervosa: An ominous variant of anorexia nervosa. *Psychological Medicine 9,* 429–448.

Schwartz, S. M., & Thompson, M. G. (1981). Do anorectics get well? Current research and future needs. *American Journal of Psychiatry, 138,* 319–323.

Strober, M., Morrell, W., Burroughs, J., Salkin, B., & Jacobs, C. (1985). A controlled family study of anorexia nervosa. *Journal of Psychiatric Research, 19,* 239–246.

13

A Lifetime Exposure to Alcohol—
The Case of
Maria Valdez

Maria Valdez, a 40-year-old Mexican-American, had been employed as an assembly line worker for a number of years. She was referred from an alcohol rehabilitation clinic to a state mental hospital so she could receive more intensive care for her alcoholism. Maria voluntarily admitted herself to the hospital to participate in a special alcohol abuse program. This was her first admission to a mental hospital.

The patient had used alcohol freely for the past 20 years and had manifested an episodic drinking pattern over that time period. She typically got drunk for one or two days on the weekend, drinking at home or in bars, and she then stayed sober for the rest of the week. Until the previous year, Maria had never reported to work drunk nor did she drink while she was working. However, she estimated that over the past ten years, she has never stayed sober for longer than two weeks at a time. Maria's only legal arrest occurred one year previously when she was charged with drunken driving.

At the time of the evaluation, Maria was separated from her husband and the youngest of her three children had recently been placed in a foster home. Maria had been fired from her job four months earlier because she had become unreliable about appearing for work. She subsisted on welfare support after she lost her job, and her welfare worker referred her to an outpatient chemical dependency clinic for treatment. However, Maria continued to have great difficulty remaining sober, and she was then referred to a state mental hospital for inpatient treatment.

Childhood Background

Maria's father was born in Mexico, and her mother was a first generation Mexican-American. When Mr. Valdez was a young man, he emigrated to the United States in search of a better job. Maria's parents were tenant farmers, and they had lived and worked in the same rural area since Maria was a child. Maria was the second youngest in a family of nine children.

Maria revealed that she had never felt close to her mother. She described her mother as a stern and religious woman who rarely showed affection toward any of her children. Mrs. Valdez also had a long history of engaging in periodic drinking bouts, and Maria clearly remembered many occasions during her childhood when her mother was drunk. The children learned to stay out of her way at such times because Mrs. Valdez would become physically and verbally abusive toward her family.

Maria recalled that her father was quite affectionate toward her and rarely punished her for misbehaving. He usually drank wine throughout the day, but she could not remember ever seeing him drunk. Maria indicated that Mr. Valdez also tried not to interact with his wife when she was intoxicated. However, after each drinking episode, he chided her about her behavior and her neglect of the children.

Maria said that she was fond of her brothers and sisters and she remembered that they always had fun together when they were growing up. An older sister took over the household chores and made sure that she had enough to eat whenever their mother was drinking.

The way of life in the rural area where Maria lived alternated between boredom and physical exhaustion during the work season. The Valdez children had very little formal schooling because they toiled in the fields during planting and harvesting time and they went to school only when they had no work obligations. Each of the children stopped attending school at the age of 14.

Maria went to live with a married sister in a large city nearby when she was 15 years old. A number of her brothers and sisters had also moved to the same city and they kept in contact with each other. However, she rarely saw one of her brothers because he was continually in jail on charges related to drunkenness. Maria was able to find work on an assembly line at an electronics factory. She occasionally went back to visit her parents, but she saw less and less of them as she established an independent life in the city. Maria indicated that no one in her family attended church very often, but she frequently prayed at bedtime.

Young Adulthood

Maria began spending her free time with the people she met at work and at local dances rather than with her relatives in the city. She said that she tried to make friends with persons of many ethnic groups and she had few Mexican-American friends. Her Chicano acquaintances reminded her too much of her parents' old-fashioned ways, and she wanted to lead the kind of life in which she could have more fun.

Maria's first sexual experience occurred at age 15 when she met Bill Harper, who was employed at the factory where she worked. Maria stated that she had had several other sexual relationships before marriage, but she liked Bill very much because he was so much fun to be with. They were married when she was 17.

Maria reported that Bill was carefree and happy during the first year of marriage. He enjoyed drinking with other persons, and Maria and Bill usually drank quite heavily on the weekend, either at someone's house or at a bar. They often drank to the point where they both had severe hangovers the next day, but this discomfort was forgotten when they began drinking again. She indicated that after several years of following this type of drinking pattern, her hangovers no longer seemed as severe.

Bill was not continuously employed because he failed to appear at the job he was holding if he did not feel like working that day. However, Maria was able to obtain fairly regular employment on an assembly line or doing simple clerical work, and she was often the sole financial provider for the family. Maria said that she was not terribly upset with her husband when he quit or was fired from a job because she was usually employed at the time. She enjoyed Bill's companionship and the lively people they met, and she did not nag him about working. Instead, she tried to humor him when he was in a bad mood or feeling the effects of drinking too much.

Maria and Bill had two children during the first three years of their marriage. These pregnancies were unplanned, and Maria revealed that she had never really enjoyed taking care of her two sons. After each child was born, she arranged for a neighbor to look after the youngsters and returned to work as soon as she felt physically able to do so. Maria stated that her finding work was fortunate; otherwise the family would not have had enough money to live on.

Three years after their marriage, Bill was arrested on a robbery charge and sentenced to four years in prison. Maria said she was surprised to find out that her husband had been burglarizing stores, but she had never questioned him about his activities or the money he spent when he was out of work. While Bill was incarcerated, Maria continued to drink on the weekends, at first with her friends and then with new acquaintances. She occasionally had sexual relationships with some of the men she met, but she did not establish a long-term alliance with anyone else.

Maria said that Bill had changed when he came out of prison. He was bitter and angry and no longer fun to be with. When they drank together, the evening usually ended in arguments and an occasional physical beating. Maria and Bill separated about six months after his release from prison, and she eventually obtained a divorce. Maria then engaged in a series of liaisons with a number of men she met at bars or through mutual acquaintances. None of these relationships lasted very long, and Maria usually found herself providing all of the financial support until she tired of that person and told him to move out.

Maria indicated that for six months she had lived with a heroin addict, although she did not know of his addiction when they first met. They were already living together when she found out, but she maintained the relationship for a while longer because he was pleasant to be with. However, Maria said that he suddenly "cracked up." He began shouting and talking irrationally, and he threatened to kill her. This bizarre behavior was extremely frightening, and she called the police. Soon after this episode, he was committed to a mental hospital.

When she was 33 years old, Maria married a man she became acquainted with at a bar. She felt Phil was the kind of person she could depend on, and he was also fun to be with. Phil was employed in the produce department of a supermarket, and he had previously worked as a cab driver. He also had a drinking problem, but he started drinking each day in the afternoon and his drinking did not markedly interfere with his job. Maria continued her well-established drinking pattern of staying sober during the week and drinking heavily on the weekend. Maria and Phil had lived together continuously for four years. They have been separated off and on for the past three years.

Maria said that her sons had always been quite unruly and difficult to discipline, and she or the man she was living with attempted to control their behavior by hitting them with a strap. She generally encouraged the boys to play outside so she would not be annoyed by their actions. She rarely asked her sons about their outside activities, even when they came home extremely late at night.

Maria indicated that Phil and her sons argued continually. Michael and Charles usually formed an alliance with each other to oppose Phil's directions, and they generally ignored Maria's attempts to persuade them to obey. Two years after their mother remarried, the boys moved out of the house following a prolonged family argument about their behavior. According to Maria, everyone agreed that the move would be beneficial. Michael and Charles were then 16 and 17 years old, respectively, and they supported themselves by working in factories.

Maria seldom saw her sons after they moved out, except when either Michael or Charles needed some money. Maria always gave them whatever funds she could spare. Maria reported that both of the boys enjoyed drinking beer, but she did not think that either of them had a drinking problem. When she was admitted to the chemical dependency program at the hospital, she had not seen Michael or Charles for several months and she had no idea where they were living or working.

Shortly after Michael and Charles moved out, Maria gave birth to a daughter. Phil, of Jewish background, voiced strong suspicions that he was not the child's father because her complexion was so dark. Even though Maria swore that Susan was Phil's child, he was not completely reassured until the youngster grew older and began to look like him.

The continual drinking and the accusations of infidelity made Maria and Phil's marital situation quite difficult. Phil was fired from several jobs because he had begun drinking at work. He also became very argumentative at home when he was intoxicated, and his drinking behavior particularly annoyed Maria during the week because she did not drink then. Phil eventually moved out of the house, but he continued to pay Maria for Susan's support when he was working. Maria said that she was sorry that Phil's drinking behavior had become so severe that they could not live together. He was the first man she had lived with who tried to support her and who took an interest in her at times other than when they were drinking.

Maria started seeing another man a few months after Phil moved out, and she said that Phil often spied on them. Phil subsequently went to a social worker and claimed that Maria was not taking adequate care of their daughter. During the following year, Susan was placed in a foster home, and Maria was given visitation rights. Maria was told that her daughter would be restored to her when she stopped drinking and was more competent to care for her. Maria was glad that Susan was well taken care of in the foster home, and she hoped that she would be able to terminate her drinking and eventually regain custody of Susan.

Phil sought help for his drinking problem after Susan was taken from Maria's custody, and with the support of Alcoholics Anonymous, he has been quite successful in abstaining from alcohol use. Maria revealed that she and Phil recently agreed to get back together again if they could both stop drinking and straighten out their lives. Phil continued to visit Susan at the foster home, and he also helped persuade Maria to seek assistance for her drinking problem

Treatment History

Maria accompanied Phil to several meetings of Alcoholics Anonymous at his insistence. She stopped attending meetings because of a reluctance to stand up in front of the group and tell them about her personal life. However, during that period Maria was unable to remain sober for longer than a few days at a time, and she could not keep a job. Several weeks after she stopped attending AA meetings, she experienced a blackout after a two-day drinking period. She could not remember anything that had happened over that time span, and the incident frightened her greatly. Maria told her welfare worker about the blackout, and the latter helped her to enroll in an outpatient chemical dependency clinic.

Maria participated in group therapy sessions at this clinic for about three months, but there was little change in her drinking behavior. The staff recommended that she receive more intensive treatment. Maria was told that she might benefit from a program of Antabuse therapy in combination with other forms of treatment, which could be started in the supervised environment of a hospital. Maria agreed to sign into a state mental hospital in order to participate in a special alcohol abuse program.

Psychological Evaluation

Maria was seen by a psychologist on the staff of the mental hospital. The patient was neatly dressed when she appeared for the interview and her dyed red hair was well combed. She spoke quietly and her conversation was free flowing and relevant to the questions asked of her. Her memory of past and current events appeared to be quite adequate. Maria conversed in a somewhat detached manner, as if the many unpleasant interactions she related had happened to someone else.

Maria became more emotionally expressive as she discussed the reasons why she had signed herself into the hospital. She said that she was unable to control her drinking sprees and found it impossible to deal with the many problems her indulgence in alcohol brought on. She stated that she did not want Susan to grow up in foster homes and she sincerely wanted to be able to take care of her daughter. Maria hoped that eventually she and her husband would be able to live together again.

The patient also revealed her fear that if she kept on drinking, she would "crack up," like the heroin addict with whom she had lived. She realized that whenever she had a day off, she could not refrain from drinking. She was also spending a greater proportion of her time drinking alone.

Maria became quite agitated as she told Dr. C. that when she signed up for the alcohol abuse program she had not realized that she would be confined to a mental hospital. This realization had occurred only after her admission on the previous day, when she observed some patients from other wards at the evening movie. She again recalled how frightened she had been when the man she had lived with became severely disturbed.

Dr. C. told Maria that persons come to the kind of hospital she was in for many different reasons, and her drinking problem did not mean she was insane. The patient was also reminded that she was on a special ward, participating in a program just for alcoholics. Despite further reassurance, Maria became visibly anxious when the psychological tests were administered to her. She felt that being asked to respond to something as peculiar as the Rorschach inkblot test indicated she was indeed mentally disturbed. She thereupon asked Dr. C. if the testing session could be terminated because she felt ill and wanted to lie down. When the patient appeared the next day to continue with the evaluation, she stated her hope that she would not have to take any more tests. Dr. C. explained that the information gained from the tests could help in determining the best course of treatment for her and Maria agreed to complete the psychological testing.

Maria's performance was at the average intelligence level. Despite rather limited formal schooling, Maria was able to correctly answer information questions about literature and geography, and she manifested adequate arithmetic skill. There were some indications that she occasionally had difficulty differentiating between her subjective thoughts and what was happening around her. However, this report of confusion appeared to be descriptive of her drinking episodes and did not suggest psychotic thought processes. There was no evidence of organic brain pathology.

On the TAT cards, the patient described relationships between men and women in terms of battles to be won. Women were portrayed as acting in a passive and dependent manner, but such behavior functioned to manipulate the man to do what the woman wanted. In addition, these relationships were superficial, with little communication of significant personal feelings. Alcohol consumption was depicted as a means of meeting people and providing a vehicle for conversation. The ingestion of liquor also functioned as an escape from the expression of strong feelings of anger, frustration, and anxiety.

Course of Hospital Treatment

Maria participated in an inpatient treatment program for persons who have been unsuccessful in staying sober while in some type of outpatient treatment. The program lasts ten weeks and the patient cannot leave for a home visit without the hospital staff's permission. The alcoholic's entire day in the hospital is structured and through the help of specially trained ward personnel, the patients are encouraged to develop greater skill and comfort in expressing their feelings. All participants in the program attend group therapy sessions and lectures about the psychological and physiological effects of alcohol. A number of patients also receive Antabuse therapy.

The Antabuse treatment procedure consists of daily administrations of this drug; the dosage is adjusted to an optimum level for that person. The medication usually has little overt effect on the individual as long as no alcohol is in the bloodstream. However, if alcohol is used when the drug is present in the body, that is, during the four or five days subsequent to the ingestion of Antabuse—the person will become violently ill. The symptoms of Antabuse in combination with alcohol include nausea, vomiting, dizziness, headache, and heart palpitations (Strecker, Ebaugh, & Ewalt, 1955).

Antabuse treatment must be initiated in a carefully controlled setting because of the strength of the physiological reaction to the drug when alcohol is ingested. For ethical as well as safety reasons, the helping professional must ensure that the patient undergoing Antabuse treatment does so voluntarily. Further, the effects of the drug must be fully explained and demonstrated to the patient.

To promote this understanding of the drug's effects, the alcoholic, while in the hospital, is given a small amount of alcohol after taking Antabuse. The individual then experiences an attenuated version of the physical symptoms associated with drinking while Antabuse is present in the body. This procedure may be repeated several times during the individual's hospitalization in order to demonstrate clearly the association between Antabuse and alcohol. For many alcoholics, Antabuse treatment has succeeded in preventing further alcohol consumption. However, Antabuse therapy may have a suppressive rather than an extinguishing effect—that is, the alcoholic will not drink after taking Antabuse but may skip the medication and consume liquor when the Antabuse is no longer present in the bloodstream.

Maria was placed on an Antabuse treatment program in order to help her terminate her drinking. She participated in the ward activities and responded well to the group milieu once she got over her initial turmoil in acknowledging that she was a patient in a mental hospital. Maria also began to take an active part in the group therapy sessions. She talked about the kinds of men she had been attracted to and how her expressed dependency on another person served to control a good part of that person's activities.

Maria continued to express the hope that she and Phil would eventually be able to solve their marital difficulties. Phil agreed to come to the hospital each day, and they participated together in a therapy group for couples with drinking problems. After two months of these sessions, Maria and Phil appeared to be somewhat more sensitive to each other's feelings. They were able to discuss alternatives to the way they usually interacted with each other.

At the end of the ten-week treatment program, Maria was hopeful that she would be able to control her drinking. She also agreed to continue on Antabuse medication as an outpatient. She and her husband decided to live together again, and they planned to petition the court to have Susan restored to them. Maria and Phil were referred to a mental health center in their area, where they could continue together in group therapy.

In light of the long-standing nature of Maria's drinking problem, the hospital staff felt that there was only a fair chance that she would be able to terminate her excessive drinking permanently. However, much could be gained if she could substantially curtail her consumption of alcohol. The prognosis for this latter possibility seemed more promising.

Discussion

The drinking pattern Maria exhibited is classified in DSM-III-R (1987) under the category of psychoactive substance use disorders, alcohol dependence. A distinction is made between psychoactive substance dependence and abuse, with dependence defined not only by physiological symptoms of withdrawal and drug tolerance, but also by cognitive and behavioral symptoms. The defining characteristic is that the individual has impaired control over the particular psychoactive substance used (alcohol, amphetamines, cannabis, cocaine, hallucinogens, etc.) and continues to use that substance despite a range of adverse consequences. The diagnostic criteria include: substance use over a longer time than intended, unsuccessful efforts to control substance use, a great deal of time spent in activities related to the substance, frequent intoxication or withdrawal symptoms evident during social, family, or work obligations, important social or other activities foregone or reduced because of substance use, continued substance use despite knowledge of problems caused by this use, symptoms of withdrawal, and symptoms of tolerance. Only three of the above criteria need be present for at least one month to make the diagnosis of alcohol dependence.

Psychodynamic theorists have suggested a number of predisposing personality traits as relevant to the etiology of chronic alcoholism. Included among these factors are unfulfilled oral dependency needs, latent homosexuality, and self-destructive impulses. However, studies comparing alcoholics with nonalcoholics have failed to reveal any consistent problem configuration in the etiology of alcoholism (Bandura, 1969; Jellinek, 1962). It also appears likely that many of the personality traits noted in alcoholic individuals are the result rather than the cause of the drinking behavior.

On the other hand, consistent evidence indicates that people with a variety of substance abuse patterns can be differentiated from those who do not exhibit these patterns by their scores on a special scale of the MMPI. This scale appears to measure a syndrome of impulsivity, high energy levels, shallow interpersonal relationships, and general psychological maladjustment (MacAndrew, 1965; Schwartz & Graham, 1979).

Alcohol has a depressant effect on the central nervous system, manifested by an inhibition of the cortical brain centers dealing with judgment and foresight. During alcohol consumption, the subcortical centers exciting strong affect are gradually released from the inhibitory control of the cortex. As a result, individuals who have ingested large amounts of alcohol can lose their critical judgment, become quite expansive in their speech, and are prone to engage in uncontrolled emotional outbursts (Snyder, 1980).

Alcohol ingestion results in a reduction of anxiety (Garfield & McBrearty, 1970), and depression in some persons. Schuckit, Pitts, Reich et al. (1969) found that a relatively high proportion of women had a history of depressive episodes either prior to the onset of problem drinking, or during periods of alcohol abstinence. For these individuals, alcohol abuse or dependence appears to be secondary to the problem of depression, and the ingestion of alcohol may serve to reduce depressive affect. However, not all persons who drink alcohol show a reduction in negative mood, which suggests individual differences in response to alcohol (Schaefer, 1978).

A number of studies have indicated a high incidence of alcoholism among family members of alcoholics (Fort & Porterfield, 1961; Tahka, 1966). Parents and other family members may model abusive alcohol use to reduce stress, as a substitute for expressing feelings, or as an integral part of daily activities. However, findings of a higher prevalence of alcoholism in the offspring of alcoholics also suggest the possibility of a biological vulnerability to alcohol dependence. This predisposition could interact with environmental factors in determining whether an offspring develops a problem drinking pattern.

Studies assessing the genetic transmission of alcoholism show relatively stronger findings for males. Goodwin, Schulsinger, Hermansen, Guze, and Winokur (1973) reported that sons of a biological alcoholic parent who had been adopted by non-relatives shortly after birth had a greater frequency of alcohol problems than a matched control group of adoptees whose biological parents had not been alcoholic. In comparing the alcoholic's sons who were adopted in infancy with the same family's nonadopted sons who were raised by the biological alcoholic parent, similar rates of alcoholism were found. For females, there were no significant differences in the frequency of alcoholism when females who had an alcoholic biological parent were compared with those who did not (Goodwin, Schulsinger, Knop, Mednick, & Guze, 1977).

Using a similar adoption strategy, Cloninger, Bohman, and Sigvardsson (1981) found a significant relationship between the biological father's recurrent alcohol abuse, criminal convictions, and low occupational status, and a moderate alcohol abuse pattern in the adopted away son. These investigators also found a higher rate of alcohol abuse among adopted daughters of an alcoholic parent, as compared with adopted daughters of biological parents who were not alcoholic (Bohman, Sigvardsson, & Cloninger, 1981). An interesting finding in these studies was an added vulnerability in the offspring if the mother was the alcoholic parent. The investigators speculate that the higher proportion of alcoholism in adopted offspring of alcoholic mothers as compared with alcoholic fathers is due to genetic factors compounded with the deleterious influence of the intrauterine environment.

Research on males who were reared in their biological families also is suggestive of possible vulnerability factors for alcoholism. Finn and Pihl (1987) studied groups of men with positive and with negative histories of alcoholism, and monitored them while they consumed a significant amount of alcohol. With alcohol, the positive family history group exhibited a marked reduction in cardiovascular reactivity to unavoidable shock, which they did not exhibit in the non-alcohol condition. The negative family history group did not exhibit cardiovascular reactivity differences to shock as a function of alcohol ingestion. Other differences in response to alcohol have been demonstrated in those with family members with alcohol problems. Schuckit (1987) found that positive family history young males rated themselves as significantly less intoxicated than did negative family history male subjects while drinking the same amount of alcohol.

The latter findings, of course, cannot separate biological vulnerability factors from family and other social experiences with alcohol. It also is important to note that the adoption studies suffer from a reliance on self-report data, a lack of careful specification of degrees of problem drinking, and a lack of objective verification of the symptoms of alcoholism (Searles, 1988). Nonetheless, the accumulated weight of these investigations suggests a statistically higher risk for alcoholism in the offspring of alcoholics. The vulnerabilities in the offspring may include increased alcohol tolerance and physiological reactivity that is reduced through the use of alcohol.

Investigations of other biological factors that might contribute to the development of alcoholism have produced negative findings. Studies of racial differences in alcohol metabolism rate demonstrated that no one group was consistently faster or slower in metabolic rate (Schaefer). In all groups, heavy drinkers had the fastest metabolic rate and nondrinkers the slowest.

Studies of alcohol sensitivity have measured responses such as flushing, heart palpitations, heavy respiration, and feelings of nausea in response to alcohol ingestion. Schaefer found a consistent trend for Asians, who have low alcoholism rates, to be highly sensitive to alcohol and become physically uncomfortable when they drink. However, the evidence regarding alcohol sensitivity and alcoholism rates is not consistent across racial and ethnic groups.

Although alcoholism has been reported to be four times as frequent in males than in females, more recent statistics suggest a closer ratio (Greenblatt & Schuckit, 1976). An interesting finding is that the alcohol absorption rate is faster for women than men, even when correcting for weight differences (Jones & Jones, 1976). Therefore, given social and psychological pressures to drink, women will reach a state of intoxication and may develop a chronic drinking problem more quickly than men. On the other hand, some women may find heavy drinking unpleasant and refrain from alcohol abuse altogether.

Social class variables have been shown to be associated with differences in attitudes about drinking by women. All social classes demonstrated less tolerance for drunken behavior in women than in men. Women of lower socioeconomic status showed a lesser approval of moderate social drinking and a greater abstention from alcohol consumption than did women of other socioeconomic groups (Lawrence & Maxwell, 1962). A related finding is that racial and ethnic groups exhibit high rates of both abstinence and heavy drinking (Lex, 1987). Other research has indicated that black women started drinking at an earlier age than white women treated for alcoholism, and were younger when they began to drink heavily and to seek treatment for their drinking (Dawkins & Harper, 1983).

The case of Maria Valdez illustrates the importance of social and family factors in the development of a particular drinking pattern. Maria grew up in a cultural setting in which there were no strong proscriptions against the consumption of liquor, although alcohol indulgence by women was less socially acceptable than in higher socioeconomic groups. Nonetheless, Maria had had the opportunity to observe both men and women engaging in excessive drinking since the time of her early childhood. Alcoholic beverages were in plentiful supply in the Valdez household, and Maria's mother provided an early model of alcohol abuse. She engaged in the type of periodic drinking that Maria adopted when she was older. Mr. Valdez usually did not drink to the point of inebriation, but he also modeled the use of liquor as an integral part of his life activities. Genetic influences in the high incidence of alcoholism among members of the Valdez family is also a possibility.

The local bar was an important recreational facility in the lower socioeconomic urban neighborhood where Maria lived. Lower social class areas also tend to be inhabited by a large proportion of alcoholics and this further increased the likelihood that the people she met would drink excessively. One of Maria's brothers who moved to the city also centered his social activities around drinking and eventually became an alcoholic.

Maria stated that she felt affection for her parents and family, but there was little evidence that she made an effort to maintain her family ties. She rarely saw her father for whom she said she particularly cared, and the longer she lived in the city, the less she saw of her other relatives.

She did not attempt to develop a warm interpersonal relationship with her sons, either, and they grew up with very little supervision and guidance. Although Maria related in a warmer and more involved manner with her daughter, her general lifestyle consisted of work, superficial relationships with male companions, and heavy drinking on the weekends. The strength and inclusiveness of this pattern left little room for extensive interactions with any family members.

With the exception of her husbands, the liaisons that Maria formed were quite transitory in nature. Her basic criterion for male companionship was that the man should be fun to be with and should spend most of his free time with her. Maria was able to control the activities of the men she lived with because she usually provided the money for food and alcohol or drugs. The threat of withholding funds until her demands were submitted to was a potent means of controlling the behavior of these individuals.

During the year before she was hospitalized, Maria's consumption of alcohol increased significantly. The intensification of her drinking may have been due to the emotional stress generated by her husband's continued attempts to intrude on her life and remove their daughter from her custody. Concomitant with the change in drinking behavior, Maria's life situation changed markedly: she lost her job, her daughter was placed in a foster home, she suffered a blackout, and she realized that she could not curtail her drinking. Therefore, the previous pattern of periodic heavy drinking lost any of its gratifying aspects because alcohol consumption was now interfering with a great many of her everyday activities. At this point, she began to consider seeking help for her drinking behavior.

Maria was further motivated to seek treatment by the example of her husband. Phil had been a heavy drinker like herself, but he had been able to terminate his drinking behavior and lead a more satisfying life. Maria found gratification in Phil's social as well as financial support and she was not permanently alienated from him by his role in having Susan placed in a foster home. Maria was influenced by Phil's pleas that she seek treatment and she eventually applied for inpatient therapy.

Although Maria entered the hospital voluntarily, she did not consider the place she was in as a mental hospital until she was confronted with the obviously psychotic behavior of some of the patients from other wards. It is possible that Maria was genuinely unaware of the nature of the hospital she came to, but it is also apparent that she did not pay attention to the cues suggesting that she was entering a mental hospital. Maria therefore continued to behave in a manner consistent with a lifelong pattern of ignoring or avoiding unpleasant environmental circumstances. When she first realized that she was in a mental hospital, she became extremely agitated because she was afraid that she also would be considered insane.

Since none of the patients on Maria's ward behaved in a disturbed manner, she gradually began to feel more comfortable in the hospital. With Phil's emotional support and shared participation in the couples' group, Maria started to make some progress in therapy. She gradually learned how to relate to others socially without liquor. She also began to verbalize and communicate her feelings, an important skill that could serve as an alternative to drinking alcohol when emotionally aroused.

Formal group therapy and other group situations such as Alcoholics Anonymous have proven helpful in modifying the behavior of excessive drinkers (Smart, 1974). The opportunity to interact with others manifesting similar problems is an important source of social support. The group can serve as an extremely powerful source of reward for sustained abstinence, as well as a source of disapproval for continued alcohol indulgence.

A number of studies have been conducted evaluating the efficacy of teaching alcoholics how to engage in controlled drinking, in comparison with focusing on a goal of total abstinence. The findings of long-term outcome studies assessing controlled drinking have been controversial, with numerous questions raised about the methodology and interpretation of the study findings. Some investigations of controlled drinking treatment procedures indicated that those who had the most positive long-term outcome progressed on their own to alcohol abstinence (Rychtarik, Foy, Scott, Lokey, & Prue, 1987). Marlatt (1979) and others have concluded that the controlled drinking paradigm seems more appropriate for persons beginning to develop alcohol problems than for those with long-standing problems of alcohol abuse.

In Maria's case, it is possible that she will be able to substantially curtail her drinking behavior if there is a change in her social interaction patterns. Therefore, it is extremely important that she avoid the situations that previously elicited alcohol intake, such as spending evenings at a bar. The use of Antabuse to suppress alcohol consumption should be particularly helpful in providing Maria with the opportunity to learn new social skills unrelated to drinking behavior.

Maria did not exhibit the depressed behavior often observed in alcoholics who have recently stopped drinking. She seemed to receive social support for avoiding alcohol consumption from a number of persons who were significant to her, including her husband and the other members of her therapy group. Further, she could perceive that her overall life situation had a strong potential for improvement if she refrained from using alcohol. For Maria and her husband, the continuation of group therapy on an outpatient basis would seem to be a crucial factor in sustaining the modification of their long-standing drinking patterns.

References

American Psychiatric Association (1987). *Diagnostic and statistical manual of mental disorders* (3rd ed., rev.) (DSM-III-R). Washington, DC: Author.

Bandura, A. (1969). *Principles of behavior modification.* New York: Holt, Rinehart, & Winston.

Bohman, M., Sigvardsson, S., & Cloninger, C. R. (1981). Maternal inheritance of alcohol abuse. *Archives of General Psychiatry, 38,* 965–969.

Cloninger, C. R., Bohman, M., & Sigvardsson, S. (1981). Inheritance of alcohol abuse. *Archives of General Psychiatry, 38,* 861–868.

Dawkins, M. P., & Harper, F. D. (1983). Alcoholism among women: A comparison of black and white problem drinkers. *International Journal of Addictions, 18,* 333–349.

Finn, P. R., & Pihl, R. O. (1987). Men at high risk for alcoholism: The effect of alcohol on cardiovascular response to unavoidable shock. *Journal of Abnormal Psychology, 96,* 230–236.

Fort, T., & Porterfield, A. L. (1961). Some backgrounds and types of alcoholism among women. *Journal of Health and Human Behavior, 2,* 283–292.

Garfield, Z. H., & McBrearty, J. F. (1970). Arousal level and stimulus response in alcoholics after drinking. *Quarterly Journal of Studies on Alcohol, 31,* 832–838.

Goodwin, D. W., Schulsinger, F., Hermansen, L., Guze, S. B., & Winokur, G. (1973). Alcohol problems in adoptees raised apart from alcoholic biological parents. *Archives of General Psychiatry, 28,* 238–243.

Goodwin, D. W., Schulsinger, F., Knop, J., Mednick, S., & Guze, S. B. (1977). Alcoholism and depression in adopted-out daughters of alcoholics. *Archives of General Psychiatry, 34,* 751–755.

Greenblatt, M., & Schuckit, M. A. (Eds.) (1976). *Alcoholism problems in women and children.* New York: Grune & Stratton.

Jellinek, E. M., (1962). Phases of alcohol addiction. In D. J. Pittman, & C. R. Snyder (Eds.), *Society, culture, and drinking patterns.* New York: Wiley.

Jones, B. M., & Jones, M. K. (1976). Women and alcohol: Intoxication, metabolism, and the menstrual cycle. In M. Greenblatt, & M. A. Schuckit (Eds.), *Alcoholism problems in women and children* (pp. 103–136). New York: Grune & Stratton.

Lawrence, J. J., & Maxwell, M. A. (1962). Drinking and socioeconomic status. In D. J. Pittman, & C. R. Snyder (Eds.), *Society, culture, and drinking patterns.* New York: Wiley.

Lex, B. W. (1987). Review of alcohol problems in ethnic minority groups. *Journal of Consulting and Clinical Psychology, 55,* 293–300.

MacAndrew, C. (1965). The differentiation of male alcoholic outpatients from nonalcoholic psychiatric patients by means of the MMPI. *Quarterly Journal of Studies on Alcohol, 26,* 238–246.

Marlatt, G. A. (1979). Alcohol use and problem drinking: A cognitive-behavioral analysis. In P.C. Kendall & S. Hollon (Eds.), *Cognitive-behavioral interventions: Theory, research, and procedures* (pp. 319–355). New York: Academic Press.

Rychtarik, R. G., Foy, D. W., Scott, T., Lokey, L., & Prue, D. M. (1987). Five-six-year follow-up of broad spectrum behavioral treatment for alcoholism: Effects of training controlled drinking skills. *Journal of Consulting and Clinical Psychology, 55,* 106–108.

Schaefer, J. M. (1978). Alcohol metabolism and sensitivity reactions among the Reddis of South India. *Alcoholism: Clinical and Experimental Research, 2,* 61–69.

Schuckit, M. A. (1987). Biological vulnerability to alcoholism. *Journal of Consulting and Clinical Psychology, 55,* 301–309.

Schuckit, M. A., Pitts, F. N. Jr., Reich, T. et al. (1969). Alcoholism. I. Two types of alcoholism in women. *Archives of General Psychiatry, 20,* 301–306.

Schwartz, M. F., & Graham, J. R. (1979). Construct validity of the MacAndrew alcoholism scale. *Journal of Consulting and Clinical Psychology, 47,* 1090–1095.

Searles, J. S. (1988). The role of genetics in the pathogenesis of alcoholism. *Journal of Abnormal Psychology, 97,* 153–167.

Smart, R. G. (1974). Employed alcoholics treated voluntarily and under constructive coercion. *Quarterly Journal of Studies on Alcohol, 35,* 196–209.

Snyder, S. H. (1980). *Biological aspects of mental disorder.* New York: Oxford University Press.

Strecker, E. A., Ebaugh, F. G., & Ewalt, J. R. (1955). *Practical clinical psychiatry* (7th ed.). New York: McGraw-Hill.

Tahka, V. (1966). *The alcoholic personality.* Helsinki, Finland: Finnish Foundation for Alcohol Studies.

14

Distress about Sexual Orientation—
The Case of
Michael Boland

Michael Boland was 21 years old when he phoned for an appointment at a local guidance clinic. He indicated that a woman friend had suggested he call. He stated that he was extremely shy and anxious, and wanted help with these problems.

Michael came from a white, lower-middle-class environment. At the time the client was seen, his father was working in a small welding shop, and his mother had died of cancer six months earlier. Michael, the youngest of three children, was the only boy in the family. His sister Patricia was 26, and another sister Carol was 23. Both were married and lived in the area. The members of the family all practiced the Catholic religion and attended church regularly.

Michael looked younger than his 21 years. His slender physique, wavy hair, long lashes, and even features, gave him an air of prettiness. He wore conspicuously stylish clothes and jewelry, with every article carefully matched. During the interviews, he spoke in an extremely low tone of voice which made it difficult to hear him across the desk.

Family Background

Michael described his mother as sweet, kind, and sensitive, and he said that he had been very close to her. Even though she had become progressively ill over a number of years, Michael found it difficult to get used to the fact that she was dead. He said that his mother had always been very protective in her relationship with him, and he missed not having the guidance and concern that his mother had continually provided.

Neither parent had given Michael any sexual information. He reported that sex was a taboo subject in his household, except for his mother's comments that premarital sexual relationships were sinful. Michael had never told his mother that he was sexually attracted to males. However, on a number of occasions he had related to her his discomfort in social situations with girls, particularly those his own age. Mrs. Boland had always responded by assuring Michael that he was still too young to worry about girls, and that it was more important for him to be concerned about his future career. She said there was plenty of time for him to go out on dates and think of marriage, and that eventually he would find a nice girl. In the meantime, Mrs. Boland felt it was important for Michael not to get mixed up with "the wrong crowd," and she encouraged him to participate in family rather than peer group social activities.

Whenever Michael went out in the evening, his mother stayed awake until he got home and she expressed relief that he had returned without any mishaps befalling him. Michael would then feel extremely guilty because his mother was ill, and worry and apprehension about his welfare had kept her awake. Michael said that his mother had not been as overprotective with his two sisters as she had been with him. She had not discouraged Carol from going out on dates, as long as she knew the people with whom Carol was going to be out. Michael felt that his mother was genuinely pleased when Carol got married at the age of 19, and he recalled that the courtship and wedding period of his eldest sister Patricia was also a happy and exciting time. The client stated that both of his sisters were happily married, but he did not feel very close to either of his brothers-in-law.

Michael characterized his relationship with his father as one of coolness and distance. He said that he had never felt a deep emotional bond with his father, and they rarely had any extended conversations. The client reported that his father had been aware of Mrs. Boland's overprotectiveness toward Michael, but Mr. Boland had never commented on this relationship nor attempted to change it.

Mr. Boland had no hobbies, and he spent a great deal of time watching television. He rarely saw the few acquaintances he had, and Michael felt that his father did not really like being with people that much because he was bitter that he had not been more successful economically. Michael never discussed vocational plans with his father. Mr. Boland made no comments about Michael's ambition to become a fashion designer, nor did he express an interest in the special courses Michael was taking in fashion design.

Since Mrs. Boland's death, Mr. Boland had become even less communicative with Michael. Although they both shared the same house, Michael and his father hardly talked to each other. Michael prepared meals for the two of them, and several times a week they ate dinner at Carol's or Patricia's house. Michael usually went out in the evenings, and his father rarely asked him where he was going or commented on what time it was when Michael returned.

Interpersonal Background

The client reported that his sisters had related to him in a protective manner ever since he was a child, and they still frequently pampered and fussed over him. He felt very close to his sisters, and thought of Patricia as a second mother. When he first started school, Carol took him to class every day and made sure that he got there on time. Mrs. Boland told Carol to be certain that Michael was neat when he got to school, and Carol always combed his hair or tucked his shirt in before she let him enter the classroom. The client stated that he was well behaved and somewhat shy throughout his school career, and he rarely got into difficulty with any of the teachers. Most of his teachers were women, and he frequently became the "teacher's pet" because of his good behavior and cooperativeness.

Michael was nonassertive with his peers, outside school as well as in. He said that he never felt the other boys accepted him because he was not good at sports. Michael stated that he had never possessed the skills necessary to play baseball or running games well, and no one had ever coached him in these games. He reported that his build had always been slender and he frequently caught colds. He found it more comfortable to follow along with one of his sisters and her friends, or play alone, than to play games with children his own age. His sisters were expected to watch him, and they encouraged him to stay with them. As a child, he would usually play with one particular boy from time to time, but he often played with girls when he interacted at all with peers.

The adolescent period was a time of great turmoil for Michael. He began to masturbate frequently, and he felt guilty because he thought he was doing something wrong that could harm him in some way. Michael was troubled with a skin problem during adolescence and he was very self-conscious about the pimples on his face. Although he recognized that most teenagers have this problem, he felt that his skin condition was more severe and noticeable than any other youngster's.

Michael revealed that when a young adolescent, he became increasingly aware that he was sexually aroused by males rather than females. He was puzzled and greatly ashamed, and did not discuss this discovery with anyone. He was intensely worried because he felt that there was something wrong with him that made him so different from his peers.

Michael made some efforts to engage in social activities with girls while in high school. He did not feel comfortable being alone with a girl in a situation that might lead to some type of sexual activity. Nonetheless, over a seven-month period during his junior year in high school, he occasionally went to the movies with a particular young woman. She was three years older than he, and they had kissed each other on occasion. Michael stated that eventually he stopped calling her because he wanted to avoid any possibility of further sexual activity.

During the high school period, Michael had maintained a relationship with another boy from school. They appeared to have been initially drawn toward each other because neither shared the interests of the other youngsters in the class. At a period when many of the boys were talking about real or fantasized sexual exploits with girls, Michael and his friend Tom had little to offer to this conversation. They tended to become anxious or embarrassed by the other boys' comments. Through being friends with each other, Michael and Tom could avoid the general discussion about girls, and they were less likely to become the target of the other boys' teasing. Tom introduced Michael to mutual masturbation, and at a later period, to fellatio and anal intercourse.

Michael indicated that he and Tom still felt a warm affection for one another, but after graduation, each had gone his separate way. Michael began to frequent homosexual bars at irregular intervals, but his mother did not allow him to spend every evening out of the house. He stated that many of the men he met at the bars were physically attracted to him, and this was a very enjoyable experience. Michael also said that he derived a great deal of physical pleasure from homosexual activity. The client had engaged in a number of homosexual encounters when his mother was still alive, and these relationships increased in frequency after her death. He said that he was not in love with any single person, but he enjoyed receiving attention and flattery from the many men he met at gay bars.

Michael reported that he was often greatly troubled by the rights and wrongs of his sexual behavior, and thought he was committing a sin. He had never been able to discuss these concerns with his parish priest, or with any members of his family. At the time Michael was seen, he had several female friends who were fellow students at the school of fashion design, and mostly older than he. He maintained friendly, platonic relationships with these women, and they appeared to enjoy his company. Michael had confided to one of them that he felt extremely guilty about his sexual orientation, and it was this woman who suggested that Michael contact the clinic.

During the clinic interview, Michael indicated that he still felt that he had a poor complexion, even though no blemishes were apparent to the interviewer. Michael stated that he always was conscious of his physical appearance, and had never thought of himself as physically attractive to females. However, he indicated that many males were attracted by his physical appearance because a slight stature is considered physically desirable in the gay community. Michael revealed that he has never experienced sexual excitement in response to females and has not attempted heterosexual intercourse.

Psychological Evaluation

Michael was seen by a female psychologist, Dr. T. The client appeared to be quite anxious during the first interview, and he tended to speak in a quavering and barely audible tone of voice. He found it difficult to maintain eye contact with the examiner, and often looked off to one side or down at his hands. He stated that one of the reasons that he had come for evaluation was to find out why he was so nervous and high-strung. The client also complained of a lack of self-confidence and of being socially naive and immature. His major concern, however, was that he was attracted to members of the same sex. Michael cooperated readily with the examiner and performed the tasks asked of him during the psychological evaluation. After his initial anxiety lessened, he smiled more frequently and began to initiate some conversation. He also helped the examiner put away the test materials at the end of the testing session.

The client completed a general personality inventory, the MMPI. He was asked to give stories to a number of cards from the Thematic Apperception Test (TAT), in order to gain more information about social relationships and interaction patterns. Michael also completed the Assertive Questionnaire (Lazarus, 1971).

There was evidence on the test material of anxiety, depression, and repetitive and bothersome thoughts. The client, however, was not overwhelmed by his personal difficulties. On the contrary, a number of his responses indicated an expectation that he would eventually be able to solve his problems and be a success in life.

Michael expressed a continued concern about behaving as one is "supposed to" or "ought to." He depicted many of the persons on the TAT cards as being punished for wrongdoings, and the punishment was viewed as an expected and justified retribution. Another theme evident in the stories he told was that of an individual who had a number of weaknesses beyond his personal control. Despite these weaknesses, the person is able to be successful and proud of himself. The following excerpt from one of the TAT stories illustrates this theme: "He is very strong and muscular, but he has other weaknesses over which he has no control. But he still thinks that he is a great person and he ends up to be a success."

Michael's responses to the test material suggested a lack of clarity about sexual identification. Some of the figures on the TAT cards were initially labeled as female, then seen as male. He did not delineate a number of other percepts seen as human figures as either masculine or feminine, but described them in the neuter gender. Older male figures were pictured as helpful persons, but individuals to whom one could not get close. He tended to view females his own age as physically unattractive and artificial, but recognized that other men might see women as desirable. Michael responded very negatively to concepts about his own body, and he described himself as physically awkward and in need of improving his appearance. He also indicated that he sometimes wished he were a girl.

The client's responses to the Assertive Questionnaire indicated that he typically interacted with others in a nonassertive manner. For example, he responded "yes" to the following items: "Are you always very careful to avoid all trouble with other people?" "When a person is blatantly unfair, do you usually fail to say something about it to him?" "Would you be hesitant about asking a good friend to lend you a few dollars?"

In general, the test results confirmed the information that had been gained from the interview.

Course of Therapy

Therapy was recommended in order to help Michael deal with his inner turmoil and guilt feelings about his sexual orientation, and to aid him in modifying his shy and dependent behavior. The goal of therapy was to enable him to make future decisions, including the selection of a sexual partner, on the basis of a more open choice, rather than because of poor interpersonal skills. Therapy with an older man was recommended, so

Michael would have a male to model his behavior after. The therapist would also be available to counsel the client on the techniques of heterosexual activity, if the client expressed an interest in obtaining this information. Michael responded quite favorably to the advice that he enter therapy, and accepted the suggestion that he see a male therapist. He expressed disappointment that he would not be continuing with Dr. T., but he was able to establish good rapport with the recommended therapist.

The initial therapy sessions were devoted to a discussion of Michael's feelings of guilt about his homosexual behavior, and his attitude that he was inferior and unattractive. Dr. E. encouraged Michael to express his feelings, and asked him to cite specific situations in which he had felt inadequate. It was apparent from Michael's comments that his feelings of inadequacy stemmed in large part from a lack of social skills in interacting with other persons, male as well as female. Dr. E. and Michael examined in detail the social events in which Michael had acted in a manner he considered inadequate. Dr. E. pointed out to Michael the effect of his behavior on other persons, and how others' responses in turn influenced the way Michael interacted with them.

The client brought up a recent event that was troubling him, and the therapist was able to demonstrate to Michael the relationship between Michael's behavior and the responses of those around him. The client described a situation that had occurred at school when he was doing some sketches of fashion designs. A young woman in his class asked to see his book of drawings, and he readily let her look at the book. She later handed in some sketches that were quite similar to the ones Michael had drawn. When the class as a whole evaluated each other's work, a number of students commented on the similarity between Michael's and Susan's drawings. Michael felt that Susan implied that she had done her sketches first, and that he had copied from her. Michael did not make any comments to Susan or to any of the other class members during the discussion and evaluation of the sketches. Further, he did not tell anyone that Susan had looked at his sketches before she had done her own.

Michael said that he was very upset by this episode, and he felt that Susan had taken advantage of him. He thought that his sketches were quite good, and felt that they had been devalued because of the suggestion that he had obtained his ideas from Susan. Michael reported that he was very angry at Susan and humiliated by the episode. He went directly home after class and stayed there for the rest of the day. His father did not notice that Michael was upset, and Michael did not say anything to Mr. Boland about the incident. When Michael saw Susan in class the next day, he made it a point to sit at the opposite end of the room from her, and in general, tried to ignore her.

Dr. E. pointed out how well this incident illustrated Michael's typical nonassertive, compliant behavioral style. Dr. E. discussed how passive compliant behavior could encourage others to take advantage of him, particularly when he made no effort to assert his rights. Because Michael's habitual response to interpersonal difficulties was to withdraw from the situation, the withdrawal reinforced Susan's behavior. Michael's withdrawal pattern also prevented him from engaging in more effective and mature ways of dealing with other persons.

Dr. E. employed the behavior therapy technique of assertion training (Wolpe & Lazarus, 1966) to teach Michael how to deal with others in a more effective and satisfying manner. He asked Michael to suggest other behaviors that he might have employed to handle the situation that was troubling him. When client and therapist then role-played a number of Michael's suggested alternatives, the inadequacies of some of Michael's initial solutions were quickly apparent. Eventually, Michael made a suggestion that seemed an adaptive, assertive response to both himself and the therapist. Michael acted out this role, while Dr. E. role-played the reciprocal changes in Susan's behavior. Michael then assumed Susan's role, and Dr. E. role-played the assertive behavior Michael had suggested. This latter procedure enabled Michael to gain a better understanding of how a change in behavior on his part would in turn affect another person's behavior. Dr. E. advised Michael to continue practicing the more assertive behavioral role when he was at home, and he also encouraged him to act more assertively in interpersonal situations. The therapist pointed out that an individual's feelings of self-esteem and self-worth depend a great deal on the way other people respond to him or her.

The issue of Michael's sexual orientation was discussed at length. The client reported that he experienced a great deal of physical gratification from engaging in homosexual behavior, and he had no interest in sexual activity with someone of the opposite sex. He said that the problem that troubled him most was his guilt feelings because of a religious belief that his sexual behavior was sinful. He also recognized the attitude of the majority of persons in our society that homosexuality is a behavior pattern to be scorned, or viewed as a sign of emotional disorder. Many of the therapy sessions were devoted to discussions about Michael's guilt feelings, and the need to differentiate between the motivation for changing his sexual orientation and the desire for societal acceptance of his behavior.

Dr. E. encouraged Michael to participate in social activities and dates with women in order to ascertain whether the lack of sexual arousal with women was due to social anxiety and poor assertive skills. He suggested that one of the ways Michael could overcome his feelings of inadequacy was through practice in the social skills necessary for interacting with others. The therapist also suggested that Michael go out with a woman whose company he enjoyed, and he should not be concerned about whether he was becoming sexually aroused by her. If the client felt physically attracted to one of the women he enjoyed dating, Dr. E. could then counsel him on heterosexual techniques.

During the course of therapy, Michael continued to frequent homosexual bars, and he engaged in homosexual activity about once or twice a week. He tended to go out with different men, rather than gravitate to a relationship with one particular individual. However, he followed the therapist's suggestion and also dated a number of women his own age. The client reported that he did not experience anxiety and these occasions were somewhat enjoyable, but he had not become sexually aroused by any of the women he had been with. He had kissed one of his female dates good night and had held her hand, but that was the extent of physical contact. Michael noted that he felt more relaxed being out with a woman than he had previously. However, he continued to express a preference for homosexual activity.

At the end of one year of treatment, Michael said that he wished to continue in therapy for a while longer. He stated that he felt more confident and less anxious than he had when he started therapy, but his major problem was still his feelings of guilt about his homosexual behavior. Although he could now enjoy himself on a date with a woman, he was not interested in sexual activities with the opposite sex. Therapy was terminated approximately two months later because Michael felt that he was able to deal with others in a more comfortable and satisfying manner.

Discussion

This case illustrates the role of societal agents including the family and religious institutions in the etiology of concerns about one's sexual preferences. It became clear during the course of therapy that Michael's anxiety, guilt, and depression were not due to a wish to change his sexual orientation. The uncomfortable emotions he experienced were due to a realistic perception of the attitudes of the greater society about his sexual behavior. Exploration in therapy indicated that his sexual preference was not a sexual *disorder* as defined by a strong motivation to change his sexual orientation. His distress was secondary to his view of family and societal attitudes about his sexual preference.

According to DSM-III-R (1987) criteria, Michael might be viewed as suffering from an identity disorder because of the severe distress he was experiencing regarding a number of aspects of his life. This diagnosis centers on uncertainty or concerns about a variety of developmental issues including one's sexual orientation, long-term goals, career choice, friendship patterns, religious and moral values, and group loyalties. These uncertainties result in difficulties in integrating aspects of oneself into an acceptable self-concept. A common age of onset of these concerns is late adolescence, as value systems change and the individual attempts to establish independence from his or her parents. A related criterion for the diagnostic classification of an identity disorder is an impairment in social or occupational functioning that results from at least three of the above concerns for a duration of at least three months.

Whether homosexual behavior is a form of psychopathology or a normal variation in sexual preference has been hotly debated by professional as well as laypersons. Changing attitudes on this issue are reflected in the 1973 decision of the American Psychiatric Association, with the strong backing of the American Psychological Association, to remove the category of homosexuality from the DSM-II (1968) classification of mental disorders. However, because of active lobbying by some practitioners who strongly believe homosexuality is a form of mental disorder, a compromise solution was reached in DSM-III (1980). At that time, ego-dystonic homosexuality was included under the general category of psychosexual disorders, defined as an unwanted sexual preference that is a constant source of distress because of a persistent concern about changing one's sexual orientation. The 1987 DSM-III-R category of sexual disorder not otherwise specified is vaguer, designating "persistent and marked distress about one's sexual orientation" (p. 296).

Psychoanalytic theory has posited that homosexuality is a pathological disorder in which the normal object (a person of the opposite sex) is replaced by an unnatural sexual object (Alexander & Shapiro, 1952). Homosexual behavior in males is proposed to be caused by the young boy's fixation on the mother, resulting in intense castration anxiety during the Oedipal period as the youngster highly fears the father's retaliation for sexually desiring the mother. The conflict is resolved by replacing the incestuous sexual object (the mother) with a sexual object of the boy's own sex.

Current research on sexual preference has focused on biological factors that influence sexual orientation. Money (1987) extensively reviewed the literature on hormonal factors in the genesis of sexual behavior in humans and in animals. He concluded that in animal studies and in human clinical data, there is strong evidence that prenatal dysfunction of maternal sexual hormones (testosterone and androgen) can influence the subsequent sexual status of the offspring as homosexual or bisexual. Money refutes the notion that sexual preference is a voluntary choice, and proposes that sexual orientation is locked into the brain through prenatal influences and experiences. If a male fetus receives too little secretion of testosterone and androgen from the mother's bloodstream, neuroanatomical changes in the fetus' brain will result in a bisexual or homosexual predisposition. Similarly, a maternal hormonal imbalance that causes the female fetus to have contact with an excess of masculinizing hormones could result in a bisexual or homosexual predisposition in the female offspring.

In humans, sexual orientation is dependent on both prenatal hormonalization and its effects on postnatal socialization. Therefore, environmental experiences are important as well as biological influences. Money suggested that hormonal imbalances in the mother may occur secondary to nutritional, medicinal, or stress-induced endocrine changes. The ultimate result in the offspring is that the releasing hormones for sexual arousal may secrete in response to same-sex rather than opposite-sex stimuli. This change in function of the releasing hormones may explain why many homosexual individuals report early experiences of sexual arousal to persons of the same sex, and a lack of sexual arousal to persons of the opposite sex.

Money's analysis places homosexual orientation within the context of hormonal rather than psychopathological influences, and also provides an explanation for why most homosexual individuals do not wish to change their sexual orientation even if they were able to do so (Weinberg & Williams, 1974). Because the releasing hormones for sexual arousal are triggered by same-sex stimuli, sexual pleasure occurs in the context of homosexual relationships, and therefore both biological and social learning processes are in operation to maintain a homosexual orientation.

The advent of the disease of AIDS (acquired immune deficiency syndrome) has drastically changed the life experiences of homosexual, bisexual, and other high risk group members. Within the past ten years, there appeared to have been a greater acceptance of homosexuality as an alternate life style, and federal statutes as well as laws in many states were enacted barring discrimination against individuals based on sexual orientation. However, at present there seems to be a backlash of prejudice against and fears of male homosexuals, related to the increasing incidence and public information about AIDS. Concurrently, the spread of illness and deaths in the gay community from AIDS and associated diseases is likely to have a significant impact on the mood and general psychological well-being of homosexual and bisexual individuals. The intense anxiety engendered in those testing positive for HIV (human immunodeficiency virus) or the fear that they will test positive at a future time also has a strong influence on current levels of stress and psychological adjustment. Therefore, studies conducted at the present time comparing the psychological well-being of homosexual and heterosexual persons will undoubtedly reflect the tremendous impact the illness of AIDS has had on the homosexual group. However, the validity of past studies of childhood and family history factors in the development of sexual orientation should not be affected by these current issues.

Michael Boland sought treatment for concerns related to his sexual orientation a number of years before the disease of AIDS was evident. Research assessing the general psychological functioning of male homosexual as compared with appropriately matched heterosexual groups prior to the advent of AIDS indicated no differences in overall present adjustment between the two groups (Bell, Weinberg, & Hammersmith, 1981; Weinberg & Williams). However, studies of male homosexuals sampled from the general population or assessed while in treatment found that a substantial proportion reported that during childhood they were fearful of physical injury and avoided physical fights and competitive games (Bieber, 1962; Evans, 1969; Thompson, Schwartz, McCandless, & Edwards, 1973). On the other hand, Siegelman (1974) found that subsamples of male homosexuals and heterosexuals who scored low on neuroticism were not significantly different in their reports of relationships with their father and mother. This array of findings emphasizes the fact that individual differences in family history and psychological functioning are evident in most groups one studies. It therefore is not scientifically valid to make generalizations about a group as if it were a unitary entity. Considering all homosexuals as comprising one homogeneous category seems just as erroneous as considering all heterosexuals as a homogeneous group.

Michael Boland's sexual orientation can be understood from the perspective of an interaction of biological and psychological processes, based on his report that he had never experienced sexual arousal in relation to females. Although there is no way at present to "prove" that this phenomenon has a strong biological basis, the research reviewed by Money is persuasive in suggesting that prenatal hormonal influences are important in the sexual orientation of the offspring. However, sexual orientation also will be influenced by one's social learning history, as it interacts with brain predispositions for the secretion of releasing hormones for sexual arousal.

An analysis of the interpersonal relationships that Michael experienced also points to the influence of the processes of reinforcement and modeling in shaping his behavior, including his sexual orientation.

Michael was in continual contact with his mother and sisters while he was growing up. He saw very little of his father, and communicated with him still less. Since Michael frequently interacted with the female members of his family, they were very potent sources of reinforcement, and behavioral role models. He learned that he would gain attention and approval from his mother and sisters when he acted in a passive and dependent manner.

Michael had very little opportunity to interact with his peers because of Mrs. Boland's overprotectiveness. He therefore was deprived of the chance to regularly observe the role behavior of male members of his peer group, outside of the school setting. He was not able to learn the social and physical play skills necessary for peer acceptance, because he did not play very frequently with youngsters of his own age. As Michael grew older, there was a greater and greater discrepancy between his behavior and what his peer group considered acceptable behavior for males. Peer group interactions were not an important source of social gratification until Michael was in high school. However, Michael always had been able to gain social approval from his mother and sisters. Throughout Michael's life, they reinforced him for behaving in a nonassertive, home-oriented manner.

In Michael's case, his body build, which is a constitutional factor, seems to have provided an additional influence on the pattern of interests and peer relationships in which he engaged. Michael was very thin and somewhat sickly as a child. These problems might have caused his mother to be more protective of him and reinforce dependency behavior more than she might have if Michael had been stronger and more active. Michael's thin stature made it difficult for him to compete in sports, and he was ridiculed because of his body build. One of the reasons that he withdrew from playing with other boys was because of this ridicule. As Michael grew older, his physical stature remained slight, and it is likely that his interests in more passive or stereotypically "feminine" activities continued to be influenced by his physical capacity as well as already learned skills.

Michael was never comfortable dating young women because of a general lack of skill in interacting with persons of his own age. He also was concerned about expectations his female dates might have about engaging in sexual activities. When he did go out with a young woman, his choice was someone a number of years older than he. Michael seemed more able to relate to a companion who was similar in age to one of his sisters, who were both predictable and nonthreatening persons in his life experience. He clearly was more comfortable with women who did not expect a sexual relationship with him.

Michael's first adolescent friendship and sexual experience with his friend Tom proved to be a pleasurable encounter. In contrast to the feelings of inadequacy and discomfort he experienced when interacting with members of the opposite sex, Michael's relationship with another male was quite satisfying. He did not think that he had to prove himself physically, and he felt accepted as he was. His friend was more sexually experienced than he and able to provide Michael with a gratifying homosexual encounter. During later sexual relationships between the two, Michael experienced even greater gratification.

Although Michael received a great deal of immediate sexual satisfaction from his homosexual activities, he felt very guilty afterwards. The guilt feelings stemmed from his strict and moralistic upbringing, which continually viewed issues in terms of good-and-evil or right-and-wrong. The client's mother emphasized that there were certain ways in which one "ought" to behave. Sexual activities, in general, were termed sinful and the result of bad peer influences. Michael also was sensitive to the attitude that many persons in our society have about homosexual behavior. When he frequented gay bars, he experienced a feeling of belonging to a group that was estranged from society. This feeling of estrangement was uncomfortable, because the rules Michael learned during his strict upbringing always stressed the importance of acting in a "good" or socially acceptable manner.

When Mrs. Boland died, Michael felt her loss quite keenly and thought of her a great deal. These thoughts included recollections of his mother's moral principles, and Michael felt very guilty because he was continuing to engage in homosexual behavior. However, the sexual gratification he received was intense and immediate, and the guilt feelings did not occur until after the homosexual encounter.

An increasingly shared belief among therapists of a number of theoretical persuasions is that each person should be free to live his or her own life as long as that person does not hurt or interfere with another's freedom (Rogers, 1961; Szasz, 1965). In this context, a client who comes for treatment because of concerns about sexual orientation but continues to express a preference for homosexual activity would not be influenced by the therapist to change to a heterosexual mode of behavior. One also might question whether sexual orientation, once strongly established, can actually be changed. One way of judging therapeutic success is whether the client is able to interact with others in a comfortable manner that does not hurt another individual, and if there is a reduction in conflict and stress by the end of treatment. In Michael's case the evidence of therapeutic success was the fact that he was more accepting of and less distressed by his sexual orientation. He also made significant progress in acting in a more assertive manner in interpersonal situations. Both of these therapeutic developments helped make his general life circumstances more comfortable.

References

Alexander, F., & Shapiro, L. B. (1952). Neuroses, behavior disorders, and perversions. In F. Alexander & H. Ross (Eds.), *Dynamic psychiatry*. Chicago: University of Chicago Press.

American Psychiatric Association (1968). *Diagnostic and statistical manual of mental disorders* (2nd ed.) (DSM-II). Washington, DC: Author.

American Psychiatric Association (1980). *Diagnostic and statistical manual of mental disorders* (3rd ed.) (DSM-III). Washington, DC: Author.

American Psychiatric Association (1987). *Diagnostic and statistical manual of mental disorders* (3rd ed., rev.) (DSM-III-R). Washington, DC: Author.

Bell, A., Weinberg, M. S., & Hammersmith, S. K. (1981). *Sexual preference*. Bloomington, IN: Indiana University Press.

Bieber, I. (1962). *Homosexuality: A psychoanalytic study*. New York: Basic Books.

Evans, R. B. (1969). Childhood parental relationships of homosexual men. *Journal of Consulting and Clinical Psychology, 33*, 129–135.

Lazarus, A. A. (1971). *Behavior therapy and beyond*. New York: McGraw-Hill.

Money, J. (1987). Sin, sickness, or status? Homosexual gender identity and psychoneuroendocrinology. *American Psychologist, 42*, 384–399.

Rogers, C. R. (1961). *On becoming a person: A therapist's view of psychotherapy*. Boston: Houghton Mifflin.

Siegelman, M. (1974). Parental background of male homosexuals and heterosexuals. *Archives of Sexual Behavior, 3*, 3–18.

Szasz, T. S. (1965). *The ethics of psychoanalysis*. New York: Basic Books.

Thompson, N. L., Jr., Schwartz, D. M., McCandless, B. R. & Edwards, D. A. (1973). Parent-child relationships and sexual identity in male and female homosexuals and heterosexuals. *Journal of Consulting and Clinical Psychology, 41*, 120–127.

Weinberg, M., & Williams, C. J. (1974). *Male homosexuals: Their problems and adaptations in three societies*. New York: Oxford University Press.

Wolpe, J., & Lazarus, A. A. (1966). *Behavior therapy techniques*. Oxford: Pergamon Press.

15

Major Depression—
"I Die a Little When I Cry"

A young woman called a local counseling center on the advice of her company physician. Angela Savanti was 22 years old, lived at home with her mother, and was employed as a secretary in a large insurance company. She stated that she had had passing periods of "the blues" before, but her present feelings of despondency were of much greater proportion. She was troubled by a severe depression and frequent crying spells, which had not lessened over the past two months. Angela found it hard to concentrate on her job, had great difficulty falling asleep at night, and had a poor appetite. She said her depression began after she and her boyfriend Jerry broke up two months previously.

Angela was dressed neatly when she appeared for her first interview. She was attractive, but her eyes were puffy and ringed with dark circles. She answered questions and related information about her life history in a slow, flat tone of voice, which had an impersonal quality to it. She sat stiffly in her chair with her hands in her lap, and moved very little throughout the interview.

The client stated that the time period just before she and her boy-friend terminated their relationship had been one of extreme emotional turmoil. She was not sure whether she wanted to marry Jerry, and he began to demand that she decide either one way or the other. Mrs. Savanti did not seem to like Jerry and was very cold and aloof whenever he came to the house. Angela felt caught in the middle and unable to make a decision about her future. After several confrontations with Jerry over whether she would marry him or not, he told her he felt that she would never decide, so he was not going to see her anymore.

Angela stated that she was both relieved and upset that Jerry had forced the issue and essentially made the decision for her. She did not attempt to contact him but became increasingly depressed. She stayed home from work several times during the past month and just sat around the house and cried.

Family Background

Angela came from a working-class family of Italian origin. Her only sibling was a sister Doreen, two years younger than she. Both sets of grandparents emigrated from Italy, and her parents were born in the United States. The Savanti family lived in a neighborhood of predominantly Italian ethnic composition and maintained ties to their relatives in the area. Both of the paternal grandparents died when Angela was quite young, and Angela's mother and father separated when Angela was 11 years old. Mr. Savanti had moved to another city, and he had never sent money to support the family, nor had he been heard from since his departure. Mr. Savanti had worked as a store salesman when he lived with the rest of the family. After he left, Mrs. Savanti got a job in a factory, and she has worked there ever since.

Angela indicated that she and her sister usually got along fairly well, but they never confided in each other. The client said that she had always had trouble expressing her emotions, and she felt that Doreen probably had the same problem. When they were younger, the only social activities they participated in together were going to church or visiting relatives. Doreen preferred playing outdoor games with boys and girls, while Angela was less active and spent more time around the house. Doreen usually got better grades in school than Angela, and Mrs. Savanti always pointed out this difference in their report cards.

Angela stated that her childhood was a very unhappy period. Her father was seldom home, and when he was present, her parents fought constantly. Sometimes the arguments became quite severe and her father would throw things and shout. Mrs. Savanti usually became sullen and withdrawn after an argument, refused to speak to her husband, and also became uncommunicative with her daughters. Angela remembered that many times as a child she was puzzled because it seemed that her mother was angry at her, too, and she did not know the reason why. Sometimes after an argument, Mrs. Savanti told her daughters that she had ruined her life by marrying their father.

Although Mr. Savanti had a poor relationship with his wife, he appeared to take some interest in his daughters. He occasionally accompanied the rest of the family to church on Sundays, and later dropped his wife off at her parents' house while he took the girls to a park or movie. Angela could not remember her mother ever expressing an interest in going somewhere with just Mr. Savanti and the girls. On the other hand, she recalled that her father could not be relied on. Many times he did not arrive to take the girls on promised outings, and he came home late in the evening instead. He always had an excuse, but he never appeared to understand how disappointed Angela and Doreen were.

Angela remembered very clearly the events that occurred at the time her father left the family. It was Angela's eleventh birthday, and her mother had baked a cake for her and invited Angela's grandparents over for dinner. Mr. Savanti was supposed to come home after work, and they delayed dinner for about a half-hour. When he did not appear, they ate without him. Mrs. Savanti did not make any comments about her husband, but Angela's grandparents made a number of disparaging remarks about Mr. Savanti's reliability.

Angela reported that she felt worse and worse at her birthday party each time one of her grandparents made a remark, but she tried not to show them how disappointed she was. Further, she began to worry that some mishap had befallen her father, as he had promised her the day before that he would be sure to be home on time for her birthday. She made a comment to her mother expressing concern about why her father had not come home, but Mrs. Savanti abruptly changed the subject. When Angela went to bed that evening, her father still had not appeared. She remembered that she had difficulty falling asleep because she was both disappointed and worried about where her father was.

Later that night, Angela was awakened by the sound of her parents arguing. She heard her mother accusing her father of being with another woman. Neither mentioned the fact that Mr. Savanti had not come home as promised for Angela's birthday. The argument increased in intensity, and Doreen woke up, too. They eventually heard their father say that he was moving out, because he did not want to live with someone who was not interested in him. Mrs. Savanti said nothing further, and Mr. Savanti packed his clothes and left the house. Doreen and Angela said nothing to each other, nor did they get out of bed and talk with Mrs. Savanti. This was the last contact they had with their father.

Angela recalled feeling very guilty when Mr. Savanti left. It seemed that if it hadn't been for her birthday party, her parents would not have argued and her father would not have gone away. She revealed that whenever she thought of her father, she always felt that she had been responsible in some way for his leaving the family. Angela had never communicated this feeling to anyone, and her mother rarely mentioned his name.

Angela described her mother as the "long-suffering type" who said that she had sacrificed her life to make her children happy, and the only thing she ever got in return was grief and unhappiness. Angela related that her mother rarely smiled or laughed and did not converse very much with the girls. She appeared to be most comfortable when they just left her alone. When Angela and Doreen began dating, Mrs. Savanti never asked them if they had had a good time, but instead commented on how tired she was because she had waited up for them. She would make disparaging remarks about the boys they had been with and about men in general.

After Mr. Savanti's departure, Angela's mother went to work in a factory near their house. Angela felt that Mrs. Savanti had taken a menial job, and that her mother had a number of skills and was qualified for some other type of work. Mrs. Savanti indicated that she did not want any other job, but nevertheless she would come home from work each day quite tired and complain about how hard she had worked. She would then put on her robe, cook dinner, and spend the evening watching television. If the girls tried to converse with her, she told them that she was tired and just wanted to be left alone. On the weekends, Mrs. Savanti generally went over to her parents' house, and she spent her time there in the same manner—fairly uncommunicative, unkempt in appearance, and seated in front of the television set.

Angela said that she liked her grandparents, but now that she was older, visiting them was no longer very pleasurable. She felt that their ideas were old-fashioned, and she had very few interests in common with them. Her grandparents and mother were very religious, and it seemed that there were always religious overtones to any discussions with them. Angela reported that she was having a great many doubts about her religious faith and beliefs, and these doubts especially troubled her around the time she stopped seeing Jerry.

At the time of the clinic visit, Doreen was attending a community college and was occupied with school activities and part-time work. Angela had decided to take business courses in high school and obtained a job directly after high school graduation. She reported that she enjoyed her position as a secretary. Both Angela and Doreen lived at home, but except for going to church with their mother on Sunday, each pursued a separate path.

Social History

Angela indicated that she had always had a number of children to play with, and she had several friends when she was a teenager. She recalled, however, that sharing her feelings with her friends and telling them about events that were troubling her had always been very difficult for her. Angela considered two of the girls she worked with as her good friends. Nonetheless, she found it hard to tell them much about her relationship with Jerry, or about her despondency after the breakup.

As a teenager, Angela had dated a number of boys. She said that she had preferred going out in groups to being alone with one boy because she did not feel so compelled to carry on a conversation when she was part of a group. Mrs. Savanti was not very friendly to any of her daughters' friends, and Angela indicated that whenever someone came to the house, she felt embarrassed by her mother's untidy appearance and distant manner.

Angela had met Jerry at a party two years earlier, when she was 20 and he was 23. She liked him from the first time they met, but she was very careful not to give any indication that she was attracted to him. She said that she was afraid Jerry would not be interested in her or would not treat her as well if he knew that she liked him.

Angela described Jerry as talkative and friendly and of similar ethnic background. She said that he too had difficulty expressing his feelings, and many times he resorted to kidding around as a means of avoiding emotional expression. They dated off and on for a number of months and then started to go steady. They continued to go out only with each other until the time of their breakup.

Jerry began to talk about getting married six months before they stopped dating. He said he had a good job and he wanted to marry Angela. Angela, however, was very ambivalent about what she wanted to do. She enjoyed being with Jerry, but her mother's indifference toward him troubled her. Mrs. Savanti made numerous comments to the effect that all men are nice before they get married, but that later their true natures come out.

Angela was confused about her feelings toward Jerry and about his feelings toward her. She was not sure whether she loved Jerry, but she knew she would be unhappy if they stopped seeing each other. When she asked Jerry how he felt about her, he became annoyed and said that it was obvious what his feelings were because he wanted to marry her.

Angela never told Jerry about the events that occurred at the time her father left the family, nor about her fear that if she did not know exactly what Jerry's feelings were toward her, she would end up in a situation similar to her mother's. Angela was not able to talk these issues over with Doreen, either. She felt that Doreen was living in a completely different world, and that the people Doreen met at college were quite different from the people with whom Angela associated.

Angela revealed that she had often been troubled with depressed moods. During high school, if she got a lower grade in a subject than she had expected, her initial response was one of anger, followed by depression. She began to think that she was not smart enough to get good grades, and she blamed herself for not studying enough. Angela also became despondent when she got into an argument with her mother or felt that she was being taken advantage of at work. However, these periods of depression usually lasted only about a day, and passed when she became involved in some other activity.

The intensity and duration of the affect that she experienced when she broke up with Jerry were much more severe. She was not sure why she was so depressed, but she began to feel it was an effort to walk around and go out to work. Talking with others became difficult, and many times her lips felt as if they were stiff, and she had to make an effort to move them in order to speak. Angela found it hard to concentrate, and she began to forget things she was supposed to do. It took her a long time to fall asleep at night, and when she finally did fall asleep, she sometimes woke up in the midst of a bad dream. She felt constantly tired, and loud noises, including conversation or the television, bothered her. She preferred to lie in bed rather than be with anyone, and she usually cried when alone.

At the point where Angela's depressed state was seriously beginning to interfere with her job, she decided she had better see the company physician. She asked the doctor to prescribe something to help her sleep, so she would not be so tired and could concentrate better. The physician suggested that Angela receive some professional help with her problems, and she was referred to a counseling center in the area.

Psychological Evaluation

Angela was seen by Dr. H., a clinical psychologist. He established good rapport with his client, and although she was hesitant at first, she eventually began to talk more freely about the events related to her breakup with

Jerry. She repeatedly stated how difficult it was for her to understand her feelings, let alone express them to someone else.

Angela cooperated during the psychological testing, and attempted to do each task asked of her. However, she did not answer any question spontaneously, and it usually took her several seconds before she gave a response. Her motor behavior, such as putting the pieces of a puzzle together or arranging blocks in a pattern, was also somewhat slow.

The client scored in the average range of intelligence. The long reaction times to verbal stimuli and the slowness of her motor responses suggested an impairment in intellectual functioning. This slowness in verbal and motor behavior is consistent with the performance observed in persons who are depressed. The client's affect, as interpreted from the test material, was constricted and controlled. She appeared to react strongly to some of the events occurring around her, but she controlled her emotions so that other people were not aware of how she felt. She was troubled by strong feelings of unhappiness and hopelessness, and a difficulty in sustaining interactions with other persons.

A theme that emerged on several of the tests was that of a person who had an unrealistically high level of aspiration, who also was extremely self-critical. As a result, this person labeled her accomplishments as poor or mediocre, no matter how hard she tried. She was constantly plagued with feelings of inadequacy, self-blame, and anger because she could not live up to her high standards of performance.

Maternal figures were depicted as controlling and lacking in empathy and warmth. The client described a scene in which a woman was forcing her daughter to perform a chore that the mother did not want to do herself. The mother did not understand or care that the daughter was not willing to do the task, and the daughter eventually complied with the mother's wishes.

Male figures were described as nice, but not to be counted on. Part of the blame for this unreliability was placed with the woman with whom the man was interacting. The woman was assumed to have the ability to modify the man's behavior, so any blame for the man's failings also had to be shared by the woman.

There were no indications of psychotic thought processes during the interviews or on the test material.

Course of Psychotherapy

The counseling center that Angela went to was staffed by a number of persons who were trained in client-centered therapy. The consensus of the staff was that Angela would benefit from this particular method of therapy because of her long-standing difficulty in expressing and accepting her feelings, and her unrealistically high level of aspiration. Angela agreed with the recommendation that she enter into a therapy program, and she met twice a week with Dr. H. for a period of ten months.

The role of the therapist in client-centered therapy is to attain the client's internal frame of reference, and to indicate to the client that the therapist is able to understand and perceive as the client understands and perceives (Rogers, 1951). Conveying this total understanding is presumed to result in the client's being able to experience himself or herself as a person having positive as well as negative emotions. The client can then accept all of these feelings without guilt, having experienced that the therapist has been able to acknowledge and respect the entire range of the client's feelings.

The therapist must provide a warm and accepting emotional climate, so the client will eventually trust the therapist and feel free to bring up the events that are causing the emotional discomfort. Rogers (1961) used the terms "empathy" and "unconditional positive regard" to describe the attitudes that the therapist should have in relation to the client. Empathy is defined as the ability to take on the client's internal frame of reference and experience the same feelings that the client is experiencing. The therapist must also be able to convey unconditional positive regard—that is, acceptance and love for the client as an individual. Rogers proposed that only in this atmosphere of empathy and unconditional positive regard will the client eventually learn self-acceptance. Through self-acceptance, the client's self-esteem is raised and the client becomes able to proceed toward greater self-actualization (the full realization of one's potential).

In client-centered therapy, the client determines the direction of each therapy session. The therapist does not ask questions or give advice, but deals only with those matters that the client brings up. Angela found it difficult to take an active role in the interactions with the therapist during the intial therapy sessions, but eventually she learned to be more assertive and bring up the issues that were troubling her. Dr. H. focused on reflecting the feelings that Angela was expressing, and on helping Angela to clarify how she felt when particular events transpired.

It became apparent to Angela that one of the reasons for her difficulty in dealing with her emotions was that she felt a great deal of hostility toward many of the persons for whom she cared. She feared that if she expressed her angry feelings, she would lose the love of these persons. Angela eventually was able to deal with the fact that she had felt very angry with her father each time he had disappointed her, and that she was also angry with Jerry for terminating their relationship.

When her father did indeed desert her, one of the reasons why Angela felt guilty was that she thought that in some way he must have known that she was angry with him. Angela began to see that she was following a behavior pattern similar to her mother's in keeping her feelings to herself and assuming a self-sacrificing attitude.

The client realized that she set unrealistically high standards of performance for herself and others, making it inevitable that she would be disappointed. She expected that both she and Jerry would be totally open and expressive with each other, and she then felt inadequate and confused when they did not achieve this type of relationship. She began to deal with her fear that there is always a loss of caring and affection after several years of marriage, and she became more aware of the characteristic ways she interacted with others.

Angela's depression eased as she began to make progress in therapy. A few months before the termination of treatment, she and Jerry resumed dating. Angela discussed with Jerry her greater comfort in expressing her feelings and her hope that Jerry would also become more expressive with her. They discussed the reasons why Angela was ambivalent about getting married, and they began to talk again about the possibility of marriage. Jerry, however, was not making demands for a decision by a certain date, and Angela felt that she was not as frightened about marriage as she previously had been.

Therapy was terminated after ten months because Dr. H. was moving to another city. Both Dr. H. and Angela agreed that substantial progress had been made in therapy. Angela made no further effort to contact the counseling center.

Discussion

Angela's despondency when she broke up with her boyfriend could well be considered a normal response to a stressful environmental event. The diagnosis of major depression, single episode, was made on the basis of the intensity and duration of the mood change. The DSM-III-R (1987) criteria specify that the depressed mood and loss of interest or pleasure in most activities reflect a change from the individual's usual state, and the depressed mood and loss of pleasure is present for most of the day over at least a two-week period. Symptoms include "appetite disturbance, change in weight, sleep disturbance, psychomotor agitation or retardation, decreased energy, feelings of worthlessness or excessive or inappropriate guilt, difficulty thinking or concentrating, and recurrent thoughts of death, or suicidal ideation or attempts" (p. 219). Slowed thinking, indecisiveness, and memory problems also are common; tearfulness, anxiety, and irritability may be evident as well. A diagnosis of major depression is not applied if the mood disturbance is a normal reaction to the loss of a loved one, unless there is also an intense preoccupation with worthlessness, thoughts of suicide, marked impairment in function, or prolonged duration of symptoms. Another exclusion criterion for the diagnosis of a major depression is a history of a hypomanic or manic episode.

Women are significantly more likely to manifest major depression than men (Weissman & Klerman, 1977); surveys report a 2 to 1 ratio of females to males. A recent study found that women were more likely than men to report increased appetite and weight gain, and feelings of anger and hostility as part of the symptom picture of depression (Frank, Carpenter, & Kupfer, 1988). It is unclear whether the greater prevalene of depression in women is due to biological factors, social processes, or an interaction of these factors.

In 1917 Sigmund Freud wrote a paper titled *Mourning and Melancholia* (1959) that had an important influence on the development of a psychological formulation of depression. In this paper, Freud posited that melancholia or depression was a result of three factors: the loss of a love object, ambivalence (i.e., love as well as hatred for the love object), and a regression of libido into the ego. He further stated that the self-blame seen in the clinical picture of depression results from reproaches against a love object being shifted onto the patient's own ego.

Psychoanalytically oriented writers agree that the essential dynamic of depression is the turning of hostile impulses originally directed against other persons back upon the self (Alexander & Shapiro, 1952; English & Finch, 1964). The regression of libido into the ego means that the individual's positive energies are withdrawn from other persons. The individual loses zest for life because interests are focused on the self, rather than on other persons or events in the environment.

In a more eclectic approach to the etiology of depression, Hofling (1968) noted that a characteristic of many types of depression is an uncertainty about one's personal worth, and a marked lowering of self-esteem. The communication of these feelings of low esteem functions to evoke expressions of reassurance from others that one is indeed a worthwhile person.

Social learning explanations of depression have focused on the availability of positive reinforcement in the individual's milieu. Ferster (1965) proposed that depression is due to the loss of major sources of reinforcement, resulting in a suppression and reduction in the ongoing behavioral repertoire. Lewinsohn also has proposed that depression is a consequence of an inadequate frequency of positive reinforcement. Supporting this thesis, Lewinsohn and Libet (1972) found an association between a low rate of positive reinforcement and the intensity of depression. However, this formulation of depression has been challenged by the findings of Nelson and Craighead (1977) and others, who have demonstrated that depressed persons tend to recall less or underestimate the amount of positive reinforcement they actually receive. The issue of self-evaluation standards in the experience of positive reinforcement is prominent in Rehm's (1977) self-control theory of depression. He proposed that depressives experience deficits in self-reinforcement because they selectively attend to negative events and set excessively stringent criteria for self-evaluation.

Seligman's (1974) learned helplessness model bridges the learning and cognitive theories of the etiology of depression. The first premise of this theory is that some persons, exposed to situations that they cannot control, develop the belief or expectancy that their future actions will have no influence over what happens to them—that is, they develop a learned helplessness. Irrespective of later experiences of exerting control over outcomes, depressed persons continue to feel that their actions do not influence what happens to them. The reformulation of the learned helplessness model of depression presented by Abramson, Seligman, and Teasdale (1978) highlighted a tendency for depressed persons to attribute negative outcomes to global, stable, and internal factors—that is, a tendency to attribute unfavorable things that happen to them to some personal characteristic that cannot be changed. Although it has generated a great deal of research, the learned helplessness model and its reformulation have received mixed empirical support. Hamilton and Abramson (1983) reported that the cognitive style evidenced by a group of depressed persons seemed more a feature of the depression itself than an enduring cognitive characteristic. On the other hand, a strong association between low perceived life control and depressive symptoms in women was reported by Warren and McEachren (1983).

The cognitive theory of depression proposed by Beck (1967, 1976) has stimulated a substantial amount of interest. Beck posited a negative cognitive triad in depression, consisting of negative beliefs about oneself, a negative view of one's world, and a negative appraisal of the future. These beliefs result in the individual's feeling of a deep, pervasive sense of loss that culminates in the sadness, pessimism, and self-criticalness of depression. The depression is sustained because the person focuses on aspects of his or her life situation that suggest loss, and glosses over other features of everyday experiences that contradict this cognitive set. Beck refers to this cognitive process as "selective attention."

In cognitive therapy based on Beck's theory, the therapist deals directly with the client's reasoning and belief systems, and actively challenges the client's negative thoughts (Hollon & Beck, 1979). The therapist also instructs the client to self-monitor mood, ongoing events, and mastery behaviors. The client is given task assignments at each session; the difficulty of each new task increases as the previous one is mastered. This mastery enables the therapist to point to the client's successful behavior, and thus disconfirm or contradict the depressive's negative thoughts about himself or herself. A further rationale of this approach is that the client will find out that her or his negative expectations are inaccurate (Beck, Rush, Shaw, & Emery, 1979). The client is also instructed to schedule pleasurable events and record anticipatory thoughts and subsequent reactions to these events. The thought distortions associated with these activities are evaluated in therapy. Hollon and Beck concluded that cognitive therapy based on the combination of cognitive and behavioral techniques just described may be particularly effective in dealing with individuals who manifest a nonpsychotic, reactive type of depression that is a reaction to a clear environmental circumstances, such as a loss or bereavement. Hollon, et al., (1988) reported that at follow-up assessment, cognitive-behavioral therapy was just as effective as antidepressant medication in the treatment of persons with a depressive disorder.

There is increasing interest in evaluating the possibility of biochemical abnormalities in persons suffering from depression. Deficiencies in the activity of neurotransmitters such as nonrepinephrine and serotonin, and abnormalities in the secretion of the neuroendocrine hormone cortisol have been examined (Andreasen, 1984; Coppen, 1971; Schildkraut, 1965). (The possible role of neurotransmitters in the etiology of mood disorders also is discussed in Chapter 16.)

Some depressed individuals show abnormalities on the dexamethasone suppression test (DST), manifested by a lack of suppression of cortisol secretion when administered dexamethasone. Dexamethasone is a synthetic hormone similar to cortisol that suppresses cortisol secretion in normal individuals. The suppression pathway occurs via chemical signals from the hypothalamus to the pituitary gland, and then to the adrenal glands. Cortisol nonsuppression in response to dexamethasone occurring in depressed persons has been viewed as an indication of a neuroendocrine dysfunction and a biological marker for endogenous depression (i.e., a biologially caused depression). At present the issue is far from clear. Only about half of depressed patients manifest this abnormality (Andreasen, 1984), and abnormal suppression has been shown to be related to factors other than depression (e.g., Nelson, Sullivan, Khan, & Tamragouri, 1986).

Further, changes in cortisol levels can occur as a response to stress (Depue, 1979) and could affect DST responding.

The study of genetic factors in the etiology of depression has been stimulated by the relatively high prevalence of depression in families with a depressed member. (Chapter 16 presents the details of many of these investigations.) A recent study assessed the psychiatric status of the families of depressed and psychiatrically normal persons who had been adopted by non-relatives shortly after birth (Wender et al., 1986). The biological relatives of the depressed adoptee group had a significantly greater prevalence of major depressive disorder (unipolar depression) and completed suicides than was found in the biological relatives of psychiatrically normal adoptees. There were no differences between the depressed and normal adoptee groups in the prevalence of unipolar depression in the adoptive relatives. These findings need to be tempered, though, by the fact that mood disorder was ascertained by hospital records rather than interview, so less severe cases of depression would not have been detected.

A causal link has been proposed between stresses associated with recent life events, and the onset of depression. For example, Paykel (1979) found that depressed patients reported an excess of events generally spread over the six months prior to the onset of depression. However, the direction of causality is not clear. Depue and Monroe (1986) pointed out that chronic disorder may generate stressful life events as well as loss of social support, so the disorder itself may precipitate negative life events.

An understanding of the family milieu in which a child grows up also is important in studying the development of psychopathology. In the most common situation, the offspring are raised by the biological parents, and here the influence can be both genetic and environmental. For example, Brody and Forehand (1986) found that mothers who were significantly depressed viewed their noncompliant children as more maladjusted than did comparison group mothers with noncompliant children. Thus, the depressed mother's more negative evaluation of her children's psychological adjustment may have a significant detrimental impact on interpersonal relationships between them.

The development of Angela's low level of self-esteem and predisposition for depression can be traced in part to genetic factors and her observations of her mother's behavior. Mrs. Savanti most likely suffered from dysthymia, a chronic, moderately depressed mood, accompanied by low low self-esteem, feelings of hopelessness, and a low energy level (DSM-III-R). Mrs. Savanti's general life pattern and attitudes suggested that she viewed herself as a worthless person, who was taken advantage of by others, and who suffered in a physically taxing job so she could support her children. Angela imitated her mother's behavior, and she began to think of herself as inadequate too. She also learned to refrain from expressing her feelings and communicating her problems to others.

Some persons have been taught that whatever happens to them is their own fault. An individual with this type of history may be extremely self-critical and manifest a lowering of self-esteem as a result of these attitudes. Bandura (1972) indicated that individuals engage in self-reward or self-punishment depending on whether their performance matches or falls short of their self-imposed standards. Thus, one might then observe the often-noted clinical picture of the depressed person who is tormented by feelings of worthlessness and self-blame (Beck) and who derives little pleasure from daily activities.

The subjective experience of depressive affect may be related to the inability to verbalize strong negative feelings in the social setting in which the events occurred. In a circumstance perpetrated by other persons, as in being denied a job or a promotion, one may be blocked from directly verbalizing one's angry feelings because the other person is in a position to retaliate; labeling and directly verbalizing one's emotions could result in another negative contingency. In other situations, the agent of the frustration may not be available for the person to direct his or her anger against.

When a person engages in activities designed to be distracting from his or her problems, there may be a temporary feeling of relief due to a lowering of the level of chronic emotional arousal. However, as soon as the distraction passes, the person is again confronted with the same problems, and the depressive state recurs. If the activity the person is engaging in is in some way problem solving and not just a distraction, then there may be a more effective alleviation of the depressive affect. The depression also may dissipate over time as the individual becomes more motivated to seek out alternate sources of reinforcement.

Angela received attention from her mother primarily when the latter was criticizing her about her behavior at school or at home. Mrs. Savanti repeatedly told her daughter that she was incompetent, and any mishaps that happened to her were her own fault. When Mr. Savanti deserted the family, Angela's first response was that somehow she was responsible. From her mother's past behavior, Angela had learned to expect that in some way she would be blamed. At the time that Angela broke up with her boyfriend, she did not blame Jerry for his behavior, but interpreted this event as a failing solely on her part. As a result, her level of self-esteem was lowered still more.

The type of marital relationship that Angela saw her mother and father engage in remained her concept of what married life is like. She generalized from her observations of her parents' discordant interactions to an expectation of the type of behavior that she and Jerry would ultimately engage in. Angela demanded that Jerry conform to her definition of acceptable interpersonal behavior, because of her belief that otherwise their marriage would not be a mutually reinforcing relationship. However, Angela set such high standards for Jerry's behavior that it was inevitable that she would be disappointed.

Angela's initial fears of marital unhappiness were probably well-founded. Before Angela entered psychotherapy, both she and Jerry were highly noncommunicative with each other. One of the results of therapy was that Angela was able to exhibit greater assertiveness and express her feelings more openly. She was also able to encourage Jerry to express his feelings. Thus, the nature of their relationship changed, with each person reinforcing the other for improved communication.

Angela was reacting to a crisis period in her life at the time she became depressed. She was at a point where she was being asked to make a decision that had far-reaching ramifications. The difficulty in deciding about marriage was exacerbated by her doubts about her religious faith, and she interpreted these doubts as another indication that she was not a good person.

Angela's uncertainties intensified when she was deprived of the major source of gratification she had, her relationship with Jerry. Despite the fact that she was overwhelmed with doubts about whether to marry him or not, she had gained a great deal of pleasure through being with Jerry. Whatever feelings she had been able to express, she had shared with him and no one else. Angela labeled Jerry's termination of their relationship as proof that she was not worthy of another person's interest. She viewed her present unhappiness as likely to continue, and she attributed it to some failing on her part. Although a short reactive depression would be quite normal under these circumstances, the intensity and duration of Angela's depressive episode suggested a process driven by more than a major life disappointment. A biological predisposition to depression, triggered by environmental circumstances, may have caused her depression to be so severe.

Psychotherapy provided Angela with the opportunity to learn to express her feelings to the persons with whom she was interacting, and this was quite helpful to her. Most important, she was able to generalize from some of the learning experiences in therapy and modify her behavior in her renewed relationship with Jerry. Angela still had much progress to make in terms of changing the characteristic ways she interacted with others, but she had already made a number of important steps in a potentially happier direction.

References

Abramson, L. Y., Seligman, M. E. P., & Teasdale, J. D. (1978). Learned helplessness in humans: Critique and reformulation. *Journal of Abnormal Psychology, 87,* 49–74.

Alexander, F., & Shapiro, L. (1952). Neuroses, behavior disorders and perversions. In F. Alexander & H. Ross (Eds.), *Dynamic psychiatry.* Chicago: University of Chicago Press.

American Psychiatric Association (1987). *Diagnostic and statistical manual of mental disorders* (3rd ed., rev.) (DSM-III-R). Washington, DC: Author.

Andreasen, N. C. (1984). *The broken brain: The biological revolution in psychiatry.* New York: Harper & Row.

Bandura, A. (1972). Modeling theory: Some traditions, trends, and disputes. In R. D. Parke (Ed.), *Recent trends in social learning theory* (pp. 35–61). New York: Academic Press.

Beck, A. T. (1967). *Depression: Clinical, experimental and theoretical aspects.* New York: Harper & Row.

Beck, A. T. (1976). *Cognitive theory and the emotional disorders.* New York: International Universities Press.

Beck, A. T., Rush, A. J., Shaw, B. F., & Emery, G. (1979). *Cognitive therapy of depression: A treatment manual.* New York: Guilford.

Brody, G. H., & Forehand, R. (1986). Maternal perceptions of child maladjustment as a function of the combined influence of child behavior and maternal depression. *Journal of Consulting and Clinical Psychology, 54,* 237–240.

Coppen, A. (1971). Biogenic amines and affective disorders. In B. T. Ho & W. M. McIsaac (Eds.), *Advances in behavioral biology* (Vol. 1). *Brain chemistry and mental disease* (pp. 123–133). New York: Plenum Press.

Depue, R. A. (1979). *The psychobiology of depressive disorders: Implications for the effects of stress.* New York: Academic Press.

Depue, R. A., & Monroe, S. M. (1986). Conceptualization and measurement of human disorder in life stress research: The problem of chronic disturbance. *Psychological Bulletin, 99,* 36–51.

English, O. S., & Finch, S. M. (1964). *Introduction to psychiatry* (3rd ed.). New York: Norton.

Ferster, C. B. (1965). Classification of behavioral pathology. In L. Krasner & L. P. Ullmann (pp. 6–26) (Eds.), *Research in behavior modification.* New York: Holt, Rinehart, & Winston.

Frank, E., Carpenter, L. L., & Kupfer, D. J. (1988). Sex differences in recurrent depression: Are there any that are significant? *American Journal of Psychiatry, 145,* 41–45.

Freud, S. (1959). *Collected papers* (Vol. 4). New York: Basic Books.

Hamilton, E. W., & Abramson, L. Y. (1983). Cognitive patterns and major depressive disorder: A longitudinal study in a hospital setting. *Journal of Abnormal Psychology, 92,* 173–184.

Hofling, C. K. (1968). *Textbook of psychiatry for medical practice* (2nd ed.). Philadelphia: Lippincott.

Hollon, S. D., & Beck, A. T. (1979). Cognitive therapy of depression. In P. C. Kendall & S. D. Hollon (Eds.), *Cognitive-behavioral interventions. Theory, research, and procedures* (pp. 153–203). New York: Academic Press.

Hollon, S. D., DeRubeis, R. J., Evans, M. D., Wiemer, M. J., Garvey, M. J., Grove, W. M., & Tuason, V. B. (1988). Cognitive therapy, pharmacotherapy, and combined cognitive/pharmacotherapy in the treatment of depression: I. Differential outcome in the CPT project. Manuscript submitted for publication.

Lewinsohn, P. M., & Libet, J. (1972). Pleasant events, activity schedules, and depression. *Journal of Abnormal Psychology, 79,* 291–295.

Nelson, R. E., & Craighead, W. E. (1977). Selective recall of positive and negative feedback, self-control behaviors, and depression. *Journal of Abnormal Psychology, 86,* 379–388.

Nelson, W. H., Sullivan, P., Khan, A., & Tamragouri, R. N. (1986). The effect of age on dexamethasone supression test results in alcoholic patients. *American Journal of Psychiatry, 143,* 237–239.

Paykel, E. S. (1979). Recent life events in the development of the depressive disorders. In R. A. Depue (Ed.), *The psychobiology of the depressive disorders: Implications for the effects of stress* (pp. 245–262). New York: Academic Press.

Rehm, L. P. (1977). A self-control model of depression. *Behavior Therapy, 8,* 787–804.

Rogers, C. R. (1951). *Client-centered therapy.* Boston: Houghton Mifflin.

Rogers, C. R. (1961). *On becoming a person.* Boston: Houghton Mifflin.

Schildkraut, J. (1965). Catecholamine hypothesis of affective disorders. *American Journal of Psychiatry, 122,* 509–522.

Seligman, M. E. P. (1974). Depression and learned helplessness. In R. J. Friedman & M. M. Katz (Eds.), *The psychology of depression: Contemporary theory and research.* New York: Wiley.

Warren, L. W., & McEachren, L. (1983). Psychosocial correlates of depressive symptomatology in adult women. *Journal of Abnormal Psychology, 92*, 151–160.

Weissman, M. M., & Klerman, G. L. (1977). Sex differences and the epidemiology of depression. *Archives of General Psychiatry, 34*, 98–111.

Wender, P. H., Kety, S. S., Rosenthal, D., Schulsinger, F., Ortmann, J., & Lunde, I. (1986). Psychiatric disorders in the biological and adoptive families of adopted individuals with affective disorders. *Archives of General Psychiatry, 43*, 923–929.

16

Bipolar Disorder—
A Cycle of Repeated Hospitalization

Bernard Jacobson was 40 years old at the time of his sixth admission to a psychiatric hospital. He had been diagnosed as manic-depressive, circular type, during his last four hospital admissions. (The designation of bipolar disorder would be the classification used according to the current DSM-III-R, 1987, nomenclature.) He was of Jewish background and he had received a bachelor's degree in education. Upon graduating from college, he had been employed for three years as a history teacher. However, his behavior subsequently became so deviant that he could no longer function in a professional setting over a continuous period of time. Bernard's wife had divorced him five years ago. The couple had no children.

The present hospitalization was at the instigation of his welfare worker, who felt that the severely depressed behavior Bernard was currently manifesting might result in his attempting to commit suicide.

Family Background

The patient was interviewed by a social worker, and the information he gave was corroborated from the records of his previous hospitalizations.

Since Bernard was extremely depressed at the time of this hospital admission, most of the facts of his life history came from his past records.

Bernard was an only child. His family was of low socioeconomic status. He and his parents had always lived with his maternal grandparents, who frequently supported them. His father had never held a regular job and was often gone from the home for long periods of time. Bernard remembered his father as aloof and withdrawn. He rarely talked to his son or other family members, although he frequently muttered to himself. As Bernard grew older, he found out that the long periods of time his father was away from home were spent at a mental hospital. (Records at that hospital indicated that the father was diagnosed as a chronic schizophrenic.) Bernard reported that, at the present time, his father was living in a board and care facility and was being maintained on medication. He apparently was functioning only marginally. Bernard indicated that when his own mood was good, he would occasionally visit his father out of a sense of filial responsibility, but he could not feel any real affection for him. He had not visited with him for some time.

Bernard felt that his mother was very unpredictable and difficult to get along with. She got angry with him very quickly, and often he was not entirely sure what she was angry about. His relationship with her had always been a stormy one. When he was growing up, she frequently shouted at him to get him to obey her, and he characteristically refused to comply despite her threats and spankings. He related that his grandmother also seemed to spend a great deal of time yelling at him and telling him that he was bad. He had difficulty remembering occasions when either his mother or his grandmother talked quietly to him. Further, his mother and grandmother argued with each other quite frequently, often about seemingly minor matters. Bernard recalled that his grandfather was rather quiet and passive and did not interfere in the various family disputes. However, he sometimes spent time quietly conversing with his grandson and occasionally took him on an outing.

School History

Bernard indicated that he had had a great deal of difficulty at school because he was continually arguing with the teachers and would not sit quietly in his seat. His classmates made fun of him because of his disruptive behavior, and he got the reputation of being a bully. The only person he felt comfortable talking to was another boy he became acquainted with in high school. However, he did not engage in any social activities with this person after school hours, nor with any other peers.

In a previous hospital admission interview, Bernard commented that during high school, he had been able to exert some self-discipline over his behavior. He found that he was genuinely interested in many of the subjects he was taking and he began to study and pay closer attention to the class material. He had learned the basic skills taught in the elementary grades despite his disruptive behavior in school. Therefore, he was not hampered academically when he wanted to learn more about a particular subject covered in high school. He enrolled in a local college after high school graduation and eventually received a bachelor's degree in education with a specialization in history. His family helped support him through college as much as they could, and he worked summers at whatever jobs he could find to help pay for his school expenses.

Social History

Bernard met his wife Sandra when they were both in college. She was also of Jewish background. He stated that he had never had any close friends, and he really did not care to participate in social activities with other persons. However, he was attracted to Sandra because she seemed to take an interest in him and went out of her way to involve him in activities with her friends and family. He said that at first he was unsure about marriage, but then he became convinced that he would be happier and more comfortable married to Sandra than he would be alone. They married one year after both had graduated from college.

Upon graduating, Bernard obtained a teaching position at a local high school. His wife also found a job after graduation, and she continued to work after they were married. He described his first year of marriage as reasonably happy but indicated that his sexual relationship with his wife was not very satisfactory. Approximately one year after their marriage, he began to manifest emotional difficulties characterized by bouts of depression and anxiety. He made few attempts to communicate with others during these episodes.

Symptom History

Over the next year, Bernard was absent from work on numerous occasions because of periods of agitated depression, and his teaching contract was not renewed for the following year. He then worked at various jobs whenever he felt able to, and at the same time obtained outpatient therapy. Bernard was almost continually in some form of outpatient treatment over the next eight years; his wife's parents provided some financial support to help pay these bills. The treatment he received generally involved supportive therapy and some form of anti-depressant medication. At one point during this time period, Bernard had been able to obtain another teaching position. Again, his contract was not renewed because of numerous absences associated with moderately severe depressive episodes.

An interview with Bernard's former wife revealed that the patient first began showing signs of bizarre behavior when he was approximately 33 years old. At that time, he became quite hyperactive and agitated and complained of receiving special messages on the radio. He spoke in whispers in the house because he was afraid that some outsider would hear him, and he often stayed up for two or three consecutive nights working without rest on a particular project that had captured his interest. He also argued a great deal with his wife and at one point threatened to jump out of the window. He then became extremely agitated and eventually agreed to enter a local psychiatric hospital. He stayed in the hospital for about a week but then signed himself out against medical advice and spent the next several months at home. He gradually became quite depressed, and four months after his previous hospitalization, he swallowed a large number of sedatives. His wife found him in a semiconscious state, and he was rushed to the emergency room of a local hospital. After his stomach was pumped and he regained consciousness, he was persuaded to return to the psychiatric hospital. He underwent a series of electroshock treatments and was discharged six weeks later, free of depressive symptoms.

Sandra reported that her former husband tried to work after his discharge from the hospital, but he was unable to keep a job for more than a week. He spent most of the next few months at home, and his behavior was generally quite belligerent. He also engaged in numerous spending sprees. Sandra said that she was the target of severe verbal abuse, usually precipitated by her objections to the amount of money her husband was spending. She felt that Bernard was not in touch with reality during this period and, for the first time, he refused to obtain psychiatric help. After a period of indecision, she finally signed commitment papers so that he could receive treatment again in a psychiatric hospital.

Bernard exhibited hallucinatory behavior when he was admitted to the hospital on this occasion, but he calmed down and became rational when placed on lithium carbonate. He spent two months in the hospital, was given a provisional discharge to a day treatment program, and was instructed to remain on the lithium medication. Sandra indicated that during this hospitalization she finally came to a decision to file for divorce since she could no longer tolerate the emotional demands her husband's erratic behavior placed on her. Bernard went along with his wife's decision without argument, and the welfare department assisted him in making arrangements to live in a boarding home.

Bernard functioned reasonably well in the boarding home and day treatment program for about four months, but he then stopped taking his medication regularly. One day he suddenly experienced an acute manic episode. He had been helping his landlord paint a room, when suddenly he began painting everything in sight, and the landlord had to wrest the paintbrush out of his hand. He roamed about the house in his underwear, talked endlessly, and insisted that nothing was wrong with him. He became extremely argumentative and unpredictable, and the welfare worker then initiated arrangements for Bernard's return to an inpatient setting.

When the patient returned to the hospital, the dosage level of lithium carbonate that he had been maintained on was increased. He then became very passive and dependent, complained about his unhappy and ineffective life, and expressed concern when he began exhibiting side effects to the medication. Other antipsychotic medications were evaluated alone and in combination with lithium carbonate, but the lithium appeared to be the most effective medication for alleviating his emotional disturbance. Bernard's mood eventually improved with hospitalization and, two months later, he was discharged back to the day treatment program. However, he resisted participating in this program and was placed in a board and care facility.

Approximately ten months later he was again hospitalized after another manic episode, which occurred after Bernard once again stopped taking his medication. Upon rehospitalization, he became quite depressed, refused to get out of bed, and insisted upon having his meals brought to his room. Various antipsychotic medications were tried, and he then was placed on lithium carbonate in combination with another antipsychotic medication. He was discharged back to a board and care home when his mood stabilized. However, he eventually discontinued the medication and gradually became increasingly depressed.

Present Hospitalization

At his welfare worker's instigation, Bernard was committed to a psychiatric hospital in order to prevent the possibility of a suicide attempt. The hospital was a different facility from the one he had been admitted to on previous occasions and recently had developed a combined medical-behavior modification treatment program. Psychological testing confirmed a significant impairment in reality testing. Bernard felt that he was physically damaged and therefore could not work. He communicated that he disliked himself, and he also stated that he regretted not having killed himself some time ago.

A continuing problem in maintaining Bernard outside the hospital was the numerous side effects he experienced when the dosage level of lithium carbonate or the other antipsychotic medications he had been placed on was too high. The side effects of lithium included ataxia (staggering gait), mild tremor, dry mouth, and sleepiness. He tended to discontinue the medication when his mood stabilized at a more normal level. The hospital treatment program included a behavior modification component aimed at reinforcing him for taking his medication and for behaving in a more socially appropriate manner. The treatment goal was to eventually extend this program to a day treatment facility.

A token system was set up in which Bernard earned points for taking the prescribed medications regularly and without argument. Points could also be earned for behaviors such as getting out of bed in the morning, shaving, combing his hair, getting to meals on time, and not complaining or crying. Points were accrued for these behaviors as monitored over specific time blocks each day. The points could be exchanged for a variety of reinforcers and privileges both on and off the ward.

Bernard was placed on lithium carbonate when readmitted because his previous history suggested that despite the side effects, he had been able to function better on this drug than on any other antipsychotic medication or combination of medications. He did not resist the request that he start taking the medication again. Bernard earned very few points during his first week in the hospital, and his behavior was observed to cycle between manic and depressed phases. After approximately seven days, at the point at which the blood levels of the drug were sufficiently high to induce a behavioral effect, he began earning points on the token system. Gradually, more socially appropriate behaviors became established. Bernard shaved and showered regularly, was well-groomed, and conversed with others about topics other than his symptoms. He also began participating in group therapy sessions. His therapist discussed with him on an individual basis the necessity of taking the medication indefinitely in order to prevent recurrences of the severe mood swings. They also discussed changes in behavior that might signal that his mood state was beginning to fluctuate more than usual and to which Bernard should be alert. He was told that if he noticed the signs of greater than average mood swings, he should contact the hospital social worker. An evaluation would then be made about whether he should be rehospitalized for a brief period of time, or whether some other treatment should be initiated.

Bernard remained in the hospital for three months. It was possible to maintain him on a lower dosage level of lithium carbonate than had been possible without the behavior modification program. He indicated that he felt a real sense of accomplishment through being able to control his behavior and monitor behavior changes by means of the token system. He was quite pessimistic about whether he would ever be able to function at a job commensurate with his intellectual ability, but he did agree to return to a day treatment program and to continue taking the prescribed medication.

Arrangements were made for the token system to be carried out at the day treatment center. Bernard would be able to earn points for social interactions with other persons, such as participating in outings, going to a movie or to the park, or engaging in other group activities. An important aspect of the program was that he continue to take his medication regularly and to report any significant mood changes to the day treatment personnel. Upon his discharge to the day treatment program, it was hoped that the combination of the medication and the behavior modification program would prevent the cycling of emotional behavior to the extremes it had in the past.

Discussion

The primary characteristic of a mood disorder "is a disturbance of mood ... that is not due to any other physical or mental disorder. Mood refers to a prolonged emotion that colors the whole psychic life; it generally involves either depression or elation" (DSM-III-R, 1987 p. 213). Affective disorder was the term used in DSM-III (1980) for this category.

Patients with bipolar disorder have a history of one or more manic episodes, and one or more major depressive episodes. The DSM-III-R diagnostic criteria for a manic episode involve a specific period of abnormally and continuously elevated, expansive, or irritable mood. A number of the following symptoms also are included: grandiosity or inflated self-esteem, decreased need for sleep, significantly greater talkativeness than usual, racing thoughts, distractibility, psychomotor agitation, and excessive involvement in high risk pleasurable activities. The DSM-III-R criteria for a major depressive episode center on evidence of a depressed mood and loss of interest or pleasure. Significant change sin weight and appetite, insomnia, psychomotor agitation or retardation seen almost daily, fatigue, feelings of worthlessness or guilt, difficulties in concentrating or indecisiveness, and recurrent thoughts of death or of suicide also are evident. A defining characteristic of bipolar disorder is the cycling of mood from the depressive, to normal, and then to the hypomanic (a subclinical or lesser intensity form of mania) or manic phase.

In some individuals, hospitalization may be necessary in only the manic or the depressive phase, because the mood swing in the opposite direction is of a subclinical intensity. Another variation of bipolar disorder is the rapid cycling type, in which there are several manic followed by depressive cycles within a 12 month period, with no intermittent normal period. According to DSM-III-R, the mood disturbance that initially precipitates hospitalization usually is a manic episode. Bipolar patients in a depressive phase are more seriously depressed at hospitalization than hospitalized nonbipolar depressed patients, and are more likely to relapse at a future time and make a serious suicide attempt (Coryell, Andreasen, Endicott, & Keller, 1987).

Bernard was suffering from a bipolar disorder, depressed phase, with psychotic features. This classification denotes that his current mood state fits the criteria for a major depressive episode, delusions or hallucinations were present, and he had a history of hypomania or mania.

There are strong indications of genetic contributions to the development of mood disorders (Angst & Perris, 1972). Elsasser (1925) found that in cases in which both parents had been diagnosed as manic-depressive there was a 32 percent risk for the emergence of manic-depressive psychosis in the offspring. The expectancy of severe affective reactions in the general population is less than 1 percent (Beck, 1967). In the group that Slater (1971) evaluated, the frequency of manic-depressive psychosis in the parents of manic-depressives was 11.5 percent, and in the children, 22.2 percent. Slater also found that the concordance rate for affective disorders in identical twins was 57 percent, while for fraternal twins the concordance rate was 29 percent. Further, significantly higher concordance rates for manic-depressive disorder in identical as compared to fraternal twins were reported by Bertelsen, Harvald, and Hauge (1977). Additional genetic evidence comes from the findings that the biological parents of manic-depressive patients who had been adopted early in life had a significantly higher frequency of mood disorders than the biological parents of a non-manic depressive group of adoptees (Mendlewicz & Rainer, 1977).

The study of high risk offspring also provides information with implications for genetic theories of mood disorders. Klein, Depue, and Slater (1985) found that 27 percent of the offspring of a bipolar parent and none of the offspring of a group of non-depressed psychiatric patients manifested bipolar forms of mood disorder. Cyclothymia, a subclinical form of bipolar mood swings, was the most frequent type of mood disorder identified in the offspring of a bipolar parent.

Two recent genetic linkage studies demonstrated important breakthroughs in research on the genetics of mood disorders. In one investigation, it wsa possible to localize a dominant gene that was a marker for a predisposition to bipolar disorder (Egeland et al., 1987); the other study found a close linkage of bipolar disorder to X-chromosome markers for color blindness and a type of glucose deficiency (Baron et al., 1987). If replicated on other samples, these findings may lead to the discovery of specific biochemical or physiological modes of action in the genes involved, which in turn can lead to a better understanding of the nature of the biological dysfunction that occurs in mood disorders.

The importance of the childhood environment interacting with predispositional factors due to heredity is demonstrated by Stenstedt's (1952) research. He found a 15 percent average incidence of manic-depressive psychosis in the parents, siblings, and children of persons diagnosed as manic-depressive. However, when these cases were categorized into good or poor childhood environments, the risk rate for the disorder was 31 percent for persons growing up in an unfavorable environment and 10 percent for those from a favorable childhood environment.

Other research on mood disorders has attempted to identify biochemical factors that are important in the etiology of these disorders. Theories have been proposed regarding a dysfunction in the action of several classes of neurotransmitters including biogenic amines such as serotonin, norepinephrine, and dopamine. Neurotransmitters are chemical substances involved in the release of a chemical signal from one neuron (the presynaptic neuron) to a second neuron or neurons (postsynaptic neurons) along a particular neuronal pathway. Most of the serotonin, norepinephrine, and dopamine systems begin in the brain stem and project up through the midbrain. The serotonin and norepinephrine systems also project into the cerebral cortex. Dysregulation of the dopamine system may be associated with deficiencies in incentive-reward motivation, and behavioral instability (Depue & Iacono, 1989). Antidepressant medications appear to affect activity in the serotonin and norepinephrine systems. Andreasen (1984) and others have suggested that irregularities in these particular neurotransmitter systems are important in the etiology of depression. However, no single neurotransmitter system has been identified that clearly causes mood disorders.

The discovery that lithium salts, used as a substitute for sodium chloride in the diets of cardiac patients, was effective in treating manic-depressive psychosis (Cade, 1949) stimulated speculation about the role of biochemical factors in the etiology of manic-depressive or bipolar disorder.

Lithium carbonate does not produce a general suppression of behavior as do sedative drugs, but instead curbs manic and hyperexcitable behavior so that the mood returns to a more normal level. However, lithium carbonate must accumulate in the blood stream over a period of a week or more before it has an effect on behavior (Gershon & Shopsen, 1973). The drug has been reported to be more effective in modifying the acute manic phase than the acute depressive phase of the disorder. Maintenance of individuals on lithium carbonate has proven effective in preventing the further recurrence of the extreme mood swings. This drug also can be effective when initially administered to bipolars during the depressive phase of the disorder (Johnson, 1975; Prien, Klett, & Caffey, 1973).

The study of human circadian rhythms is of interest in the search for other biological parameters that might influence the etiology of mood disorders. Circadian rhythms are the approximately 24-hour "biological clock" cycles of various physiological processes as well as activity patterns. These processes include sleep-wake patterns, body temperature changes, and a large number of daily hormonal changes, particularly secretions of the endocrine system (Wehr & Goodwin, 1981).

Initial studies have begun on the possible involvement of circadian rhythm disturbances in mood disorders. Some of the characteristics of depression that suggest circadian rhythm disturbances are early morning awakening, the variation during the day in symptom severity, the seasonal nature of rates of hospital admissions for depression, and the cyclicity of the disorder itself. A significant biological factor influencing the onset and course of affective disorders will be demonstrated if research findings eventually confirm an involvement of the circadian system in these severe mood disturbances.

More recent interest in cyclical patterns of depression has centered on the specification of the phenomenon of seasonal affective disorder, most often manifested by winter depression and summer hypomania (Rosenthal et al., 1984). Light treatment at a specific intensity simulating summer light-dark time patterns has proven effective in alleviating the winter depression (Rosenthal et al., 1985), with a recurrence of symptoms with light of a lower intensity. These findings strongly point to a biological basis for this type of mood disorder.

The studies reviewed thus far suggest a biological component to the etiology of bipolar disorder. Future research may more clearly identify abnormalities in neurotransmitter and other biological systems that affect mood, and may find that these dysfunctions are inherited mechanisms. However, the contribution of environmental factors also needs to be considered. A child's exposure to a parent's psychopathological behavior provides an environmental as well as a possible genetic influence on whether the child will develop a disordered behavior pattern. Children living with a disturbed parent who do not develop alternate sources of interaction with peers and other adults may be less likely to learn socially appropriate interactional skills than children who seek out persons outside of the family (Beardslee & Podorefsky, 1988). Thus, the strength of the biological predisposition, as well as the environmental stressors encountered may determine the incidence and the severity of a disorder in the offspring.

The life history of Bernard Jacobson includes the possibility of genetic influences interacting with the factors of an unfavorable environment in the development of a psychotic disorder. Bernard's father was diagnosed as a chronic schizophrenic and, throughout his adult life, functioned in society in a minimally effective manner. Bernard's childhood experiences were dominated by tensions between his mother, grandmother, and himself, and neither his mother nor grandmother seemed to interact with him in a warm and supportive way. Bernard's grandfather was extremely passive and rarely got involved in the arguments among the other family members. The role model he presented to his grandson was also that of an ineffectual and minimally involved male figure.

The persons in Bernard's home neither taught nor reinforced him for engaging in the social skills necessary for interacting harmoniously with his peers and other persons. His argumentative behavior in school earned him a negative reputation and as a result he had no friends. His fighting and verbally abusive behavior also precluded him from the opportunity to observe how others interact in a cooperative manner. Therefore, Bernard did not learn more effective social abilities, and he was unable to gain gratification through social interactions with his peers.

Nonetheless, Bernard's life was not completely chaotic and strife-filled, and he did acquire some social skills, perhaps in large part from his relationship with his grandfather. Further, his intelligence level was high enough to enable him to profit from the academic material presented in his elementary school classes despite minimal attention on his part. When he became interested in the subject matter offered in high school, the gratification derived from learning was apparently self-reinforcing. He applied himself to mastering the subject material assigned to him, and he did well in school. As he grew more interested in learning and his classroom behavior correspondingly changed, the responses of other persons in the environment changed as well. In college, he was able to establish a relationship with both the woman he eventually married and her family. Indeed, the time interval between high school and college graduation was the only relatively tranquil period in his life.

Bernard did not appear able to cope with the responsibilities of relating to a wife and interacting with his colleagues and pupils. It is also possible that he was unable to deal with the sexual and social demands of a sustained relationship. Within a year after his marriage, he manifested signs of emotional disturbance and sought professional help for his difficulties. Despite eight years of almost continuous therapeutic support and treatment with various medications, his functioning gradually became more inadequate and disturbed.

The symptoms clearly characteristic of a manic-depressive or bipolar disorder first became obvious at age 33, when Bernard became hyperactive, hallucinatory, and highly suspicious of others. The first onset of this disorder generally occurs between ages 20 and 30, and in other respects, the natural course of Bernard's bipolar disorder is similar to the descriptions found in the clinical literature. The episodes of mood swings, although sometimes occurring quite suddenly, followed a consistent escalating or de-escalating pattern in cycling between the manic and depressed phases. Somewhat less usual than the reported normative pattern was Bernard's tendency to move through the entire mood cycle in a period of several days. At first, he had insight into the fact that he needed help from others to cope with these mood disturbances. However, as these episodes recurred and became more severe, he began to blame others for his problems. Bernard became unwilling to be hospitalized either for treatment or for his own safety and the protection of others.

Various types of antidepressant, sedative, and antipsychotic medications as well as electroconvulsive treatments were ineffective in completely preventing the recurrences of the mood disorder. However, the various treatments did decrease the severity of the symptoms manifested and shortened the episodes of disturbed behavior. Bernard functioned somewhat more adequately on lithium carbonate medication than he had on other drugs. However, a continuing problem was finding an effective dosage level of lithium while keeping the drug's side effects to a manageable level. A further difficulty was to convince Mr. Jacobson to take the medication indefinitely even when his mood was normal.

The incorporation of a behavior modification program with the lithium therapy regimen appeared to increase the probability that further recurrences of severe mood swings could be prevented or attenuated. The annoying drug side effects functioned to make the indefinite maintenance on medication an extremely aversive experience. Bernard could be maintained on a lower dosage level of lithium when the drug was used in combination with the behavior modification program. Therefore, one can be more optimistic that he will continue taking the medication in his present-day treatment setting, because of the reduced side effects.

It would be unrealistic, however, to suggest that the behavior modification program served as anything more than a supplement to the drug therapy regimen. Bernard did not respond at all to the token program until he had taken lithium for several days. The cumulative effect of the drugs eventually resulted in blood levels of lithium that were high enough to show a pharmacologic effect on mood and behavior. Only then was it possible to modify other aspects of his behavior in a more socially effective direction. Nonetheless, the overall effectiveness of the treatment program was enhanced because of Bernard's ability to earn tokens and gain social reinforcement for engaging in socially appropriate behaviors. His history indicated that he had not had the opportunity to receive social approval for positive behaviors in quite some time.

The extension of the behavioral program to the day treatment center and to other aspects of the nonhospital environment appeared to be a significant step in the treatment process. In addition, training Bernard to respond to the early signals of a greater than usual change in mood was important in preventing further extreme mood swings. The monitoring procedure also functioned to give him some feeling of self-control and direction to his life. Through continued self-reinforcement and the reinforcement of others for compliance with the medication and behavioral treatment regimen, perhaps Bernard will be able to stay out of the hospital for longer periods of time and experience a more satisfactory life.

References

American Psychiatric Association (1980). *Diagnostic and statistical manual of mental disorders* (3rd ed.) (DSM-III). Washington, DC: Author.

American Psychiatric Association (1987). *Diagnostic and statistical manual of mental disorders* (3rd ed., rev.) (DSM-III-R). Washington, DC: Author.

Andreasen, N. C. (1984). *The broken brain: The biological revolution in psychiatry.* New York: Harper & Row.

Angst, J., & Perris, C. (1972). The nosology of endogenous depression. Comparison of the results of two studies. *International Journal of Mental Health, 1,* 145–158.

Baron, M., Risch, N., Hamburger, R., Mandel, B., Kushner, S., Newman, M., Drumer, D., & Belmaker, R. H. (1987). Genetic linkage between X-chromosome markers and bipolar affective illness. *Nature, 326,* 289–292.

Beardslee, W. R., & Podorefsky, D. (1988). Resilient adolescents whose parents have serious affective and other psychiatric disorders:

Importance of self-understanding and relationships. *American Journal of Psychiatry, 145*, 63–69.

Beck, A. T. (1967). *Depression: Clinical, experimental and theoretical aspects.* New York: Hoeber Medical Division, Harper & Row.

Bertelsen, A., Harvald, B., & Hauge, M. (1977). A Danish twin study of manic-depressive disorders. *British Journal of Psychiatry, 130*, 330–351.

Cade, J. F. J. (1949). Lithium salts in the treatment of psychotic excitement. *Medical Journal of Australia, 36*, 349–352.

Coryell, W., Andreasen, N. C., Endicott, J., & Keller, M. (1987). The significance of past mania or hypomania in the course and outcome of major depression. *American Journal of Psychiatry, 144*, 309–315.

Depue, R. A., & Iacono, W. G. (1989). Neurobehavioral aspects of affective disorders. *Annual Review of Psychology, 40*, 457–492.

Egeland, J. A., Gerhard, D. S., Pauls, D. L., Sussex, J. N., Kidd, K. K., Allen, C. R., Hostetter, A. M., & Housman, D. E. (1987). Bipolar affective disorders linked to DNA markers on chromosome 11. *Nature, 325*, 783–787.

Elsasser, G. (1952). Ovarial function and body constitution in female inmates of mental hospitals; special reference to schizophrenia. *Archives of Psychiatry* (Berlin), *188*, 218–225.

Gershon, S., & Shopsen, B. (Eds.) (1973). *Lithium: Its role in psychiatric research and treatment.* New York: Plenum Press.

Johnson, F. N. (Ed.) (1975). *Lithium research and therapy.* New York: Academic Press.

Klein, D. N., Depue, R. A., & Slater, J. F. (1985). Cyclothymia in the adolescent offspring of parents with bipolar affective disorder. *Journal of Abnormal Psychology, 94*, 115–127.

Mendlewicz, J., & Rainer, J. D. (1977). Adoption study supporting genetic transmission in manic-depressive illness. *Nature, 268*, 327–329.

Prien, R. F., Klett, C. J., & Caffey, E. M., Jr. (1973). Lithium carbonate and imipramine in prevention of affective disorders. *Archives of General Psychiatry, 29*, 420–425.

Rosenthal, N. E., Sack, D. A., Carpenter, C. J., Parry, B. L., Mendelson, W. B., & Wehr, T. A. (1985). Antidepressant effects of light in seasonal affective disorder. *American Journal of Psychiatry, 142*, 163–170.

Rosenthal, N. E., Sack, D. A., Gillin, J. C., Lewy, A. J., Goodwin, F. K., Davenport, Y., Mueller, P. S., Newsome, D. A., & Wehr, T. A. (1984). Seasonal affective disorder: A description of the syndrome and preliminary findings with light treatment. *Archives of General Psychiatry,* *41,* 72–80.

Slater, E. (1971). The parents and children of manic-depressives. In J. Shields, & I. I. Gottesman (Eds.), *Man, mind, and heredity: Selected papers of Eliot Slater on psychiatry and genetics* (pp. 55–68). Baltimore: Johns Hopkins Press.

Shields, & I. I. Gottesman (Eds.), *Man, mind, and heredity. Selected papers of Eliot Slater on psychiatry and genetics.* Baltimore: Johns Hopkins Press.

Stenstedt, A. A. (1952). A study in manic-depressive psychosis: Clinical, social, and genetic investigations. *Acta Psychiatrica et Neurologica Scandinavica,* Suppl. 79.

Wehr, T. A., & Goodwin, F. K. (1981). Biological rhythms and psychiatry. In S. Arieti & K. H. Brodie (Eds.), *American handbook of psychiatry* (2nd ed.) Vol. 7 (pp. 46–74). New York: Basic Books.

17

Chronic Schizophrenia— "I Can't Think or Talk Straight"

A young woman appeared one evening at a walk-in crisis intervention center and told the person interviewing her that she had come to the center because "I've been feeling really weird. I can't think or talk straight, and it's really a scary feeling. . . . It seems like everything is falling apart in my head. I hear voices telling me I'm 'no good'." The woman's appearance was disheveled; her long brown hair hung down to her shoulders and was uncombed and matted. She looked at the interviewer with an open-eyed, fixed stare, and throughout the discussion her gaze never moved from the interviewer's face. She indicated that she had heard of the center from the staff and fellow residents of a half-way treatment house in which she had recently been.

The young woman's name was Diane Franklin; she was 22 years old. She revealed that she had been in a number of psychiatric treatment facilities since the age of 14, and she had learned to seek help of some type whenever she felt that she could not cope with life on her own. Diane indicated that her family lived in the same city, but she had been trying to be somewhat independent of them. She currently shared a small apartment with another young woman whom she had met at the half-way house.

Diane was the youngest in a family of three children; her 29-year-old sister, a college graduate, was married and had two children; Diane's brother was 26, also a college graduate, and employed as an accountant. Diane's mother had been hospitalized periodically over the past 20 years and was diagnosed as paranoid schizophrenic. Mr. Franklin divorced his wife 11 years previously and subsequently remarried. The family was white, of middle-class, Protestant background.

The counselor at the walk-in clinic suggested that Diane sign herself into an acute psychiatric care facility associated with the center. Diane readily agreed to do so and she was hospitalized on a psychiatric inpatient ward of the hospital.

Family Background

Diane was interviewed by a psychiatry resident. She described her childhood as unhappy and sometimes scary, and recalled the many arguments her parents had had. She indicated that often the heated verbal exchanges between her parents escalated to the point where her mother would grab her father by the shoulders and begin shaking him until her father would have to forcefully push his wife away from him. Diane remembered her mother as being extremely unpredictable, one moment calm and conversing quietly, the next moment becoming quite angry and shouting. Diane felt that her mother had almost always provoked the arguments with her father, often for no reason apparent to Diane.

Diane recalled that during her childhood, her mother was periodically away from home for varying periods of time. Something was always mysterious about these absences; her father typically would only state that Mrs. Franklin had gone for "a rest," and was vague about where his wife had gone to or how long she would be away. These absences increased in frequency and length during the time Diane was in elementary school. Generally, Mr. Franklin's sister came to the house and helped with the family chores when Mrs. Franklin was away. However, she usually did not come to visit when Mrs. Franklin was at home.

Diane indicated that the other members of her family generally "babied" her. She described her father as quite warm and indulgent with her during her childhood when he was not preoccupied with personal problems relating to his wife. She remembered that her older sister made sure Diane ate properly and she also helped Diane prepare her clothes for school the next day. She felt that her sister and brother generally made extra efforts to be nice to her. They often let her have her way and even took care of some of the household tasks that she was supposed to do, if

Diane did not feel like doing them. She said that her aunt also tended to give in to her whims.

The family situation became even more confusing to Diane around the time of her tenth birthday. She recalled that her mother had been particularly argumentative and suspicious, and her parents had engaged in a series of intense arguments. Diane's maternal grandparents, whom she had not seen in several months, came to the house unexpectedly one day. More arguments ensued, and then her parents left with them. Her father returned home later in the day and told Diane and the other children that their mother had been hospitalized for her "nerves" and would be in the hospital for some time. Diane stated that as it turned out, her mother did not come back to live them. Mr. Franklin's sister and his parents became more involved in caring for the family, but the children rarely saw their maternal grandparents.

Several months after Mrs. Franklin left the house, Mr. Franklin told his children that he and their mother were getting a divorce. Diane recalled this period of time as an extremely bewildering one for her. She became even more confused when a number of months later her father brought a woman named Betty Sanders to the house, and told the children that he would like them to meet her. Diane said that Betty seemed rather distant and uncomfortable with her, and Diane felt the same way. This mutual feeling did not change as Betty visited the home more frequently. Diane recalled that when her father told the children that he and Betty were going to be married, she quietly accepted this announcement. However, she felt very frightened and perplexed because she had not seen her mother since she had been hospitalized, and did not know what was going to happen to her mother.

Diane was around 13 years old when she saw her mother for the first time since her hospitalization. Diane described this visit as extremely upsetting because her mother had seemed very distant and uninterested in being with her children. The visit took place at some sort of boarding home, and Diane remembered that a number of the other persons there had stared at her and her sister and brother but had not attempted to converse with them. Diane had felt frightened and uncomfortable for several weeks following this visit, and none of the children had gone out of their way to see their mother after that time. Further, Mr. Franklin discouraged these visits because he felt that they were too upsetting for everyone involved. Their mother rarely called them or made overtures to be with her children.

A social worker conducted several interviews with Mr. Franklin while Diane was hospitalized. Diane's father indicated that living with his wife had become impossible. For the children's benefit as well as his, he had obtained a divorce and custody of the children. Their mother has continued to alternate between the hospital and maintenance on medications in community treatment settings. She apparently was having increasing difficulty communicating with others, and at the time of the evaluation, the Franklin children had not seen their mother in some time. Mr. Franklin revealed that he was content in his second marriage, but wished that his second wife could have been more affectionate and less strict with the children.

Mr. Franklin could recall nothing unusual in Diane's birth or early development, nor had she ever had any unusual medical diseases or significant injuries. Mr. Franklin appeared to be genuinely concerned about his daughter and frustrated and uncertain about how he could help her. He expressed the fear that Diane had fallen into the same pattern of repeated hospitalizations that her mother exhibited. Mr. Franklin stated that his two eldest children were happy and functioning quite adequately, and did not manifest the emotional instability that Diane did. Mr. Franklin confirmed that Diane had been treated as the baby of the family and had not been encouraged to be as independent and self-reliant as she might have been. He recalled that he always was somewhat bewildered by Diane's behavior and had difficulty deciding how to deal with her. As a child, she seemed especially sensitive and hurt by criticism or verbal reprimands, while as an adolescent she sometimes seemed impervious to reprimands or the loss of privileges. Diane and her stepmother argued frequently, and the latter accused Mr. Franklin of being too lenient with his daughter. In retrospect, Mr. Franklin felt that the family pattern that had developed in dealing with Diane was one of inconsistency and indulgence.

School and Peer Relationships

Mr. Franklin indicated that Diane did fairly well in school, although she occasionally went through periods when she appeared confused and "didn't seem to have her two feet on the ground." Her several hospitalizations during adolescence interfered with her school progress, but she nonetheless graduated from high school and had taken some further course work. However, she generally lost interest in her college courses about half-way through the semester, and often did not appear for the final examination.

Diane had a number of male and female friends during high school and she seemed to enjoy being with them. However, Mr. Franklin felt that Diane often did not take a stand about her own wishes and ideas, and she sometimes followed the poor judgment of the persons she was with. In addition, she seemed to go through periods of confusion and inefficiency that often required some type of professional help. During these periods, she seemed to lose interest in her friends and surroundings.

Diane also mentioned that she had enjoyed interacting with other teenagers "when my head was straight." She said that during adolescence she had used marijuana in group settings with her friends and had tried some "downers," but these experiences usually made her feel "weird" afterwards. Her first heterosexual experience occurred when she was 16. She had intercouse on a number of occasions with a boy she had known and liked for some time. These experiences were satisfying, and Diane did not feel guilty about sexual relationships before marriage as long as there was affection involved in the relationship. She has occasionally had sexual relationships with other young men since that time.

Symptom History

The information gained from Diane and her father indicated a long-standing pattern dating back to the period of elementary school in which Diane exhibited poorly organized thinking and behavior, confusion, and inefficiency. Diane periodically experienced difficulties in concentrating and completing her school assignments, and she was evaluated a number of times by a school psychologist. These several evaluations were consistent in finding that Diane was of above average intelligence, but her responses to the test material were often quite unusual and bizarre in comparison with the ideas and associations exhibited by most persons her age. Her uneven concentration on the tasks she was working at also interfered with her performance on the tests.

At 14, Diane saw a psychologist for several months because her complaints of feeling "weird," her forgetfulness, and her confusion about recent events had become quite noticeable. For example, she had taken a test in school the previous week and had received a C- on this examination. Diane later told her father that she could not compete academically with her classmates and she was certain she was not going to pass. She said that the test she had taken was a college entrance examination, and her failing grade would prevent her from continuing in school. However, the teacher indicated to Mr. Franklin that the examination had only involved a class assignment.

The weekly sessions with the psychologist did not improve Diane's behavior and her confusion continued to intensify. Diane was then hospitalized for six weeks in a psychiatric hospital. Under a structured schedule including daily classroom activities, her confusion and feelings of unreality gradually decreased and she was able to return to her regular school.

A similar episode of confusion and concentration difficulties occurred when Diane was 16, and she was hospitalized again. Mr. Franklin was told that Diane was exhibiting many signs of a schizophrenic process. She again complained that she could not think straight, that she had difficulty following through on tasks she was involved in, and that she felt extreme anxiety because it seemed as if she were unable to control the things she said or did. The structured hospital milieu, set up so that events happened on a routine schedule, plus the antipsychotic medication she was placed on, proved helpful. Diane was discharged from the hospital three months later, maintained on the medication. She was enrolled in a different high school and did well for the next year.

After graduation from high school, Diane seemed to drift for a period of over a year. She was involved in activities with her friends from time to time, but she could not decide whether to go to college full-time or get a job. She had stopped taking the antipsychotic medication prescribed for her because she felt the drugs masked her true personality. She again experimented with marijuana and on a number of occasions, cocaine. She was hospitalized at age 20 for several months when her confusion and feelings of unreality intensified again. At this time, she was placed on a different kind of antipsychotic medication. When she had improved to the point where she could be released from the hospital, arrangements were made for her to live in a half-way treatment facility in the community. She stayed at the community facility for a number of months and then moved into an apartment with an acquaintance from the half-way house. She functioned reasonably well in this arrangement for approximately six months, and regularly participated in activities with persons her age. She then stopped taking the prescribed medications, and gradually the confusion and feelings of unreality returned. At this point, she sought help at the walk-in clinic.

Course of Hospitalization

Diane was under the general treatment supervision of a clinical psychologist, Dr. G. He met briefly with Diane on a daily basis, and saw her for more intensive discussions once a week. When first admitted, Diane indicated that she heard voices telling her that she was bad and worthless, and that she might be better off dead. She would look at Dr. G., but then suddenly glance in the opposite direction, almost as if she were checking to see whether someone was behind her. Her body movements at other times during the initial interviews appeared somewhat hesitant. She was quiet and cooperative, but when she tried to answer questions she was unable to get words and coherent sentences out. She would then become confused and unable to talk. Diane eventually was able to state that she did not believe that she was trying to get better. She felt that she was not letting herself think clearly or get straightened out. She also indicated that she did not feel that Dr. G. could understand what she was trying to say because even she could not understand herself.

Psychological testing corroborated that Diane was functioning at a psychotic level, with poor reality testing, unusual and bizarre thought associations, and an impaired ability to concentrate and communicate with others. She was diagnosed as suffering from schizophrenia, undifferentiated type. However, the occasional evidence of delusions of persecution and ideas of reference were suggestive of a paranoid dimension.

Dr. G. worked in consultation with the ward psychiatrist, and various types of antipsychotic medications and combinations of medications were tried and evaluated in terms of their effectiveness in improving Diane's concentration and lessening her feelings of unreality. A structured daily activity plan also was initiated, in which special events and privileges were used as reinforcers for being involved in ward activities such as housekeeping chores, serving meals, interacting with others, and attending group meetings. Diane gradually became more involved in the daily activities on the ward. She began to participate in group therapy sessions and contribute to decisions about ward procedures. She also began establishing positive relationships with the staff and other patients, and exhibited less helplessness and dependency.

Diane's difficulties with memory, concentration, and processing information began to lessen. Her comprehension and abstract abilities improved, and she was able to function with much less external structuring. She still exhibited occasional misperceptions of the events happening around her, but she became increasingly able to recognize her own inappropriate thought processes. When she became aware that her thinking was confused, she was capable of redirecting her attention to the concept she was trying to formulate. She no longer heard voices inside of her and her anxiety level decreased markedly as her functioning improved.

Diane indicated to Dr. G. that a long-standing and still present problem was a personal sense of emptiness and a lack of awareness of her own preferences, goals, and personal strengths. She questioned the continued use of medication and indicated again that the medication prevented people from perceiving her as an individual person. However, Dr. G. explained that the medication was quite important in helping Diane to concentrate, think clearly, and generally function more effectively. He expressed his belief that without the medication Diane would find it difficult to maintain her considerable improvement.

Arrangements were made for Diane to return to a structured half-way house setting in the community. She would reside at this home and work during the day on jobs in the local area. The prognosis for the maintenance of her improved functioning was considered poor, because of the chronic nature of her thought disorder and her tendency to stop taking whatever antipsychotic medication she was on as soon as she began to function more effectively. In the past, she had been unable to deal with the stresses of the ordinary environment when she moved outside of a sheltered, structured setting, and this pattern did not bode well for the future.

Discussion

The DSM-III-R (1987) criteria for schizophrenia include evidence of characteristic psychotic symptoms during the active phase of the disorder, and overall functioning below the highest level the individual previously achieved, for a duration of at least six months. There is a "tendency toward onset in early adult life, recurrence, and deterioration in social and occupational functioning" (p. 187). Characteristic psychotic symptoms consist of disturbances in the following areas: content of thought (delusions), form of thought (loosening of associations, or thoughts shifting rapidly from one topic to another), perception (hallucinations, most commonly auditory), affect (no emotional expression or inappropriate affect), sense of self (confusion about one's identity), volition (disturbance in goal directed activities), interpersonal functioning (social withdrawal, emotional detachment), and psychomotor behavior (reduction in motor activity, bizarre posturing, stereotyped movements). The full range of symptoms is not required for the diagnosis of schizophrenia to be made. The criteria for the undifferentiated type of schizophrenia include prominent psychotic features such as delusions, hallucinations, incoherence, or highly disorganized behavior, not meeting the DSM-III-R criteria for other types of schizophrenia.

The active phase of the schizophrenic illness is often preceded by a prodromal phase marked by an obvious deterioration of functioning. General indicators include social withdrawal, peculiar behavior and affect, unusual thought and perceptual experiences, and deterioration in personal grooming. Often, a residual phase is present after the active period, similar to the prodromal phase. According to DSM-III-R, schizophrenics usually do not return to their highest level of functioning before the onset of the disorder.

In Diane's case, the diagnosis of schizophrenia, undifferentiated type, reflected her long-standing thought disorder and associated history of increasingly impaired functioning, combined with an acute presentation of psychotic symptoms. Her present difficulties involved an intensification of a state of confusion, and an inability to concentrate. Her verbalized feelings of unreality and the hallucinations and misinterpretations of events in the world around her were also extremely debilitating to her general functioning.

To a great extent, one can view the thought disturbance as a primary factor, and Diane's interpersonal and school difficulties as secondary to her problem with processing information and thinking in an organized manner. Her feelings of anxiety and poor self-esteem appear to be largely a result of her inability to control her thoughts and communications with others, and an inability to accurately comprehend what others are communicating to her.

A number of studies have been conducted on the interaction patterns of parents with a schizophrenic child, based on the theory that disturbed family relationships and communications cause the development of schizophrenia in the offspring (e.g., Bateson, Jackson, Haley, & Weakland, 1956; Farina, 1960; Lidz, Cornelison, Fleck, & Terry, 1957). On the other hand, Liem (1974) found that difficulties in communicating with a schizophrenic son in an experimental situation were the result of the poor verbal communications and inappropriate conceptualizations of the youngster, rather than of the parents. This finding suggests that the disturbed communication processes noted in some family interaction studies might be a result of the child's thought disorder, rather than the cause of it.

Jacob (1975) reviewed the studies involving the direct observation of family interactions in disturbed and normal families. He concluded that these investigations have failed to identify specific family patterns that differentiate schizophrenic from normal families. Jacob also felt that these studies shared a methodological fallacy in considering all schizophrenic families as a unitary group.

The importance of evaluating subgroups of schizophrenic families was demonstrated by Roff and Knight (1981). They were able to differentiate two childhood family patterns associated with unfavorable outcome in adult schizophrenics. The first pattern, found in intact families, consisted of a situation of aversive maternal control—that is, anxious, neglectful childrearing practices by the mother. The second pattern associated with relatively poor adult outcome was found in disturbed and disorganized, usually nonintact families. The maternal practices in this type of family milieu were characterized as irresponsible, indifferent, and cold. The demonstration by Roff and Knight of different family environments with different maternal interaction patterns points to the danger of generalizing about schizophrenia as a disorder with invariable environmental influences.

The evaluation of a possible genetic contribution to the development of schizophrenia has been approached from the study of the incidence of schizophrenia in identical (monozygotic) and fraternal (dizygotic) twins, and in families (Gottesman & Shields, 1976). In a careful and extensive investigation, Gottesman and Shields (1972) found that the concordance rate for schizophrenia in monozygotic twins varied between 40 percent and 58 percent. The concordance rate also was affected by the level of severity of the disorder in the proband. For dizygotic twins, the concordance rate varied between 9 percent and 12 percent. Heston (1966) conducted a follow-up of the children of severely schizophrenic mothers who had been separated from their mothers shortly after birth and reared in foster homes. An evaluation of the adult status of these adoptees indicated a high degree of psychiatric and sociopathic disability, in comparison with adoptees of mothers without psychiatric problems. All cases of schizophrenia occurred in the group with a schizophrenic mother.

Further evidence of a biological familial pattern in the incidence of schizophrenia was reported by Kety, Rosenthal, Wender, and Schulsinger (1976). They assessed biological relatives of schizophrenic and psychiatrically normal individuals who had been adopted by nonrelatives shortly after birth. The biological relatives of the schizophrenic adoptees exhibited a significantly greater prevalence of schizophrenia and related disorders than the biological relatives of the control group adoptees. The adoption studies are of interest in their demonstration of the presence of similar disorders in biologically related persons who had no contact with each other. One should view these findings with some caution, though, because some of the adoptee studies have methodological problems centering on a poor evaluation of evidence of psychopathology in the foster parents and in the more general adoptive environment.

A study of the development of schizophrenia in children raised by schizophrenic mothers was begun in Denmark in 1962 (Mednick, Schulsinger, & Schulsinger, 1975). By 1967, two subgroups of these high-risk children could be distinguished: in one, high-risk subjects had already been admitted to psychiatric hospitals or had received psychological treatment; a second high-risk group, was judged to be well over the five-year, follow-up period. Analysis indicated that the mothers of the sick group manifested a greater severity of schizophrenia and had been hospitalized earlier in the child's life than the mothers of the well group.

Differences between the sick and well group children in physiological reactivity, maternal pregnancy problems, and birth complications were found in the initial testing but were not substantiated in a later follow-up (Schulsinger, 1976). Group differences on these variables also were not demonstrated in other studies of high-risk offspring (Erlenmeyer-Kimling, 1975; Hanson, Gottesman, & Heston, 1976).

Several studies have indicated that some high-risk children manifest various attentional and information processing impairments not found in groups of low-risk children. A follow-up study of high-risk children by Hanson, Gottesman, and Heston found that 17 percent of the schizophrenic offspring group and none of the control group youngsters manifested enduring patterns of maladjustment. A number of children in the high-risk group also exhibited several of the signs often associated with the premorbid histories of schizophrenics, such as poor motor skills, large intraindividual performance inconsistencies on cognitive tasks, and apathy and emotional instability. Marcus (cited in Garmezy, 1975) found that the children of schizophrenic mothers manifested attention and reaction time deficits, which were not manifested in the children in the low-risk groups.

Other evidence of attentional and perceptual deficits in high-risk children has been reported. Nuechterlein (1983) found a deficit in signal detection during vigilance in the offspring of schizophrenic mothers, indicating a lowered perceptual sensitivity. Rutschmann, Cornblatt, and Erlenmeyer-Kimling (1986), using a different type of visual tracking task, reported a similar deficit in the high-risk group they studied. In a review of the research on children at risk, Garmezy (1981) concluded that deficits in sustained attention were among the most significant findings in the high-risk group. These attentional difficulties may be related to the Danish findings that the high-risk males who became schizophrenic as adults were described by their teachers as disciplinary problems and as exhibiting poor inhibitory control (John, Mednick, & Schulsinger, 1982).

Some years ago, Meehl (1962) postulated that clinical schizophrenia was the end point of a process involving both genetic and social learning factors. He used the term *schizotaxia* to refer to an integrative neural defect, which he felt was the only thing inherited. The imposition of any type of social learning history on a schizotaxic individual resulted in a personality organization that he called the schizotype. However, if the interpersonal situation was favorable and the person also inherited a low anxiety readiness, the schizotaxic individual would function reasonably adequately. Meehl stated that only a subset of schizotypic personalities would decompensate into clinical schizophrenia, and he felt that the most crucial factor in this decompensation was a schizophrenogenic mother. Other constitutional weaknesses also were posited but the necessary condition for the manifestation of clinical schizophrenia was the inheritance of the integrative neural defect.

Current research has failed to substantiate the universality of that much maligned lady, the schizophrenogenic mother (Fontana, 1966; Hirsch & Leff, 1975). On the other hand, Meehl's concept of the interaction of inherited neurological deficits and environmental stress factors in the manifestation of clinical schizophrenia appears quite appropriate in light of the findings of the follow-up research on high-risk children discussed in a previous paragraph. Further, research on neural and perceptual characteristics related to eye-tracking performance of schizophrenic and other patient groups demonstrated a specific eye movement pattern in schizophrenic patients that was not found in the other groups (Iacono & Koenig, 1983). Schizophrenic patients and a high percentage of their first degree relatives (parents, siblings, or offspring) consistently demonstrated a dysfunction in smooth-pursuit tracking, that is, following a slowly moving target that is in continuous motion (Iacono, 1988). These findings may be quite important in eventually identifying a neurological mechanism through which attention deficits are manifested, and perhaps in identifying a perceptual "marker" that might be suggestive of risk for schizophrenia in nonpatient groups.

The history of the development of Diane's schizophrenia strongly suggests that genetic influences operated in conjunction with environmental stresses in the onset and course of her difficulties. If schizophrenia could be explained entirely as an inherited disorder, one would expect to find a monozygotic twin concordance rate of 100 percent. However, there is little evidence for a concordance rate that high. Therefore, the development of Diane's disorder will be discussed with the assumption that she inherited a biological predisposition to schizophrenia. However, the social learning influences in her life are seen as interacting with this biological dysfunction in the development of clinical schizophrenia.

The presence of a schizophrenic mother during Diane's formative years suggests both genetic and social learning influences. As the research literature strongly indicates, Diane was at a higher than normal risk for the development of schizophrenia because of genetic factors. These genetic influences, possibly in the form of a deficit in neural transmission or in neural integration, could have been manifested by difficulties in concentrating, processing information, and thinking in an organized fashion. In addition, environmental pressures were plentiful. The family was subjected to an intense degree of emotional stress because of the arguments between the parents, the mother's unpredictable behavior, and the frequent verbal abuse she directed toward her children. Diane had ample opportunity to observe her mother's behavior and perhaps adopt some of her mother's poor reality testing and confused view of other people's motives.

Although Diane reported that she engaged in friendly interactions with her peers, she seemed to drift from person to person and group to group. The lack of enduring friendships might have resulted partly from Diane's poor social skills. Further, Diane's mother was an inadequate female role model for teaching her child how to relate harmoniously with other persons. Mr. Franklin's second wife was described as cool, aloof, and authoritarian, and also might not have provided Diane with a role model from which she could learn how to relate to others in a positive way. On the other hand, Diane learned some social skills and during adolescence was able to function well enough to graduate from high school, despite two hospitalizations. Although her mother's behavior resulted in emotional stress and poor learning opportunities for prosocial behavior, it is possible that other adequate role models were present in Diane's life, particularly her sister and brother. She also was able to gain social reinforcement from interactions with her father, who seemed to be genuinely concerned about his daughter and appeared to interact with her in a warm and supportive manner. Diane's siblings and paternal aunt also appeared to be supportive figures in her life.

Diane related to her family in a highly dependent manner, and this dependency behavior was reinforced by all of the persons around her except for her mother, and later her stepmother. Diane's relatives attributed the reinforcement of her dependency behavior to the fact that she was the youngest in the family, and certainly this might have been a significant factor. However, an interesting question is whether the family's avoidance of reinforcing independent behavior was the cause of Diane's dependency or the result of their observation of Diane's early difficulties in processing environmental information. If Diane, from birth on, had exhibited an inappropriate and confused coping style, then the family's initial efforts to protect her and act for her might have been elicited by Diane's own behavior. However, over time these early family interactions became a highly learned pattern of relating to one another, and later in life Diane continued to be reinforced for acting in a helpless manner. This dependent and helpless behavior pattern was also noted in the hospital and was changed in that setting through the use of medication and a behavior modification program.

An unknown factor is why Diane's schizotypic personality decompensated into clinical schizophrenia, while her brother and sister, if they were schizotypes, remained competent and functioned quite well. It is possible that Diane had a greater genetic loading for whatever the inherited mechanism(s) are that constitute the biological predisposition for schizophrenia. From a social learning perspective, the timing of Diane's birth also could have been crucial in her later development of schizophrenia. Her mother's symptoms were reported to have become markedly worse around the time of Diane's birth and in the ensuing years. Therefore, Diane's siblings were older when their mother showed a deterioration in functioning, and they had a longer opportunity to develop more effective social skills. If they already had been able to establish some relationships with peers, they would have been less dependent on interacting with their mother than Diane was when Mrs. Franklin's behavior became quite disturbed. Therefore, their relationships with other persons could have remained essentially normal. The association of Diane's birth and the intensification of the mother's symptoms suggests that Mrs. Franklin might have been quite rejecting of Diane and particularly unsupportive in her interactions with her youngest daughter.

The question remains, "What about Diane's future?" Her history is consistent with Phillips's (1953) designation of the individual with a poor adjustment prior to the development of schizophrenia. Her stressful family history, difficulties in school and in forming enduring relationships with peers, and the gradual worsening of her symptoms over time all suggest the poor premorbid history associated with an unfavorable prognosis.

Diane's treatment history indicated that various kinds of antipsychotic medications were helpful in alleviating the symptoms of her thought disorder. This improvement in communicating with others was associated with a greater responsiveness to material and social reinforcements and the development of more assertive and independent behaviors. However, a continuing problem with the use of antipsychotic medications is the individual's tendency to stop taking these drugs as soon as he or she is functioning better. As the thought disturbance again becomes more severe, the individual may be unable to pay attention to, or might be uninterested in, the kinds of social support opportunities they would be responsive to if they were in a less agitated state. This is not to imply that the behavior of schizophrenics can be modified only when they are on medication. There has been ample demonstration that token economy programs can increase the skills of institutionalized chronic schizophrenics (Neale & Oltmanns, 1980). However, these patients usually were not in a highly agitated state at the time that a particular program was instituted.

It seems that an appropriate treatment strategy was chosen for Diane when she left the hospital. Her behavior could be monitored in a half-way house setting and she could receive social approval for taking her medication. Long-term placement in this structured community facility also seems extremely important in increasing her social skills and in alleviating some of the stresses of coping with an unpredictable environment. Further, the vocational training and job placement with others from the half-way house could give her a sense of accomplishment and self-esteem. However, it is unlikely that Diane would be willing to remain in this setting for an indefinite period of time. Therefore, Diane might experience repeated hospitalizations throughout her life because of the stress of interacting with persons in the natural environment, plus the insidious nature of the chronic schizophrenic process. The ultimate hope, of course, is that the continuing study of biological and psychological factors predictive of schizophrenia will result in the development and application of more effective prevention and treatment techniques.

References

American Psychiatric Association (1987). *Diagnostic and statistical manual of mental disorders* (3rd ed., rev.) (DSM-III-R). Washington, DC: Author.

Bateson, G., Jackson, D. D., Haley, J., & Weakland, J. (1956). Toward a theory of schizophrenia. *Behavioral Science, 1,* 251–264.

Erlenmeyer-Kimling, L. A. (1975). A prospective study of children at risk for schizophrenia: Methodological considerations and some preliminary findings. In R. D. Wirt, G. Winokur, & M. Roff (Eds.), *Life history research in psychopathology* (Vol. IV) (pp. 23–46). Minneapolis: University of Minnesota Press.

Farina, A. (1960). Patterns of role dominance and conflict in parents of schizophrenic patients. *Journal of Abnormal and Social Psychology, 61,* 31–38.

Fontana, A. F. (1966). Familial etiology of schizophrenia: Is a scientific methodology possible? *Psychological Bulletin, 66,* 214–227.

Garmezy, N. (1975). The experimental study of children vulnerable to psychopathology. In A. Davids (Ed.), *Child personality and psychopathology: Current topics* (Vol. II) (pp. 171–216). New York: Wiley.

Garmezy, N. (1981). The current status of research with children at risk for schizophrenia and other forms of psychopathology. In G. A. Allen & D. A. Regier (Eds.), *Etiology of Schizophrenia* (pp. 23–39). NIMH and U.S. Government Printing Office, Washington, DC 20402.

Gottesman, I. I., & Shields, J. (1972). *Schizophrenia and genetics.* New York: Academic Press.

Gottesman, I. I., & Shields, J. (1976). A critical view of recent adoption, twin, and family studies of schizophrenia: Behavioral genetics perspectives. *Schizophrenia Bulletin, 2,* 360–401.

Hanson, D. R., Gottesman, I. I., & Heston, L. L. (1976). Some possible childhood indicators of adult schizophrenia inferred from children of schizophrenics. *British Journal of Psychiatry, 129,* 142–154.

Heston, L. L. (1966). Psychiatric disorders in foster home reared children of schizophrenic mothers. *British Journal of Psychiatry, 112,* 819–825.

Hirsch, S. R., & Leff, J. P. (1975). *Abnormalities in parents of schizophrenics.* Maudsley Monograph No. 22. London: Oxford University Press.

Iacono, W. G. (1988). Eye movement abnormalities in schizophrenic and affective disorders. In C. W. Johnston & F. J. Pirozzolo (Eds.), *Neuropsychology of eye movements* (pp. 115–145). Hillsdale, NJ: Lawrence Erlbaum.

Iacono, W. G., & Koenig, W. G. R. (1983). Features that distinguish the smooth-pursuit eye-tracking performance of schizophrenic, affective-disorder, and normal individuals. *Journal of Abnormal Psychology, 92,* 29–41.

Jacob, T. (1975). Family interaction in disturbed and normal families: A methodological and substantive review. *Psychological Bulletin, 82,* 33–65.

John, R. S., Mednick, S. A., & Schulsinger, F. (1982). Teacher reports as a predictor of schizophrenia and borderline schizophrenia: A Bayesian decision analysis. *Journal of Abnormal Psychology, 91,* 399–413.

Kety, S. S., Rosenthal, D., Wender, P. H., & Schulsinger, F. (1976). Studies based on a total sample of adopted individuals and their relatives: Why they were necessary, what they demonstrated and failed to demonstrate. *Schizophrenia Bulletin, 2,* 413–428.

Lidz, T., Cornelison, A. R., Fleck, S., & Terry, D. (1957). The intrafamilial environment of schizophrenic patients: II. Marital schism and marital skew. *American Journal of Psychiatry, 114,* 241–248.

Liem, J. H. (1974). Effects of verbal communications of parents and children: A comparison of normal and schizophrenic families. *Journal of Consulting and Clinical Psychology, 42,* 438–450.

Mednick, S. A., Schulsinger, H., & Schulsinger, F. (1975). Schizophrenia in children of schizophrenic mothers. In A. Davids (Ed.), *Child personality and psychopathology: Current topics* (Vol. II) (pp. 217–252). New York: Wiley.

Meehl, P. (1962). Schizotaxia, schizotypy, schizophrenia. *American Psychologist, 17,* 827–838.

Neale, J. M., & Oltmanns, T. F. (1980). *Schizophrenia.* New York: Wiley.

Nuechterlein, K. H. (1983). Signal detection in vigilance tasks and behavioral attributes among offspring of schizophrenic mothers and among hyperactive children. *Journal of Abnormal Psychology, 92,* 4–28.

Philips, L. (1953). Case history data and prognosis in schizophrenia. *Journal of Nervous and Mental Disease, 117,* 515–525.

Roff, J. D., & Knight, R. (1981). Family characteristics, childhood symptoms, and adult outcome in schizophrenia. *Journal of Abnormal Psychology, 90,* 510–520.

Rutschmann, J., Cornblatt, B., & Erlenmeyer-Kimling, L. (1986). Sustained attention in children at risk for schizophrenia: Findings with two visual continuous performance tests in a new sample. *Journal of Abnormal Child Psychology, 14,* 365–385.

Schulsinger, H. (1976). A ten-year follow-up of children of schizophrenic mothers. Clinical assessment. *Acta Psychiatrica Scandinavica, 53,* 371–386.

18

Paranoid Schizophrenia — The Case of Carlos Rivera

Carlos Rivera, a 47-year-old Mexican-American, was committed by the court to a maximum security hospital for the criminally insane with a diagnosis of schizophrenia, paranoid type. This was his sixth commitment to a state mental hospital in the last 15 years, and his fourth stay at a hospital for the criminally insane. The present commitment procedures were initiated after Carlos was apprehended for burglarizing a cocktail lounge and pistol-whipping the owner when the latter attempted to resist. A patron in the bar recognized Carlos, and the patient was arrested shortly thereafter.

Carlos stated that he was hazy about what happened in the bar, and he could not remember the details of the burglary. He only remembered that he had taken benzedrine and wine before the alleged event, and "my mind blanked out. You lose your reasoning power. I took all that wine and I woke up in jail." He did not recall repeatedly shouting, "You're not going to control me; you're not going to control me!"

The police report indicated that Carlos had "gone berserk" when the police officers attempted to arrest him. He struggled forcefully with them and threatened to kill anyone who came near him. He was eventually overpowered when a policeman came up behind him and knocked the gun he was brandishing out of his hand. Carlos and several other persons received minor injuries as a result of the struggle.

Carlos had been married twice. His first marriage lasted for five years, and a daughter born during this time was the patient's only child. She was approximately 19 years old at the time of the evaluation. Carlos and his second wife separated after they were married for two years, and at the time of the arrest, Carlos was unsure of where his wife was living.

Carlos had an arrest record that dated back to when he was 12 years old. He was apprehended on numerous occasions for various types of theft, and he was also arrested several times for assault with a dangerous weapon. Since his first arrest at age 12, Carlos had spent a total of 23 years in either penal institutions or mental hospitals.

Social History

Carlos grew up in a poverty-stricken Mexican-American area in a large city on the West coast. His parents emigrated from Mexico to the United States in hopes of bettering their economic status. Carlos was the youngest in a family of five boys and two girls. All of the children were born in the United States.

The Riveras' standard of living had always been marginal because Mr. Rivera was never able to obtain steady employment. He was only hired for seasonal jobs that involved unskilled, manual labor. Mrs. Rivera was employed occasionally as an assembly line worker, but her time was limited by family responsibilities, and in addition there were frequent layoffs at the factories.

Carlos described his father as a stern man with a quick temper. His father often expressed bitterness and disappointment because of the difficult life the family had in the United States, and he spent much of his time talking and drinking with the other men in the area. Mr. Rivera reacted quickly when any of his children misbehaved, and he frequently punished Carlos and his siblings by hitting them with a strap. Mrs. Rivera rarely punished the children for misbehaving. She usually waited until her husband was home, then told him about any problems with the youngsters. Mr. Rivera would then administer some form of physical punishment.

The patient was born with a deformed foot and had always walked with a limp. Carlos had a dark complexion, and he said that his siblings and the neighborhood children constantly teased him because he was skinny and black, and because he had a crippled foot. He stated that his parents rarely intervened when his siblings teased him, and his mother did not treat him in a special manner because he was the youngest child. On the contrary, it seemed that his mother was preoccupied with so many problems that his difficulties were always overlooked in the usual turmoil at home.

The patient revealed that he was tormented by the children's taunts about his physical appearance, and he was also distressed by the harsh punishment he received at his father's hands. There was little he could do to prevent his father from hitting him, but he found that he could make the other youngsters stop teasing him if he fought back or gave them some food. Carlos quickly developed a skill at fighting, and he indicated that he began to enjoy the knowledge that some of the children were afraid of him.

Having enough to eat was a real problem in the Rivera household. Carlos related that he often was hungry when he left the table after a meal. He began stealing food from stores in the neighborhood when he was about six or seven, and he occasionally shared the food with his siblings or other children. Carlos's first official difficulty with the police occurred in relation to stealing food: he was arrested at age 12 for breaking into a food store. As a result, he was sent to Juvenile Hall and was kept there for two weeks.

The patient said that some older boys taught him how to masturbate when he was about six years old, and he had continued this activity since that time. His first heterosexual experience occurred when he was about 14. According to Carlos, this episode was the result of a dare by some boys because they expected that he would be unable to perform sexually. Carlos revealed that he had surprised the other boys when he attracted a girl and then successfully engaged in sexual intercourse.

The patient indicated that he had had many heterosexual experiences since adolescence, during the times when he was out of institutions. He stated that these experiences were pleasurable, but he did not feel that sex had ever been a strong necessity in his life. He had also had a number of homosexual propositions over the course of his life. He occasionally submitted to homosexual advances when he was in prison, usually when he feared for his physical safety if he did not submit. However, he stated that homosexual encounters nauseated him and he tried to avoid them if at all possible.

Educational Background

Carlos quit school when he was 15 years old. He was in eighth grade at the time, and he felt that he had not learned much in school. His teachers never took the time to listen to the ideas he was trying to express, and they failed to help him when he was having difficulty with a particular subject. Carlos also indicated that he disliked standing up and reciting in front of the class. He was ashamed that he was so skinny, and the other youngsters made unfavorable comments about his physical appearance when he spoke in class. Carlos said that no matter what he did in school, he could not win. If he knew the answer to a question the teacher asked him, the children called him "smarty," and if he was unable to answer the question, they called him "burro."

Delinquency Record

During his adolescence and young adulthood, Carlos was in and out of juvenile detention homes, reform schools, and prisons. He was confined to a state mental hospital for several days when he was 14. According to the patient, he was hospitalized briefly for observation because he faked a suicide attempt in order to get out of reform school. On another occasion, he escaped from a police station while he was being charged with possession of marijuana, and the police never traced him. Carlos was made a ward of the Juvenile Court at age 15 because of his numerous arrests.

As a teenager, Carlos was unruly and drank a great deal. He said that he has frequently been intoxicated, and during these periods, he "feels like a zombie. No reasoning power. I go to sleep." The patient also stated that he had taken benzedrine for many years because the drug pepped him up and he enjoyed this feeling. He denied ever using heroin.

Carlos became a member of an antisocial neighborhood gang when he was 17. The gang members drank a great deal and committed various crimes including burglary and physical assault. Carlos said that he had to go out of his way to be daring and tough, because he had to continually prove to the others that he was not a weakling. Carlos and some other gang members were caught in the midst of a burglary, and Carlos sustained a bullet in his arm in a shoot-out with the police. He was 19 years old at the time.

Carlos continued to engage in antisocial activities each time he was released from prison. He said that the prospect of imprisonment did not frighten him, because the food was good, and he had a chance to continue his education. Carlos indicated that he spent his free time in prison reading, and for the first time in his life he felt that he was gaining important knowledge. Carlos read many books dealing with metaphysical and religious subjects, and he also had become very intrigued with occult topics.

Marital History

Carlos got married when he was 20; his wife was three years younger than he. Carlos stated that they got along fairly well, except for a constant concern about financial matters. After his marriage, Carlos continued to steal cars and other objects in order to gain money for his daily needs. He said he was too skinny to earn a living by any other means.

Carlos had been married for two years when he received a five-year prison sentence for auto theft. His wife divorced him while he was in prison, because she had found another man with whom she wanted to live. She also told Carlos that this person would be a good father to Carlos's daughter. Carlos agreed to the divorce and he had not seen his wife or daughter since.

The patient remarried when he was 28 years old. He indicated that he and his second wife, Maria, had a good relationship and they were sexually compatible. Carlos said that they enjoyed living in some rooms of their own, even though the house in which they resided was quite dilapidated. Carlos continued to steal cars and burglarize stores because he was always short of funds. He stated that employers still would not hire him for manual labor, and he had no skills for any other type of job. Carlos was apprehended again after he and Maria had been married for two years, and this time he was sentenced to a four-year prison term for theft. When Carlos was sent back to prison, his wife went to visit some relatives in the Midwest. Carlos had neither seen nor heard from her since.

Religion

The patient was raised as a Catholic and attended church regularly with his mother and siblings until he was 14 years old. Carlos indicated that for a period of time after he remarried, he considered himself a Protestant because he felt that the Catholic church had too many sins. He said that he still did not believe in different churches because there is only one God.

The patient decided to regard himself as a Catholic again when he was 34 years old, just after his release from prison. He began to attend church from time to time, and he indicated that he prayed every night, which he believed was more important than going to church. Carlos related that he usually prayed to God to help him overcome the evil forces that made his life so full of misery and sadness. He stated that he had been confused many times during the past few years, because it seemed to him that God and the Devil were one Being, or that God had joined with the Devil in tormenting him. Carlos felt that the only defense he had was prayer, even though he was not sure whether God's intentions toward him were good or evil.

Later Antisocial Record

Carlos reported that over the past few years his activities had become increasingly associated with heavy drinking, and he was frequently arrested. While drinking he became very angry about his current situation, because he felt that other persons were preventing him from having the kind of life he wanted. Carlos indicated that if he then got into a fight or was caught stealing something, he "went crazy" and had to be forcibly subdued because he wanted to kill anyone who annoyed him.

Carlos was 35 years old when he was sent to a state mental hospital for the criminally insane for the first time. He was apprehended while in the process of armed robbery, and he became physically violent and incoherent when the police attempted to arrest him. He had spent the previous few hours drinking, and he indicated that he did not clearly remember what he did after leaving the bar.

During his second confinement to a hospital for the criminally insane, Carlos was described as disoriented and physically violent, and he was given a total of thirty electroconvulsive treatments. A marked improvement in his behavior was noted after the course of shock therapy. Carlos revealed that the shock treatments were quite frightening to him, and during that period he believed that the doctors were trying to kill him. The patient was confined to the same hospital for varying periods over the course of the next ten years, and at each discharge, he was continued on antipsychotic medications. However, he did not follow the medication regimen once he was released from the hospital.

Interview and Psychological Evaluation

Carlos was referred for psychological testing in order to determine whether he was mentally competent to stand trial. He appeared to the examiner to be younger than 47 years of age and of more robust build than the patient's descriptions indicated. Carlos looked directly at the psychologist during the interview, and he spoke to her in a forceful tone of voice. Although the patient completed the tests administered to him, he repeatedly commented that he did not like taking the tests because everyone would then be able to read his mind.

The patient had difficulty remembering a number of past events that were documented in his files. He was also unable to remember the name of the hospital he was confined in, and he was disoriented about what season, month, and year it was. His conversation was hard to follow at times because he tended to interject comments that to a casual listener would appear irrelevant to the topic discussed.

Carlos scored within the dull-normal range of functioning on an individually administered intelligence test. There was evidence of an impairment in abstract reasoning due to the intrusion of distracting thoughts. Also, the patient's responses on items measuring judgment in social situations were quite deviant from the responses given by persons on whom the test was standardized. Carlos was also asked to draw a picture of a person. He drew a figure with long hair and said that the picture was "Jesus Christ. Full of suffering."

Several other tests were administered, and the results substantiated the clinical impression that Carlos had difficulty distinguishing between reality and fantasy. There was also evidence suggesting that Carlos experienced a great deal of anger that he did not overtly express. Further, he attributed hostile intentions to the persons around him. There was no evidence of organic brain pathology. If there had been, brain changes caused by excessive alcohol or drug use might have been suspected in the etiology of Carlos's thought disorder and violent behavior.

Carlos told the examiner that as he became more aware of how other persons lived, he became more certain that he would never be able to change his life. He stated that the forces in the world around him seemed too strong and powerful for him to fight. When he tried to overcome his problems by stealing or fighting, he found himself in further difficulty. In addition, Carlos saw no hope for himself in terms of a job, and having enough money to buy food was a very real problem for him. The patient stated that he could see no path that would allow him to rise above the misery of his present existence.

Carlos attributed his problems primarily to "the Gringoes." He felt that white persons were in control over him; they owned the factories or fields where he worked, the house he lived in, and the stores where he bought food and clothes. The laws were made by Gringoes, and it was the white lawyer and the white judge who conspired to sentence him to jail. It seemed to Carlos that no matter where he turned, he could find no evidence of Chicanos having control over their own fate. It was outsiders who did not understand or care about him who were causing him so much difficulty.

The patient also felt that members of his own ethnic group were persecuting him. Carlos stated that early in life he had learned never to trust anyone and always to rely on himself. He had to be constantly on the alert so others would not cheat or hurt him. Carlos said that his parents and his brothers and sisters were against him too, and they would hurt him also if they had the opportunity to do so. He remembered numerous occasions during his childhood when he was teased or hit by another youngster and none of his siblings came to his aid. Instead, they joined in the teasing and added further to his misery. Carlos recalled that his mother never intervened to help him either, even though some children might have been hitting him, or his father severely beating him.

Carlos became extremely agitated as he related these events. He spoke in an increasingly loud tone of voice and he gesticulated with his hands and arms in large sweeping movements. He ignored the examiner's questions and comments and in his discourse began to mix Spanish words with English. He repeated over and over again that he was intelligent and resourceful and he deserved more in life than to be locked up in hospitals and prisons because persons were purposely tormenting him. Even God, he felt, had allied Himself with the Devil in order to persecute him.

The patient reported that he could hear voices laughing at him and telling him to do evil things. The voices also made fun of him because he was so skinny and ugly, and they told him that it was impossible for a woman to be attracted to him. Many times he became enraged by the voices he heard, and before he knew it, he was involved in a physical dispute with someone. Carlos indicated that the voices seemed to bother him more when he was in his home environment than when he was confined in a hospital. The patient revealed that he also had special powers that made it possible for him to hear what other persons were thinking about him. He said that he knew some of the doctors were trying to kill him.

On the basis of the interview and test material, the psychologist concluded that Carlos Rivera was not able to take care of himself and his property, and therefore he was not mentally competent to stand trial (California Probate Code Annotated, 1971).

Ward Behavior

The patient was described as "suspicious and hostile" because he interpreted many of the ward procedures as in some way an attempt to control his mind. The nursing personnel noted that even though Carlos was occasionally confused about what day it was or why he had been committed, he was extremely alert to his immediate environment. He promptly noticed any change in the hospital routine and became angry when there was any modification in procedure. He also questioned very closely any new persons admitted to the ward, in order to find out why they were there and if they had heard of him in some way. No one came to visit Carlos while he was at the hospital.

The patient often muttered to himself in Spanish, and when he was asked what he was saying, he replied that he was talking to the voices. However, the patient's reports of auditory hallucinations declined the longer he stayed in the hospital. Carlos was maintained on large doses of antipsychotic medication, and he became less agitated and suspicious over time.

After he was hospitalized for several months, Carlos was assigned to an indoor paint crew. He appeared to enjoy this job, and it was noted that he learned very quickly, worked carefully, and took pride in his work. His supervisor commented that the patient was agile, despite his limp.

Carlos had a very poor relationship with the other members of the paint crew. An incident was recorded in which another patient accused Carlos of being careless with the paint equipment, and Carlos reportedly became enraged and threatened to kill the other person. Carlos also accused the other worker of being unfair to Mexicans, even though the latter was himself a Mexican-American. Carlos had to be forcibly brought back to the ward after this incident, but several days later he was allowed to rejoin the work crew. There was no further mention of the altercation when Carlos went back to work.

Course of Therapy

Three months after Carlos was admitted to the hospital, the staff physician recommended that Carlos participate in group therapy in addition to continuing on the antipsychotic medication. The patient regularly attended the meetings of an ongoing therapy group, but he did not participate very often in the discussions. He became extremely disturbed if someone criticized him, and he would then start shouting vehemently in Spanish until the session ended, or until the focus of attention was diverted to someone else.

The therapist reported that there had been little change in the patient's attitudes or behavior in the group in the course of four months of therapy sessions. However, Carlos attended the meetings regularly, and the therapist felt that eventually Carlos would learn how to communicate more effectively with the other group members. The patient also remained on the paint crew. This work was considered beneficial because it kept Carlos active and involved with other persons, and because it provided him with an occupational skill should he be discharged from the hospital. However, the prognosis for a long-term improvement in functioning was considered poor, because of the extensive nature of the patient's interpersonal difficulties and his thought disorder.

Discussion

The DSM-III-R (1987) diagnostic criteria for schizophrenia refer to disturbances in thought processes, motor activity, and affect, with continuing signs of dysfunction present for at least six months. (See Chapter 17 for more details.) Work, social relations, and self-care behaviors are below the highest level achieved before the onset of the acute phase of this disorder. The six-month period of disturbance can include a prodromal phase in which a deterioration in functioning was clearly evident, but not to the degree of severity seen in the active phase.

The criteria for the paranoid type of schizophrenia specifically include "preoccupation with one or more systemized delusions or with frequent auditory hallucinations related to a single theme," and specifically exclude "incoherence, marked loosening of associations, flat or grossly inappropriate affect, catatonic behavior, grossly disorganized behavior" (DSM-III-R, p. 197). Therefore, paranoid schizophrenics present a clinical picture that is relatively more intact than the disorganized thought and behavioral patterns exhibited by patients with other types of schizophrenia.

According to DSM-III-R, paranoid schizophrenics may not show a marked impairment in functioning if the delusional material is not acted upon. Thus, an individual who feels that he or she can perceive another person's thoughts but does nothing about this, might not exhibit an obvious impairment in daily activities. The age of onset of paranoid schizophrenia tends to be later than the usual onset of other types of schizophrenia, and there often is a more stable symptom pattern from one acute phase of the illness to the next. Further, the prognosis may be more favorable than in other types of schizophrenia.

Other diagnoses that would be applicable in Carlos Rivera's case are psychoactive substance use disorder, and antisocial personality disorder. The latter classification refers to the long-standing delinquency pattern he exhibited, and reflects an extensive personality disturbance that was evident for many years before the onset of the schizophrenic disorder.

Psychodynamic formulations of the development of paranoid schizophrenia place strong emphasis on the individual's use of the defense mechanism of projection. The paranoid individual ascribes to others characteristics that cannot be accepted in the self, particularly strong sexual and aggressive impulses (Wolman, 1965). A commonly held belief since the writings of Sigmund Freud (1959) is that the paranoid employs the defense mechanism of projection to guard against homosexual impulses. The projection of these impulses to other persons is assumed to be unconscious and an indication of an impairment of reality testing.

An analysis of Carlos's ability to relate to other persons is important in assessing the traditional psychodynamic viewpoint that paranoid schizophrenia, particularly in males, is a result of latent homosexual impulses. The patient exhibited a general orientation, based on an aversive life experience, of viewing all persons in the environment as hostile and devious. There was no one with whom Carlos had ever been able to establish a warm emotional relationship. His description of his two marriages indicated that very little shared communication had occurred.

His sexual behavior was dependent on availability, and he chose female partners when he had the opportunity to do so, despite his feelings that his body was unattractive. He at times submitted to homosexual advances in prison, but he did not find these experiences gratifying. Carlos had never learned the interpersonal skills necessary to form a close relationship with any person, male or female. It therefore seems more consistent with the facts to interpret the patient's disturbed behavior as the result of an inability to communicate with others, rather than as resulting from the influence of latent homosexual impulses.

Carlos Rivera's life history indicates that his psychopathological behavior fell into two somewhat different patterns. Antisocial activities associated with adequate reality testing were more typical of the earlier part of his life, and stealing and physical violence in conjunction with confused reality testing was a pattern that developed at a later period. This history is consistent with 30-year follow-up data demonstrating that for some individuals, child and adolescent antisocial behavior was a precursor to an adult form of schizophrenia (Robins, 1966).

Theft became an established behavior pattern when Carlos was still a young child. He was reinforced for stealing by the gratification he received from the food he ate when he was hungry, and by the esteem he earned from his peers when he stole something they valued. The persons in his social environment communicated the attitude that one could do little to improve one's life, because the rules and regulations that governed one's existence were in the hands of fate or the Gringoes, and therefore outside of one's personal control. Any act that flaunted the establishment's rules, such as skipping school or taking things that did not belong to one, was highly reinforcing because it made fun of or contradicted the perceived hold institutional forces and alien persons had on one's life.

When Carlos was 35 years old, the quality of his antisocial acts changed and he was then confined for periods of time in mental hospitals rather than in prisons. The thefts that he carried out became more interpersonal in nature. Instead of stealing cars or appliances, he began to burglarize establishments when other persons were present, and he frequently engaged in physical violence during these burglary attempts. As he became more emotionally involved in the conviction that everyone was against him, he began to attribute hostile intentions to all persons with whom he came into contact. The poor reality testing associated with this belief system eventually became delusional in quality because it was so pervasive and it aroused such intense affect. As Carlos began to pay more attention to his covert thoughts and less attention to objective aspects of the environment, he also began to report that he had heard voices talking to him.

The psychologically crushing effect of an economically deprived environment has been documented in a number of studies demonstrating a strong relationship between socioeconomic class and mental illness (Hollingshead & Redlich, 1958; Pasamanick, Roberts, Lemkau, & Krueger, 1964; Srole, Langner, Michael, Opler, & Rennie, 1962). The various studies are consistent in finding the highest rates of schizophrenia in the lowest social class (Neale & Oltmanns, 1980). Economic change also appears to influence hospital admissions (Brenner, 1973), suggesting that the stresses associated with economic adversity and unemployment can precipitate the overt symptoms of schizophrenia that necessitate hospitalization.

Thus, individuals of the lowest socioeconomic stratum are confronted with physical and psychological stressors that are related to continual economic insecurity. Their childhood environment may contain little love, protection, and stability; the risk of physical or sexual abuse is significantly higher for lower socioeconomic class children and adults (Baldwin & Oliver, 1975; Finkelhor, 1984). Many of the poor grow up experiencing a lifetime of neglect and rejection, first by parents and siblings, and later by society as a whole.

The problem of severe emotional disturbance in economically and socially deprived persons is therefore one of significant proportion. The adverse environmental conditions experienced by the poor may result in a lowering of resistance to stress. Further, Langner and Michael (1963) reported that lower status persons tended to agree with statements suggesting feelings of futility, resignation, alienation from group and society, and social isolation. Psychological difficulties, antisocial behavior, and the use of chemical substances as an expression of alienation and as an escape from adverse living conditions seem likely to ensue from these life experiences.

Minority group members have been concentrated in the lowest economic strata of our society, and the increase in black young adult suicide rates (Goodstein & Calhoun, 1982) has been attributed to these feelings of futility about the possibility of improving one's socioeconomic status. Minority group members with few realistic hopes of upward mobility may express an external control orientation (Rotter, 1966), that is, that they are not the masters of their own destinies, and that the events that happen to them are a matter of luck or a result of forces outside their personal control. Phares (1972) suggested that many instances of criminal behavior may be the result of behavior motivated by this external control orientation.

Lefcourt and Ladwig (1972) studied a group of white and minority group inmates who came from similar socioeconomic backgrounds and who were imprisoned for similar crimes, generally car theft. Their findings indeed indicated that the minority group inmates exhibited a relatively greater expectancy that their fate was controlled by forces outside of their personal control than did the white inmates. Thus, antisocial behavior could be reinforced by peers if these individuals shared an attitude that one must take what one can get, because hard work will not change one's status in life.

Carlos was born with a number of physical characteristics over which he had no personal control, and his life experiences seemed consistently outside his control from that point on. He discovered that because he had a darker skin and was more vulnerable than others around him, his family and peers imitated the behaviors and attitudes they had learned from the majority group. Through ridicule, they behaved toward Carlos as the majority group behaved toward them.

Carlos was able to protect himself and actively gain social approval from persons in his social milieu only through imitating the aggressive behavior he observed around him. His environment was one in which aggression was reinforced and modeled by his father, siblings, and peer group. Bandura and Walters (1959) had similarly found that the fathers of delinquent boys modeled physical aggression and reinforced their youngsters for acting in an aggressive manner toward other children.

The haven that Carlos eventually found from the realities of his life was the sheltered world of the prison and the mental hospital. During his first stay at Juvenile Hall, Carlos enjoyed the food, and he found the sleeping accommodations more comfortable than what was available at home. The routine of prison life may have been monotonous and at times violent, but Carlos also derived a great deal of reinforcement from being confined. He had the opportunity to further his education, and he found this to be a rewarding experience.

Carlos's behavior became more psychopathological as he grew older. This deterioration in functioning was associated with a worsening of the interpersonal and economic circumstances of his life. It is unclear whether Carlos also suffered from some type of biological predisposition for schizophrenia that interacted with the stresses of his life and eventually resulted in the psychotic behavior he manifested. When Carlos was released from prison at age 34, he was separated from his second wife and had lost contact with his daughter. He rarely saw his parents or any other family members. There was no one who could offer him emotional support, and there was no one to converse with as a means of testing social reality. Carlos increasingly believed that life was unjust and that the persons existing in the world had hostile intentions toward him. These beliefs could not be compared with an external standard of judgment or tested for social consensus, because Carlos spent so much of his time alone. He usually interacted with other persons while he was drinking heavily in a bar, and these occasions were not conducive to rational evaluations of social reality. As his life became more unhappy, Carlos turned to religion, in a confused interaction between himself and a deity.

As he grew older, Carlos also experienced a greater need to obtain a job where he would be regularly employed and be able to live above the poverty level. He therefore became more and more frustrated as he compared his present existence with his aspirations for a happier and more comfortable life. He was faced with the realization that his life would never be any better than it was at the present time. Carlos responded to these feelings of isolation and economic frustration in the way that he had learned to respond to negative emotions in the past: he became extremely angry, and he was frequently involved in fights. He found some relief from the negative emotions engendered by his evaluation of his life situation through using alcohol and drugs. He therefore drank until he reached a state in which he was amnesic about his activities during the drinking episode.

Carlos's response to alcohol and benzedrine was shaped by his bothersome thoughts and individualized interpretations of his surroundings. Physical aggression and theft were the most frequent behaviors he engaged in to deal with his problems, and he did not discriminate between his fellow Mexican-Americans or white persons in the expression of antisocial behavior. Carlos frequently became physically violent while drinking, and he engaged in burglary as a means of enhancing his economic situation. These behaviors were also self-reinforcing because they functioned as an attack on external society, which Carlos perceived as responsible for his personal plight. A further reinforcement for antisocial behavior was the improvement in his economic and social situation through confinement.

Carlos's reports of auditory hallucinations were of relatively recent origin, and their emergence signalled a more serious phase of his illness. Auditory hallucinations have been shown to be elicited by the patient engaging in and listening to his or her own subvocal speech (Bick & Kinsbourne, 1987). The hallucination is the experience of this subvocalization as a voice that emanates from other persons. The messages of the subvocal speech reflect the patient's disordered thought processes.

Carlos's record indicated that he had received a series of electroconvulsive treatments during one hospital confinement, and a reduction in physical violence and a diminishment of verbal delusional behavior were concomitant with the shock treatments. In subsequent hospitalizations, he responded to the antipsychotic medication with a diminishment of actively disturbed behavior.

The development and extensive use of various forms of antipsychotic medication has dramatically changed the treatment of psychotic individuals. There has been an associated marked decline in the use of electroshock or insulin convulsive treatments, as well as the surgical procedure of prefrontal lobotomy, in which the nerve fibers between the prefrontal and frontal lobes of the brain are severed. A number of carefully controlled studies have indicated that antipsychotic medications do not act simply as tranquilizers, but have an effect on the thought disorder itself (Cole & Davis, 1969; Davis, 1978). Some of the reported benefits of these medications are improved verbal communication in previously incoherent patients, and restored mental clarity in those who were disoriented and confused. In some patients, hallucinations and delusions are eliminated, while in others hallucinations still may be present, but the patient reports that he or she is not bothered by these experiences. A number of theories currently are being tested to ascertain why some schizophrenics improve on particular types of antipsychotic medications while others do not. However, present findings are not definitive.

A significant factor in a patient's compliance in the use of antipsychotic medications is the presence of drug side effects. Dizziness, dry mouth, and constipation are frequently reported complaints across a range of antipsychotic medications, and cardiac irregularities and sexual dysfunction have also been documented. However, the most serious complications stem from a dysfunction of the movement regulating systems of the brain (Snyder, 1980). The symptoms include tremors, shuffling gait, drooling, chewing and lip movements, and finger and leg movements. One particularly noticeable motor complication, involving severe facial and other movements, is called tardive dyskinesia. This condition appears to be permanent, and reducing the drug dosage level may conversely increase the intensity of these symptoms.

An alternative procedure for teaching schizophrenic patients to develop greater self-sufficiency has been evaluated by Gordon Paul. Chronic patients in a mental institution were placed either in a social learning program that included a token economy, or in a milieu (social community) therapy program (Paul & Lentz, 1977). The goal of the social learning program was to provide patients with the basic interpersonal and work habit skills that would enable them to function in the community. However, multiple factors appear to be crucial in determining long-term results. One issue is the adequacy and availability of facilities in the community. A more general issue is the psychological and economic supportiveness of the environment to which the person returns.

That chronic schizophrenics can be helped to live in a more productive manner in the community is demonstrated by the findings of a 32-year longitudinal study of chronic psychotic patients who were placed in a comprehensive rehabilitation program. This extensive intervention program consisted of community treatment that included halfway houses, outpatient clinic treatment, and job placement (Harding, Brooks, Ashikaga, Strauss, & Breier, 1987). Long-term follow-up demonstrated that one-half to two-thirds of the patients were considerably improved or recovered.

For those patients returning home after hospitalization, the family environment to which the patient returns is also an important component of outcome. The presence of negative family attitudes toward discharged schizophrenic patients has been demonstrated to be a predictor of unfavorable long-term status. Criticism and over-involvement as expressed by a key relative was the strongest predictor of relapse nine months after hospital discharge (Vaughn, Snyder, Jones, Freeman, & Falloon, 1984). Therefore, both the family environment and resources in the community in which the discharged patient lives have an effect on outcome.

In Carlos's case, the absence of a supportive family milieu to which he could return likely exacerbated his adjustment problems. The result was a worsening of his disorder, whether or not he continued to take antipsychotic medications when he was discharged from the hospital.

Carlos obviously required help and instruction in many areas of functioning, and group therapy was one method of accomplishing behavior change. However, a treatment strategy that does not deal with the social environment will not be successful. Carlos needed training in specific job skills, but he also had to be able to obtain a job so he could use these skills to improve his economic situation.

The interpersonal and environmental difficulties that Carlos Rivera faced were many. His problems required modification in many areas, so the prison and the mental hospital would no longer have to serve as a refuge from the harsh realities of his existence. Hopefully, in a supervised community setting with monitoring of his medications, an improvement in general functioning could occur. However, given the extent of psychopathology evident and the meagerness of environmental resources, the outlook for the future seems poor.

References

American Psychiatric Association (1987). *Diagnostic and statistical manual of mental disorders* (3rd ed., rev.) (DSM-III-R). Washington, DC: Author.

Baldwin, J. A., & Oliver, J. E. (1975). Epidemiology and family characteristics of severely-abused children. *British Journal of Preventive and Social Medicine, 29,* 205–221.

Bandura, A., & Walters, R. M. (1959). *Adolescent aggression.* New York: Ronald.

Bick, P. A., & Kinsbourne, M. (1987). Auditory hallucinations and subvocal speech in schizophrenic patients. *American Journal of Psychiatry, 144,* 222–225.

Brenner, M. H. (1973). *Mental illness and the economy.* Cambridge: Harvard University Press.

California Probate Court Annotated. Sec. 1460 (1959 ed.), 1971 pocket supplement.

Cole, J. O., & Davis, J. M. (1969). Antipsychotic drugs. In L. Bellak & L. Loeb (Eds.), *The schizophrenic syndrome.* New York: Grune & Stratton.

Davis, J. M. (1978). Dopamine theory of schizophrenia: A two-factor theory. In L. C. Wynne, R. L. Cromwell, and S. Matthysse (Eds.), *The nature of schizophrenia: New approaches to research and treatment.* New York: Wiley.

Finkelhor, D. (1984). *Child sexual abuse: New theory and research.* New York: Free Press.

Freud, S. (1959). *Collected papers.* Vol. 2. New York: Basic Books.

Goodstein, L. D., & Calhoun, J. F. (1982). *Understanding abnormal behavior.* Reading, MA: Addison-Wesley.

Harding, C. M., Brooks, G. W., Ashikaga, T., Strauss, J. S., & Breier, A. (1987). The Vermont longitudinal study of persons with severe mental illness, I: Methodology, study sample, and overall status 32 years later. *American Journal of Psychiatry, 144,* 718–726.

A. B., & Redlich, F. C. (1958). *Social class and mental illness.* New York: Wiley.

Langner, T. S., & Michael, S. T. (1963). *The midtown Manhattan study.* Vol. II. *Life stress and mental health.* New York: The Free Press of Glencoe.

Lefcourt, H. M., & Ladwig, G. W. (1972). The American Negro: A problem in expectancies. In J. R. Rotter, J. E. Chance, & E. J. Phares (Eds.), *Applications of a social learning theory of personality* (pp. 424–433). New York: Holt, Rinehart, & Winston.

Neale, J. M., & Oltmanns, T. F. (1980). *Schizophrenia.* New York: Wiley.

Pasamanick, B., Roberts, D. W., Lemkau, P. W., & Krueger, D. B. (1964). A survey of mental disease in an urban population: Prevalence by race and income. In F. Riessman, J. Cohen, & A. Pearl (Eds.), *Mental health of the poor.* New York: Free Press.

Paul, G. L., and Lentz, R. J. (1977). *The psychosocial treatment of chronic mental patients.* Cambridge: Harvard University Press.

Phares, E. J. (1972). A social learning theory approach to psychopathology. In J. R. Rotter, J. E. Chance, & E. J. Phares (Eds.), *Applications of a social learning theory of personality* (pp. 436–469). New York: Holt, Rinehart, & Winston.

Robins, L. (1966). *Deviant children grown up.* Baltimore: Williams and Wilkins.

Rotter, J. B. (1966). Generalized expectancies for internal versus external control of reinforcement. *Psychological Monographs, 80* (Whole No. 609).

Snyder, S. H. (1980). *Biological aspects of mental disorder.* New York: Oxford University Press.

Srole, L., Langner, T. S., Michael, S. T., Opler, M. K., & Rennie, T. A. C. (1962). *The midtown Manhattan study* (Vol. I). *Mental health in the metropolis.* New York: McGraw-Hill.

Vaughn, C. E., Snyder, K. S., Jones, S., Freeman, W. G., & Falloon, I. R. H. (1984). Family factors in schizophrenic relapse: Replication in California of British research on expressed emotion. *Archives of General Psychiatry, 41,* 1169–1177.

Wolman, B. B. (1965). Schizophrenia and related disorders. In B. B. Wolman (Ed.), *Handbook of clinical psychology* (pp. 976–1029). New York: McGraw-Hill.

19

Catatonic Schizophrenia and Resistance to Treatment— The Case of John Cronholm

John Cronholm was 28 years old at the time of his most recent hospital commitment. This was his fourth commitment in six years to a state mental hospital, and his seventh psychiatric hospitalization. During the period of his latest admission, he sat without moving for many hours at a time. He seemingly made an effort to speak and moved his lips when someone asked him a question, but he was only able to articulate several words in sequence.

John was tall and thin and his eyes had a vacant stare, even when he tried to talk. His hair hung down over his shoulders, and his general appearance was one of dishevelment. He was willing to dress only in hospital-issued pants, top, and slippers during the first part of his hospital stay.

Two weeks prior to his commitment, John had been taken by the police to the emergency room of a county hospital after they noticed him wandering in traffic. He was dirty and malnourished, suffering from a severe cough, and apparently living in the streets. John spent a week in the hospital on antibiotic treatment for viral pneumonia, and during this period he was essentially mute. When the pneumonia cleared, he was transferred to the hospital psychiatry unit and placed on a 72-hour hold to keep him in the hospital for psychiatric observation. He was diagnosed at that time as suffering from schizophrenia, catatonic type.

The county hospital staff were able to identify John through some papers in his possession. John previously had been hospitalized at the same facility, and the prior case records contained the names and address of his parents. His parents lived in another city, and they were informed that John was in the hospital. They did not come to visit him, but kept track of his progress through calls to the nursing station. His parents were notified when the staff physician initiated the 72-hour hold proceeding. The legal requirement for such a proceeding is that patients must be judged in imminent danger of harming themselves or others if released. John received a copy of the required form as part of the procedure, and his parents agreed that the hold was appropriate to John's welfare. However, John refused to agree to a voluntary transfer to the state mental hospital for more extended treatment. At that point his father, on the advice of the county hospital psychiatric staff, submitted a petition for judicial or involuntary commitment. After a hearing in which the family and John were each represented by attorneys, the judge ruled that John should be committed to the state hospital for an indefinite period because he was mentally ill and not competent to care for himself.

Family Background

John was the oldest of the three children in the Cronholm family. He had a brother Paul who was three years younger than he, and a sister Suzanne five years younger than John. The family was Caucasian, of middle-class socioeconomic background, and resided in a large city in the Northwest. Mr. Cronholm held a middle management position in an industrial firm, and Mrs. Cronholm worked for a smaller company as a financial accounts specialist. The family was of Protestant religious affiliation and attended church services from time to time while the children were growing up. Paul and Suzanne were both college graduates, and lived in different cities in California. Suzanne worked in a stock brokerage office, and Paul worked for an engineering firm. Both were single and according to their parents, usually participated in social activities. Each shared an apartment with several other roommates.

Because of John's muteness at his respective hospital admissions, information about his childhood, family history, and current activities was obtained almost entirely from the parents. They described their children as getting along quite well during their childhood, and stated that the family did many things together. Both Mr. and Mrs. Cronholm had relatives who lived in the area, and they visited with them frequently.

The parents indicated that John's interactions with his brother and sister during adolescence became somewhat distant. John did not seem terribly interested in his siblings' activities. He rarely initiated conversations with Suzanne and Paul, and he also did not get into fights with them. Correspondingly, Paul and Suzanne did not make any extra effort to involve John in their conversations or activities. However, John usually said hello to Paul and Suzanne when he came home from school or other places, and he conversed with them more extensively from time to time. Both parents indicated that Paul and Suzanne had a much closer relationship with each other than either had with John. Mr. and Mrs. Cronholm stated that their children had had no problems with drug or alcohol use, disobedience, or problems at school when they were adolescents.

There is no family history among the parents, siblings, or extended relatives of outpatient treatment or hospitalization for schizophrenia, mood disorders, or other psychiatric disorders. There is also no family history of suicide attempts or substance abuse problems.

School and Peer Relationships

John was described by his parents as an exceptionally able student in junior and senior high school, and they indicated that he had several male and female friends. John was on the soccer team from eighth grade until high school graduation, and he generally was a good athlete who enjoyed participating in both organized and informal sports activities. He also was a talented artist, and many of the pictures that he painted while in high school were hung at home and at his church. There was no information available regarding John's sexual experiences, and he consistently refused to answer questions on this topic when asked during his various hospital interviews. His parents indicated that to their knowledge he had never gone on a date with just one person.

John attended a university in another city and did well academically for about one semester. However, he stopped going to classes during the second semester of his first year, and moved from his dormitory residence to another part of the same city.

Psychopathology History

It is unclear whether a trained observer would have noticed early signs of schizophrenia when John was in high school. While John's parents indicated that he had a group of friends throughout this time, John later described himself as a loner during high school. There is a consensus that John began having significant difficulties in functioning several months after he started college.

John worked at a succession of unskilled jobs subsequent to dropping out of college. He remained at each job for progressively shorter periods, and began to spend a greater amount of time between jobs staying in his room in the rooming house in which he now lived. His parents continued to phone him regularly and encouraged him to come back home. However, John indicated that he preferred living alone.

John's parents stated that about a year after he dropped out of college, John took a bus to the East Coast to see that part of the country. However, he did not inform his parents that he was leaving. They found out he was gone when they attempted to phone and were told that he had moved. Shortly thereafter, John sent a postcard to his parents telling them that he was in New York City, but he did not include an address or phone number. Mr. and Mrs. Cronholm indicated that they were extremely worried about John's psychological condition. They were greatly relieved when several weeks later he returned to the city where he had attended college and called his parents from there. Although John lived 500 miles away from his parents, they almost immediately drove to see him at his rented room.

The Cronholms reported that John seemed greatly changed. He was not very communicative, nor was he responsive to suggestions that he look for a job. John apparently had worked from time to time in New York, and he had about $30 in his possession. It seemed to Mr. and Mrs. Cronholm that something extremely upsetting had happened to John in New York. He alluded to some "bad things happening," looked visibly upset, and then sobbed for a minute or two. However, he would not discuss any details about what had occurred.

John's parents insisted that he undergo some sort of psychological evaluation, and he reluctantly agreed. His parents were able to set up an appointment at a local clinic for the following week, with all three attending. Because John was 19 years old and no longer a minor, the clinic staff had to obtain his permission to convey to Mr. and Mrs. Cronholm their assessment of John's psychological status. John gave permission for the staff to do so, and the parents were informed that the professional consensus was that John would benefit from short-term hospitalization and individual therapy. The staff felt it important to further observe and evaluate John's behavior, and that making a formal diagnosis at this point was premature.

John remained in an inpatient facility for 30 days. The staff felt that it was likely he was manifesting the early signs of schizophrenia, and he was placed on an antipsychotic medication with the recommendation that he continue taking the medication after discharge. John was somewhat more communicative when he was released from the hospital. The psychiatric resident who had seen him twice a week in therapy indicated that these sessions had been helpful in encouraging John to find a job and be more socially active.

John returned to his rooming house and worked from time to time, but he lived primarily on welfare assistance. He stopped taking the prescribed medications as soon as he left the hospital, stating that taking medications was contrary to his ethical values. Over the next two years he was hospitalized two more times when his parents persuaded him to seek treatment for his deteriorating condition. He now was diagnosed as suffering from schizophrenia, undifferentiated type. He had become less and less communicative, more isolated, and disheveled in appearance. He spent most of his time wandering in the streets. At these subsequent evaluations and short-term hospitalizations, he again was placed on antipsychotic medications. John showed an improvement while in the hospital, but each time he left the hospital prematurely against medical advice. Upon leaving, he immediately stopped taking the prescribed medications and his condition again worsened.

At age 22, John was legally committed to a state mental hospital for the first time. The staff consensus was that his symptoms were now consistent with a diagnosis of schizophrenia, catatonic type. He had been living in the streets or at shelters for the homeless for the past several months, and he was barely communicative. He still did not want to live in the same city with his parents, and they were finding it more and more difficult to keep in contact with him. They initiated involuntary commitment proceedings in hopes that a longer course of treatment would help him. Over the next five years, John was committed to a state hospital two additional times. Commitment proceedings were initiated by John's parents in cooperation with the county hospital staff because John was judged not competent to make a decision about his need for treatment. Although John did not strongly object to hospitalization, he did not voluntarily agree. He was released from the hospital on both occasions after several months of treatment, when his condition stabilized with maintenance on antipsychotic medications.

While in the hospital, John refused to take the medications prescribed for him. After each refusal, the physician in charge of his case initiated procedures for the use of nonemergency forced medication, requiring John to take these drugs against his will. During his second commitment, John developed dystonic torticollis, a contraction and twisting of the neck that sometimes occurs with the use of antipsychotic medications. This symptom reflects a dysfunction of the extrapyramidal motor system, a system that includes brain structures that modulate movement. During his third commitment, John experienced severe side effects from a different antipsychotic medication. He now developed a larger number of symptoms of dysfunction of the extrapyramidal motor system, including tremor, motor restlessness and pacing, and muscle spasms of the arms and legs causing them to twist to one side. With both episodes of severe medication symptoms, lowering the drug dosage level alleviated these problems. However, the motor system side effects that John experienced suggested that he was highly sensitive to antipsychotic medications.

Current Hospitalization

John's parents were interviewed as part of the information obtained for the present commitment proceedings. Mr. and Mrs. Cronholm indicated that John had functioned extremely well after his last hospital discharge and seemed almost normal again. However, when he came home for a family occasion about three months previously, it was apparent that he was "starting to slip again." He exhibited hesitancy in speech, throwing his head back and blinking his eyes, and slept a great deal, symptoms typical of his illness in the past. A month later, Mr. and Mrs. Cronholm visited John and noted that when he began to speak, the words just drifted off and he then became silent. He brought food up to his mouth, set it back down on his plate, and then rapidly stuffed a large amount into his mouth. Sometimes he then took the food out of his mouth and put it back on his plate. He had not worked in several months, and his parents described him as very unkempt, wiping his nose on his hat and scarf when they went outside. Mr. Cronholm pleaded with John to resume taking his medications, but John responded "what for?"

Over the past two months, John apparently began living on the streets and in shelters for the homeless, and eating very little. He was significantly underweight at the time he was picked up and hospitalized with viral pneumonia.

After John was treated for pneumonia and the commitment was approved, he was transferred to the same state hospital in which he had been treated on three previous occasions. John agreed to cooperate in a mental status examination conducted by a medical student and staff psychiatrist, but he did not respond verbally to most of the questions asked. However, he appeared to be trying to cooperate. His facial expression suggested distress when he could not give a verbal response to a particular question, and he smiled occasionally when he was able to articulate an appropriate response.

The treatment plan was to place John again on antipsychotic medications, and a medication that might prevent the motor side effects. The goal was to alleviate his muteness and withdrawal through the use of medications. After John became more verbal, he could then gain additional treatment benefit through participation in ward meetings and other group activities aimed at increasing social awareness and interpersonal skills.

John refused to take the prescribed medications, communicating that he did not like the way the medications made him feel. As in the past, the hospital staff then recommended that he be placed on non-emergency forced medications. One week after admission, this recommendation was approved by the hospital treatment review panel. Approval was granted because John had shown marked improvement with antipsychotic medications during his prior hospitalizations. Further, the drug side effects he had experienced previously markedly diminished when he had been placed on a lower dosage level of the drug.

Interview and Psychological Evaluation

John was seen by Dr. H., a clinical psychologist on the staff of the state hospital. The patient was now more mobile than he had been when admitted to that hospital ten days previously. He no longer sat unmoving in one position for hours at a time; he walked in a slow but awkward manner. John nodded his head in response to a question by Dr. H., indicating that he was willing to talk. However, he still had great difficulty articulating words and sentences. John was able to communicate to Dr. H. that she should ask him direct questions. When she followed this procedure, he then was able to give simple responses. There was no overt evidence that John was experiencing delusions or hallucinations, and he indicated that he had never experienced these symptoms in the past.

At a later interview with Dr. H. in which he was more verbal, he spoke in a quiet and halting manner. He stated that he was unsure what had caused him to become mute and withdrawn after his last discharge from the hospital, but he thought his behavior was related to the fact that he had been sick with a cold. He revealed that he did not like the situation at his rooming house because the building was noisy and dirty, and he was about to be evicted for nonpayment of rent. He dealt with these problems by living in the streets rather than looking for another place to live, even though he did have enough funds to rent another room.

John had definite views on who at the hospital he did or did not get along with, which he shared with Dr. H. He had not liked the physician and social worker who had been assigned to him at his last hospitalization, and he also specified which nursing personnel he preferred to others. He was adamant that his family not be contacted for treatment planning. He stated his belief that problems with his family which he would not detail were causing much of his current difficulty in functioning.

At this second interview, John agreed to participate in psychological testing. However, after reading the MMPI test booklet for several minutes, he indicated that he could not complete the MMPI because it was not possible for him to choose a true or false answer to each of the test items. He also had great difficulty generating descriptions for the various projective test stimuli administered to him. After approximately 15 minutes of testing, he told Dr. H. that he was not able to participate in any further testing because he could not express his thoughts clearly enough.

Dr. H. recommended that in the near future John be transferred from the locked ward to a less restrictive ward. She felt that the current risk that John would wander off the hospital grounds was minimal, and the open ward offered a behavior modification program more specifically focused on enhancing interpersonal skills. Dr. H. also suggested that as John became more communicative, one-to-one supportive therapy aimed at helping him with the tasks of daily living might be of benefit. John was judged not to be a good candidate for insight-oriented therapy aimed at personality reconstruction. He was not able to verbalize his feelings and goals, and he had poor social skills. The therapeutic help he needed was on a more concrete, situational level.

Hospital Treatment

John was transferred to an open ward with a step-wise behavior modification program. Patients at the first step of the program earn points for privileges such as snacks, cigarettes, and toilet articles. The patients earn points by making their beds, combing their hair, going to meals on time, or attending group sessions. With each successive step in the program, a greater amount of prosocial behavior is required to earn points. These more complex behaviors include speaking in group sessions and initiating requests for activities. After the patients accrue a designated number of points, they move on to the next and succeeding steps, in which they progressively earn more freedom and independence, including going to the canteen in another building, being allowed out on the hospital grounds unescorted, and attending evening movies at the hospital.

With the treatment review panel's consent, John was started on a combination of a phenothiazine (major tranquilizer) antipsychotic medication and a drug to reduce motor side effects of this drug. John did not experience any motor symptoms at the dosage level he was on. His mental condition improved noticeably, and he accepted without protest the medications he was under order to take each day. However, after he had been hospitalized for about a month, he appealed the treatment review panel's decision forcing him to take medications against his will. The review panel interviewed John, discussed his request to rescind the forced medication order, and upheld his appeal. The panel members agreed that John's mental condition had improved to the point where he was able to make an informed decision regarding the continued use of medication. However, after the medication order was lifted, John did agree to take the medications voluntarily even though he stated as he had in the past, that taking these drugs conflicted with his ethical values.

John steadily improved. In the individual and group sessions, he learned more effective skills for caring for himself. He role-played acting in a more assertive manner in situations he might encounter outside of the hospital, such as living in an apartment with noisy neighbors next door. In the individual sessions, the therapist and John explored ideas about the type of job for which John could apply when he was released from the hospital. The challenge was to focus on jobs that were interesting to him, and that he had a realistic chance of obtaining.

John decided that he would make use of the social service assistance available at the hospital to obtain a more intellectually stimulating job than the ones he had held previously. He also was considering taking some college courses, but he did not want to enroll as a full-time student. Because he was reluctant to ask his parents for financial assistance for tuition, he realized that it was especially important for him to become more financially independent and not rely on welfare assistance.

John was discharged after a six-month stay. He agreed to live in a half way house in the community after his release, the first time he had been willing to do so. The personnel in this semi-structured setting should be helpful in providing continued support for John to interact socially and to hold a job, and helpful as well in overseeing John's medical regimen.

Discussion

The DSM-III-R (1987) criteria for the classification of schizophrenia are presented in detail in the Discussion sections of Chapters 17 and 18.

According to DSM-III-R, the diagnosis of the catatonic type of schizophrenia requires at least one of the following: catatonic mutism or stupor, catatonic negativism marked by a resistance to instructions by others or attempts by others to move the individual, maintaining a rigid posture against efforts to be moved (catatonic rigidity), excited motor activity not influenced by obvious external stimuli (catatonic excitement), and the assumption of strange postures. Alternation between the extremes of catatonic excitement and rigidity can occur. Mutism is a common feature of this disorder, and malnutrition and exhaustion may be evident as well. Individuals require close supervision to avoid hurting themselves or others. Although once fairly common, catatonic schizophrenia is now quite rare in North America and Europe.

The recent psychiatric literature reflects an interest in positive and negative symptoms in schizophrenia, with some reports of differential long-term outcome. Positive symptoms of schizophrenia are active processes engaged in by the patient, such as hallucinations, delusions, bizarre behaviors, and some type of thought disorder (Carpenter, Heinrichs, & Wagman, 1988). Negative symptoms involve a lessening or avoidance of engagement with the environment. These symptoms include restricted affect and emotional range, poverty of speech, diminished social interests, and the constriction of ideas. Positive symptoms may fluctuate over time, while the presence of negative symptoms is seen as an enduring feature of schizophrenia.

Andreasen and Olsen (1982) reported that negative symptom schizophrenics were less educated, had a poorer premorbid adjustment, enlarged cerebral ventricles as assessed through CT (computerized tomography) scan, and higher ratings of impairment at both admission and discharge in comparison with positive symptom schizophrenics. Schizophrenic patients with the poorest long-term outcome manifested more severe negative symptoms than chronic schizophrenic patients who had episodes of remission and a more fluctuating course of disorder (Keefe, et al., 1987). The clinical picture of negative symptoms in schizophrenia is similar to the early descriptions by Kraeplin (1883) of what he termed dementia praecox, described as an insidious disorder beginning in adolescence and resulting in progressive deterioration over time.

Findings of sex differences in the incidence and course of schizophrenia suggest an interaction between biological vulnerability and social factors in the etiology and outcome of this disorder. A prospective study identifying all cases of first onset psychosis in a large catchment area identified three times as many males as females with a first diagnosis of schizophrenia (Iacono & Beiser, 1989). Further, schizophrenic women had a somewhat better outcome after 18 months than schizophrenic men.

Goldstein (1988) reported relatively better outcome for women in a ten-year follow-up. Differences in sex-role expectations for males and females to act in an independent manner, as well as a greater availability of social support for females may be important social influences in the differential sex ratio of disorder and outcome.

A number of investigations have assessed the size of the brain ventricles (fluid spaces within the brain) and cortical atrophy in schizophrenic patients. The goal of these studies is to ascertain whether there are brain structure abnormalities that might account for the schizophrenic disorder. Some studies reported that a greater proportion of the schizophrenic than comparison groups exhibited lateral ventricular enlargement according to a CT scan measure of ventricle-brain ratio (VBR) (Losonczy et al., 1986; Schulz et al., 1983). However, the interpretation of VBR differences is not absolutely clear. The Losonczy group did not find a relationship between lateral VBR and severity of positive or negative symptoms, or response to antipsychotic drug treatment. Iacono reported that schizophrenic patients experiencing their first onset of psychosis had larger third ventricles, but did not exhibit larger lateral ventricles than other first onset psychotic groups, and normal subjects (Iacono et al., 1988). In addition, the Iacono group found no differences between groups on a measure of cortical atrophy.

Generalizations cannot be made currently about the presence and site of brain tissue shrinkage and ventricle enlargement, and its relationship to the etiology of schizophrenia. Smith and Iacono (1986) concluded that whether a study reported significant lateral VBR differences between schizophrenic and comparison groups depended on the particular comparison group chosen. While the VBR for the schizophrenic patients generally remained similar across the studies reviewed, the medical patients chosen as a control group in studies that reported ventricular enlargement in schizophrenia had relatively smaller ventricles than control subjects chosen in studies that did not find enlargement.

The dopamine hypothesis positing an excess of dopamine activity is another biological process proposed to be important in the etiology of schizophrenia. Dopamine is a neurotransmitter that travels in a specific pathway throughout the limbic system, a brain system involved in emotional expression (Andreasen, 1984). A large number of dopamine receptors are located in the limbic system and the basal ganglia, the latter important in modulating motor activity. The action of the phenothiazine antipsychotic medications is to block the transmission of dopamine in the brain by occupying dopamine receptor sites. Because of this process, the extrapyramidal and other motor side effects of antipsychotic medications may be due to their action in occupying dopamine receptors in the basal ganglia. However, the evidence supporting the dopamine hypothesis is conflicting. A study comparing the post-mortem brains of schizophrenics and nonschizophrenics found a higher level of dopamine activity in the schizophrenic group (Wise & Stein, 1973), while another study failed to find group differences (Wyatt, Schwartz, Erdelyi, & Barchas, 1975). A more recent study that directly measured dopamine receptors found significantly higher densities of these receptors in the brain tissue of schizophrenic than control group subjects (Seeman, et al., 1984).

The role of genetic factors in the etiology of psychopathological disorders is a subject of current interest. The family history literature covered in previous chapters in reference to schizophrenia, mood disorders, and alcoholism might lead to the impression that all or most individuals manifesting a particular disorder will have a relative who also fits diagnostic criteria for the same disorder. However, in John Cronholm's case as well as the case of paranoid schizophrenia presented in Chapter 18, there was no reported evidence of schizophrenia in family members.

The prevalence rates of psychopathology in close relatives of diagnosed patients must be looked at in perspective. A study of the first degree relatives (i.e., parents, siblings, or offspring) of catatonic schizophrenics found that these particular family members had a 5.6 percent morbid risk for any type of schizophrenia, a 5.7 percent morbid risk for nonaffective psychotic disorders, and a 12 percent morbid risk for affective disorders (Kendler, Gruenberg, & Tsuang, 1988). For individuals diagnosed as paranoid schizophrenic, the morbid risk for any type of schizophrenia in first degree relatives was 3.9 percent, for nonaffective psychotic disorders, 10.8 percent, and for affective disorders, 6.7 percent. Therefore, although the prevalence rates for schizophrenia and other disorders in first degree relatives are substantially higher than the base rates in the general population, the majority of close relatives of schizophrenic patients do not exhibit a psychotic disorder.

The findings regarding possible morphological abnormalities in the brains of schizophrenic individuals, and the importance of other biological processes point to some fascinating directions for further exploration and clarification. It is not likely that a single structural, physiological, or neurological abnormality will be identified that can explain entirely the etiology of schizophrenia. However, research findings may eventually enable one to identify particular types of schizophrenia in which brain shrinkage or other biological processes are significant etiological agents. Perhaps the presence in an individual of a high ventricle-brain ratio in a particular area of the brain may eventually prove to be a marker of a vulnerability or predisposition for the later development of schizophrenia.

In considering the cause of catatonic schizophrenia in John's case, one is struck by the gradual and insidious nature of his illness. Following a diathesis-stress model, it is possible that there was an interaction between some type of brain dysfunction and environmental stress in precipitating his disorder. However, the stressors may have been those associated with normal developmental or maturation processes such as family and societal expectations for more independent behavior in adolescence and young adulthood. There was no recorded evidence in John's childhood history of severe disturbances in family interaction patterns, or reports of other external stress factors that might be causally linked to the onset and progression of his disorder.

Although John's childhood development appeared fairly normal, the information obtained regarding his adolescent years is ambiguous. All informants agreed that he participated in organized and informal sports activities. However, Mr. and Mrs. Cronholm reported that John had a circle of friends, and John indicated that he was a loner. They all may be correct. Although John attended social functions, he already may have been experiencing the interpersonal anxiety and emotional estrangement from others that is one of the characteristics of a schizophrenic process. His apparent sexual inexperience may have been another early sign of discomfort and withdrawal from others. John's decision to attend a college in a city away from his family, while certainly not unusual in and of itself, also may have been an aspect of his emotional and social withdrawal.

When John left home, he was required to function in a more autonomous manner. He had to make financial decisions on his own and monitor his expenditures. There also were increased academic demands, and he had to cope with the sometimes aversive behaviors of neighbors and strangers. His response to these pressures was withdrawal from others, coupled with gradually worsening difficulties in verbal communication.

As John's illness became more severe, the manifestations were more obvious. He exhibited an unconcern about personal hygiene, lived in the streets, and was oblivious to traffic. He was not overtly sensitive or interested in how others responded to his behavior, and eventually he became mute. John's poor nutritional status and the fact that he came to the notice of the police because he was wandering in the street indicates that he had reached the point where his illness was a threat to his health and safety.

John's trip to New York at an earlier phase of his disorder contains a number of unexplained elements. Apparently, something very traumatic happened to him about which he was unable to talk. He did communicate to his therapist that the episode involved other males. If sexual activity was involved in this encounter, John's general withdrawal from others makes it unlikely that the experience was voluntary or enjoyable. John may have been subjected to a sexual assault or physically beaten. His clearly distressed behavior in alluding to these events illustrates the vulnerability of mentally ill persons to exploitation and assault, particularly when living in conditions in which they may be confronted by antisocial persons.

John exhibited a number of negative symptoms of schizophrenia, including restricted affect and range of emotions, withdrawal from others, and impoverished speech. There were no signs of positive symptoms of hallucinations or delusions during the periods when he was more verbally fluent, or any behavioral signs of responding to voices when he was mute. According to the research literature, the predominance of negative symptoms suggests a relatively poor long-term outcome. Because John never had undergone brain imaging tests, one does not know whether he exhibited ventricle enlargement or signs of cortical atrophy. However, at the present time, the relationship of these factors to vulnerability to schizophrenia and ultimate prognosis is not clear.

An important and troubling feature in John's treatment history is the fact that he consistently stopped taking his medications whenever he left the hospital, despite his marked improvement while on the drug regimen. The distressing motor and other side effects he experienced at times likely contributed to his repeated decisions to discontinue medication usage. However, the negativism and resistance that is part of the catatonic schizophrenic disorder also seems a factor. John may not have wanted to comply with the wishes of others. It also is likely that he experienced reality, with its expectations for independent living and communication with others, as an aversive experience. John may have been more comfortable psychologically in his withdrawal, and found it reinforcing to return to this noncommunicative state. His lack of interest after his previous hospitalizations in living in some type of supervised community facility seems to be a consequence of a need to withdraw from others.

At the present time, John interacted minimally with his sister and brother, and there was little evidence of closeness between them. It is possible that they were embarrassed and frightened by John's behavior and felt alienated from him because he would not stay on his medications even though these drugs obviously helped him to function better. John's parents were highly concerned about him, and in the earlier stages of his illness attempted to maintain close contact. However, after dealing with a chronic illness of almost ten years' duration, they realistically felt helpless to change John's behavior or convince him to stay on his medications. It also seems inevitable that eventually his family would feel rejected by John's lack of interest in communicating with them.

An important ethical question is how far health professionals and other societal agents can go in forcing someone to take medications against their will, even if there is clear improvement in their condition with the medication. Do patients have a right to their mental illness? Some have taken the attitude that mentally ill persons, by virtue of their disorder, are unable to judge what is beneficial for them and should be forced to take medications indefinitely because they have a right to treatment. Others argue that after the patient's mental status has improved so that he or she can make a reasonably informed decision about the continuance of medication, he or she has the right to refuse treatment. The latter position is based on the premise that a patient's right to receive treatment is separate from the right to refuse treatment.

An additional consideration in treating patients with antipsychotic drugs is the fact that continued use of these medications can result in significant physical problems. Each has a number of side effects (some dependent on dosage level) and complications. The most serious complication is tardive dyskinesia, an often permanent and extremely noticeable disorder characterized by writhing movements of the tongue and face, and writhing and twisting motions of the neck, arms, and hands. Approximately 20 percent of patients receiving antipsychotic medications develop tardive dyskinesia; in the majority of studies the risk increased with the length of drug exposure (Kane & Smith, 1982).

The right of involuntarily committed mental patients to refuse medication was established by judicial order in Massachusetts in 1975 (*Rogers* v. *Okin*, 1979), and confirmed in that state in trial court in 1979. A number of states currently have adopted a procedure of judicial review for hospitalized patients who refuse to take prescribed medications (Appelbaum, 1988). A judge then makes a decision whether the administration of the medication is in the patient's best interest, and/or whether a competent patient would have agreed to accept the medication. Because this is a relatively new procedure, it is difficult to predict its ramifications. In Massachusetts, 90 percent of patient refusals were overruled at judicial hearing (Appelbaum).

Ethical and social questions also occur when a patient leaves the hospital. One might assume that a legally committed patient discharged from a hospital has been judged by the professional staff to be competent to manage his or her own affairs, or at least not in need of a custodial setting. However, many patients do require after-care. Indeed, the closing down of many large state hospitals as part of the community mental health movement of the 1960s was predicated on the assumption that adequate care facilities would be available in the community in which the patient lived. However, the increase across the country in the number of the homeless mentally ill shows that community care services are not adequate.

It is possible that John will need some type of community-based supervised care indefinitely, irrespective of whether he remains on antipsychotic medications. It is crucial that adequate societal resources are available to care for those who by virtue of the deteriorating course of their illness, are unable to protect themselves from harm. There need to be some alternatives between commitment to a state hospital and living on the streets.

References

American Psychiatric Association (1987). *Diagnostic and statistical manual of mental disorders* (3rd ed., rev.) (DSM-III-R). Washington, DC: Author.

Andreasen, N. C. (1984). *The broken brain: The biological revolution in psychiatry.* New York: Harper & Row.

Andreasen, N. C., & Olsen, S. A. (1982). Negative v. positive schizophrenia: Definition and validation. *Archives of General Psychiatry, 39,* 789-794.

Appelbaum, P. S. (1988). The right to refuse treatment with antipsychotic medications: Retrospect and prospect. *American Journal of Psychiatry, 145,* 413-419.

Carpenter, W. T., Heinrichs, D. W., & Wagman, A. M. I. (1988). Deficit and nondeficit forms of schizophrenia: The concept. *American Journal of Psychiatry, 145,* 578-583.

Goldstein, J. M. (1988). Gender differences in the course of schizophrenia. *American Journal of Psychiatry, 145,* 684-689.

Iacono, W. G., & Beiser, M. (1989). Age of onset, temporal stability, and eighteen-month course of first-episode psychosis. In D. Cicchetti (Ed.), *Rochester symposium on developmental psychopathology* (pp. 221-260). Hillsdale, NJ: Lawrence Erlbaum: Cambridge University Press.

Iacono, W. G., Smith, G. N., Moreau, M., Beiser, M., Fleming, J. A. E., Lin, T-Y., & Flak, B. (1988). Ventricular and sulcal size at the onset of psychosis. *American Journal of Psychiatry, 145,* 820-824.

Kane, J. M., & Smith, J. M. (1982). Tardive dyskinesia. *Archives of General Psychiatry, 39,* 473-481.

Keefe, R. S. E., Mohs, R. C., Losonczy, M. F., Davidson, M., Silverman, J. M., Kendler, K. S., Horvath, T. B., Nora, R., & Davis, K. L. (1987). Characteristics of very poor outcome schizophrenia. *American Journal of Psychiatry, 144,* 889–895.

Kendler, K. S., Gruenberg, A. M., & Tsuang, M. T. (1988). A family study of the subtypes of schizophrenia. *American Journal of Psychiatry, 145,* 57–62.

Kraeplin, E. (1883). *Compendium der psychiatrie.* Leipzig: Abel.

Losonczy, M. F., Song, I. S., Mohs, R. C., Small, N. A., Davidson, M., Johns, C. A., & Davis, K. L. (1986). Correlates of lateral ventricular size in chronic schizophrenia, I: Behavioral and treatment response measures. *American Journal of Psychiatry, 143,* 976–981.

Rogers v. *Okin,* 487 F Supp 1342 (D Mass, 1979).

Schulz, S. C., Koller, M. M., Kishore, P. R., Hamer, R. M., Gehl, J. J., & Friedel, R.O. (1983). Ventricular enlargement in teenage patients with schizophrenia spectrum disorder. *American Journal of Psychiatry, 140,* 1592–1595.

Seeman, P., Ulpian, C., Bergeron, C., Riederer, P., Jellinger, K., Gabriel, E., Reynolds, G. P., & Tourtellotte, W. W. (1984). Bimodal distribution of dopamine receptor densities in brains of schizophrenics. *Science, 225,* 728–731.

Smith, G. N., & Iacono, W. G. (1986). Lateral ventricular size in schizophrenia and choice of control group. *Lancet, i,* 1450.

Wise, C. D., & Stein, L. (1973). Dopamine-β-hydroxylase deficits in the brains of schizophrenic patients. *Science, 181,* 344–347.

Wyatt, R. J., Schwartz, M. A., Erdelyi, E., & Barchas, J. D. (1975). Dopamine β-hydroxylase activity in brains of chronic schizophrenic patients. *Science, 187,* 368–370.

20

Primary Degenerative Dementia of the Alzheimer's Type— A Case of Early Onset

Lewis Edwards was 53 years old when he was seen in consultation by a staff neurologist at a Veteran's Administration hospital. At the time of the evaluation, he was on sick leave from his job as a post office supervisor because he was experiencing memory difficulties and problems with depression. The psychiatrist treating him requested a consultation to ascertain whether there might be an organic process causing or exacerbating the memory problems associated with his depression.

Mr. Edwards was of medium height and build, and dressed neatly in slacks and a shirt. His facial expression seemed sad, and he spoke slowly, in a quiet and sometimes halting manner. His wife accompanied him to the clinic appointment, and after Mr. Edwards was seen, she was asked to join him in the examining room to provide additional information.

Mr. Edwards had been under the care of a psychiatrist for the past year. He indicated that the various antidepressants prescribed for him had not been of benefit, and the memory problems he experienced over the last year or two were still present. He also stated that he sometimes had problems at work filling out required forms and keeping track of the activities of those whom he was supposed to supervise.

Mrs. Edwards reported that her husband occasionally had problems finding his way around familiar streets. She revealed that Mr. Edwards was finding it difficult to carry out and finish projects around the house that required a great deal of planning and organization, such as expanding the outdoor shed on which he had been working for the past several weeks. He also was having trouble estimating the appropriate amount of materials he needed to purchase for tasks such as painting the house or house repairs, projects he had enjoyed doing in the past. Other family members in addition to Mrs. Edwards noted these difficulties because Mr. Edwards always had performed these jobs extremely well.

Family Background

Lewis Edwards and his wife Gladys were black, and both had grown up in poor families in the same large southern city. They were of Southern Baptist religious affiliation. They had two daughters, Christine, age 31, who was married and had three children, and Delores, age 26, who was single. Both lived in neighborhoods close to their parents.

Mr. Edwards enlisted in the army when he was 18 years old, and he and Mrs. Edwards got married while he was in military service. He earned his high school equivalency degree during his army career, and he also received specialized training in clerical work and typing. After Mr. Edwards had been on active duty for six years, he decided not to reenlist because he did not like being transferred so frequently. Also, his last assignment in Germany necessitated a separation from his family because the Army did not provide transportation or housing for spouses, and the Edwardses could not afford the expenses involved for Mrs. Edwards and Christine to join him overseas. He left the Army with the rank of Sergeant First Class, reflecting consistent promotions while in military service.

Mr. Edwards moved back to his home town after his tour of duty was completed, and obtained a postal service job. Over the years, he was promoted to his current position of postal supervisor. He indicated that he was pleased with his job, and hoped to be able to continue working at the post office until he reached retirement age. Mrs. Edwards worked for many years as a beautician, and at present continued to do so on a part-time basis. She usually cared for her grandchildren in the afternoons when Christine went to work. The family lived in a middle-class, primarily black area of the city. Much of their social life, as well as that of their daughters Delores and Christine, centered on church activities.

Mrs. Edwards described her husband as a devoted family man who always took an interest in others. His mother was still alive and living with Mr. Edwards's sister in the same city. He often visited them as well as his other relatives, and frequently did repairs and other odd jobs around their houses. He spent much of his spare time working around his own house, or attending church activities with the rest of the family.

Mr. Edwards described himself before he was troubled with depression and memory problems as usually in good spirits. He related that if he occasionally felt "down in the dumps," these gloomy periods did not last very long. When questioned about alcohol use, he indicated that he drank only occasionally, and his wife did not drink at all. Mr. and Mrs. Edwards both reported that there was no one in his immediate or near family who had been diagnosed as mentally ill, alcoholic, or who had committed suicide. There also were no family members with significant memory problems, except for two of Mr. Edwards's aunts who became somewhat forgetful as they grew older. Neither Mr. nor Mrs. Edwards felt that the memory problems these aunts manifested were anything more than normal aging.

Recent Status

Mrs. Edwards had urged her husband to go to the V.A. hospital for a checkup the year previously. At that time, he appeared to be lacking in energy and not as interested in outside activities as he usually was. He often seemed to be thinking about something else rather than paying attention to what was happening around him. He also was noticeably forgetful at times. Neuropsychological testing conducted at that time did not reveal any abnormalities suggestive of organic cerebral dysfunction. Mr. Edwards was diagnosed as manifesting a depressive disorder, and his memory and concentration problems were perceived as part of his mood disorder. The psychiatrist who examined him felt that the etiology of the depression was biologically rather than situationally determined, and placed him on an antidepressant medication. Mr. Edwards later was given medication trials with several other antidepressants, but he did not show an improvement with any of these drugs.

Neurological and Mental Status Evaluation

A neurological and mental status examination was conducted at the current clinic visit by Dr. C., the consulting neurologist. The neurological examination did not reveal any abnormalities in reflex functioning, and the CT (computerized tomography) brain scan and EEG (electroencephalogram) brain wave tests were within normal limits. The patient's gait was normal, which also indicated no obvious neurological impairment.

The mental status examination revealed that the patient was oriented as to time and place, but he was in error by one day of the week when asked what day it was. Memory testing demonstrated that Mr. Edwards could not remember what school he had attended, the date of World War I, or the name of the past president of the United States. However, he did know the current president, and the date of World War II. He could not remember three words he had been told to remember five minutes earlier, and he had some difficulties in naming objects that were placed in front of him. His arithmetic skills were adequate.

Neuropsychological Evaluation

Mr. Edwards was evaluated by Mr. T., a psychology intern who was supervised by a staff psychologist. The patient's verbal responses demonstrated that he generally was able to find the right words to express himself, and he used appropriate grammar and syntax. Intellectual assessment suggested selective decline, as verbal abilities were relatively intact but nonverbal abilities were moderately reduced. For example, the patient was quite able to define vocabulary words but less able to match geometric designs. Such results are characteristic of primary dementia (memory disorder), in which concrete verbal abilities typically are less affected than abstract nonverbal abilities.

Mild deficits were evident on tests of immediate or short-term memory, such as the ability to recall words and drawings that had been presented moments earlier. Long-term memory for verbal and nonverbal materials was somewhat more impaired. These abilities were measured by several tests, including one counting the number of details the patient recalled from a story passage read to him one hour previously, and another measuring the number of figures recalled that were learned at an earlier point in the testing.

The mild but consistent memory and visual spatial deficits manifested on the current neuropsychological testing were more consistent with the performance of someone with an organic mental disorder than a nonorganic mood disorder. However, not all of the test results were consistent. The patient was administered an auditory verbal learning task in which a person hears a list of words and then is asked immediately to repeat as many of the words as he or she can remember. The same procedure is repeated over several more trials. Mr. Edwards performed better on earlier than on later trials of this task. This type of performance is often interpreted as suggestive of a problem in motivation or attention, more typical of depression than organic cerebral dysfunction.

Case Conference

After the evaluations were performed by each of the professional staff, a case conference was held to discuss whether Mr. Edwards's basic disorder was one of depression or a primary organic memory disorder. The physical examination and laboratory tests tended to rule out alternative organic causes such as stroke, a brain tumor, or Parkinson's disease. However, a differential diagnosis between depression and a primary memory disorder still was not entirely clear. Dr. H., the psychiatrist, noted that Mr. Edwards continued to exhibit classic signs of depression such as loss of weight and appetite, and a loss of interest in everyday activities. He also continued to manifest a dysphoric or sad mood state. On the other hand, both the neuropsychologist and the neurologist felt that the various test and clinical findings were more suggetive of a primary organic memory disorder such as early onset or presenile Alzheimer's disease.

The treatment plan agreed upon was for the patient to remain under the primary care of Dr. H., who would place him on a different type of antidepressant medication. Mr. Edwards would then return to the outpatient psychiatry clinic on a monthly basis in order to have his progress monitored and medications adjusted as needed. If differential diagnosis still remained an issue, the neurological and neuropsychological evaluations would be repeated in six months to ascertain whether there had been a deterioration in functioning over this time period. A further option was to repeat the CT scan and EEG brain studies at that time.

Course of Illness

Mr. Edwards exhibited an improvement in mood over the next two months associated with the antidepressant he had been placed on. Both he and his wife stated that there had been some memory improvement as well. Based on these findings, the psychiatrist, in consultation with the neurologist, recommended that his sick leave be terminated and that he return to work.

Mr. Edwards had extreme difficulty functioning at his job. He could not remember the names of his co-workers, nor could he carry out any of his required duties. He went to work over a three-day period, but it was evident to him that he could not perform the tasks he needed to do. He was extremely sad and distressed to hand in his resignation, but he felt that he had no alternative.

Mr. Edwards was referred to Dr. C. for a neurological re-examination after he stopped working. It was her judgment that despite the moderate improvement with antidepressant medication, the basic problem was an organic one consistent with the diagnosis of an early onset primary degenerative dementia. It had been reasonable to ascertain whether Mr. Edwards could function at work when his depression lessened. However, it now was clear that the difficulties he encountered were substantial, irrespective of his mood state, and he could not perform as needed at his job. Dr. C. also felt that it was highly likely that Mr. Edwards's functioning would continue to deteriorate over time.

Both Dr. C. and the psychiatrist, Dr. H., concurred in transferring Mr. Edwards's primary care from the outpatient psychiatry to the outpatient neurology clinic. Further neuropsychological testing just two months after the last testing was judged not necessary, particularly when the symptoms of a primary organic memory disorder were clearer than they had been previously. The plan was to continue to monitor Mr. Edwards at periodic intervals through visits to the outpatient neurology clinic.

Three-Month Status

Mr. Edwards and his wife returned to the neurology clinic for a scheduled appointment three months later. He was taken off of the antidepressant medication because there no longer was an improvement in mood, and he now was experiencing drug side effects. A mental status examination revealed that Mr. Edwards was unable to state the precise date or time of day. He could not recount any current events, even though his wife indicated that he always watched the news on television. Further, he could not remember the details of a minor automobile accident his daughter Delores had been in.

Mrs. Edwards commented that her husband exhibited substantial variations in his level of functioning; he sometimes was unable to carry out a particular task that he was able to perform quite well on a later day. One morning he told his wife that he was unable to operate the toaster, and he was extremely distressed about this. He also was experiencing periods of confusion and marked changes in mood, and on several occasions he refused to bathe.

Mrs. Edwards related that Mr. Edwards continued to attend church functions with the family. She was saddened, though, by the fact that their friends commented that Lewis was not the same person he used to be. He now was passive and quiet in social situations outside of the immediate family. He tended to sit in one place simply listening to the conversation of others, although he did respond when someone asked him a question. His answers usually were one or two sentence communications, but the response was appropriate to the question asked.

Dr. C. prescribed a daily medication whose most frequent use is in treating hyperactive children. However, this drug also can be helpful in improving concentration and decreasing confusion in patients with memory disorders. Mr. Edwards was scheduled for a return appointment in three months to further evaluate his condition and to assess the efficacy of the drug just prescribed. Dr. C. asked Mrs. Edwards to call her if Mr. Edwards complained of any physical symptoms that might be side effects of the medication. Mrs. Edwards also was given the phone number of the social work department at the hospital to use as needed. Spouses and other close family members of patients with Alzheimer's disease often require psychological as well as practical help in dealing with the management problems that occur during the course of this illness.

Six-Month Status

At the subsequent three-month visit, Mr. Edwards's condition was unchanged. He was taken off the previously prescribed medication because there was no improvement evident in concentration or memory. Mr. Edwards demonstrated an awareness of his deficits, and was appropriately sad about his disabilities. Mrs. Edwards appeared to be extremely supportive of her husband, and seemed to exercise supervision over his activities without becoming overprotective. In private conversations with Dr. C., she expressed her concern about her husband's future, in what was now clear to both professionals and family members to be a progressive illness. She also conveyed her sorrow that Mr. Edwards, at age 54, was so young to be suffering from the memory problems and general deterioration of functioning that he was experiencing.

Two-Year Status

Over the next year and a half, Mr. Edwards participated in two separate experimental drug studies of cholinergic replacement drugs for treating

Alzheimer's disease that recently had been approved by the Federal Food and Drug Administration. However, there was no improvement in his condition over either of these drug trials, and he continued to exhibit a gradual deterioration of functioning. Mrs. Edwards reported that her husband now seemed more irritable and much more difficult to manage. Further, he was having difficulty finding dishes and utensils in the kitchen, and while he still was able to drive, he only did so when Mrs. Edwards was in the car with him giving directions.

During his appointment with Dr. C., Mr. Edwards constantly asked the same questions over and over, even though Dr. C. answered his queries each time. He also seemed to Dr. C. to be interacting in a rather argumentative manner. The plan was to continue following Mr. Edwards in the neurology clinic at four-month intervals.

Two-Year-and-Four-Month Status

The major change in the patient's condition during this four-month period was that he now was having difficulty in dressing himself. On the mental status examination, his performance was uneven. He knew the year he was born, but could not give the exact date or place of his birth. Although he correctly stated who the president was, he could not give any other details of current events. Other functions were more intact. He was able to copy a cube quite well, indicating that he possessed some spatial relationship abilities. He also was able to serially subtract from 100 by sevens, a task that he had been unable to carry out at an appointment seven months previously. Mrs. Edwards continued to work part time, and one of her daughters or a neighbor checked on Mr. Edwards when she was out of the house. Mr. Edwards seemed to enjoy having his grandchildren come to visit him. He smiled at them and attempted to initiate some play activities. Mrs. Edwards was becoming increasingly frustrated with her husband's poor memory, but in general she appeared to Dr. C. to be coping reasonably well.

Two-and-One-Half-Year Status

Mrs. Edwards requested an appointment before their next scheduled visit, stating that her husband was now extremely irritable and difficult to manage. She also was concerned that on one occasion he had failed to recognize their daughter Delores. However, he consistently recognized his wife and addressed her by name.

The irritable behavior Mrs. Edwards described also was evident during the mental status examination with Dr. C. Mr. Edwards became very annoyed at some of the questions asked, and said that he did not want to answer. With gentle prodding, he did respond to the questions, although his response often was that he did not know the answer.

Dr. C. placed Mr. Edwards on an antipsychotic medication that sometimes reduces confusion and irritability in patients with dementia. The irritable behavior manifested by people with memory disorders often serves as a means of disguising confusion, and this seemed to be the case with Mr. Edwards. After several months, his irritable behavior was substantially diminished; Dr. C. discontinued the medication at that point because it no longer seemed needed. The irritability and management difficulties did not recur, perhaps because the patient no longer was perceiving his intellectual impairment.

Three-and-One-Half-Year Status

Mr. Edwards continued to deteriorate slowly in function. He now tended to get lost in the house, could not get dressed by himself, and had some episodes of urinary incontinence. He did not go outside when there was no one home, and his overall mood was quite placid. There was no evidence of the irritability he had exhibited the previous year. Through the efforts of the social service staff at the hospital, Mr. Edwards attended a day care facility for several weeks. However, this activity was discontinued because he was resistant to going and seemed agitated at the end of the day. Mrs. Edwards stated that while it was difficult having her husband at home in his present condition, she was able to manage with the help of other family members and friends from church. She indicated that she did not want to place Mr. Edwards in a nursing home.

Four-Year Status

Mr. Edwards continued to live at home. He no longer recognized his daughters, but he still recognized his wife. A mental status evaluation revealed that he knew his and his wife's name and the state they lived in. However, he did not know any other facts of orientation.

Five-and-One-Half-Year Status

Mr. Edwards was now 59 years old. He lived at home and was able to walk unassisted. However, he could not eat by himself, and had to be fed his entire meal. He recognized his wife, but he did not know her name. He could state his own name, and spoke fluently in response to questions, using appropriate grammar and syntax. However, there was little content or information conveyed in his comments. He was incontinent most of the time.

Although Mr. Edwards's condition continued to deteriorate, Mrs. Edwards indicated that it was still possible for her to manage him at home. The nursing assistance she received from family and friends enabled her to continue to work part time to supplement Mr. Edwards's disability pension. In addition, the time out of the house provided her with a respite from caring for her husband. Mrs. Edwards was realistic in her appraisal of her husband's progressive deterioration, but she stated that she was willing to care for him at home as long as she could.

Discussion

The primary characteristic of dementia is an impairment in immediate and recent memory. Loss of cognitive function also is demonstrated in the areas of judgment, reasoning, or abstract thinking; personality changes may be evident as well. The extensive nature of the dysfunction in this disorder has a significant impact on work, social activities, and other aspects of interpersonal relationships.

The DSM-III-R (1987) diagnostic criteria for primary degenerative dementia of the Alzheimer type, also known as Alzheimer's disease, are dementia with a gradual onset and a progressively deteriorating course in intellectual, social, or occupational functioning, and the exclusion of all other specific causes of dementia including major depression and other psychiatric disorders, and specific organic conditions such as Vitamin B_{12} deficiency, Parkinson's disease, and hypothyroidism. The exclusion of other organic factors can occur through laboratory tests, physical examination, or patient history. Primary degenerative dementia of the Alzheimer's type can be specified as occurring with depression, delusions, or delirium; the latter symptoms are judged secondary to the primary disorder of dementia. For persons age 65 or younger, presenile onset of the disorder is designated.

Primary degenerative dementia of the Alzheimer's type progresses to the point of muteness, immobility, and eventual death. According to DSM-III-R, the symptoms of dementia tend to be relatively stable over a several month period, although some fluctuations in memory ability may occur within a shorter time span. At a mild stage of dementia, depression or anxiety may be part of the clinical picture because the individual is able to recognize his or her impairment. In addition, cognitive deficits can be exacerbated by situational changes (e.g., moving or vacations) which require the patient to perform new tasks in unfamiliar surroundings, or by psychological stressors related to other life changes.

Epidemiological surveys of Alzheimer's disease cannot be conducted with precision because the diagnosis can be confirmed only through autopsy. Surveys of adult populations, usually age 65 and older, have reported prevalence rates of senile dementia of 0.6 to 1.8 percent (Henderson, 1986). Surveys of dementia in persons under age 65 have not been carried out. Prevalence estimates broken down according to age over 65 indicate that the range of severe dementia varies from less than 1 percent for persons age 65 to more than 15 percent for those over age 85 (Katzman, 1986).

The characteristic brain changes of Alzheimer's disease once were thought to occur only in presenescent individuals (below age 65), but now are known to occur in those over age 65 (Katzman, 1986). Indeed, the prevalence rates noted above suggest that these changes are more common after rather than before age 65. The average duration of life from disease onset to death is approximately seven to eight years in those age 54 and younger, eight and one-half years in patients 55 to 74, and five to six and a half years in patients 75 and older (Heston, Mastri, Anderson, & White, 1981). Presenile onset dementia has been described as having a more severe course until death primarily because of the relatively early age of onset, and a presumed shorter course until death. Early mortality in patients over 75 probably is caused by other diseases such as cancer, infection, or heart disease.

Neuropsychological tests and mental status examinations have been helpful in distinguishing between some of the clinical features of dementia and depression, that is, differentiating between memory loss and inattention. Because dementia can be caused by a large number of disorders such as brain tumors, neurosyphilis, Pick's disease, and strokes, laboratory tests also are of diagnostic importance. However, a conclusive confirmation of the diagnosis of Alzheimer's disease can only be made at autopsy through the identification of particular structural changes in the brain that are characteristic of this disorder (Alzheimer, 1907).

The major changes in the brain noted at autopsy and considered definitive of Alzheimer's disease are neurofibrillary tangles and neuritic plaques. Neurofibrillary tangles are abnormal neurons in which the cytoplasm of the nerve cell is filled with fibers or filament structures that are tightly wound around each other in a paired and twisted fashion (Wisniewski, Narang, & Terry, 1976). A neuritic plaque is a cluster of degenerating nerve endings (dendrites and axons) with a central core containing filaments with chemical and structural characteristics of amyloid protein.

The appearance of tangles and plaques is associated with cerebral atrophy and a reduction in brain weight (Brun, 1985).

The pathological changes in Alzheimer's disease occur in a typical pattern and distribution in the brain. In the cerebral cortex, the parietal and temporal areas show the most extensive changes, while the sensorimotor areas are relatively more intact (Brun, 1985; Katzman, 1986). Changes and cell loss also have been noted in the hippocampus, entorhinal cortex, and the amygdala, areas crucial for memory function.

Although neurofibrillary tangles and plaques are found in nondemented elderly persons, the large number of these structural changes, their co-occurrence, and their concentration in particular areas of the brain are characteristic of Alzheimer's disease. Group differences have been demonstrated between Alzheimer's disease patients and those without dementia or other diseases on measures of cerebral atrophy and brain weight. However, it is important to note that loss of brain tissue also can occur during the normal aging process.

Research on the activity of specific neurotransmitters suggests that some neurotransmitter systems are involved in the pathology of Alzheimer's disease. A decrease in choline acetyltransferase activity in the amygdala, hippocampus, and cerebral cortex has been demonstrated in Alzheimer's disease patients (Davies & Maloney, 1976). This finding is significant because choline acetyltransferase is a neurotransmitter that is extremely important in human memory. Additional evidence suggesting a relationship between this neurotransmitter and memory is the relatively high correlation found between changes in scores on mental status examinations and loss of choline acetyltransferase (Katzman, 1986). The brains of Alzheimer's disease patients also show a decrease in somatostatin, a peptide neurotransmitter present in neurons in the hippocampus and the cerebral cortex, areas involved in memory and intellectual functioning.

The prevalence data reviewed earlier suggests that the major risk factor for Alzheimer's disease is age. However, family history studies suggest a genetic influence. Heston et al., (1981) studied the relatives of patients with autopsy-confirmed Alzheimer's disease, and found a significantly increased risk of the disorder in parents and siblings. Approximately one-third of the families of Alzheimer's disease probands had relatives with this disorder. The risk was relatively high in families of probands with a more severe disorder, that is, an earlier onset and shorter course. When age of onset in the proband was age 70 or older, the risk in relatives was no different from that of the control group.

The Heston group also found an increased risk of Down's syndrome and lymphomas primarily in the relatives of Alzheimer's disease probands with a more severe course of disorder. Older Down's syndrome patients have a similar distribution of plaques, neurofibrillary tangles, and loss of choline acetyltransferase to that found in patients with Alzheimer's disease (Katzman, 1986). Because Down's syndrome patients also are highly likely to develop Alzheimer's disease (Brun, 1985), there may be a commonality in the genetic bases and pathological mechanisms of these two disorders.

The specific types of memory loss that occur in Alzheimer's disease are a subject of current research. Deficits in immediate and recent memory are typical features of the disorder, and encoding and attentional deficits seem a component of these deficits. The extent of short-term memory impairment is correlated with clinical ratings of the severity of the dementia, and age, with younger Alzheimer's disease patients tending to show relatively greater short-term memory deficits (Morris & Kopelman, 1986). Impairment in long-term memory and the recall of remote events appear to be even more severe, and are reflected in deficiencies in the recall of previously learned information and personally experienced events. Morris and Kopelman (1986) concluded from their review of experimental studies of memory function in Alzheimer's disease that the long-term memory deficit in this disorder seems caused in part by poor organization in memory (encoding problems) along with information processing deficiencies.

Semantic memory (an understanding of the meaning of words and the principles of their relationships) also seems impaired in Alzheimer's disease. This impairment is reflected in speech hesitancies, the inability to recall the names of persons or objects, and losses in complex verbal comprehension. Vocabulary comprehension is relatively unimpaired, and semantic knowledge about category membership (e.g., fruit) appears intact (Morris & Kopelman, 1986). However, there is evidence of impairment in the ability to differentiate between items in a category (e.g., apples vs. oranges).

Implicit memory has been studied and seems relatively intact in Alzheimer's patients at mild or moderate levels of illness severity. Implicit memory refers to enhancement or priming effects for later memory based on prior exposure to relevant stimulus material. Knopman and Nissen (1987) demonstrated that the performance of Alzheimer's disease patients on a reaction time task involving response to a repeating sequence was enhanced by prior experience with that sequence. Hartman (1987) found that Alzheimer's disease patients had intact semantic memory and intact knowledge of relationships between words on a semantic priming task. These findings suggest that the neural systems involved in implicit learning may be different from those involved in explicit or recognition and recall tasks.

Prospective studies of language in Alzheimer's disease patients have demonstrated that in the early stages, there is little impairment in the form of conversational speech; phrase length, grammar, and articulation are relatively normal. Abnormalities are demonstrated in the content of speech, consisting of word naming problems and reliance on common phrases (Kaszniak & Wilson, 1985). Comprehension on auditory tasks and in reading is poor, although the ability to read is preserved (Huppert & Tym, 1986). Disorders of written language also are common, as are impairments of visual spatial perception. Progressive impairment in language and spatial relationship abilities are a reflection of the continued deterioration that is a major defining characteristic of Alzheimer's disease.

Research on the development of an effective treatment for this disorder has been stimulated by the evidence of cholinergic transmitter system depletion in Alzheimer's disease patients, and findings that cholinergic blockade produces a marked memory impairment in normal subjects (Kopelman, 1986). However, clinical studies using cholinergic replacement drugs as a treatment for Alzheimer's disease have produced disappointing results thus far. Other types of pharmacological agents have been effective in modifying some of the secondary symptoms of Alzheimer's disease, particularly irritability or confusion. However, the disease eventually progresses beyond the stage where these particular symptoms are problematic. Unfortunately, at present there is no effective treatment to prevent, arrest, or reverse the insidious progression of this disorder.

Some investigators have pointed to the importance of treating the symptoms of depression in Alzheimer's disease through psychopharmacological and other treatment methods, even though the depression might be secondary to the patient's recognition that she or he is suffering from a progressive memory disorder. Lazarus, Newton, Cohler, Lesser, and Schweon (1987) found that 41 percent of patients with primary degenerative dementia manifested mild to severe depression at the beginning to middle stages of the disorder, reflected in symptoms such as depressed mood, anxiety, feelings of helplessness, worthlessness, and hopelessness.

Questions about depression and differential diagnosis were prominent in the early phase of Mr. Edwards's disorder, and it is possible that when he first was seen, he was suffering from both depression and early dementia. It is unclear whether the depression at the beginning stage of his illness was secondary to a perceived loss of function related to the dementia, or whether Mr. Edwards was manifesting two coexisting disorders. Laboratory tests indicated that there was no specific organic cause of the memory problems such as a brain tumor. While Alzheimer's disease was initially diagnosed through the exclusion of these other causes, over time the primary degenerative dementia process became clearer.

The symptoms of depression that were evident when Mr. Edwards was first evaluated disappeared as the dementia became more pronounced. The irritability that occurred several years after the onset of the illness likely was due to an increasing frustration with being unable to cope with environmental demands. These feelings and behaviors also dissipated over time. The apathy and blunting of emotional expression that took the place of the irritability are characteristic of still later stages of the disorder.

Mr. Edwards exhibited an insidious and progressive deterioration. After at least a five-and-one-half-year course of the disorder, he no longer could feed or dress himself, and he was incontinent. However, he still was able to speak and his gait was relatively normal.

The problems in eating and dressing appear to reflect conceptual difficulties accentuated by minor visual-spatial coordination problems. For example, the act of putting on one's shoes involves a recognition that the object one is looking at is a shoe, and a recollection of the function that shoes serve. Further, the individual must make a discrimination between a shoe that goes on the right foot and one that goes on the left. There also needs to be an awareness that a prior step in the sequence, putting on one's sock, already has occurred. The eye-hand coordination involved in putting on a shoe and tying the laces also must be intact for this act to be carried out. Going through the sequence of completely dressing oneself is infinitely more complex. Similarly, the urinary incontinence at this stage of Mr. Edwards's illness may have been due to the inability to process the signals of bladder distension, or coordinate these signals with all of the behaviors necessary to urinate in the toilet. Therefore, while physical strength may be present, the execution of complex tasks can be highly impaired.

Mr. Edwards was at the stage in his illness where he was unable to recognize familiar individuals such as his daughters or recall his wife's name. Facial recognition is one aspect of the processing and discrimination of visual information, and the inability to provide the name of a particular person is part of a more general difficulty in naming objects. These relatively severe difficulties in recognition and naming are characteristic of later stages of Alzheimer's disease. Since the names of close relatives and friends is highly overlearned within a person's memory, an impairment in the ability to recall the names of familiar individuals should occur at a later point than the inability to recall the names of less familiar persons or objects.

Mr. Edwards was extremely fortunate to be living in a highly supportive and predictable environment. The fact that there were familiar individuals available to care for him at home may have been an important influence in preventing a more rapid progression of his disorder. Attendance at a day care facility proved disruptive to his functioning, possibly because he was unable to process the new information regarding the people with whom he now had to interact, or the layout of the building that he was in. While day care activities can be beneficial for some, in the patient's case and at the point in his illness in which day care was attempted, it had a deleterious effect.

The treatment of Mr. Edwards involved the administration of numerous medications that varied in their usefulness at different points of his illness. To a certain extent, medications were given on a trial and error basis at the beginning of his disorder because the cause of his difficulties was not clear. The various antidepressants prescribed during the early stage of his disease usually did not produce a significant change in his condition. After the possibility of situational causes of the depression was explored and ruled out, psychotherapy or counseling was not considered because the depressive symptoms were viewed as biological rather than psychological in origin. However, as the primary dementia became clearer, it might have been helpful for Mr. Edwards to have had the opportunity to participate in some type of counseling to ventilate his sorrow and anxiety about his progressive illness.

At a later stage in his disorder, Mr. Edwards manifested irritability and confusion, which were treated through the use of other medications. Mrs. Edwards did not avail herself of social work assistance at that time, most likely because she seemed to be coping with these problems reasonably well, and she also had a strong social support network. When the symptoms of irritability or mood swings abated, medications whose action has an effect on these behaviors were no longer necessary. Mr. Edwards's physician was appropriately sensitive to the behavioral changes in the natural cycle of this disorder and did not overmedicate him. Unfortunately, Mr. Edwards's participation in drug trials with two different cholinergic replacement drugs produced no change in his condition.

The development and use of cholinergic replacement drugs is a logical step in finding an effective treatment for primary degenerative dementia of the Alzheimer's type because of the demonstration of a depletion of the cholinergic transmission system in this disorder. However, this neurochemical dysfunction is but one of a number of changes that have been demonstrated in this illness. The accumulation of structural changes in the brain such as neurofibrillary tangles and neuritic plaques, if irreversible, would also seem to have an important effect on memory and general intellectual functioning. Psychosocial stressors such as removal from one's home, and the associated absence of familiar persons are additional influences on the overall functioning of Alzheimer's disease patients. Therefore, it may be expecting too much to assume that a drug whose action is on a single system of the body, and administered after several years' progression of the disorder, will cause a dramatic improvement in functioning. It is hoped that pharmacological agents will be developed at a future time that can be effectively used to arrest at early stages or reverse the course of this disease.

The outlook for Mr. Edwards is bleak. A continued deterioration in functioning to the point of muteness and immobility seems inevitable, with a future life expectancy of about three years.

References

Alzheimer (1907). Über eine eigenartige Erkrangkung der Hirnrinde. *Allg Z Psychiat, 64,* 146–148.

American Psychiatric Association (1987). *Diagnostic and statistical manual of mental disorders* (3rd ed., rev.) (DSM-III-R). Washington, DC: Author.

Brun, A. (1985). The structural development of Alzheimer's disease. *Danish Medical Bulletin, 32* (Suppl 1), 25–27.

Davies, P., & Maloney, A. J. F. (1976). Selective loss of central cholinergic neurons in Alzheimer's disease. *Lancet, 2,* 1403.

Hartman, M. (1987). A cognitive-neuropsychological study of semantic representation in dementia of the Alzheimer's type. Unpublished doctoral dissertation, University of Minnesota, Minneapolis.

Henderson, A. S. (1986). The epidemiology of Alzheimer's disease. *British Medical Bulletin, 42,* 3–10.

Heston, L. L., Mastri, A. R., Anderson, V. E., & White, J. (1981). Dementia of the Alzheimer type: Clinical genetics, natural history and associated conditions. *Archives of General Psychiatry, 38,* 1085–1090.

Huppert, F. A., & Tym, E. (1986). Clinical and neuropsychological assessment of dementia. *British Medical Bulletin, 42,* 11–18.

Kaszniak, A. W., & Wilson, R. S. (1985). Longitudinal deterioration of language and cognition in dementia of the Alzheimer's type. Paper presented at the 13th Annual Meeting of the International Neuropsychological Society. San Diego, CA.

Katzman, R. (1986). Medical progress. Alzheimer's disease. *New England Journal of Medicine, 314,* 964–973.

Knopman, D. S., & Nissen, M. J. (1987). Implicit learning in patients with probable Alzheimer's disease. *Neurology, 37*, 784–788.

Kopelman, M. D. (1986). The cholinergic neurotransmitter system in human memory and dementia: A review. *Quarterly Journal of Experimental Psychology, 38A*, 535–573.

Lazarus, L. W., Newton, N., Cohler, B., Lesser, J., & Schweon, C. (1987). Frequency and presentation of depressive symptoms in patients with primary degenerative dementia. *American Journal of Psychiatry, 144*, 41–45.

Morris, R. G., & Kopelman, M. D. (1986). The memory deficits in Alzheimer-type dementia: A review. *Quarterly Journal of Experimental Psychology, 38A*, 575–602.

Wisniewski, H. M., Narang, H. K., & Terry, R. D. (1976). Neurofibrillary tangles of paired helical filaments. *Journal of Neurological Science, 27*, 173–181.

Author Index

Subject Index

A

Aggression, 57, 61-62, 68, 71, 121, 157, 168-169, 174, 313, 314. *See also* Conduct disorder
Agoraphobia, 84, 85
AIDS, 243-244
Alcohol
    abuse, 157, 159-160, 162, 168, 172, 215-230, 304, 306, 314
    effects of, 224-225
    idiosyncratic intoxication, 169
Alcoholic parent, 143-145, 151, 153, 154, 199, 209-210, 216, 225
Alcoholics Anonymous, 220, 229
Alzheimer's disease, 337-353
    brain changes in, 347-348

    genetic factors, 348-349
Amenorrhea, 182, 187, 190
Amphetamine(s)
    -induced psychoses, 169-170
    toxic effects of, 171-172
Androgeny, psychological, 51-52
Anger, 257, 262, 306, 307, 314
Anorexia nervosa, 179-193, 207. *See also* Bulimia nervosa
Anoxia, 22, 34
Antabuse therapy, 220, 222-223, 229
Antisocial behaviors, 68
Antisocial personality disorder, 157–176, 310
Anxiety, 203–204, 224
    castration, 50, 242
    disorders, 85–86. *See also* Phobias
    hierarchy, 82–83

Heart disease and "Type A"
  behavior patterns, 137
Homosexuality, 233–247, 303
  biological factors, 242–243
  discrimination against, 243–244
Human circadian rhythms, 276
Hyperactivity, 68, 160, 189. *See
  also* Attention-deficit
  hyperactivity disorder
Hyperventilation, 118

I

Illusions
  auditory, 283, 288–289, 290,
    291, 308, 309, 315
  visual, 149, 151, 163–164,
    169, 170–171
Immune functioning and stress,
  138–139
Implicit memory, 349
Implosive therapy, 86
Impotence, 126, 131, 134
Incest, 143–155
Infantile autism. *See* Autistic
  disorder
Infantile psychosis, 11–13. *See
  also* Autistic disorder
Information processing theory
  obsessive-compulsive
    disorder, 106
  phobias, 84–85
Intelligence
  evaluation, 57, 59, 63, 166–167
  quotient and delinquent
    behavior, 72–73
Interpersonal skills, therapy for
  enhancing, 326–327
In vivo exposure to phobic
  stimulus, 86–87, 99, 105–106
Irritable behavior, 344–345,
  350, 351, 352

Irritable colon, and psychological
  factors affecting physical
  condition, 125–141

L

Labor and delivery problems, 22,
  29, 33, 34
Language. *See* Speech
Learned helplessness model, 259
Learning theory
  autistic disorder, 12
  depression, 259
  development of
    psychophysiological
    disorders, 136–137
  phobias, 84–85, 86, 87
  See also Social learning theory
Life changes
  and development of physical
    and mental diseases, 138
  and onset of depression, 261
Lithium carbonate, 270, 271,
  272, 273, 275–276, 278–279
Lobotomy, 315
LSD, 157, 163, 169–171

M

Manic-depression. *See* Bipolar
  disorder
Marijuana, 164
Marital discord, 129, 130
  of parents, 41, 47, 53, 94–95,
    159–160, 199, 250–252,
    262–263, 284, 285–286
Masturbation. *See* Sexual
  activity
Medication
  antidepressant, 270, 271,
    337, 339, 341, 342, 352
  antipsychotic, 272, 273,